Research Methods for Digital Work and Organization

Research Methods for Digital Work and Organization

Investigating Distributed, Multi-Modal, and Mobile Work

Edited by
Gillian Symon
Katrina Pritchard
Christine Hine

OXFORD
UNIVERSITY PRESS

OXFORD
UNIVERSITY PRESS

Great Clarendon Street, Oxford, OX2 6DP,
United Kingdom

Oxford University Press is a department of the University of Oxford.
It furthers the University's objective of excellence in research, scholarship,
and education by publishing worldwide. Oxford is a registered trade mark of
Oxford University Press in the UK and in certain other countries

Published in the United States of America by Oxford University Press
198 Madison Avenue, New York, NY 10016, United States of America

British Library Cataloguing in Publication Data

Data available

Library of Congress Control Number: 2021937363

ISBN 978–0–19–886067–9 (hbk.)
ISBN 978–0–19–886068–6 (pbk.)

Printed and bound by
CPI Group (UK) Ltd, Croydon, CR0 4YY

Acknowledgements

We initially formulated the concept for this book in the context of our own collaborative research on methods for capturing emerging forms of digital work. As we explored these ideas we ran a two-day symposium 'Research Methods for Digital Work: Innovative Methods for Studying Distributed and Multi-modal Working Practices' at the University of Surrey (2017). We are very grateful to the University of Surrey's Institute of Advanced Studies and NEMODE (RCUK's New Economic Models in the Digital Economy Network Plus) for the funding provided to support this event. We would also like to thank all the presenters and attendees for their input to this project.

Of course, much has changed since 2017, and when we started work on this volume none of us anticipated that the book would itself be developed, written, and produced through entirely digital means. We are indebted to all those who have contributed to this book, recognizing that taking on the additional task of authoring a chapter during the pandemic is a considerable commitment and we are very grateful for all their hard work. We are also very grateful for support from Oxford University Press throughout the process.

Gillian would like to thank Brian and Jamie whose patience with absence and forgetfulness really knows no bounds.

Katrina would like to dedicate this book to Bill and her family, of both the two and four-legged variety.

Christine thanks Simon, Esther, and Isaac for being so reassuringly analogue when everything else turned digital.

Contents

List of Figures

List of Tables

The Editors and Contributors

Editors

Gillian Symon is Professor of Organization Studies in the School of Business and Management at Royal Holloway, University of London. Her research focuses on understanding digital work and organization as sociomaterial practice, and she specializes in qualitative approaches to analysing and understanding work and organization. She has co-edited four compendia of qualitative methods in this area, including *The Essential Guide to Qualitative Methods in Organizational Research* (Cassell and Symon, 2004, Sage Publications), and *Organizational Qualitative Research: Core Methods and Current Challenges* (Symon and Cassell, 2012, Sage Publications). She is also co-founding editor of the journal *Qualitative Research in Organization and Management* (Emerald Publishing, with Catherine Cassell).

Katrina Pritchard is a Professor in the School of Management, Swansea University. She is a qualitative researcher who embraces methodological diversity and innovation. She has published widely on topics ranging from digital ethics, ethnography, and visual studies to multi-method research, drawing on her research in organization studies across the topics of identity, diversity, and technology use at work. With Rebecca Whiting, she recently authored *Collecting Qualitative Data using Digital Methods* (2020, Sage Publications).

Christine Hine is Professor of Sociology at the University of Surrey. She is a sociologist of science and technology who has a particular focus on the role played by new technologies in the knowledge construction process. She has a major interest in the development of ethnography in technical settings and in the use of the Internet in social research. In particular, she has developed mobile and connective approaches to ethnography that combine online and offline social contexts. She is author of *Virtual Ethnography* (2000, Sage Publications*), Ethnography for the Internet* (2015, Bloomsbury), and *Understanding Qualitative Research: The Internet* (2012, Oxford University Press), editor of *Virtual Methods* (2005, Berg) and co-editor of *Digital Methods for Social Science* (2016, Palgrave).

Contributors

David Antons is a Professor and co-director of the Institute for Technology and Innovation Management (TIM) at RWTH Aachen University, Germany. He held visiting appointments at the universities of Cambridge and Melbourne. His research interests include knowledge sharing across organizational, spatial, and disciplinary boundaries; psychological influences on decision-making; individual learning from feedback; and text mining approaches. Recent contributions have been published in journals such as *Academy of Management Review, Journal of*

Management, Academy of Management Perspectives, Research Policy, Journal of Service Research, Organizational Research Methods, and *Journal of Product Innovation Management.*

Mario Aquino Alves is Associate Professor and Associate Dean for the Graduate Program in Public Administration and Government at FGV EAESP, Brazil, He held visiting appointments at HEC Montréal, ESSEC Paris, and Cardiff Business School. He is also President-Elect of the International Society for Third Sector Research. His research interests include civil society and social movements organizations, uncivil social movements, political corporate social responsibility, and discourse and narrative analysis. Recent contributions have been published in journals such as *Journal of Business Ethics, Research in the Sociology of Organizations, British Education Research Journal, Social Policy and Society,* and *Revista de Administração Pública.*

Adam Badger is an interdisciplinary PhD student (Geography and Management) at Royal Holloway, University of London, where he also works as a research associate. His work focuses on the intersections of technology and contemporary gig work in order to explore the lived experiences workers have of their jobs; foregrounding sociomaterial elements of the work amidst the broader backdrops of urban space. In addition to studying the experience of work, Adam is dedicated to investigating how workers can collectivize and resist in these seemingly atomizing conditions. As such, he has studied trade union activism and challenges to platform narratives and has intervened in British and European policy debates.

Diane E. Bailey is the Geri Gay Professor of Communication in the Department of Communication at Cornell University,

where she studies technology, work, and organization. Her current research interests include precision agriculture, artificial intelligence, computational technologies, digitized artifacts, and metrics/audit cultures. With an expertise in organizational ethnography, she conducts primarily large-scale, team-based empirical studies. She authored, with Paul Leonardi, the MIT Press book, *Technology Choices, Why Occupations Differ in Their Embrace of New Technology.* She has won best paper awards in communication, management, engineering, and library studies.

Frank G.A. de Bakker is Full Professor of Corporate Social Responsibility in the Department of Management and Society at IESEG School of Management, Lille, France where he is a member of a CNRS research laboratory (LEM-CNRS UMR 9221) and coordinates the IESEG Centre for Organizational Responsibility, ICOR. He is co-editor of *Business & Society* and sits on several editorial boards. His research focuses on the interactions between activists and firms on issues of sustainability and corporate social responsibility. His work appeared in journals such as *Academy of Management Journal, Academy of Management Review, Journal of Management Studies, Organization Studies,* and in several other journals and edited volumes.

David Barberá-Tomás is Associate Professor in Ingenio (CSIC-UPV), Universitat Politècnica de València, Spain. His academic research deals with different areas of innovation, such as medical innovation, innovation policy, innovation in creative sectors, or innovation and social entrepreneurship. The results of his research have been published in high impact journals in the fields of Innovation Studies and Management, such as *Academy of Management Journal* and *Research Policy.*

His current work tries to understand the organizational and discursive configuration of socio-technical systems related to Covid-19 testing and artificial intelligence in medical imaging.

Stephen R. Barley is the Christian A. Felipe Professor of Technology Management at the College of Engineering at the University of California Santa Barbara. He is also the Richard Weiland Emeritus Professor of Management Science and Engineering at Stanford University. Barley co-founded and co-directed the Center for Work, Technology and Organization at Stanford's School of Engineering from 1994 to 2015. He was editor of the *Administrative Science Quarterly* from 1993 to 1997 and the founding editor of the *Stanford Social Innovation Review* from 2002 to 2004. Oxford University Press published his latest book, *Work and Technological Change*, in 2020.

Eber Betanzos is a Professor at the National Autonomous University of Mexico (UNAM) and currently works at Mexico's Federal Audit Office (ASF). Previously, he worked as Vice-Minister of Public Administration to Mexico's presidency, as well as Deputy Attorney General in Human Rights to the Office of the Attorney General. He holds a PhD in Human Rights, masters in Critical Theory and Public Policy, as well as a Law degree. Dr Betanzos is currently researching with Dr Savage how to audit digital labour platforms to quantify the conditions of workers to better regulate the platforms and ensure better conditions for workers.

Claudine Bonneau is Associate Professor at UQAM School of Management in Montréal, Canada. She is a member of the Laboratory for Communication and the Digital (LabCMO). Her current work focuses on new work practices, social media uses, and online collaboration. She is also interested in methodological issues related to qualitative research and online ethnography. Besides her contributions to edited books (such as *Experiencing the New World of Work*, Cambridge University Press, 2020 and the *Handbook of Social Media Research Methods*, Sage, 2017), her work has been published in journals such as *Educational Technology Research and Development* and *Communication, Research & Practice*.

Eliane Bucher is an Associate Professor with the Nordic Centre for Internet and Society at BI Norwegian Business School in Oslo, Norway. She completed her doctorate in management at the University of St Gallen in Switzerland where she is currently also a lecturer for digital media and communications management. Her research centres on new forms of work and organizing, algorithmic management, and digital platforms. In particular, she is interested in harnessing automated forms of text analysis and machine learning to understand voice and inequality in large-scale online discourses. This includes inquiries into online spaces as catalysts for social movements.

Itziar Castelló is Senior Lecturer at Surrey Business School in the UK. Itziar's research offers insights on how business, entrepreneurs, and the civil society lead change towards more sustainable societies in the digital economy. She looks at the discursive and governance challenges and opportunities. Itziar has published in peer-reviewed journals such as *Academy of Management Journal, Journal of Management Studies, Research Policy, Journal of Business Ethics, Business & Society*, amongst others. Her research frequently appears in venues such as *The Huffington Post* and *Deusto-Harvard Business Review*. She is Associate Editor of *Business & Society*.

Tania Pereira Christopoulos is Associate Professor in the post-graduation programme in Sustainability and in the Bachelor's degree in Marketing at the University of São Paulo. Tania has a post-doctorate qualification in social business from HEC Montreal and another from the University of Lisbon. She has Phd in business management and a degree in public administration from FGV EAESP, Brazil. Her research agenda emphasizes microfinance, social entrepreneurship, and digital narratives. Tania has published in peer-reviewed journals such as *Business and Society, Journal of Business Ethics, Culture and Organization Journal*, and *Journal of Innovation and Learning*. Her current research focuses on critical organization studies about social finance and sustainability.

Claudio Coletta works as a Senior Assistant Professor at the Department of Philosophy and Communication Studies, University of Bologna (IT). He holds a PhD in Sociology and Social Research (University of Trento). Claudio's research revolves around the fields of science and technology studies, urban studies, and organization studies. Previously, Claudio investigated smart city development processes in the EU and the USA, following the interplay of networked infrastructures and metropolitan-regional governance through qualitative and ethnographic approaches. Currently he coordinates the project 'INFRATIME' focusing on data infrastructures, ecological transitions, and the formation of sustainable smart urbanism timescapes.

Cami Goray is an Information Science PhD Student at the University of Michigan. Previously, she earned her master's degree in Information Science at the University of North Carolina Chapel Hill where she studied User Experience. She is interested in researching the ethical impacts of algorithms on society and finding ways to support people's emotional well-being on social technologies.

Francisca Grommé , PhD, is Assistant Professor in Organisational Dynamics in the Digital Society at the Erasmus University Rotterdam. Her research focuses on digitalization in relation to organizational knowledge practices: how digitalization changes the way data are collected, analysed, and verified by the state and in the digital economy. Francisca is interested in what comes to count as 'good knowledge' for governance, who decides on this, and how this changes relations between citizens and the state, and between professions. Central research themes in Francisca's work are: surveillance, identity, digital work, organizational formats, experiment, expertise, occupations, materiality, participation, and citizenship.

Eduard Grünwald works as a Data Scientist at the Institute for Technology and Innovation Management at RWTH Aachen University (RWTH TIM). There, he is responsible for various data science projects in a consulting capacity, which mainly revolve around the topics of data mining and text mining. His main job is currently at SPORT1 GmbH as a Data Scientist, where he combines his passion for data and sports. His most recent publication dealt with the application of text mining methods within innovation research.

Steve Huckle (https://glowkeeper.github.io/) is a Senior Developer at Minima Global Ltd, a blockchain startup. He also teaches in the Informatics Department at the University of Sussex, which includes convening an Undergraduate module on programming within 3D environments. Steve completed his PhD in 2020, where his thesis asked whether blockchains can help overcome some of the most urgent problems facing humanity. In short, he concluded that they could, but it is impossible to solve all of humanity's issues by diversifying technical operations; we need to change political, economic, and cultural goals, too. Steve is an experienced computing professional, which includes several years of creating websites using Drupal, the content management system that is the focus of Steve's contribution to the book.

Mohammad Hossein Jarrahi (https://www.jarrahi.com) is an Associate Professor at the University of North Carolina at Chapel Hill. His research focuses on the use and consequences of information and communication technologies (ICTs) in extra-organizational contexts, and flexible work arrangements (e.g. mobile work, digital nomadism, and online freelancing). He is also interested in the role of artificial intelligence (AI) in the future of work. In recent years, he has explored the use of novel methodologies such as digital diaries or app-based, passive data collection approaches for capturing people's work practices outside the organization.

Dariusz Jemielniak is Full Professor and head of Management in Networked and Digital Environments (MINDS) department, Kozminski University, and faculty associate at Berkman-Klein Center for Internet and Society, Harvard University. He is a corresponding member of the Polish Academy of Sciences. His recent books include *Collaborative Society* (2020, MIT Press, with A. Przegalinska), *Thick Big Data* (2020, Oxford University Press) and *Common Knowledge? An Ethnography of Wikipedia* (2014, Stanford University Press). His current research projects include climate change denialism online, anti-vaxxer internet communities, and bot detection.

Paul Leonardi is the Duca Family Professor of Technology Management at the University of California, Santa Barbara. He received his PhD from Stanford University. His research and teaching focus on helping companies explore new ways to create and share knowledge effectively using advanced information technologies. In addition to publishing many articles in journals across the fields of Management, Communication, and Information Systems, he is the author of two books, *Car Crashes Without Cars* (MIT Press, 2012) and *Technology Choices* (MIT Press 2015; co-authored with Diane Bailey) on innovation and organizational change and the editor of two volumes on materiality and expertise (both published by Oxford University Press).

Richard Rogers is Professor of New Media & Digital Culture, Media Studies, University of Amsterdam. He is director of the Digital Methods Initiative, known for the development of software tools for the study of online data. Rogers also directs the Netherlands Research School for Media Studies. He is author of *Information Politics on the Web* (MIT Press, 2004), awarded best information science book of the year by the American Society for Information Science and Technology (ASIS&T) and *Digital Methods* (MIT Press, 2013), awarded outstanding book of the year by the International Communication Association (ICA). Rogers has received research grants from institutions including the Open Society Foundations, Ford Foundation, MacArthur Foundation and Gates Foundation. His most recent books are *Doing Digital Methods* (Sage, 2019) and the edited volume (with Sabine Niederer), *The Politics of Social Media Manipulation* (Amsterdam University Press, 2020).

David Rozas (https://davidrozas.cc) is a postdoctoral researcher at the Universidad Complutense de Madrid (Spain). He is currently involved in the ERC EU project P2P Models, in which he is exploring the potentialities and limitations of blockchain to experiment with alternative models of governance and distribution of value in the platform economy. David's previous research as a PhD student at the University of Surrey (UK) focused on individual involvement and group dynamics of Commons-Based Peer Production communities, studying the Free/Libre Open Source Software community Drupal, in the context of the FP7 EU project P2Pvalue. You can find him on Twitter @drozas.

Saiph Savage is an Assistant Professor at Northeastern University and co-director of the Civic Innovation Lab at the National Autonomous University of Mexico (UNAM) where she uses AI and Human Centered Design to create intelligent systems for empowering the invisible workers in our AI industry (e.g. to increase their wages or skills). Dr Savage is one of the 35 Innovators under 35 named by the MIT Technology Review, Center for Democracy & Technology Fellow, and is a former tech worker. Her work has been featured on the BBC and in the *New York Times*, and she holds a PhD in Computer Science from the University of California.

Peter Kalum Schou is an Associate Professor in Strategy and Management at BI Norwegian Business School. He holds a PhD from Copenhagen Business School. Peter's research focuses on organizational development and change in science-based ventures, how digital technology transforms entrepreneurial behaviour as well as the future of work. Currently, his work centres around voice behaviour of gig workers and social movements in online communities.

Viviane Sergi is Associate Professor in Management in the Department of Management at ESG UQAM in Montréal, Canada. Her research interests include process thinking, performativity, the transformation of work, leadership, and materiality. Her recent studies have explored how communication is, in various settings, constitutive of organizational phenomena, such as new work practices, strategy and leadership. She also has a keen interest for methodological issues related to qualitative research. Her work has been published in journals such as *Academy of Management Annals, Human Relations, Scandinavian Journal of Management, Long Range Planning, M@n@gement* and in *Qualitative Research in Organizations and Management*.

Agata Stasik is Assistant Professor in Management at Koźmiński University (Poland) with a background in sociology and science and technology studies (STS). She investigates the intersection of society and energy in the context of fossil fuel production and pathways of post-carbon energy transition. The main focus of her current research lies in the connection between technology, the creation of knowledge for transition, and innovations in politics and governance. Most recently, Agata published in *Energy Research and Social Science* and the *Journal of Risk Research*.

Carlos Toxtli is a PhD candidate in Computer Science at Northeastern University and a visiting research scientist at UNAM's Civic Innovation lab Carlos' PhD thesis focuses on using artificial intelligence to improve the workplace. He has designed intelligent virtual assistants that help managers delegate work to employees, as well as intelligent interfaces that use deep learning to learn to detect when an employer is being unfair to workers. Carlos has worked at Microsoft Research, Google, and the United Nations. He is also an Amazon Twitch Research

Fellow and has founded several startups in Latin America.

Matthias Waldkirch is an Assistant Professor and Director of the Entrepreneurship and Family Firm Institute (EFFI) at EBS University Germany, and an affiliated researcher at the Centre for Family Entrepreneurship and Ownership (CeFEO) at Jönköping International Business School, Sweden. His research focuses on innovation and professionalization processes in family firms, broader dynamics around ownership, and how organizational phenomena unfold in digital spaces. He was a visiting researcher at Stanford University and the University of British Columbia. His research has been published in journals such as Journal of Business Venturing, *Human Resource Management Review*, and *Organization*

Andrew Whelan is a Senior Lecturer in Sociology at the University of Wollongong in New South Wales, Australia. His research interests include the online circulation of music in digital formats, contemporary university administration and governance, and the use of digital document formats in organizations. He is currently researching user experiences of online social welfare claim portals. He has published in journals such as *Critical Sociology, Social Media and Society, Communication and Critical/Cultural Studies, Popular Communication, Critical Social Policy, Open Cultural Studies*, and *Sociological Research Online*.

Nina Willment is a PhD researcher in the Department of Geography at Royal Holloway, University of London. Nina's PhD research seeks to advance understanding of contemporary work cultures within the creative economy, through an empirical case study of British travel bloggers. Her research interests include aesthetic labour, the spatialities of

creative work, and how digital technologies are changing the landscape of work. She has recently published papers in *Geography Compass* and *Information Technology and Tourism*.

Adriana Wilner is Lecturer in Scientific Writing, Assistant Editor at GV-executivo and researcher in critical organization studies at FGV EAESP, Brazil. She specializes in discourse and narrative analysis. Her current research focuses on hidden narratives in social media and the internet. She has published in journals such as *Journal of Business Ethics, Culture and Organization*, and *The Learning Organization*. She is also a journalist with experience in the main print media in Brazil, such as Folha de S.Paulo, O Globo, Exame, CartaCapital, and Pequenas Empresas & Grandes Negócios.

Yinglong Zhang is a Quantitative UX Researcher at Google. Previously, he obtained his PhD degree from the University of North Carolina at Chapel Hill. As a User Experience researcher, he is interested in using quantitative and qualitative methods to understand users' needs and motivations for designing technologies that can better support users' day-to-day work.

Stephanie Zirker is a Business Consultant at IBM and is based in Dublin, Ireland. In 2016, she received her bachelor's degree in Information Science from the University of North Carolina at Chapel Hill. In 2018, she moved to Ireland to do a master's programme in Digital Innovation at the Michael Smurfit Graduate Business School. Previously, she was a Business Analyst on the Continuous Improvement team at Cisco in North Carolina. She enjoys working on the user-focused aspects of technology projects and ensuring that users are adequately represented in the design of a solution.

1

Introduction

The Challenge of Digital Work and Organization for Research Methods

Gillian Symon, Katrina Pritchard, and Christine Hine

Introduction

Even within traditional contexts of employment, many people now move between different sites during the working day or week, and switch between offline working and diverse forms of online work. In addition, some forms of work occur almost wholly online, such as the digital labour of crowdsourcing platforms like Amazon's Mechanical Turk. Organizationally-sanctioned online communications and digital repositories are used alongside extra-organizational resources such as social media and informal face-to-face conversations. Professional and personal activities share communication channels and the line between what is regarded as work and what is not is increasingly blurred. Online work activities may be hidden from view whilst also being subject to new forms of surveillance. This shift in working practices was accentuated through the Covid-19 pandemic which, apart from large-scale business failure, has seen a rapid increase in remote working (often from home, Nagel 2020) and a general restructuring of labour markets (e.g. van Barneveld et al. 2020). It remains to be seen how far these pandemic-induced working patterns will endure over the longer term, an issue we come back to in the concluding chapter. In general, however, digital technologies are associated with the transformation of work organizationally, interpretively, spatially and temporally and, as a consequence, research on digital work is of considerable strategic importance to the field of business and management studies and beyond.

Research methods must continually evolve if researchers are effectively to capture and understand contemporary (digital) working practices. This provides many challenges for the researcher, requiring the tracking of activities and their meanings across multiple modalities often connected in an unpredictable fashion. An array of innovative methodologies are emerging to address these challenges. We bring together some of these techniques in this volume as a sourcebook for management, business organizational and work researchers, capturing the latest thinking and practice in an emergent field of enquiry. We anticipate this volume will be invaluable to a

Gillian Symon, Katrina Pritchard, and Christine Hine, *Introduction*. In: *Research Methods for Digital Work and Organization*.
Edited by Gillian Symon, Katrina Pritchard, and Christine Hine, Oxford University Press.
© Oxford University Press (2021). DOI: 10.1093/oso/9780198860679.003.0001

wide range of researchers as they are faced with understanding new ways of working which do not fit well with traditional research methodologies.

In this introductory chapter, we first outline what we mean by 'digital work' and why this creates new methodological challenges. Subsequently, we consider some of the issues associated with accessing and interpreting digital data specifically. We end the chapter with an overview of the 16 core chapters of the volume which comprise reflexive accounts of researchers' own experiences in developing methods that capture digital aspects of work and organization.

Digital Work

There has been an (often unexamined) assumption that work as an activity is spatially and temporally contained within an identifiable workplace and carried out by people who can unequivocally be labelled as workers (Huws et al. 2018). Consequently, many of our existing research methods aim to collect relatively homogenous data to interrogate a defined work situation. However, contemporary work practices and workplaces, involving various forms of digital technologies, are much less well-defined. We have titled our volume specifically 'research methods for *digital work and organization*' to highlight the potential new methodological challenges raised by digital technologies in a work context. However, it is important to note that 'digital work' now hardly exists as a separate category of work:

> the 'digital' no longer serves as a useful separable feature distinguishing a type of work. Work today always entails the digital; even where the work itself doesn't directly involve a computing device, most contemporary work relates to digital phenomena.
>
> **(Orlikowski and Scott 2016, 88)**

Consequently, our goal in producing this volume does not rest on an assumption that some work is 'digital' while other work is not. While some forms of work may be only lightly touched by digital interventions, much contemporary work—at least in the Global North—involves or is impacted by digital technologies of some kind and to some extent. This requires that our research methods capture these aspects of work if we want to understand the experience of work, management, and organization in the twenty-first century. The contributions to this volume interpret digital work as not just immediate and individual interaction with digital technologies but also: the use of shared online platforms to execute work activities; the presentation and management of (work) selves online; the online support of work; the ways in which work is represented and discussed online; and the structures of organization produced through digital work.

Importantly, we focus on the everyday practice of work. Many authors have discussed large scale changes to the nature and type of work said to be due to digitalization, often through the medium of surveys and involving international comparisons (e.g. Huws et al. 2018; Kässi and Lehdonvirta 2018). Whether utilizing a qualitative or quantitative approach, our focus is on exploring ways of capturing the 'doing' of work (Barley and Kunda 2001) as it is experienced by workers. By workers we include, for example, the self-employed, full-time employees, contract workers and volunteers, including new kinds of workers seemingly formed through the coming together of economic goals and digital technologies (e.g. 'gig workers', the 'precariat', etc. Crouch 2018). In the rest of this section we consider what new methodological issues are raised by digital work and organization under four main headings: blurred boundaries and the visibility of work; mobile working; individualized yet distributed working; the management and surveillance of work.

Blurred boundaries: Identifying digital work as work

One of the defining features of (digital) work in the twenty-first century—and one that has stimulated much debate—is the blurring of boundaries between what is regarded as 'work time' and what is regarded as 'leisure time'. Much of this blurring is associated with the use of digital technologies and may occur because we use the same devices and platforms for work as we do for non-work activities (e.g. smartphones, Facebook, etc.). Concerns are raised that, because employees are reachable through their devices, they will be expected to work after hours and indeed this may become a norm of employee interaction (Mazmanian et al. 2013). Additionally, the intermingling of work/leisure activities online makes distinguishing between different personae (employee, colleague, friend, mother) problematic (Ollier-Malaterre et al. 2013). This raises methodological issues around research access (entering private spaces for research purposes) and identifying content that is (supposedly) work-related as opposed to leisure-related on digital platforms.

The muddied distinctions associated with merged places and timings of work are taken a step further when activities previously regarded as 'leisure' are monetized (Scholz 2013). For example, 'micro-influencers' have turned everyday domestic and personal activities into work by posting videos on YouTube whose embedded advertisements are watched by many thousands of followers (Törhönen et al. 2019). In a similar vein, in this volume, Willment focuses on travel bloggers who have turned holidaying into entrepreneurial labour. Conversely, workers may be providing free labour, particularly where activities are seen as a 'public good'. For example, Hine explores the experience of the digital volunteer who works without recompense in leisure time, and Rozas and Huckle consider the work of developers involved in producing open source software. In these cases and others, they demonstrate how our research methods need to effectively capture merged activities and help us learn more about what work means in the twenty-first century.

The issue of merged work and leisure is related to the growing 'invisibilization' of work: the 'major reorganization of work which expands and depends on many kinds of activities that are occurring out of sight' (DeVault 2014, 777). Most (in)famously associated with housework, the potential for invisible work is extended through the use of digital technologies as our activities are centred on a silent communion between individual and device, as human work is hidden behind anonymized platform labour (Irani and Silberman 2013) and as digital technologies require additional support tasks not recognized as work (Whiting and Symon 2020). When we are not aware of or cannot see the work practices, when the management of such practices is not visible even to those engaged in the work, how can such work form the focus of our research methods? Capturing apparently invisible activities is a recurrent theme within this volume, ranging from Bailey and colleagues, Grommé, and Coletta peering over the shoulder of the employee at their PC to capture the daily doing of digital work, through the autoethnographies of Badger and Hine, to Savage and colleagues' activist research 'visibilizing' work practices to empower workers themselves.

Some of these new methodological approaches capitalize on the tendency that, at the same time as making work invisible, digital technologies also mean that we leave a record of our online work activities behind us (van Dijck 2013). Paradoxically, then, our work is also made *more* visible online either through our own actions (e.g. providing comments on Reddit) or because we are referenced by others (e.g. being tagged on Instagram) (Leonardi and Treem 2020). Such traces are invaluable to the researcher interested in digital work (Hine 2008) but how can we capture these insights and how do we interpret their significance? Devising methods to capture newly visibilized activities of digital work is also a recurring theme of this volume, from the scraping of social media (Bucher and colleagues, Jemielniak and Stasik, and Wilner and colleagues) to the detailed analysis of comments left using track changes within a digital document (Whelan). On the way, contributors also identify and analyse new forms of digital work such as the practice of online audience engagement (Rogers), including curating online material (Willment) and encouraging alignment to a cause (Castello and colleagues). We revisit these recurring themes of invisibilization and visibilization when we describe the content of this volume in more detail towards the end of this chapter.

Mobile working: Capturing the fluidity of workspaces

Elliott and Urry (2010) identify mobility as one of the defining features of contemporary lifestyles, including working practices. What has the potential to constitute a 'workplace' is now much more varied, being nearly any venue in which we can use WiFi. In an early study, Halford (2005) drew attention to the spatial 'hybridity' of workspaces enabled by digital technologies and which might include organizational, domestic, and 'cyber' spaces: 'Hybrid workspaces are not simply relocated or dislocated, but multiply located' (Halford, 2005, 22). Additionally, there is the duality of 'workplace' that takes place simultaneously within an online setting and in the location where the worker is bodily present. The research challenge is not only identifying shifting places of work but also understanding work 'on the move' as it is supported by digital devices. Ironically, in a study of commuters dependent on supportive technology to work as they travel, Hislop and Axtell (2015) highlight all the issues that work against effectiveness in these circumstances, including loss of signal and cramped spaces.

These developments raise methodological issues around how we can capture the potential fluidity of work and organization. In order to investigate digital work and organizing, sometimes our methods will rely on analysing various forms of digital trace data and taking part in digital interactions, but sometimes we will observe or participate in the worksites in which such labour and organizing takes place—and to do so requires methodological creativity in order to address both the physically present and digitally distributed aspects of such work. Within this volume, ethnographers Grommé, Coletta, and Badger, with an embodied presence in the field, grapple with the challenges of taking account of the nature and experience of work that depends upon and orients to digitally enabled infrastructures. When we are following a particular work practice, we need to be able to go where the practice goes, discouraging a priori method or site choices: adopting 'multi-sited and multimodal research strategies, which move between sites ... focusing on practices in specific situations. In this way [we are] captur[ing] how technology, humans, symbols and discourses are linked together in practice' (Plesner and Phillips 2014, 4). This includes considering how we can capture the shift between 'worlds'. To address this challenge the Digital Brain Switch project employed video methodology so research participants could record moments when they switched between different roles in their lives, including between online and offline activities (Whiting et al. 2018). In this volume, Jarrahi et al. discuss digital diaries as one potential way of tracking the work experience of 'digital nomads' (Makimoto and Manners 1997) in particular.

Individualized yet distributed working: Tracking networks of work

In global virtual work teams, work colleagues are brought together (potentially) entirely in cyberspace to work collaboratively on shared tasks. This development reflects the growing globalization of work, partly enabled by the use of digital technologies. Research into virtual teams has been ongoing for many years, highlighting both the potential benefits (Malhotra and Majchrzak 2014) and challenges (Au and Marks 2012) of this mode of digital work. However, more recently, we also see the rapid growth of forms of distributed work including crowdsourcing and digital platform work. In contrast to virtual teams, such workers may be working on the same task but unaware of others working with them (Irani and Silberman 2013): individualized yet distributed work. Such digital work may be freely given or paid for. As an example of the first case, digital 'citizen science' (Heigl et al. 2019) asks individuals to volunteer to take part in large-scale science projects where huge datasets need to be analysed but for which there is as yet no effective automated Artificial Intelligence (AI) system. Similarly, the systematic reviews of scientific studies required for evidencing valid medical interventions needs to cover a vast array of publications, and health professionals volunteer their time to undertake this painstaking work (Lefebvre et al. 2019). These examples raise again the issue of what now counts as 'work'. In both cases, participation is unpaid and voluntary but in the second case, scientific publishers profit from the publication of this 'voluntary' work. In both these cases, individuals come together online to work fairly independently on projects. However, such crowdsourced work may also form a virtual organization. In this volume, for example, Rozas and Huckle highlight the particular governance and coordination issues of online collaboration for writing open source software code, and present their own methodological solution for understanding networks of work.

Forming a more concentrated focus for research currently is the growth of digital labour platforms as part of the (so-called) gig economy. At base, digital platforms are organizations that broker and support links between (so-called) independent contractors and clients requiring their services. These can be services that are location-based—mediated through the platform but physically performed in the local environment (e.g. Uber)—or entirely digitally-based, where 'clickworkers' perform often repetitive small tasks online like checking through visual images for particular patterns (e.g. Amazon's Mechanical Turk) or where the outsourcing of more complex work is managed through the platform (e.g. Upwork) (Berg and de Stefano 2018). The take-up of platform work of this kind in Europe currently represents the main income of an average of only 2.9 per cent (Huws et al. 2018) and is largely combined with more traditional forms of labour. However, it may be more significant as a form of work in the Global South (Graham et al 2020) and it may be a growing source of income with rising unemployment levels post-pandemic (ONS 2020). Crowdwork's global reach tends to encourage worker surveys, but what kind of methods can we develop to capture the multi-modal experience of engaging in this digital work? In this volume, Badger describes his own autoethnography of such platform work as a valuable method of understanding the worker's perspective. This kind of work is very low-paid and precarious in nature, with the lack of contact between workers helping to keep wages low and collective action difficult. This has consequently led to more activist research methods (Irani and Silberman 2013) and Savage and colleagues in this volume report on the kinds of interventionist methods employed to support workers engaged in clickwork.

Management and surveillance of work: Detecting invisible actors

As above, for location-based platform workers, digital mediation has fundamentally altered the labour process (Gandini 2019). Food couriers, although described by platform companies as independent contractors, have little autonomy because they are micro-managed through phone-based apps utilizing algorithm-based technology (van Doorn and Badger 2020). In the same way as the time and motion studies of Taylor (1911), algorithms suggest the most efficient ways of completing tasks. The rise of algorithms to manage or deliver work raises new issues about how we can capture these elements of twenty-first century work practices, particularly given they 'seem to operate under the surface or in the background' (Introna 2016, 25). Badger, in this volume, details his own methodology aimed at capturing how algorithmic management affects the everyday experience of platform workers. This (invisible) management of work through digital means (algorithms) involves continual performance monitoring and evaluation—what Ursula Huws has termed 'logged labour' (Huws 2016), for example:

> Upwork, the online freelance marketplace offers its clients the option of paying by the hour as it can monitor the workers by recording their keyboard strokes and mouse clicks and taking random screen shots.
>
> **(Berg and de Stefano 2018, 181)**

Not only does the technology itself monitor performance but customers are also encouraged to provide anonymous online evaluations (e.g. Scott and Orlikowski (2012) on TripAdvisor; Wilner and colleagues, this volume, on Glassdoor). Such evaluations are deliberately made public (for informed consumer choice) and therefore are easily accessible to the researcher; however, this raises important questions about the ethics of digital data collection. All the contributors to this volume debate the ethical issues raised by their research and we return to consider this issue in more detail in the concluding chapter.

As van Doorn and Badger (2020) have argued (and see Badger in this volume), workers employed through digital platforms may begin a process of *self*-monitoring in order to increase personal efficiency. Indeed, society as a whole has begun to take up digital technologies as a means of self-monitoring in pursuit of a cultural orientation to self-knowledge, self-entrepreneurialization and responsibilization (Lupton 2020). Powered by Fitbits, smartphone apps and confessional social media, such digital technologies begin to construct life itself as work—something we must labour at. The data generated by such self-monitoring has become a lucrative commodity to be bought and sold by corporate bodies; through digitalization our personal lives now form the basis of venture capital. Rogers in this volume proposes that we critically engage with these traces, and the metrics based upon them, and re-purpose for less individualized goals; turning instead to increasing an awareness of important social issues. Coming full circle here, the boundaries between the activities of work and those of leisure are unclear and researching digital work appears almost boundary-less, with the potential to touch on so much of human life.

Digital Data

In the previous section, we identified why digital work may raise some issues for research methodology. As a response, we have seen the development of 'digital' defined as 'the use of online and digital technologies to collect and analyse research data' (Snee et al. 2016, 1). Such methods are often described as either traditional methods that have 'been digitalised' (Veltri 2020, 28) or methods that have emerged as a specific response to the kinds of data and manipulations available online (e.g. text-mining algorithms, as discussed in this volume by Jemielniak and Stasik and by Bucher and colleagues). In addition, Rogers (2013, and see this volume) argues that researchers should exploit the existing functionality of the internet to define new research methods (e.g. utilising embedded hyperlinks). In this volume, Badger describes in detail how the functionality of the smartphone can be put to use in the capture of research data, and Savage and her colleagues designed plug-ins that can open up crowdwork platforms to additional data capture. However, it is important to recognize some of the issues that new methods of digital data capture highlight, particularly in relation to the nature and quality of digital data. It is essential that we take a critical perspective on the nature of digital data and its role in the research process.

Digital data may be commonly thought of as 'big data' producing 'topographical maps of internet phenomena, illuminating the overall shape and form of the issues under consideration' (Whiting and Pritchard 2020, 4). As such, Veltri (2020, 15) argues that 'collectively, human society is assembling massive amounts of behavioural data …'. For quantitative researchers, the availability of vast online datasets means the possibility to address previously unanswerable questions and to feel greater confidence in the generalizability of their conclusions. However it poses particular problems for qualitative research online, and Hine argues that 'the availability of Internet archives and the ability to search data en masse accentuates the sense of the task's enormity in relation to the individual researcher's capacities' (2013, 12) concluding that 'we may yet see qualitative researchers more broadly accepting the possibility that various forms of automatic coding, data coding and visualisation could inform their work' (Hine 2013, 129). In this volume, we see examples of this in the work presented by Bucher and colleagues, and Castello and colleagues, and combining qualitative and quantitative work is advocated by several contributors. Beyond this, however, it is important to note that the association between digital data and big data obscures other perspectives (e.g. online ethnography) and other issues around digital data. Additionally, the multi-modal nature of digital data may well be over-looked. Digital data may often be assumed to be textual or numerical but in fact encompasses images, sound and relational data embedded in links likes and follows. There is a requirement to develop methods that can also capture these aspects and, additionally, to develop new multi-modal methods of *presenting* our research, beyond the table or graph. Rogers in this volume provides some examples of innovative visual ways of presenting data analysis that is both revealing and impactful.

There is a continuing debate about whether work behaviours online are naturalistic (or as Veltri, 2020, puts it 'organic'), as in data that are not artificially generated for research purposes but that can be observed and collated without influence. However, they are, of course, still shaped by the context of production, as are all data. As users, we are aware that the internet is panoptical, that we are observed, judged, and our data collected by external agencies. So we may shape our digital presences accordingly. This impression management may be more pronounced when we are interacting online in our capacity as an employee, manager, entrepreneur, etc. (Ollier-Mallaterre et al. 2013). Additionally data are shaped by digital platforms and by underlying algorithms (Scott and Orlikowski 2012). That is, these sites have already constituted the nature of the data we can access (Ruppert et al 2013). Partly this is about the shaping of digital data by platform design choices and hidden operations (Orlikowski 2007) but it also concerns the source of these data. It is difficult to know whether the data we access online were produced by humans, automated processes or artificial intelligence (Gerlitz and Weltevrede 2020). Consequently 'the critical eye that social scientists have learned to exercise needs to be sharp in a research domain in which digital data have become the most valuable asset for very large sectors of the economy …' (Veltri 2020, 7). However, this does not render these data valueless, as long as we recognize their context and either make this the focus of our attention or reflexively account for it in our data interpretation (as further discussed by Jemielniak and Sustik in this volume).

This realization emphasizes the sociomateriality of the research endeavour; the need to take into account the entanglement of the social and the material in our everyday work practices (Orlikowski and Scott 2008). Our digital work is sociomaterial, not just because we use (digital) tools to accomplish work but because the distinction between human and material actions is contested in digital work. In relation to the object of our research practices, we must be concerned with how sociomaterial relations produce digital work and not only how (human) workers are working digitally: 'digital platforms reconfigure human/non-human dichotomies into a more complex continuum and therefore challenge certain methodological assumptions' (Gerlitz and Weltevrede 2020, 9). With respect to our research practices, we must also be concerned with how the research object has been sociomaterially produced through the entanglement of researchers, participants, digital platforms, digital research tools, etc:

> Methodological approaches might look to engage with … the kind of analysis … that works to expose and acknowledge the active and constitutive role of technology, both in the domains being researched, as well as in the methods themselves.
>
> (Knox 2016, 184–5)

Various contributors throughout this volume draw attention to the ways in which data are presented to us by the internet—shaped by platform regulation and underlying algorithms—and reflexively explore the ways in which they accounted for this 'pre-packaging'.

Drawing attention to the context of the production of digital data is thus pertinent not just to the way in which research participants mould their presence online and how digital data are shaped by the digital environment, but also to how we, as researchers, are active in creating the 'data' we then study. In a digital environment this can literally mean that we find ourselves in our own data as Whiting and Pritchard (2020) indicate. In their research using digital alerts and search engines to explore the discursive construction of age and work online (Pritchard and Whiting 2014), they found their own blogs and tweets appearing in the data they were gathering. However, we also mean by this that whatever methods we choose to investigate the experience of digital work create a representation of that experience in a particular way. Just because we are scraping data rather than dynamically constructing it through interviews does not mean that the data offer a transparent reflection of a phenomenon. The way we go about 'observing', in itself, creates particular windows on the phenomenon: 'particular methods mediate the object of study, rendering it visible for science in particular ways' (Plesner and Phillips 2014, 7). Hence the need for ongoing critical appraisal in this research as much as any other (Whiting and Pritchard 2020). This kind of reflexive analysis of methodological choices and processes is a feature of the chapters in this volume.

We have suggested that digital data may be more easily available than other forms of data we may seek to collect. Additionally, of course, it may be easier to access some participants if research is conducted online (e.g. shift workers, Morgan and Symon 2004). However, this suggestion needs qualification, given that digital data are an important potential source of income revenue. The availability of data for scraping is a matter for digital platforms to determine. Such access as is provided via social media platforms, utilizing an application programming interface (API), has been subject to change without warning. In the past, collecting historical data from Twitter has entailed employing particular data mediators and paying large sums for access (Bruns and Burgess 2016).[1] So the idea that online data are readily available could be limited by financial considerations, raising the important issue of the potential restriction of online research to those institutions, organizations and research groups that can afford to purchase datasets, and undermining the argument that online research is necessarily cost-efficient.

Additionally, of course, when our focus is digital work, our access to relevant digital data is severely constrained by organizational firewalls and privacy considerations. Directly accessing, for example, organizational email systems, while it has been accomplished by some researchers, is problematic when interchanges may be personal or expose the inner workings (or even commercial secrets) organizations may prefer to keep hidden. Employees may set up Facebook or WhatsApp groups in which they discuss the intimate workings of their own organizations and which are purposefully closed to outsiders to encourage free sharing of views. Famously, the UK Parliament is awash with MPs' cross-party WhatsApp groups discussing everything from TV programmes to shared hobbies to specific Government policies, and which are not subject to any parliamentary regulation much less open to researchers' analysis (Elgot 2017). Indeed, it is these very hidden areas of organizations in which researchers may be most interested! However, we may find ourselves even more firmly locked out of organizational digital data than the difficulties already well known in accessing real-time observational data in face-to-face settings. We may then rely on reports of such data in traditional interviews or access employee voice through personal views reported on Twitter (Conway et al. 2019) or through (anonymous) blogs (e.g. Ellis and Richards 2009). New kinds of negotiations and ethical undertakings may be required to access such organizational digital data. Ethical issues of working in this area are discussed by many of our contributors and we return to this in our concluding chapter.

However, as we have already noted, there are only a few types of work that are exclusively digital, many have some sort of digital aspect but workers tend to move across digital and non-digital worksites. So relevant research methods for digital work are not only confined to online data capture. Conversely, 'offline' methods are useful for capturing certain aspects of online work. Indeed, a combination of online and offline methods may be useful in many contexts, especially if we are seeking to understand the everyday practice of work holistically. Indeed, we may question 'how far the online–offline boundary is defensible for bounding an object of study, whether that be for principled or pragmatic reasons' (Hine 2013, 13). This is a further example of a twenty-first century blurring of boundaries that once were thought to be a given.

Drawing on these observations, there are some important aspects to keep in mind concerning our use of digital data to inform our understanding of digital work:

- recognizing the multi-modal nature of digital work and consequently the need to capture not just text but visual and other sensory modes of digital interaction and data interconnections;
- not getting 'carried away' by the nature and availability of digital data into analysis simply because the data exist but to keep focused on the work practice in which one is interested, which may take us out of the digital sphere;
- remaining aware of the constructed nature of digital data and its context of production in our interpretation, including restrictions on access which shape what data can be collected and from whom;
- orienting to the sociomaterial performance of work more explicitly (Symon and Pritchard 2015).

In the conclusion we return to reflect on the range of skills that the authors of our chapters have deployed in defining, accessing and analysing their chosen forms of data.

Overview of the Volume

This volume provides 16 chapters each showcasing an individual method or package of methods in the context of research conducted by the chapter's author(s). This is not predominantly a text book, which aims to produce templates for knowledge production (see Pratt et al. 2020 for limitations of this approach), but rather seeks to present the methods in the context of empirical research projects, illustrating the distinctive intellectual contribution to business and management studies that such approaches can make. In each case our contributors demonstrate methodological adaptability and creativity as they seek to capture work practices in fast-moving multi-modal working environments. As such, the research work presented in this volume is at the forefront of methodological innovation in understanding digital work. In addition, this volume highlights the importance of insights from a range of different disciplines. A focus on digital work as interdisciplinary opens up a wide range of studies conducted by sociologists, geographers, computer scientists, social anthropologists, etc. As our research becomes increasingly recognized as sociomaterial (Woodward 2020), so combining different outlooks becomes more enlightening and disciplinary boundaries become less helpful.

The core 16 chapters are organized into four parts, each part focusing on a particular aspect of digital work. It is important to emphasize, however, that these sections are not mutually exclusive. Chapters are sited in particular parts in relation to their predominant theme but the content also often overlaps with other parts, and readers interested in a particular platform or method may wish to consult the index to identify that focus. Each part is described below.

Part I Working with screens

This section presents research approaches seeking to understand digital work through the detailed analysis of individual and group interactions with computer artefacts, as it were 'through the screen', including work with multiple and hand-held screens. As this group of authors argue, capturing the nature of that digital work is particularly difficult because, as we have already stressed above, it can appear 'invisible'. All these researchers approached this methodological challenge by adopting some form of observational or ethnographic approach, such that they are physically present at the research site. However, the different ways they go about this illustrate the wide array of methodological possibilities available to the researcher interested in digital work.

In their analysis of changes to engineers' working practices with increasing computerization, Bailey, Barley, and Leonardi adapted to the challenge by creating multi-modal innovative techniques to capture work experience, and it is through the rigorous application of this range of methods that they are able to identify important processes of digital work which may have otherwise seemed invisible. While Bailey et al. were in the role of observers of the action, visiting offices at regular intervals, Grommé's chapter describes sustained, co-located fieldwork, addressing the invisibility of screenwork by capturing the minutiae of digital work as it unfolds. Among her methodological strategies is a focus on making visible the role of the screen itself in 'bringing into being objects of study and intervention', taking a sociomaterial approach in identifying the agency of screens in performing digital work.

Taking the embodied presence a step further, Badger provides an autoethnography of the gig work of becoming a food courier in London. This makes available to him the complex everyday working practices which are largely invisible to consumers. While apparently very much physical work (cycling around the streets of London), Badger's account draws attention to the digital artefacts which coordinate this work, as delivered through the smartphone interface. In so doing, he illustrates the way in which the functionality of the digital device can be turned to research purposes and he develops the practice of autoethnography in the process. Here, then, the digital is simultaneously a focus of research interest and the method through which research insights are captured. Like Bailey et al., the research is multi-method and multi-modal, but in this case, this multi-faceted investigation is occurring through one device, as Badger concludes 'smartphones are undoubtedly a Swiss Army knife in the qualitative researcher's toolkit'. Coletta shares a focus on 'urban rhythms' with Badger. However, while Badger is experiencing this firsthand on the seat of his bicycle, Coletta's ethnographic fieldsite is situated within Dublin's traffic control centre. The screenwork that is Coletta's interest is that which mediates traffic controllers' understanding of urban traffic movement. Coletta's focus on the temporality of this work again encompasses its sociomaterial expression (here algorithms) and emphasizes how the research both has its own temporality and also becomes attuned to the 'heartbeat' of the site. In this way, Coletta's insights on digital work also expands our understanding of ethnography as method in space and time.

Ultimately this group of chapters, while concerned with digital work specifically, also illustrates how even a focus on screenwork requires an understanding of the larger sociomaterial workspace: both zooming in to the screen to understand how larger processes are enacted, and panning out to the fieldsite to understand how screenwork is implicated in performing digital work. The chapters illustrate that while work may have apparently moved online, the embodied presence of the researcher in the fieldsite is still of significant value in making visible what might otherwise go unnoticed.

Part II   Digital working practices

The chapters in this section focus on capturing the detail of how contemporary digital working practices unfold from the workers' points of view. In each case the challenge is to find ways of following work that is 'temporally and spatially unpredictable' (Hine) and that occurs outside the traditional 'territorialized workspace' (Willment). As in Section I, this can make the work difficult to observe and the contributors to this section all strive in different ways to make these practices more transparent, whether that be to researchers or to workers themselves.

Mobility of working practices is the focus of Jarrahi, Goray, Zirker, and Zhang's study of 'digital nomads', professionals who work outside traditional offices and usually in a variety of different contexts, as enabled by digital technologies and connectivity. For mobile work, we need mobile research methods and Jarrahi and colleagues utilize digital diaries for experience sampling, capitalizing on the functionality of existing worktools as vehicles for their research by delivering their diaries through participants' smartphones and laptops. Willment's travel bloggers are similarly engaging in explicitly hyper-mobile work, and she is able to capture this through a netnography of their emergent blog accounts, as a contemporary form of autobiographical diary. Hine addresses the challenge of following the unpredictable working practices of digital volunteers through an autoethnography of her own experience, including the affective and tacit elements of that experience. Additionally, in this section, Savage, Toxtli, and Betanzos-Torres take an activist perspective seeking to improve the working practices of crowdworkers through providing digital means for mutual support and development. This requires capturing largely tacit and invisible processes of online working, and they detail various digital tools they have developed to both log the work and provide real-time interventions for improving individual working practices through learning and development. Overall, these accounts reveal the complexity of such practices as workers move on- and offline and as they bring together different digital artefacts and operate across different digital platforms in a form of 'articulation work' (Jarrahi et al.).

In each case, the authors explain how they have adapted existing methods for digital work, often capitalizing on existing worktools as vehicles for research. However, all the authors also argue for additional methods. Hine supplements her individual autoethnographic experience by interviewing other digital volunteers with different backgrounds and motivations, while both Jarrahi and colleagues and Willment chose to also interview their diary keepers and blog writers to add explanation to observed phenomena, in both cases using the diaries and blogs themselves as prompts in 'object-elicitation interviews' (Woodward 2020). Savage and her colleagues design opportunities for information sharing, but also conduct experiments to check that their interventions are having a positive effect.

While the focus here is on individual experience of digital working practices, the unavoidably (digitally) interconnected nature of those practices is also highlighted. Willment's bloggers rely on audience engagement to create revenue, and Hine is conscious of co-workers and the larger organization through the digital traces of their work activities, even if rarely interacting with them. Savage et al.'s very purpose is to turn what appears to be the atomized experience of crowdsourced work into a collective support network and community of practice: 'computationally orchestrating crowd workers to actively drive positive change'.

These chapters are based on very different case examples, illustrating the digital working practices of a wide variety of occupations and highlighting how the digital both shapes and is shaped by these practices. As in our opening comments, we see how the boundaries between 'work' and 'leisure' are increasingly blurred: as workers' spatial and temporal flexibility incorporates spaces once thought of as leisure-oriented (e.g. coffee shops); as travel bloggers' apparently leisure-lifestyle obscures the hard work that goes into the production of attractive blogs; as volunteering is increasingly organized online; and as 'clickwork', once thought of as temporary and part-time, becomes an opportunity for career development. Our contributors here demonstrate that our research methods can be creatively adapted and new methods developed to capture these changing contexts.

Part III Distributed work and organizing

In this section we turn to examples of distributed forms of digital work, whereby work is conducted and organized through digital interconnections, giving rise to new kinds of organizational forms and practices. Rozas and Huckle provide an insider ethnography of an online community of open source software engineers, Drupal, whose interconnected, heterogeneous and somewhat invisible digital work raises the issue of what is identified and valued as a work contribution. Concentrating on a similarly 'volunteer' workforce, Jemielniak and Stasik explore the Wikipedia community and, through an analysis of debates on Twitter, investigate how the entries produced by these digital workers are constructed as reliable. Bucher, Schou, Waldkirch and colleagues also 'scrape' data from a public social media site (Reddit) to access the discussions of a distributed work community—freelance professionals using the digital platform Upwork, identifying a new kind of community-driven self-organization. Again new kinds of organizing on the internet form the focus of the research as Castello, Barberá-Tomás, and de Bakker explore the emotion-symbolic work of a social movement organization working through social media platforms to generate public support for their cause.

Many researchers in this section have used existing social media platforms to collect data, taking advantage of both the longevity and real-time nature of these data (prefiguring the focus on 'digital traces' in the subsequent section). They describe various forms of 'big data' analysis and introduce us to automated tools for data collection. But they also highlight the limitations to such approaches, advocating that big data collection be understood as an initial stage and automated tools as predominantly a way of narrowing down a focus which can then be explored more qualitatively. Jemeilniak and Stasik label this phenonemon as 'thick big data' and suggest a further form of 'elicitation' interview (see the outline of Part II) which could be termed 'big-data elicitation' as the results of the overarching analysis are brought into a more focused interaction.

In this section, we become further aware of the mutual shaping of digital work, academic theory, and research practice. Rozas and Huckle utilize Activity Theory as their analytical framework, illustrating how this both opens up a perspective on digital work but is itself modified as a result of the rise of digital work and organization. Similarly Castello and colleagues draw on existing theory on emotion-symbolic work but demonstrate how this is altered in a digital environment and particularly through visual methods of communication. As noted above, we see the sociomateriality of data and research processes as data 'scraping' tools are disabled by changes made to social media platforms (Jemielniak and Stasik) and Castello and colleagues emphasize how the digital platform shapes the timing of interactions that are then captured by researchers.

Overall, in this section, we are again reminded of the blurring of boundaries highlighted through research into digital work. The boundary between work and recreation is blurred as volunteers provide flexible digital labour to important social projects; the boundary between being inside and outside the organization is blurred as workers take to public social media to discuss their working practices or organizational work processes are discussed externally; and the boundary between qualitative and quantitative research is blurred as big data and qualitative analysis become entangled. Taken together these chapters encourage us to focus on not just the blurring of boundaries but the (re-)drawing of boundaries of both work and research about work in the light of digital technologies.

Part IV Digital traces of work

Many of the chapters in this book concern 'digital traces of work' to the extent that researchers may be capturing online content. In Section IV, however, we focus on how digital traces left by digital workers are re-purposed for research objectives. The digital work highlighted in Rogers' chapter is the work of encouraging public engagement with online content. Rogers critiques the digital traces of likes, views and followers at an individual level (the 'vanity metrics' of identity performance) and substitutes with an analysis of degree of engagement with social issues through creative visibilization of digital traces. Sergi and Bonneau's analysis is similarly multi-modal, while also visibilizing a previously undocumented practice specific to the online environment—'working out loud'. This practice encapsulates workers' postings (particularly on Instagram) of mundane aspects of their everyday work. In a university setting, Whelan's analysis of the 'track changes' function of Word similarly focuses on an (apparently) mundane and everyday work practice, the 'digital residue' of annotating an organizational document. Whelan interprets track changes as the site of a critical negotiation of stakeholder perspectives on the issue of work-load planning. Wilner, Christopoulos and Aquino Alves also focus on aspects of work difficult to express openly through their analysis of worker opinions on working in self-managed organizations, often 'romanticized' as ideal work sites. Wilner and colleagues track and analyse the digital traces left by employees as they review their organizations through the Glassdoor platform.

In all cases here, we see again the intertwined process of visibilizing and invisibilizing in digital work and in research on that work. Both Whelan and Wilner and colleagues argue that the digital may provide the means for exposing sensitive organizational issues and giving voice to difficult to express opinions—often opinions that are critical of the organization or organizational members—whether that be in the 'backchannel marginalia' (Whelan) of an organizational document or the anonymous space of an online review platform. Sergi and Bonneau bring to light a practice not previously identified and reflexively emphasize how it is through their creative capturing and analysis of this practice that the practice itself becomes a 'phenomenon', including establishing the boundaries of the concept. Indeed, they are also keen to detail their own 'mundane' research practices in order to expose the invisible 'messiness' of everyday research practice. Rogers re-purposes and re-presents data on the internet using creative visual techniques that take advantage of existing internet functionality to expose aspects of issue engagement not otherwise visible.

Again our attention is brought to the sociomateriality of research practice. Wilner and colleagues highlight the ways in which Glassdoor's structuring of reviews produces particular accounts. This structuring is inevitably reflected in their own interpretation of the antenarratives they assemble. Whelan also emphasizes the role of MS Word software in producing organizational effects, as some text is retained while marginalized comments are later deleted, thus invisibilizing earlier traces of debate and opposition. Rogers' central argument is how digital functionality shapes issue presentation and Sergi and Bonneau highlight the complex interaction between their data collection (including the use of hashtags), its structuring, and their consequent presentation.

Overall in Section IV our attention is brought to the existence of a variety of available digital traces of work that may not be self-evident but whose excavation provides important insights into work and organization; as long as we have the imagination as researchers to envisage the methodologies that might capture such insights, and the reflexivity to recognize the sociomaterial shaping of our research accounts.

Conclusion

Several recurring themes permeate the chapters contributed to this volume and can be considered emergent features of the methodological landscape of investigating digital work. We note here particularly how the invisible activities of digital work may be 'visibilized' through: the embodied presence of a researcher paying acute attention (including through autoethnography); the assembling or re-visualization of diverse digital contributions which, by being brought together, provide new insights; or through tracking activities as they unfold online, uncovering unseen interconnections. This highlights for us the importance of being aware of who and what is potentially detrimentally exposed by our practice and giving due attention to dealing with the new ethical challenges that arise, which we explore further in the concluding chapter.

We note also the blurring of boundaries, not just between aspects of digital 'work' but between traditional methodological commitments (e.g. quantitative and qualitative), research disciplines (e.g. computing science and social science) and the traditional online/offline distinction of research foci. Linked to this is a revitalized creativity in inventing new methodological tools as solutions to the challenges provided by seeking to capture digital work and organization, and an orientation to synergy and efficiency in repurposing existing digital artefacts for research objectives. In the concluding chapter we will return to the potential new skills and sensibilities required of researchers interested in understanding digital work and organization. Overall, we appreciate the ongoing need for reflexivity in our research endeavour, recognizing this as a sociomaterial practice shaped not just by our actions but entangled in the multi-modal materiality of the world.

All of these are important aspects of research practice for investigating digital work which, in a post-Covid world, is likely to take up even more of our research focus. Our concluding chapter considers further this new post-Covid research scene.

Notes

1. In 2000, Veltri argued that 'the age of free and relatively unregulated access of social media platforms' API to obtain data is over' (page 46). However, in January 2021 Twitter granted academics full access to public data https://www.reuters.com/article/us-twitter-product-idUSKBN29V2B1. As we comment, the situation is changeable but depends on the ongoing cooperation of social media platforms with the needs of researchers.

References

Au, Y., and Marks, A. 2012. 'Virtual teams are literally and metaphorically invisible': Forging identity in culturally diverse virtual teams. *Employee Relations*, 34(3): pp. 271–87.

Barley, S. R., and Kunda, G. 2001. Bringing work back in. *Organization Science*, 12(1): pp. 76–95.

Berg, J. and de Stefano, V. 2018. Employment and regulation for clickworkers. In Neufeind, M., O' Reilly, J. and Ranft, F. (eds). *Work in the Digital Age: Challenges of the Fourth Industrial Revolution*. (pp 175–184). London: Rowman and Littlefield International.

Bruns, A., and Burgess, J. 2016. Methodological innovation in precarious spaces: The case of Twitter. In Snee, H., Roberts, S., Hine, C., Morey, Y., and Watson, H. (eds), *Digital Methods for the Social Sciences* (pp. 17–33). London: Palgrave Macmillan.

Conway, E., Rosati, P., Monks, K., and Lynn, T. 2019. Voicing job satisfaction and dissatisfaction through Twitter: Employees' use of cyberspace. *New Technology, Work and Employment*, 34(2): pp. 139–156.

Crouch, C. 2018. Redefining labour relations and capital in the digital age. In Neufeind, M., O'Reilly, J., and Ranft, F. (eds). *Work in the Digital Age.* (pp. 187–98). London: Rowman and Littlefield International.

DeVault, M. L. 2014. Mapping invisible work: Conceptual tools for social justice projects. *Sociological Forum*, 29(4): pp. 775–790.

Elgot, J. 2017. WhatsApp: The go-to messaging tool for parliamentary plotting, *The Guardian*, 12 June. Accessed 19 January 2021.

Elliott, A., and Urry, J. 2010. *Mobile Lives*. London: Routledge.

Ellis, V., and Richards, J. 2009. Creating, connecting and correcting: Motivations and meanings of workblogging amongst public service workers. In Bolton, S. C. and Houlihan, M. (eds), *Work Matters: Critical Reflections on Contemporary Work.* (pp 250–68). Basingstoke: Palgrave Macmillan.

Gandini, A. 2019. Labour process theory and the gig economy. *Human Relations*, 72(6): pp 1038–1056.

Gerlitz, C., and Weltevrede, E. 2020. What happens to ANT, and its emphasis on the socio-material grounding of the social, in digital sociology? In Blok, A., Farias, I., and Roberts, C. (eds), *The Routledge Companion to Actor-Network Theory.* (pp. 345–56). London: Routledge.

Graham, M., Woodcock, J., Heeks, R., Mungai, P., Van Belle, J. P., Du Toit, D., ... and Silberman, S. M. 2020. *The Fairwork Foundation: Strategies for Improving Platform Work in a Global Context*. Geoforum.

Halford, S. 2005. Hybrid workspace: Re-spatialisations of work, organisation and management. *New Technology, Work and Employment*, 20(1): pp. 19–33.

Heigl, F., Kieslinger, B., Paul, K. T., Uhlik, J., and Dörler, D. 2019. Opinion: Toward an international definition of citizen science. *Proceedings of the National Academy of Sciences*, 116(17): pp. 8089–8092. https://www.pnas.org/content/116/17/8089

Hine, C. 2008. Virtual ethnography: Modes, varieties, affordances. In Fielding, N., Lee, R., and Blank, G. (eds), *The SAGE Handbook of Online Research Methods* (pp 401–15). London: Routledge.

Hine, C. 2013. *The Internet*. Oxford: Oxford University Press.

Hislop, D., and Axtell, C. 2015. The work-related affordances of business travel: A disaggregated analysis of journey stage and mode of transport. *Work, Employment and Society*, 29(6): pp. 950–68.

Huws, U. 2016. Logged labour: A new paradigm of work organization? *Work Organisation, Labour & Globalisation*. 10(1): pp. 7–26.

Huws, U., Spencer, N. H., and Syrdal, D. S. 2018. Online, on call: The spread of digitally organised just-in-time working and its implications for standard employment models. *New Technology, Work and Employment*, 33(2): pp. 113–29.

Introna, L. D. 2016. Algorithms, governance, and governmentality: On governing academic writing. *Science, Technology, & Human Values*, 41(1): pp 17–49.

Irani, L. C., and Silberman, M. S. 2013. April. Turkopticon: Interrupting worker invisibility in Amazon Mechanical Turk. In *Proceedings of the SIGCHI conference on human factors in computing systems* (pp. 611–20). New York: ACM Press.

Kässi, O., and Lehdonvirta, V. 2018. Online labour index: Measuring the online gig economy for policy and research. *Technological Forecasting and Social Change*, 137, pp. 241–8.

Knox, J. 2016. What's the matter with MOOCs? Socio-material methodologies for educational research. In Snee, H., Roberts, S., Hine, C., Morey, Y., and Watson, H. (eds), *Digital Methods for the Social Sciences*. (pp. 17–33). London: Palgrave Macmillan.

Lefebvre, C., Glanville, J., Briscoe, S., Littlewood, A., Marshall, C., Metzendorf, M. I., … and Wieland, L. S. 2019. Searching for and selecting studies. In Higgins, J., Thomas, J., Chandler, J. et al (eds), *Cochrane Handbook for Systematic Reviews of Interventions*. (pp. 67–107). Chichester: Wiley..

Leonardi, P. M., and Treem, J. W. 2020. Behavioral visibility: A new paradigm for organization studies in the age of digitization, digitalization, and datafication. *Organization Studies*, Online-First.

Lupton, D. 2020. *Data Selves*. Cambridge: Polity Press.

Makimoto, T., and Manners, D. 1997. *Digital Nomad*. Chichester: Wiley.

Malhotra, A., and Majchrzak, A. 2014. Enhancing performance of geographically distributed teams through targeted use of information and communication technologies. *Human Relations*, 67(4): pp. 389–411.

Mazmanian, M., Orlikowski, W. J., and Yates, J. 2013. The autonomy paradox: The implications of mobile email devices for knowledge professionals. *Organization Science*, 24(5): pp. 1337–57.

Morgan, S. and Symon, G. 2004. Electronic interviews in organizational research. In Cassell, C. and Symon, G. (eds), *Essential Guide to Qualitative Methods in Organizational Research*. (pp 23–33). London:Sage.

Nagel, L. 2020. The influence of the COVID-19 pandemic on the digital transformation of work. *International Journal of Sociology and Social Policy*. Online First.

Ollier-Malaterre, A., Rothbard, N. P., and Berg, J. M. 2013. When worlds collide in cyberspace: How boundary work in online social networks impacts professional relationships. *Academy of Management Review*, 38(4): pp. 645–69.

ONS 2020. Earnings and employment from Pay As You Earn Real Time Information, UK https://www.ons.gov.uk/employmentandlabourmarket/peopleinwork/earningsandwo rkinghours/bulletins/earningsandemploymentfrompayasyouearnrealtimeinformatio nuk/latest (November).

Orlikowski, W. J. 2007. Sociomaterial practices: Exploring technology at work. *Organization Studies*, 28(9): pp. 1435–48.

Orlikowski, W. J., and Scott, S. V. 2008. Sociomateriality: Challenging the separation of technology, work and organization. *Academy of Management Annals*, 2(1): pp. 433–74.

Orlikowski, W. J., and Scott, S. V. 2016. Digital work: A research agenda. In Czarniawska, B. (ed.). *A Research Agenda for Management and Organization Studies*. (pp. 88–95). Cheltenham: Edward Elgar Publishing.

Plesner, U., and Phillips, L. 2014. Introduction: Approaching the Study of Virtual Worlds. In Plesner, U. and Phillips, L. (eds), *Researching Virtual Worlds* (pp. 1–15). London: Routledge.

Pratt, M. G., Sonenshein, S., and Feldman, M. S. 2020. Moving beyond templates: A bricolage approach to conducting trustworthy qualitative research. *Organizational Research Methods*, Online First.

Pritchard, K., and Whiting, R. 2014. Baby boomers and the lost generation: On the discursive construction of generations at work. *Organization Studies*, 35(11): pp. 1605–26.

Rogers, R. 2013. *Digital Methods*. Cambridge, MA: MIT Press.

Ruppert, E, Law, J. Savage, M. 2013. Reassembling social science methods: The challenge of digital devices. *Theory, Culture & Society*, 30(4): pp 22–46.

Scholz, T. (ed.). 2013. *Digital Labour: The Internet as Playground and Factory*. New York: Routledge.

Scott, S. V., and Orlikowski, W. J. 2012. Reconfiguring relations of accountability: Materialization of social media in the travel sector. *Accounting, Organizations and Society*, 37(1): pp. 26–40.

Snee, H., Roberts, S., Hine, C., Morey, Y., and Watson, H. (eds). 2016. *Digital Methods for the Social Sciences* (pp. 17–33). London: Palgrave Macmillan.

Symon, G., and Pritchard, K. 2015. Performing the responsive and committed employee through the sociomaterial mangle of connection. *Organization Studies*, 36(2): pp. 241–63.

Taylor, F.W. 1911. *The Principles of Scientific Management*. New York: Harper & Brothers.

Törhönen, M., Hassan, L., Sjöblom, M., and Hamari, J. 2019. Play, playbour or labour? The relationships between perception of occupational activity and outcomes among streamers and YouTubers. *Proceedings of the 52nd Hawaii International Conference on System Sciences* (pp 2558–67). Washington: IEEE Computer Society.

Van Barneveld, K., Quinlan, M., Kriesler, P., Junor, A., Baum, F., Chowdhury, A., ... and Rainnie, A. 2020. The COVID-19 pandemic: Lessons on building more equal and sustainable societies. *The Economic and Labour Relations Review*, 31(2): pp. 133–57.

Van Dijck, J. 2013. *The Culture of Connectivity: A Critical History of Social Media*. Oxford: Oxford University Press.

Van Doorn, N., and Badger, A. 2020. Platform capitalism's hidden abode: Producing data assets in the gig economy. *Antipode*, 52(5): pp. 1475–95.

Veltri, G. A. 2020. *Digital Social Research*. Cambridge: Polity Press.

Whiting, R., and Pritchard, K. 2020. *Collecting Qualitative Data Using Digital Methods*. London: Sage.

Whiting, R., and Symon, G. 2020. Digi-housekeeping: The invisible work of flexibility. *Work, Employment and Society*, 34(6): pp. 1079–96.

Whiting, R., Roby, H., Symon, G., and Chamakiotis, P. 2018. Participant-led diaries. In Bryman, A. and Buchanan, D. (eds), *Unconventional Methodology in Organization and Management Research*. pp 190–211. Oxford: Oxford University Press.

Woodward, S. 2020. *Material Methods*. London: Sage.

PART I

WORKING WITH SCREENS

2

Wrestling with Digital Objects and Technologies in Studies of Work

Diane E. Bailey, Stephen R. Barley, and Paul M. Leonardi

Introduction

Any historian of the first and second industrial revolutions will tell you that technologies have been altering the landscape of jobs, skills, employment, and organizations in multiple ways since the mid-seventeenth century. Historians of technology would argue that technologies have been significantly changing what people do and how they do it for longer than that. But what most social scientists have not considered is what changes in technology and work imply for the methods we use to study work.

That such changes in method are necessary is illustrated by the history of industrial engineering, a field originally founded on the study of work and work practices.[1] In the late 1890s and the first two decades of the twentieth century, industrial engineers began to study human motion and the effective use of tools with the aim of improving the efficiency of production systems (e.g. Taylor 1903, 1911; Gilbreth 1912; Gilbreth and Gilbreth 1916). Needing precise temporal data, industrial engineers pioneered stopwatch studies and analysing films of people at work with chronometers to capture and analyse workers' movements.

As industrial engineering matured, it began to emphasize effectiveness and human welfare in addition to efficiency, giving birth to the study of human factors or ergonomics.[2] The military catapulted human factors into prominence during World War II when it became clear that designing more effective human–machine interfaces could reduce errors in operation and fatigue as well as save lives (Chapanis 1976). Confronting physical machines, ergonomists initially treated human beings as biophysical entities. Early ergonomists were concerned with such phenomena as reach, body posture, reaction time, and perception. Because the design of controls could be altered to improve humans' physical interactions with machines, ergonomists needed a different method than those who studied the processes and tools associated with time and motion studies. They began to rely largely on experiments to recommend changes in technology.

With the coming of computers and digital interfaces, ergonomists could no longer treat humans as biophysical entities only. To deal effectively with human–computer

Diane E. Bailey, Stephen R. Barley, and Paul M. Leonardi, *Wrestling with Digital Objects and Technologies in Studies of Work.*
In: *Research Methods for Digital Work and Organization.* Edited by Gillian Symon, Katrina Pritchard, and Christine Hine,
Oxford University Press. © Oxford University Press (2021). DOI: 10.1093/oso/9780198860679.003.0002

interactions, ergonomists also had to consider humans as cognitive beings who processed and made sense of information. Hence, a new branch of ergonomics emerged: Human–Computer Interaction (HCI). Although experts in HCI continued to employ experiments, they also began to make extensive use of interviews, videotapes, and observation (Card et al. 1983). With the coming of computer-based communications and the internet, which allowed people to work together in groups whether collocated or at a distance, practitioners of HCI realized that work was social and collaborative as well as cognitive, thus giving rise to a subfield known as Computer-Supported Cooperative Work (CSCW). CSCW scholars continued to use older research methods but also began to do ethnography in work settings and to work with trace data that people generated when using computer programs(Crabtree 2003).

As with early industrial engineers, sociologists and anthropologists studied work that was mostly physical and interactional before computers became widespread, and for this they long employed primarily surveys, interviews, and participant observation. However, the growing ubiquity of computers, the increasing power of algorithms, and the advent of remote control and simulation technologies, among other developments, have rendered problematic sociologists' and anthropologists' reliance on these standard methods. The shortcomings of standard methods are particularly apparent when researchers aim to study technical work, which poses at least three new problems for them.

First, technical workers such as engineers, scientists, and technicians speak technical languages with which the typical sociologist or anthropologist is unfamiliar; complicating matters, technical workers often truncate this jargon when writing on paper documents, typing commands at the computer, labelling digital artefacts, or speaking with colleagues. Second, many technical tasks are now executed (and information processed and transformed) by algorithms. Technical work processes are, therefore, typically invisible to an observer except for the portion that entails a worker entering a command, writing a script, or selecting an icon on a computer or device (Leonardi 2015). Third, technical work may or may not involve an entwining of physical and digital objects. This entwining occurs, for example, when engineers create digital representations of automotive parts and then test the representations in a computer simulation, hoping for virtual results that match the physical testing of the physical parts in an experimental bay.[3] Accordingly, it is difficult for sociologists and anthropologists of work to rely on standard methods if they wish to understand what technical workers do or to document work practices that rely on complex digital technologies.

For almost three decades, the three authors have been involved in field studies of technical work and technical occupations. In the process, we have been forced to devise novel approaches and techniques so that we might better study work practices that involve digital objects and digital technologies. In many ways, the methods that we devised blend the attention given to the precise details of movement pioneered by industrial engineers with the note taking of ethnographers, allowing us to analyse our data both structurally (e.g. counting types of events) as well as thematically (e.g. identifying and understanding meanings and behaviours). Our objective in this chapter is to describe the methods that we have developed in the hope that our experiences will prove useful to others who wish to study digital and technical work.

Our Approach to Studying Digital and Technical Work

We explain and illustrate our methods in the context of a decade-long field research project that originated in conversations at the Center for Work, Technology and Organization at Stanford and was funded by the National Science Foundation and General Motors Corporation. In our project, we sought to make theoretical contributions to studies of work and technology primarily in organization studies journals but also in information systems, communication, and engineering journals. To that end, we asked research questions about how the use of emerging advanced computer technologies was changing how engineering work was done, including how the work was organized, who performed it, what skills and knowledge it required, and how roles, practices, status, power, and other attributes of engineering work life were altered.

We studied three types of engineers: structural engineers who designed building structures, automotive engineers who designed vehicles, and hardware engineers who designed microprocessor cores and peripherals. For structural and hardware engineers, we conducted our study at three American firms each. For automotive engineering, we studied three engineering groups in one US firm located across eight countries (Australia, Brazil, Germany, India, Korea, Mexico, Sweden, and the USA). We typically employed a grounded theory approach (Glaser and Strauss 1967; Glaser 1978; Strauss and Corbin 1990) that looked to the data rather than the academic literature for direction.

We found that engineers used digital objects and digital technologies least in structural engineering and most in hardware engineering, with automotive engineering falling somewhere in between. We discuss each of the ends of this continuum first (structural and hardware engineering) before proceeding to the middle (automotive engineering), an order that matches how we studied the three occupations and that tracks the evolution of the methods we devised. Table 2.1 summarizes the 14 methods that we developed and that we discuss in this chapter.

New Methods for Studying Structural Engineers

We begin our discussion with a structural engineer named Sally,[4] pictured at work in Figure 2.1. Whereas many studies of work and technology focus on the implementation and use of a single technology, our work took a broader approach out of necessity: Sally's workplace, for example, featured over 150 types of technologies

Table 2.1 Methods developed to study engineering work across three occupations

Developed when studying this occupation	Method	Purpose
Structural engineering	1. Office and technology layouts	To physically position technologies, artefacts, and people in reference to each other
	2. Dual observers	To capture otherwise missing and unfamiliar technical terms in the context of use
	3. Glossary of technical terms	To provide official and practical definitions of unfamiliar technical terms
	4. Informant/observer recaps of events	To understand events that transpired during observations
	5. Fieldnotes that recorded a stream of behaviour	To capture in words and illustrations everything that engineers said or did while working
	6. Retrieval and documentation of artefacts	To facilitate the study of objects (often created using technology) in conjunction with the reading of fieldnotes
	7. Project phase descriptions	To create a temporal portrayal of tasks and technology use
	8. Task table	To describe how and why a set of actions were typically undertaken and with what technology
	9. Technology inventory	To document a history of technology purchases and creation, the task purposes of each technology, alternative technologies, and the like

Table 2.1 *Continued*

Developed when studying this occupation	Method	Purpose
Hardware engineering	10. Project summaries	To create a temporal history of codebases and a linearity of work, products, and engineers
	11. Observation summaries	To provide quick references to help track action across multiple observations of the same informant
	12. Highly structured coding	To tease out how and why engineers employed technologies and made technology choices
Automotive engineering	13. Digital artefact database	To quickly see and read about the objects that engineers created as separate from but tied to the written fieldnote accounts of talk and action
	14. Technology and organizing timelines	To show how technology use prompted changes in work organization (e.g. roles, location)

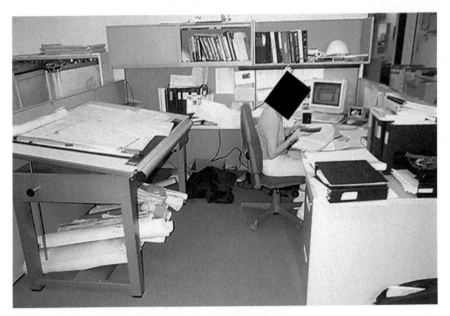

Fig. 2.1 Sally, a structural engineer, at work in her cubicle

whose use she wove together to accomplish her work. Our first task was to determine how all those different technologies operated in relationship to each other.

Office and technology layouts (Method 1)

Many of the technologies that Sally employed were physical, as the numerous arte-facts scattered about her cubicle in Figure 2.1 attest. On the drafting table behind her we see flattened as well as rolled-up drawings. The bookshelf along the back wall held textbooks from her master's programme in civil engineering that she often retrieved; their pages were marked throughout with yellow highlights. Also on the bookshelf were vendors' catalogues (featuring building elements and specifications) plus a hardhat for when Sally visited building sites. Beside her on her desk were black binders full of calculations and communications from past and current projects. In her hand she held a calculator. Laid out before her were calculation sheets and an open structural engineering design manual. Her computer was pushed into the far corner of her desk.

We documented the physical and digital artefacts in Sally's cubicle as well as the cubicles of other engineers whom we observed in our study by drawing layouts that indicated where technologies and other artefacts were stored and used. The fact that we recorded the titles of most of the textbooks on Sally's and the other engineers' bookshelves gives a sense of the level of detail we sought to capture.

In comparison to the physical artefacts in Sally's office, digital work artefacts were less common. The position of the computer on Sally's desk reflected her short and infrequent use of it. Sally typically used her computer to run quick analyses of building forces to ensure that the structural elements she had chosen (e.g. beams, columns, bolts, welds) were of sufficient heft to withstand the physical loads placed on them. These analyses took no more than a minute or two to run. As a result, Sally rarely spent more than an hour on the computer at any one time. Computer use was so infrequent, in fact, that the screen of her computer and those of the engineers around her were often dark for more than half the day before their first use.

Structural engineers' limited use of computers did not mean that their work was easy for us to understand and study. The work's technical content made it challenging. In describing our remaining methods for studying Sally, her colleagues, and engineers in the other occupations, we will sometimes dwell on the technical aspects of the work as well as the digital. Often, the two were inseparable. We think that this is not uncommon in digital work.

Dual observers (Method 2) and glossary of technical terms (Method 3)

When we first began observing structural engineers our fieldnotes were peppered with missing words, including nearly all the nouns, which were foreign to us. In the engineering settings we studied later we found that we understood quite a bit about computers (e.g. programs, clocks, simulations) and knew the parts of a vehicle (e.g. brakes, engine, fender), which made listening to conversations among automotive engineers and hardware engineers relatively straightforward. But buildings were a mystery to us even though we worked and lived in them and, for this reason, we struggled to follow the structural engineers' conversations. While we were mentally processing what we thought we just heard ('Was that catenary?' 'Did I hear purlin?'), we missed the engineers' next words. Worse still, we realized that so many missing words meant that we had no quotes that we could analyse and, hence, no findings we could publish.

Luckily, the missing words were usually technical terms. To better capture technical terms in use, we decided to use dual observers to document each observation. The first observer captured action, the second manually recorded words, spelling them phonetically. These phonetic spellings proved close enough to the correct spelling for us to locate the term in a structural engineering dictionary that we purchased for this purpose. Asking a single observer to simply capture the spoken words with a digital recorder did not work given soft-spoken engineers, mumbled terms, and background noises. Moreover, the second observer could sometimes confirm phonetic guesses in real time with another engineer while the first observer continued to capture the shadowed informant's action. We then built our own glossary of technical terms. This glossary included each term's dictionary definition as well as examples from our notes of engineers using the term in conversation. By the time we had added about 50 terms to our glossary, we felt comfortable enough to revert to single-observer observations.

Informant/observer recaps of events (Method 4)

Despite these efforts, we often still had only a vague idea of what happened and why as we watched structural engineers at work, which hindered our ability to answer research questions around how engineering work and its organization were changing with the use of advanced, emerging digital technologies. To improve our understanding, we began asking shadowed engineers at the end of an observation to recap all the events that had occurred. To our disappointment the engineers typically used the same language or offered the same rationale in their end-of-day explanations that they had used during the observation, leaving us none the wiser. We decided that we had no choice but to risk losing credibility with our informants by letting them know just how little we understood. Therefore, we changed our protocol and began recapping for the engineers what we thought we saw, using our laymen's terms. Our accounts often made the engineers laugh as they realized the extent of our confusion. But by revealing our ignorance, we helped them realize the level at which and the terms with which they needed to explain their actions to us. These recaps, in conjunction with our expanded vocabulary, quickly increased our understanding. Soon we went back to our prior practice of having the engineer recap the observation for us at its conclusion. Eventually, we needed no recap at all.

As a side note, when we moved to the highly digital work of hardware engineering, recaps at the end of observations proved incredibly important to help us catch actions, events, and tasks that we might have otherwise missed. In hardware engineering, actions, events, and tasks occurred quickly at the computer prompt and programs ran 'in the background' while engineers did other work on the screen. In other words, the methods we developed to study mostly physical technical work were useful when technical work became nearly completely digital. The methods made transparent what we did not see, because we either did not understand it (structural engineering) or were not observant enough to see it (hardware engineering).

Fieldnotes that recorded a stream of behaviour (Method 5) and retrieval and documentation of artefacts (Method 6)

Having finally come to understand the structural engineers' jargon and what they did in their offices, we could take decent fieldnotes. Our conceptualization of what constituted decent fieldnotes drew significantly upon Barker's (1963) ideas for recording a stream of behaviour.[5] In essence, we sought to write down everything the engineer did or said in our notes from each day's observation. Recording time in ten-minute increments, we noted what technologies the engineer employed, for what purpose, and for how long. We used digital voice recorders whenever we could not keep up with a dyad's conversation with a pen and paper or when more than two people conversed.

We paid particular attention to the retrieval and documentation of work artefacts. We made screenshots, asked for copies of digital files, and made photocopies of paper artefacts. We sketched physical objects that engineers used that we could not take with us (smartphones were not yet widely available, and we moved around enough to make lugging cameras impractical). We recorded the engineers' indexical gestures to drawings in design meetings by describing in our notes the place on the drawings where the engineers pointed, stabbed, circled, or otherwise indicated. Afterwards, on copies of the drawings that we made and took with us, we labelled such places with capital letters to more efficiently refer to them in our finalized notes (e.g. 'he pointed to the weld at 'A' on Attachment #1 as he talked').

Our observations lasted three to four hours at a stretch. We took, on average, two and a half days to type up the fieldnotes from a half-day's observation. Figure 2.2 presents an excerpt from our fieldnotes to provide an idea of the level of detail that we captured.

Project phase descriptions (Method 7) and task table (Method 8)

In the course of our observations, we learned that structural engineering projects have phases, with specific tasks and technologies associated with each phase. We

9:25 a.m.

Sally writes a note in red on the lefthand side of the sheet: "NEW TS PEDESTAL @ 5'-0" o.c., @ ea. ROW OF 2-P5000, TYP." She removes sheet two and begins sheet three. She erases something at the top of sheet one. She writes in the project name and job number. She uses a real, short straight edge to make a line at the bottom of sheet three. She uses her scale ruler to measure off a distance. She uses her straight edge to fill in the sides of what is becoming an elevation view of the floor. She uses it to make dashed lines. She attaches labels to the members. She pulls out the Unistrut supplier manual to get some dimensions of objects called channels from page 53. (See Att. #2 for this page and other relevant pages from the manual.)

Now Sally surprises me by lifting a power-drill eraser from her desk, where I had not seen it, to erase something on her sheet. The tip is green; it is a lighter-looking model than Victor's. She sets the eraser down and picks up her calculator. She punches in some numbers and then contemplates her sketch.

Me: What did you just calculate, Sally?
S: I have two Unistruts. I am trying to figure out how much room is remaining, hanging out over the edge, for the member below.

Fig. 2.2 Notes from observing as Sally erases, measures, retrieves, and calculates

	Task	Description	Technology
SD	Design alternative gravity systems for typical floor	Commonly the first subsystem designed. SE determines appropriate gravity loads and applicable performance constraints. Using first principles, SE conceptualizes alternate gravity load path configurations: highly simplified models showing beam and column locations and sizes for the typical floor. Models must work within architectural and MEP desired conditions. Subtasks: • determine architectural, geographical, MEP, and other constraints on floor geometry • determine gravity loads • determine performance specifications for gravity subsystem (e.g. deflection and stress limits) • develop very simple conceptual model of beam and column locations and sizes for typical floor • perform calculations (by hand) to determine global performance of subsystem • design original elements • design details from architect's sketches • (**if renovation**) interpret and analyze existing gravity load path from original blueprints	AutoCAD, Excel, hard copy drawings, pocket calculator, previous project records, ruler, manuals

Fig. 2.3 Task description for 'designing alternative gravity systems'

built a table describing project phases. We also constructed tables to sort out tasks by phase to help us make sense of the temporality of the work and the interdependencies among tools and tasks. Figure 2.3 provides an example from a task table detailing the task of designing alternative gravity systems for a floor in a building. This task occurred in the schematics design (SD) phase of a structural engineering project; the typical technologies employed appear in the final column.

Technology inventory (Method 9)

In addition to describing project phases and constructing task tables, we built technology inventories in which we described a technology's use or purpose; the alternatives that engineers might use; the technology's history in terms of when it was acquired and upgraded; whether it was purchased, developed by someone in the firm, or given to an engineer by a professor during their education, and other relevant information. In constructing these inventories, we were surprised by the number of home-grown digital technologies we found (i.e. digital technologies created by an engineer in the firm and then shared with colleagues). An example was an Excel template for single angle connections in which some numbers in cells were fixed (meaning they appeared when engineers opened the spreadsheet and could not be changed), some were parameters that engineers entered to solve their current problem, and others were calculated based on fixed and entered quantities that only appeared after engineers had entered the necessary parameters. We often did not catch all those differences in the course of our observation, but because we asked the engineers to share their work files with us, we were able to explore the files back in our offices. Through such exploration, we could trace the actions that we observed in our notes and recreate the entries in the templates, allowing us to better understand what values engineers knew at the time of use and which ones they sought.

Digital technologies that structural engineering firms purchased generally had rudimentary interfaces and were inexpensive. These technologies had pull-down menus and iconic buttons that enabled engineers to conduct fairly straightforward analyses that they could view schematically in black 3-D windows, as shown in Figure 2.4. Because engineers had to point the mouse and make selections in this interface, and because their use of the software was relatively infrequent, they proceeded at a pace that permitted us to track and record their choices as we observed. Even so, engineers typically opened purchased technologies, ran their analyses, and closed the technologies in just a few minutes. In their world, there was no such thing as running a program 'in the background' while they did something else on the screen. Every action required their undivided attention and immediate interactions with the software.

Among the purchased technologies, the most expensive at the time of our study cost $25,000 USD per licence. Only one firm among the three firms in our study owned it. Most technologies that we saw engineers using cost much less. Because purchased technologies were governed by licensing agreements, we could not get copies of work files to take back for examination in the same way that we could with home-grown templates in common software applications. Instead, we asked for screenshots

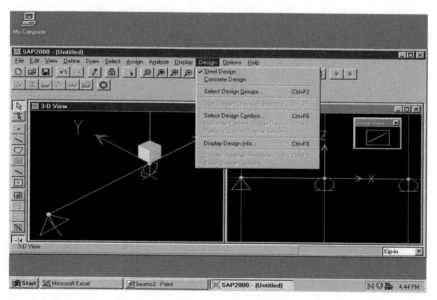

Fig. 2.4 Screenshot of a structural engineering analysis software application

along the way and later reconstructed events with the screenshots. If we were still unable to understand how the work had unfolded, we would ask the engineer during our next observation.

Additional New Methods for Studying Hardware Engineering

Most technologies used by hardware engineers were digital, which meant that most of the physical artefacts on their desks were not work-related. The desk of a hardware engineer named Eric, shown in Figure 2.5, was typical in this respect. Plastic action figures in the likenesses of Agents Mulder and Scully were propped up on Eric's desk beside a photo from his wedding; a row of Beanie Babies adorned the top of his computer monitor. Along the back wall of his office was a bookshelf that, like Sally's cubicle, contained books from his master's programme. Whereas Sally's books featured heavily highlighted pages, the pages of Eric's books were pristine. And while Sally frequently used her books at work, Eric, like his fellow hardware engineers, almost never used his. Hardware engineers told us that if they turned to a textbook, it meant that they were doing something extremely hard, a rare event. In contrast to Sally, who arranged items reflective of physical work (pens, pencils, erasers, white-out liquid, staplers) along the back of her desk (out of view in Figure 2.1), Eric had few such items. The diagram drawn on the whiteboard along the back wall of Eric's office remained unchanged during the three months we spent onsite, and we never

Fig. 2.5 The office of Eric, a hardware engineer

witnessed him writing on the board. Eric told us the diagram provided a high-level visualization of the functionality of the microprocessor he was creating. Although Eric was not present when we took this photo, he was working: He was running programs 'in the background' while he fetched a (free) morning snack from the firm's break room.

In contrast to structural engineering, most technologies in hardware engineering were expensive, often costing as much as US$1M each. High costs meant that hardware engineers typically had only one option available to them when selecting a technology to complete a given task, as compared to the many options of the structural engineers. Thus, our job was simpler in hardware engineering in that we had fewer technologies to understand.

However, because hardware engineers rarely moved from their keyboards and screens, their work was often barely visible to us. By comparison, structural engineers punched numbers into calculators and wrote the results on paper that we could photocopy. They pulled down books and turned to page numbers that we could record. They drew sketches by hand that we could reproduce or copy. At a computer, they selected pull-down menus and buttons in software applications with their mouse at a pace that we could follow and record. Hardware engineers primarily typed commands quickly at computer prompts and talked to their colleagues. Therefore, knowing the technical jargon they employed proved critical for understanding their typing and their talk. Accordingly, we built a glossary of terms much as we did in structural engineering. Although we knew many of the terms they employed, in our glossary we found ourselves defining new verbs ('to sync') in addition to nouns ('build/config'). We also built a technology inventory for each firm as we had in structural engineering.

Project summaries (Method 10) and observation summaries (Method 11)

To understand the work of hardware engineering, we also adopted a new practice: creating project summaries. Both structural and hardware engineers worked on projects (for example, a new building project for structural engineers, a new microprocessor core project for hardware engineers). But whereas buildings were almost always unique, microprocessors evolved as new versions were built on the base of an earlier product's code. Each new project in the evolution of a codebase in hardware engineering was named after the new version of the microprocessor it would create. To understand the engineers' actions, we needed to keep project names straight across this evolution because the engineers also named computer directories by project (and, hence, product). Thus, when engineers entered a directory, the project (product) name was part of the prompt on their screen, providing a clue to what work was being done. To see the prompt was to know in which codebase the engineer was working.

Date	Primary Events	Technology
08/09	Denis is responding to a customer support case. Also, he is designing a co-processor interface. For that, he has to first simulate a co-processor. He has a discussion with Tomas where they talk about details of technical issues. Tomas later drops by for another discussion about the email (subject: primary path) that he just sent to Denis.	• Post-it notes • Verilog • SupportDesk • Automatic Test Generator Program • VCS • Specification manual (soft copy) • Core Processor Interface Specification (soft copy)
08/15	Denis compiles some information for the marketing department by running some tests. He has trouble opening an emailed PowerPoint presentation. He runs some tests to evaluate a CAD tool to see whether it gives the same performance as at the vendor's site. Some time is wasted because he does not have the root permission for a machine. He is learning Verilogy by attending a training class. He writes a program to design a counter.	• PowerPoint • Postscript viewer • Specs document • Windows • Excel • Handheld calculator • Html document • Verilog • Quickstart Verilog (book)

Fig. 2.6 Two observation summaries detailing events and technologies employed

We also created summaries by observation in hardware engineering to help us draw connections across time and engineers by tracking what technologies which engineers were using when. Figure 2.6 provides two examples from observations of an engineer named Denis. Unlike structural engineers, hardware engineers frequently interrupted each other during the day, as illustrated by Denis's interactions with Tomas. They did so precisely because the code for one microprocessor core drew from the code of its predecessor. An engineer responsible for redesigning a component of the microprocessor would begin with code a colleague created for a prior version of the microprocessor. When the code written by the engineer doing the redesign failed, he often suspected that the problem lay not in his own code, but in the code he inherited. Because engineers often failed to 'comment' their code (that is, they did not provide text explanations of how the code worked within the code itself), other engineers struggled to decipher how the inherited code worked. It was easier for engineers to ask the prior code's creator for an explanation of how the code worked than to spend hours puzzling it out alone. When observing conversations that interruptions prompted, we often found it difficult to follow which code was in question. Observation summaries helped in that respect, especially if we read them prior to our next observation. The summaries also provided a sense of how the engineers used technologies across time, tasks, and projects.

All this summarizing and table-building amounted to a preliminary analysis that helped us as we sought to explain differences in the technology choices that engineers made across the occupations we studied. We had noticed, for example, that hardware engineers would write scripts to automatically turn the output of one technology into the input for the next. In contrast, structural engineers connected their technologies manually by, for example, typing the output values from one technology as input into another technology's user interface. In other words, unlike hardware engineers, structural engineers never wrote scripts to automatically link technologies.

Highly structured coding (Method 12)

To understand how and why engineers did or did not automatically link their technologies, we defined a 'technology gap' as the space between two technologies across which the output of the first technology became input for the second.[6] In our fieldnotes we flagged every episode in which an engineer encountered a technology gap. Figure 2.7 provides an example from an observation of a structural engineer.

The example in Figure 2.7 shows the highly structured coding process that we employed. By highly structured, we mean that we applied the same ten code families to each episode. The resulting ten codes told us, for example, the 'action' the engineer took at the gap (crossing the closed gap in the first instance or bridging the open gap in the second one shown in Figure 2.7) and the technologies that lay on either side of the gap (the 'tech out' code family denoted the technology whose output became the input for 'tech in', the code family for the second technology).

We could determine from this highly structured coding that engineers in different occupations chose different ways to manage technology gaps. With these analyses in hand we could query our notes and conduct interviews to better understand the factors that rendered technology gaps different across structural and hardware engineering and that enabled or hampered the automation of engineering work. For example, in interviews, senior structural engineers told us that engineers straight out of university programmes were skilled in computer analysis but lacked a basic understanding of building materials and loads. The senior engineers feared that if they automated the movement of designs across technology gaps, new engineers would never take the time to carefully consider their assumptions about how loads travelled through, and were handled by, the elements of the building. Because the technologies in structural engineering had no means to check these assumptions, having correct assumptions was key to performing valid analyses and remained a job for a human. Hardware engineers, on the other hand, had faith in their technologies' ability to test for all possible design failures, leaving them with few fears of automating handoffs across technologies. In this manner, the methods listed in Table 2.1 through hardware engineering provided the foundation on which we could pursue our research questions with respect to automation and engineers' technology choices.

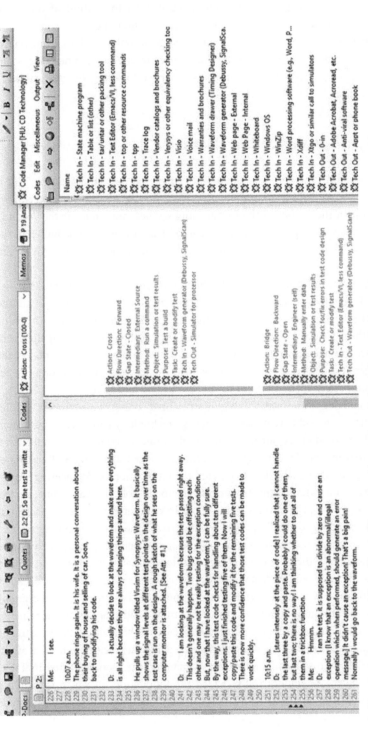

Fig. 2.7 Structured coding of 'technology gaps' in an observation of a hardware engineer

Yet More New Methods to Study Automotive Engineering

Automotive engineers inhabited a middle ground between the structural engineers' infrequent use of computers and the near-constant use of computers by hardware engineers. Figure 2.8 shows Arvind, an automotive engineer in India who built digital simulation models for testing vehicle performance. As one might expect in the work setting of an engineer who builds digital simulations, Arvind's computer took a central place in his cubicle. There were very few other physical artefacts in the cubicle, either work-related or playful ones. Arvind shared his office with another engineer who worked on a second shift, sitting in Arvind's chair and using his computer. The phone, the schematic of a vehicle tacked to the cubicle wall, and the email directory tacked directly below it served both engineers equally well.

Unlike hardware engineers, automotive engineers, even ones devoted to creating digital simulations, needed a thorough understanding of physical objects and their interactions (especially when simulating crashes) to complete their tasks on the computer. For this reason, automotive engineers who built digital simulations depended greatly on physical tests. If engineers could validate their simulation—if they could get their simulated vehicle to respond just like a real vehicle in a physical test—then they would be more confident of their results when running the simulation with different parameters for which there were no data from physical tests. In one case we encountered, the engineer who built a simulation of a vehicle crash

Fig. 2.8 Arvind, an automotive engineer, sitting in his shared-across-shifts cubicle

neglected to model the airbag flap over the passenger grip. As a result, the virtual passenger in the simulation experienced greater forces than did the dummy passenger in the physical test. In other words, the engineer's simulation did not accurately represent the physical test results.

Digital artefact database (Method 13)

In automotive engineering, therefore, we needed to understand not just the digital, as we did in hardware engineering, or the digital as a bit player, as in structural engineering, but digital representations in conjunction with the physical phenomena they represented. To help us do so, we built an artefact database that made it easy to summon to our screen digital objects that we had retrieved from the field. We could sort columns of metadata in the database—such as whether the object was 2D, 3D, or text—to help us formulate an understanding of the engineers' work. For example, we could see the part displayed in Figure 2.9 if we clicked on its associated row in the database. The part in Figure 2.9 was one of 17 artefacts we retrieved the morning we observed one of the automotive engineers. The written notes from that day's observation spanned 14 pages of single-spaced text, with additional pages describing the 17 artefacts as attachments. In Figure 2.9, the description identifies the object (a 3D solid model), describes what it models (the inner belt extension and the inner belt

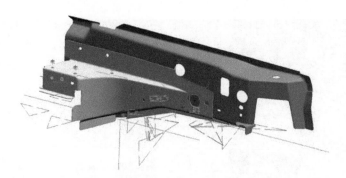

ATTACHMENT 3

[engineer"s name] 07/25/03
This is a 3 dimensional – solid model of the inner belt extension, depicted by the yellow, and the inner belt reinforcement, depicted by the orange taken from Unigraphics – Modeling. This is what the part looked like before [engineer"s name] made any modifications to it.

Fig. 2.9 An example of a linked, stored artefact in the automotive engineering database

reinforcement), notes the technology that produced it (Unigraphics), and shows its state at the time of capture (before the engineer modified it that day).

Technology and organizing timelines (Method 14)

Through our detailed inspection and contemplation of the digital work artefacts that we retrieved, stored, and analysed, as well as our work observations and interviews, we were able to build timelines of technology and organizing that reflected how occupational roles and the location of work evolved with the use of emerging digital and computational technologies.[7] To begin, when finite element analysis techniques enabled digital simulations that closely resembled real vehicles to replace box-and-spring models that were purely schematic representations, the modelling function was shifted from R&D into engineering. This shift proved useful because it placed workers in the newly created role of simulation engineer in close contact with the physical parts that they modelled. Eventually, however, as the verisimilitude of digital models improved and their results became more accurate, managers mistakenly assumed the need for physical referents had disappeared. Consequently, managers offshored modelling's base tasks—building but not analysing simulation models—to India with the creation of two new roles: simulation modellers (in India, who were distant from physical parts) and simulation analysts (in the USA and other engineering centres worldwide, who were close to physical parts). Our detailed methods of engineers' technology use helped us to document how and why this geographical and role separation between the digital and the physical became problematic for engineering analysis in this firm.

Obstacles, Benefits, and Disadvantages Associated with Our Approach

All methods for studying technical and digital work encounter obstacles, and all have advantages and disadvantages. Throughout this chapter, we have detailed many of the obstacles we encountered, including missing words, technical jargon, incomprehensible tasks, physical and digital artefacts, invisible work, and nearly motionless workers. We have also discussed how we overcame those obstacles by improvising new methods. We now address what we see as the main benefits and disadvantages of our methods.

Benefits of our methods

Perhaps the most striking benefit of our methods was that they enabled us to conduct deep investigations across multiple topics in the study of digital and technical work. To wit, we have explored a range of topics including technology choices and automation (Bailey and Leonardi 2015), learning (Bailey and Barley 2011), organizational change (Leonardi, 2012), interdependence (Bailey et al. 2010), distributed collaboration (Leonardi and Rodriguez-Lluesma 2013), occupational changes (Bailey et al. 2012), brokerage (Leonardi and Bailey 2017), social networks (Leonardi 2013), boundaries and boundary objects (Leonardi 2011b; Barley et al. 2012; Leonardi et al. 2019), technology adoption and adaptation (Leonardi 2009 2011a), and knowledge (Leonardi and Bailey 2008; Gainsburg et al. 2010), all drawing on data collected in the same large study.

Moreover, our methods led to findings that were not tied to individual technologies, thereby achieving a kind of generality. For example, as long as workers continue to employ a series of technologies to accomplish a task, there will be technology gaps no matter what technologies lie on either side of each gap. As a result, we think that many of the conclusions in our papers are unlikely to come undone with the appearance of new technologies in the engineering fields that we studied.

In addition, the methods we devised yielded rich comparisons rooted in the details of the numerous episodes of work on which we based our claims As a result, they allowed us to speak knowledgeably and deeply about engineering work across occupations. We could draw upon the many visualizations of work artefacts and episodes of talk and action that our methods yielded to relay our understanding of this work to our readers. As digital technologies come to underlie more and more occupations, the methods that we devised thus have the further benefit of being applicable to a broad range of studies of technical and digital work.

Disadvantages of our methods

These significant benefits notwithstanding, our methods had disadvantages as well. To begin, they took time. We spent years in the field and then in the office: The project took ten years in total. Worse still, our intensive methods led to few early publications. Had we decreased the scale of our project—for example by limiting our sample to one or two engineering occupations rather than three—we surely would have reduced the time it took. In this respect, our methods remain appropriate for projects smaller than ours. Moreover, in studies of occupations whose technical jargon has become commonplace, speed might be gained. As we noted, we were able to gain an understanding of the work faster in hardware engineering and automotive engineering than we were in structural engineering because the language of coding and vehicles was familiar to us, while that of buildings was not. Nevertheless, our methods are time intensive. If one is diligent at understanding and detailed in recording technology use, then it is likely to take days to write up a complete record of the talk and action that occur during a half-day observation. Intermediate research products such as technology inventories and project summaries stretch out the time it takes to understand tasks and roles by months.

Supporting our team of researchers also took funding, in our case over US$2M distributed across a decade. Smaller projects should require less funding, but time-intensive methods do require considerable support for a research team's time.

Although our methods were not overly invasive (in part because our equipment needs were minimal since we did no video recording), they did raise ethical concerns related to the act of shadowing informants at work. For us, these concerns arose primarily at the beginning of our project during our fieldwork in structural engineering, where junior engineers had low status relative to their seniors.[8] A few junior structural engineers were noticeably made anxious by our observations, presumably because they feared we would report on their performance to their seniors. For junior engineers not calmed by our reassurances of confidentiality, we found innocent reasons (e.g. 'saw that task enough in prior observations') to end their participation in our study. Status issues arose again in our observations in India, whose culture commonly associates status with seniority; we dealt with anxious informants there in the same manner as we had in structural engineering.

Beyond the issue of anxious informants, which is not uncommon in workplace observations of any type, the primary ethical issue that our methods raised was that anonymization of our fieldnotes was impossible. Details of the engineer's desk, interactions with colleagues, projects, and at times the technologies employed meant that a manager or colleague might guess the engineers' identities even if names were removed. For this reason, we refused to share our data despite escalating pressure to do so on US federally funded research projects.

No study of work is ever a simple matter. Perhaps studies of digital work are particularly complicated because it takes so long to identify the important details of what is going on, why it is going on, how it unfolds, and who is involved. We hope that by sharing our methods we might save readers' time by not repeating our mistakes. But beware! Our methods are laborious and protracted, but we believe our approach yielded findings and theoretical notions that we could not have otherwise achieved.

Notes

1. For an extended discussion of how industrial engineering's approaches to studying work have changed see Bailey and Barley (2005). Barley and Kunda (2001) issued an earlier call for sociologists of organizations to again attend to how work, and by extension forms of organizing, are changing.
2. Students of human factors and ergonomics can now be found in psychology departments as well as departments of industrial engineering.
3. On the importance of the physical to the digital in technical work, see Bailey et al. (2012).
4. All names in this account are pseudonyms. The examples we give are based on actual individuals, not fictionalized accounts or aggregations of behaviours and actions across our sample.

5. See Bailey and Barley (2011) for details of our translation of Barker's ideas of recording physical behaviour in social, home, and educational settings to our project's technical and digital work context.
6. See Bailey et al. (2010) for details of this concept and our analysis.
7. See Bailey et al. (2012) for our analysis of changes in occupational roles over time in automotive engineering and for an example of our technology and organizing timelines presented via multiple table panels.
8. Seniority-based status differences were not as striking when we moved on to our second occupation, hardware engineering. Status differences (or their absence) were rooted in differences in the rate of knowledge change across the two occupations. Junior structural engineers had to gain competence in a vast domain of relevant and largely static and centuries-old knowledge of materials, physics, components, and structures, whereas the fast pace of knowledge change in hardware engineering often favoured recent college graduates over senior engineers. See Bailey and Barley (2011) for details.

References

Bailey, D.E., and Barley, S.R. 2005. Return to work: Toward a post-industrial engineering. *IIE Transactions*, 37: pp. 737–52.

Bailey, D.E., and Barley, S.R. 2011. Teaching-learning ecologies: Mapping the environment to structure through action. *Organization Science*, 22(1): pp. 262–85.

Bailey, D.E., and Leonardi, P.M. 2015. *Technology Choices: Why Occupations Differ in Their Embrace of New Technology*. Cambridge, MA: MIT Press.

Bailey, D.E., Leonardi, P.M., and Chong, J. 2010. Minding the gaps: Understanding technology interdependence in knowledge work. *Organization Science*, 21(3): pp. 713–30.

Bailey, D.E., Leonardi, P.M., and Barley, S.R. 2012. The lure of the virtual. *Organization Science*, 23(5): pp. 1485–504.

Barker, R.G. 1963. *The Stream of Behavior*. New York: Appleton-Century-Crofts.

Barley, S.R., and Kunda, G. 2001. Bringing work back in. *Organization Science*, 12(1): pp. 76–95.

Barley, W.C., Leonardi, P.M., and Bailey, D.E. 2012. Engineering objects for collaboration: Strategies of ambiguity and clarity at knowledge boundaries. *Human Communication Research*, 38(3): pp. 280–308.

Card, S.K., Moran, T.P., and Newell, A. 1983. *The Psychology of Human–Computer Interaction*. Hillsdale, NY: Erlbaum.

Chapanis, A. 1976. Engineering Psychology. in M. D. Dunnette (ed.), *Handbook of Industrial and Organizational Psychology* (pp. 697–744). Chicago: Rand-McNally.

Crabtree, A. 2003. *Designing Collaborative Systems: A Practical Guide to Ethnography*. London: Springer.

Gainsburg, J., Rodriguez-Lluesma, C., and Bailey, D.E. 2010. A 'Knowledge Profile' of an engineering occupation: Temporal patterns in the use of engineering knowledge. *Engineering Studies*, 2(3): pp. 197–219.

Gilbreth, F.B. 1912. *Primer of Scientific Management*. London: Constable and Company.

Gilbreth, F.B., and Gilbreth, L.M. 1916. *Fatigue Study: The Elimination of Humanity's Greatest Unnecessary Waste*. New York: Sturgis and Walton Company.

Glaser, B.G. 1978. *Theoretical Sensitivity: Advances in the Methodology of Grounded Theory*. San Francisco: The Sociology Press.

Glaser, B.G., and Strauss, A.L. 1967. *The Discovery of Grounded Theory: Strategies for Qualitative Research*. Chicago: Aldine.

Leonardi, P.M. 2009. Why do people reject new technologies and stymie organizational changes of which they are in favor? Exploring misalignments between social interactions and materiality. *Human Communication Research*, 35(3): pp. 407–41.

Leonardi, P.M. 2011a. When flexible routines meet flexible technologies: Affordance, constraint, and the imbrication of human and material agencies. *MIS Quarterly*, 35(1): pp. 147–67.

Leonardi, P.M. 2011b. Innovation blindness: Culture, frames, and cross-boundary problem construction in the development of new technology concepts. *Organization Science*, 22(2): pp. 347–69.

Leonardi, P.M. 2012. *Car Crashes without Cars: Lessons about Simulation Technology and Organizational Change from Automotive Design*. Cambridge, MA: MIT Press.

Leonardi, P. M. (2013). When Does Technology Use Enable Network Change in Organizations? A Comparative Study of Feature Use and Shared Affordances. *MIS Quarterly*, 37(3), 749–775.

Leonardi, P.M. 2015. The ethnographic study of work in an age of digitization. In Hargittai, E. and Sandvig, C. (eds), *Research Confidential: Digital Methods* (pp. 103–38). Cambridge, MA: MIT Press.

Leonardi, P.M., and Bailey, D.E. 2008. Transformational technologies and the creation of new work practices: Making implicit knowledge explicit in task-based offshoring. *MIS Quarterly*, 32(2): pp. 411–36.

Leonardi, P.M., and Bailey, D.E. 2017. Recognizing and selling good ideas: Network articulation and the making of an offshore innovation hub. *Academy of Management Discoveries*, 3(2): pp. 116–44.

Leonardi, P.M., and Rodriguez-Lluesma, C. 2013. Occupational stereotypes, perceived status differences, and intercultural communication in global organizations. *Communication Monographs*, 80(4): pp. 478–502.

Leonardi, P.M., Bailey, D.E., and Pierce. C.S. 2019. The co-evolution of objects and boundaries over time: Materiality, affordances, and boundary salience. *Information Systems Research*, 30(2): pp. 665–86.

Strauss, A.L. , and Corbin, J.M. 1990. *Basics of Qualitative Research: Grounded Theory Procedures and Techniques*. Thousand Oaks, CA: Sage.

Taylor, F.W. 1903. *Shop Management*. New York: Harper and Brothers.

Taylor. F.W. 1911. *The Principles of Scientific Management*. New York: Norton.

3

Screen Mediated Work in an Ethnography of Official Statistics

Screen Theories and Methodological Positions

Francisca Grommé

Introduction

On 28 February 1959, a vacancy with the heading 'Computer' appeared in a Dutch newspaper with the following announcement: 'To resolve critical technical issues related to processing statistical data, Statistics Netherlands will acquire a computer'. It went on to encourage 'clever youngsters' with the ability to use this 'electronic mathematical miracle' to apply.[1] Today, the purchase of a single computer would hardly be regarded as a miracle. In fact, any visitor to a national statistical institute (NSI) would see computers everywhere. Working behind screens, statisticians do not only clean and analyse data, they also email colleagues, video conference, and search for background literature. In addition, they use WhatsApp on their cell phones, take part in LinkedIn groups, and follow the news on Twitter. Finally, employees at Statistics Netherlands (SN) record news items for television and social media.

The current omnipresence of computers has consequences for researchers interested in observing the work of professionals specialized in the collection, analysis, and dissemination of data. One of these consequences is that, very often, people will be engrossed in their screens. This chapter focuses on the role and presence of screens in ethnographic fieldwork. Screens are electronic, flat displays on which an image can appear. They can be part of laptops, PCs, mobile phones, or other devices. Through computers and mobile phones, screens are connected to larger technological configurations, including devices and infrastructures such as an organizational intranet, a platform, or a shared database. As a verb 'screening' can have contradictory meanings: something is shielded and made invisible, or something is projected and made visible (Merriam-Webster 2021). In accordance, how screens affect their environment is not fixed; they can enable or constrain actions depending on (informal) rules, regulations, and other artefacts.

Francisca Grommé, *Screen Mediated Work in an Ethnography of Official Statistics*. In: *Research Methods for Digital Work and Organization*. Edited by Gillian Symon, Katrina Pritchard, and Christine Hine, Oxford University Press.

The increasing relevance of screens as part of digital work makes it worthwhile to address two questions in this chapter: first, given the connection of screens to a variety of other devices and their varying roles on the work floor, how should we conceptualize the role of screens in digital work? Second, how to approach screen mediated work as part of ethnographic fieldwork? This second question is motivated by the practical difficulties of deciding how and when to observe the role of screens, and by the additional difficultly of observing screen mediated work when figures, messages, and graphs appear only briefly, and often out of view. In answering these questions, my focus will be on the role of screens in knowledge practices (e.g. the collection and analysis of data). While screens can serve as a heuristic for social inquiry (Winthereik et al. 2011), for instance, by studying how some practices are metaphorically 'screened off' or by focusing on 'displays', in this chapter I focus on electronic screens as material devices, primarily computer monitors. I take it as a given that screens do not operate on their own. For instance, a screen can display the result of a computer calculation. Furthermore, when discussing screens, one might refer to the effects of visualizations presented on interfaces or video displays. However, the screens discussed in this chapter are different from visualizations precisely because they are connected to a technical configuration that transmits data or produces graphs.

In this chapter I will take a few steps towards answering the above questions by drawing on an ethnographic project called ARITHMUS, or 'How data make a people'. In this project, six researchers observed digital work in statistical offices and conference venues across Europe to observe such aspects as organizational discussions, changes in work routines, and tacit assumptions.[2] At a time when statistical offices are experimenting with the uptake of new data types and analytical possibilities (e.g. social media data and machine learning), our question was: how do these new methods affect how statisticians delineate, define, analyse, and present populations? In statistics, a 'population' denotes a group of people linked to a bounded territory, often the nation state or sub-divisions of it (Curtis 2001; Foucault 2009). However, populations are not stable or natural entities. In this research project, the central premise was therefore that populations do not exist in advance. Instead, making populations through statistical practices requires, among other activities, the continuous work of collecting and analysing data, demonstrating the veracity of the data and the validity of analyses, negotiating population definitions, and so on (Law 2008; Ruppert 2011). We considered it relevant to study changes in how statisticians define, measure, modify, and enact populations because this also has consequences for how people identify with them. Furthermore, it affects expert roles and how policies are designed. To illustrate, a population can change when a new data source is adopted. If an NSI normally defines a population using registered *residency* in a country, this would no longer be possible if it started using Twitter geotags. Now populations would be defined based on *presence* in a country (possibly complemented by other data sources) (Daas et al. 2011).

Because of the project's orientation towards everyday practices, we mainly conducted co-located, face-to-face fieldwork.[3] Although face-to-face work is the focus of this chapter, this work continues in online environments (for instance, we also followed social media pages and wikis), and ethnographic projects can benefit from combining face-to-face and virtual, online or digital methods as described in other chapters in this book (also see Hine 2015). Drawing on fieldwork at Statistics Netherlands, I retrospectively distinguish five methodological positions. Instead of defining methodology as a top-down disciplinary system of rules, procedures, methods, and logics, I refer to methodological positions as the concepts, methods, and practical foci that can guide and enrich ethnographic research in screen mediated work places (I will refer to these as 'small m' methodologies). Fostering awareness of the methodological positions we occupy can support attuning ethnographic research along the way, as will be shown here for the research activities of screen demonstrations, observation, and participation. Before elaborating on this point, I will discuss five ways in which screen mediated work and its effects have been theorized beyond the ARITHMUS project. The chapter can therefore be read in two parts: a theoretical introduction to screens, followed by practical starting points for research in screen mediated environments.

Conceptualizations of Screen Mediated Work: From Synthetic Situations to Oligopticons

Broadly conceived, screens have been in use since people started displaying images on a flat surface. Shadow plays and early cinema can both be thought of as screened phenomena. However, the screens central to this chapter, computer monitors, are a relatively recent invention. Until the 1970s, mechanical displays or light bulbs would inform users of a computer's calculation result. In an often-recited episode of computer history, Xerox developed the first device comparable to a computer monitor as we know it today. The idea was eventually (and controversially) brought to Apple via Steve Jobs, where it was made possible for the first time to interact with and through computers through visual interfaces (Isaacson 2015). Whereas the first computer screens were mainly used to interact with the system through code, they were increasingly integrated into a wide variety of applications. Screens are now part of our communication and entertainment systems, medical practices, scientific research, police surveillance, and more. Moreover, touch screens have added a mode of interaction on top of the visual.

The variety of screen applications in knowledge practices can complicate conducting an ethnography of screen mediated work. Malte Ziewitz' reflection on his research illustrates some of the challenges. Below, he reflects on the role of screens in an interview with a content moderator (Helen) for an online forum. In the interview, Helen pointed at her computer screen to explain her activities. Looking back, Ziewitz asks:

> The 'screen' may be mentioned here in conversation, but it is surely not the 'screen' Helen is concerned with? Doesn't she also mention the keyboard and the mouse? And aren't these entities just employed as a literary figure of *pars pro toto* [referring to a larger whole], enacting a computer system the workings of which will soon be explained in greater detail? And what actually is so special about adjusting the screen? Didn't I also need to move the mouse—and in fact the mouse pad!—across the table to operate it?
>
> **(Ziewitz 2011, 213)**

Ziewitz asks whether the screen was relevant to the conversation. His hesitation can be partly explained by the fact that, even if we are not interested in screens as part of digital work, they very often take part in organizing this work. Therefore, even if our research does not immediately concern the role of screens in digital work, work practices may still be shaped by them. He furthermore wonders what we talk about when we talk about screens. Aren't we really talking about computation systems behind them? Indeed, it is by no means clear in advance how screens should be conceptualized: as singular artefacts, as part of larger systems, or perhaps as the outcomes of capacities we project onto them.

The fundamental openness of ethnographic methods makes this 'slipperiness' of screens difficult to manage. Ethnographers attempt to understand the *in situ* practices of actors (Clifford 1983; 1988). This means ethnography is based on a form of 'immersion' or closeness to the research object, in contrast to methods based on distant observation, such as survey research. Through interviewing, observation (participant or more passive), and studying documents we can learn, for instance, about routines, strategies, and artefacts deployed at a site of practice, including their tacit and unwritten conventions or logics (Latour and Woolgar 1986). The intention to examine time and location specific ('situated') practices also implies that the exact events to be observed and research activities to be deployed cannot be fully determined beforehand. Instead of determining every aspect of a study in advance, many ethnographers let (parts of) their methods, research aims, and theories emerge together.[4]

Research characterized by such openness of design can benefit from more clarity about methodological positioning to navigate the conceptual and methodological slipperiness of screens. Methodological positioning includes considerations about how we choose our research object, what we make observable, and how screens are conceptualized accordingly. The next section will suggest five methodological positions based on fieldwork conducted in ARITHMUS. Before turning to these, I will first elaborate on how screens have been implicitly and explicitly conceptualized beyond this project. I discuss five theoretical traditions that ethnographers interested in knowledge practices in organizations such as laboratories and companies can draw on: (1) symbolic interactionism; (2) ethnomethodology; (3) panoptic theories of power; (4) actor-network theories; (5) sociomateriality in organizational processes. This overview is not comprehensive but rather makes a start at highlighting the role of screens in five related theoretical traditions. I will predominantly review conceptualizations of screens *as part of* knowledge work (e.g. data analysis, knowledge communication, and coordination) in science and technology studies (STS) and related fields.[5] My focus will be on screens as part of assemblages of different technologies and practices, instead of considering screens apart from their contexts of usage. A final caution is that screens focus our attention on the visual aspects of knowledge work. However, ethnographers may also want to take acoustic and sensory aspects into account (cf. Mody 2005; Myers 2008).

A first conceptualization of screen mediated work by Karin Knorr Cetina and Urs Bruegger draws on symbolic interactionism. Following this tradition, these authors examine screens in the context of interactions between actors, and the meanings, symbols, and realities emerging from these interactions. Knorr Cetina and Bruegger contend that social interactions are no longer situated in local, geographically restricted spaces. Screen mediated work, such as currency trading, produces global social forms in which people do not need to be physically present. Instead, they need to be available for timely and short-term interaction ('response present') (Knorr Cetina and Bruegger 2002a; Knorr Cetina 2014). In sectors such as banking, workers predominantly orient towards global realities (in this case markets) through monitoring, responding, interacting, and coordinating their activities through screens. Knorr Cetina and Bruegger refer to this social situation as a 'synthethic situation' that no longer requires physical presence, and is augmented and coordinated by 'scopic media' (Knorr Cetina 2014, 47).

Screens (as part of scopic media) are essential to synthetic situations because they present visually what are otherwise geographically dispersed events; they present events in a streaming temporal order; and they collect and focus heterogeneous activities on a single surface. Furthermore, they foster mutual awareness because they act as 'mirrors' that reflect workers' real-time actions next to the actions of others (Knorr Cetina and Bruegger 2002a). The authors suggest this constant stream of action represented on screens is what makes them engrossing and demanding of our attention. Even though the screen is conceptualized as 'a building site on which a whole economic and epistemological world is erected' (Knorr Cetina and Bruegger 2002b, 167), this line of theory also warns that ethnographers need to be aware of the organizational work behind screens. For instance, screens can only fulfil their role as a 'building site' because professionals have formatted the information in ways that foster trust. In addition, workers' engagements with screens also depend on face-to-face interactions taking place on the work floor.

In ethnomethodological approaches, the analytical focus shifts from social inter-action to the object of knowledge (e.g. microbes or crime) (cf. Garfinkel 2002). The point of departure is that perception does not take place in the 'individual brain', but can be understood as a distributed sociomaterial process in which screens participate (Goodwin 1995, 256). Lucy Suchman, for instance, shows that in the design of roads and infrastructures, the visual interface of a screen makes it possible for engineers to imagine distant cities and highlight particular features. Their understanding of the world outside of their office emerges through embodied interactions with screens: through pointing, an engineer physically interacts with a screen to conceptualize the work that needs to be done to build a road (Suchman 2000, 12). Next to pointing and gesturing, discursive practices and professional expertise are relevant to how an image on a screen is interpreted (Goodwin 1994). Accordingly, the screen 'is not sim-ply a flat inscription, a place where information is to be apprehended through vision alone, but the basis of a three-dimensional work area, something that can be touched and manipulated' (Goodwin 1995, 258). Finally, screens also shape analytical work. Because screens present simplified and standardized representations of reality ('in-scriptions', such as graphs), they allow different areas of observation and expertise to be combined. They are not just 'windows' into a reality out there, but they allow diverse spaces with diverse properties to be analyzed in relation to each other. On the other hand, screens can remove much of the 'clutter' that otherwise contextual-izes events because they allow for cropping images, creating stills out of video, and backgrounding audio streams (Goodwin 1994, 622).

Another relevant engagement of ethnographers with screen mediated work draws on Michel Foucault's account of the panopticon as a model for the exercise of a particular form of power. The panopticon is a prison architecture that allows a single guard from a watchtower to observe the prison population in surrounding cells (a well-known design by Jeremy Bentham). However, prisoners can never be sure they are watched. As a consequence, they internalize rules of behaviour and the exercise of power becomes 'automatic'; this is what Foucault calls disciplinary power (Foucault 1995 [1977], 201). Panoptic theories have been adopted by con-temporary researchers to examine current forms of electronic surveillance by video cameras or image recognition, leading to theories of the 'neo-panopticon' or 'hyper-panopticon' (Armstrong and Norris 1999; Lyon 2007). They examine screens as part of the physical architecture enabling this exercise of power. For disciplinary power to be exercised, this architecture can be complemented by among others professional and everyday knowledge, and statistical and disciplinary techniques (e.g. the confes-sion). Importantly, not only authorities participate in surveillance but surveillance can also take place 'from below' by individuals and citizen organizations (Mann et al. 2002; Timan and Oudshoorn 2012). Foucault's work and influence range well be-yond this discussion of screens.[6] In the context of this chapter, however, I suggest that panoptic theories can sensitize ethnographers to the role played by screens in the constitution of power relations within the field.

In ethnographies that take up insights from actor-network theory (ANT) the notion of screens as part of a panopticon from where a comprehensive overview can be obtained from a small space is moderated. As in ethnomethodological approaches, the focus is on how objects of knowledge are made. Ethnographers are interested in observing the mutual shaping of human and non-human entities in the ongoing formation of relations that bring into being objects of knowledge, such as populations or microbes. As also explained in the introduction, the knowledge practices (e.g. data analysis) observed by ethnographers are performative: they do not represent reality but bring it into being (Latour 1993).

Bruno Latour and Emilie Hermant (2006) describe how Paris, a dynamic and complicated metropole, is essentially unknowable in its full complexity but is constituted in different ways in 'centres of calculation'. As part of control rooms, laboratories, planetary observatories, and offices, screens visualize and assemble inscriptions that simplify the real world (Latour 2012). Yet screens do not present a bird's eye view; we did not move from micro to macro. Instead, they take part in specified and simplified enactments of Paris (cf. Haraway 1988). Control rooms and other screened environments therefore function as oligopticons instead of panopticons: they show very little (*olig*), and this is why we use them. Work inspired by ANT and related approaches (post-ANT, material semiotics) furthermore demonstrate contingencies and fragilities characterizing the operation of screens in practice (Dubbeld 2005; Pols 2011; Ziewitz 2011). For instance, in an examination of organizational communication infrastructures used by scientists, Janet Vertesi adopts notions of mess and heterogeneity to hightlight the enduring contingencies and misalignments among different elements (routines, schedules, technology parts) that make up these infrastructures (cf. Law, 2004). For screens to make people co-present consequently takes constant work and effort, and it is exactly this work that is relevant for who is included and excluded (Vertesi 2014).

Finally, sociomaterial theories of organizational processes (often related to ANT approaches) start from the assumption that the roles of technologies and humans in organizational practices are relational and in constant rearticulation (Orlikowski 2010). Although screens are not explicitly theorized, two examples give an insight into how screen mediated work has been addressed. First, Barbara Czarniawska examines a press office where part of the work has been automated and screens are always present to inform journalists about the most recent global press releases. Monitors constantly display a stream of news, offering

> ' ... the opportunity to monitor what others [other journalists] are doing. ... In the old days apparently, journalists tried to figure out what the others were writing by sounding out their colleagues in face-to-face encounters. Now they can save themselves the ordeal, as well as the uncertainty about whether the information they gathered was correct or not. The screen will tell them soon enough. '
>
> (Czarniawska 2012, 183).

As in Knorr and Bruegger's work, screens thus allow for constant observation and awareness of colleagues elsewhere (Knorr Cetina and Bruegger 2002a, 2002b; Knorr Cetina 2014). However, how screened devices rearrange organizational practices depends on how the narratives framing screened devices are negotiated. Focusing on the use of smartphones, Katrina Pritchard and Gillian Symon (2014) show that the introduction of smartphone photography to share images prompted a renegotiation about what counts as good evidence within an organization. By following how conventions change, we learn that even though smartphones have the capacity to reconfigure work practices, how they affect digital work depends on organizational processes of meaning making.

To summarize, we can understand screens as part of the ongoing production of synthetic situations they enable and constitute; as part of embodied practices of analysis; as part of architectures of disciplinary power; as part of fragile and messy actor-networks or oligopticons; and as part of organizational processes that (re)configure screens through meaning making processes. Different roles can be distinguished: in some approaches screens are central because they are understood to have a 'scopic' effect. In other approaches, screens are more malleable: their roles and effects are outcomes rather than givens. This conceptual variety suggests different methodological positions towards studying digital work. I suggest that making these positions more explicit can enrich fieldwork. The next section aims to offer a resource for methodological (re)positioning based on research in the screen mediated environment of official statistics.

Methodological Positions for Fieldwork in Screen Mediated Environments: Insights from an Ethnography of Statistical Practices

Ethnographic fieldwork is often organized as one long fieldwork period (for instance, six months) and a return visit. In the case of ARITHMUS fieldwork at SN was spread over thirteen visits ranging from a day to four weeks between 2015 and 2020. Spreading fieldwork allows researchers to follow projects over a longer period, and to share findings with other researchers in the project along the way. Research activities included observing everyday work, work meetings and conferences, interviewing, and collecting relevant documents. In addition, we followed mailing lists, wikis, and social media pages. My primary fieldwork locations were SN in The Hague, in particular the innovation laboratory, and a field office of SN in Bonaire, the Caribbean Netherlands.

Drawing on fieldwork moments and situations, this section distinguishes between five different methodological positions. These are 'small m' methodological positions that each present an approach to screens, including whether screens are understood to shape: the observed work practices; a particular research activity (e.g.

interviewing); and the main research interest or object. In brief, these methodological positions each present a focus for conducting fieldwork in a screen mediated workspace. The central concern of the research project was how populations are constituted through everyday practices. Conceptually, it was predominantly informed by elements of ANT, particularly performativity, and ethnomethodological attention to the embodied interactions with screens in analytical work. While these theories inform the methodological positions described below (mainly positions 1 and 2), they did not limit the range of positions adopted. Instead, the ARITHMUS project shows that varying positions may be adopted depending on opportunities and observations in the field.

Position 1: Focus on screen interfaces as integral to digital work

The fieldwork included interviewing statisticians about how they clean, interpret, and analyse data. Interviewing was a research activity allowing me to understand these practices in greater detail. Visual observations of work practices, in this instance, were less suitable because this work is generally less visible and many of the data analysed by statisticians are confidential. Accordingly, I conducted open-ended and semi-structured interviews. Semi-structured interviews either involved a topic list or a list of questions that guided rather than fixed conversations.

Interviewing enabled learning about the changing nature of statistical work. Familiarizing myself with the modes of analysis, data types, and everyday routines used by statisticians was a relevant part of eventually understanding how populations are brought into being through these procedures. When I first started talking to statisticians about the making of demographic statistics (e.g. birth rates), I was often told this process was almost fully automated. Many analyst positions had disappeared, and a lot of work seemed to concern updating the software rather than data analysis. To learn more about actual work processes in the context of automation I often included screen demonstrations in the interviews so I would get an impression of how the software operated and how statisticians interpreted screen interfaces. A screen demonstration is an interview technique where an informant is asked to demonstrate their interfaced work (Suchman 2000). When I asked a statistician to show me how they usually checked and validated statistics before publication, the following happened:

> The statistician pointed at a few highlighted cells in an Excel file. She explained that these cells are highlighted because the values in these cells are especially relevant to compare with those of the previous year. 'That's funny', I said, 'I was told this was all automated'. '"Automated" should be understood between quotation marks', she responded, as she continued to demonstrate how she made graphs to verify whether the statistics are correct.

Automation, the example suggests, did not make the statistician redundant. While everyday work floor discourse emphasized the absence of 'handwork', screen demonstrations allowed for observation of the work practices that remained relevant. Through this interview technique I also learned about other details of statistical production, for instance, about the types of data included in the population register and the steps between the collection of data and publication.

The example illustrates the methodological position adopted to examine data cleaning, editing and interpretation: a focus on screen interfaces as integral to and co-constituted with digital work. This means screens shape digital work practices (in this case analysis) and cannot be understood in isolation from them. In fact, many artefacts of statistical practice, such as population registers, do not seem to exist separately from screen interfaces. Statisticians' repeated use of manual drawings of interfaces (e.g. the cells of a population register) to explain their work when a computer screen was not present also indicates this. We might then conclude that screen demonstrations make interviewing easier because informants are not required to abstract their practices from their everyday engagement with screens. Being aware of the co-constitution of screens and digital practices and artefacts can make interviewing easier in different ways. For instance, when I conducted an interview about the production of census statistics, it was helpful to ask my informant to explain this by walking me through the file structure (the on-screen icons of files in Windows File Explorer).

Position 2: Focus on screen interfaces as constitutive of objects of knowledge

Screen demonstrations were furthermore used to learn about the embodied processes of constituting populations. In ethnomethodologist Charles Goodwin's words, they are 'the basis of a three-dimensional work area, something that can be touched and manipulated' (1995, 258). In this project, we also studied the performance of population in various statistical practices. Here I will illustrate this part of the research with a statistical project that, for the first time in the Netherlands, used internet data (URLs, website information collected through scrapers) to determine the characteristics and size of the 'digital economy'. In the following fragment from a screen demonstration a statistician explains how she compiled a database of all relevant companies:

> Scrolling through the database with companies, she pointed out 'a difficult one': hartendief.com.[7] 'The company number is on the website, look, but it's in English so it cannot be scraped automatically, I now have to use this number and connect to another file'. Next, she pointed at another example, Bobbakker.com, and opened the website on another screen. A 'flat' website appeared that only showed a screen size portrait picture of someone, probably Bob Bakker. 'There are so many pointless websites', she commented.

The fragment points out that analytical work is not a purely individual cognitive process; instead, it involves talk and interaction with interfaces. Through clicking, pointing, and commenting the statistician demonstrated who is part of a population of Dutch 'digital companies' and who is not. This moment can be read as an instance of 'doing' population through interactions between bodies and screens. When a team of statisticians later convened to discuss the progress of the project, similar enactments of the population together with screens took place. On this occasion, one of the statisticians pointed at data suggesting that many participants in the digital economy are small web shops. Consequently, he argued, the digital economy was characterized by a 'typically Dutch' entrepreneurial spirit—referring to an imaginary of a nation of small traders and shopkeepers.

These findings are of interest because they demonstrate the integration of new data types (URLs) in the performance of population. New data types helped to extend a population of 'typically Dutch' economic actors to the digital realm. Similar to position 1, the methodological position underlying this research practice is an understanding of screens as constitutive of digital work. Instead of focusing on understanding work practices, the main research interest here is on how populations came into being through interacting with interfaces. Alternatively, as I will describe next, screens can also be bracketed off from the primary focus of attention in fieldwork observation.

Position 3: Bracketing off screens

Another central research activity was observation. In this sub-section I discuss a passive type of observation, as opposed to participation (see position 5). Part of the research consisted of sitting at a desk in, among others, the SN innovation laboratory in The Hague and the analysts' room at Statistics Caribbean Netherlands. During these days, I would arrange my interviews, study documents, and join office chat. One of the aims of 'hanging out' is to arrive at a richer, *in situ*, understanding of the routines, issues, tasks, bodies of knowledge, organizational discourses, and technologies that are part of a statistical office.

Such open-ended immersion also made it possible to identify research topics I had not determined beforehand. Fieldwork conducted at Statistics Caribbean Netherlands helps to illustrate this. The Caribbean Netherlands are an overseas territory of the Netherlands consisting of the islands of Bonaire, St Eustatius, and Saba. A field office in Bonaire collects and analyses data about the 26,000 people living on these islands using similar standards and methods to those used in the office in The Hague. At the time of a large survey, office chat developed around WhatsApp conversations among the Statistics Caribbean Netherlands fieldworkers. Some of these conversations concerned the high rate of incorrect addresses in the population register—a data infrastructure that helps determine who should be in the survey sample. In response, a statistician would consult Google Maps for the correct address of a potential interviewee or call to check their details.

Data infrastructures, this suggests, do not work by themselves. Instead, statisticians drew on different data sources and workarounds to make the register operational. What is more, without this everyday work the population register could not be used in constituting the Caribbean Netherlands population. We might even consider these small everyday acts of consulting platforms to confirm addresses as 'political' in the sense that they supported a 'politics of method' (cf. Scheel and Ruppert 2019): they supported the constitution of population through registers originally developed for the context of the continental Netherlands.

Methodologically, something different is happening here compared to positions 1 and 2. Even though screens were everywhere in this office, I did not take them into account as constitutive of the practices I was studying. This did not mean they were not part of the field. In fact, screens were part of the social fabric. On receiving an email message, some statisticians would immediately utter comments that made us part of the stream of events projected by the screens (for instance by stating 'this is incredible'). Yet, in this part of my fieldwork the methodological position is best described as 'bracketing off' screens in my analysis. Bracketed off are the interactions (e.g. pointing, reading from the screen) in which screens and digital practices shape each other, as highlighted by the ethnomethodological stance in position 2 above. Furthermore, this methodological position is not concerned with how screen mediated work is shaped through organizational negotiations, as in sociomaterial theories of organizational processes (Pritchard and Symon 2014). Instead, screens are backgrounded even though they are part of office chat and work practices. This example thus illustrates that we can recognize that screens are relevant parts of digital work, and yet choose a different focus. In the end, the ethnographer decides when and how to focus on screens in line with their research objectives.[8]

Position 4: Focus on the role of screens in shaping (inter-) organizational power relations

As is implied by the open-endedness of ethnographic observation, a methodological position can also be abandoned in the interest of pursuing different analytic directions. Continuing with the example of the Caribbean Netherlands, positioning screens in yet another way can improve our understanding of our field sites. When observing video calls with The Hague from Bonaire, I learned that the room with a large screen for video calling was rarely used for any other purpose. In practice, it was dedicated to coordinating and discussing the production of statistics with the main office in The Hague. Also configuring the role of this room in cross-Atlantic coordination was the picture of the Dutch King and Queen in the same room (see Figure 3.1). Through the presence of screens and this picture, the room was positioned as a node of Dutch central government in the Caribbean Netherlands. In SN Heerlen, a statistical office also outside of the administrative centre of The Hague, screens were given a similar role. Here, a set of screens was always on stand-by, so statisticians could see and contact each other any time of day. Pointing at the screen, one statistician explained that it was like 'a connection to researchers on Antarctica, and Antarctica, that's us'.

At the time of the research, I did not theorize these observations extensively. Rather, they were part of my effort to improve my understanding of the power relations in a field. Looking back, however, we can think these observations through with Janet Vertesi's work on the messy and negotiated infrastructures of communication used by Spanish and American scientists (inspired by, among others, the ANT tradition discussed in the previous section). In her ethnography of everyday scientific work, Vertesi observes a laptop on the floor of a Spanish office. On closer inspection, an American sticker and power socket reveal that the casual scene can also be read as a location of American power established through the everyday actions and technologies that intertwine Spanish and American communication infrastructures. The case of the Caribbean Netherlands illustrates yet other, postcolonial, relations established through and with screens. In the examples discussed above, this happened not through maintaining

Fig. 3.1 Room dedicated to conference calls (picture of the King and Queen on the left wall)

messy, heterogeneous socio-technical relations but through the everyday usage of symbols such as a photograph of the King and Queen and the image of Heerlen as 'Antarctica'.

The methodological position I want to highlight here is that, whether extensively theorized or not, ethnographers can also focus on screens to improve their grasp of the power relations that may be present at a field site. In this case, thinking this through helped to connect statistical institutes across the Atlantic as part of a postcolonial state system instead of thinking of them as separate field sites. A fieldwork practice may therefore also consider screens as a starting point for thinking through a myriad of intergovernmental or interorganizational relations, and thereby make it easier to understand and navigate the power relations characterizing geographically dispersed organizations (cf. Grommé, forthcoming).

Position 5: Focus on the making of screen mediated work

So far, we have discussed screens as part of digital work practices. We can include them as constitutive of digital work, bracket them off, and consider their role in shaping field sites. But there is another methodological position: a focus on the *making of* screen mediated work. I implicitly adopted this methodological strategy when I got the opportunity to conduct a more participative mode of observation. Participation in digital work can offer opportunities to experience the hidden, tacit, and affective aspects of this work. Through reflecting on and making sense of our individual encounters with routines, assumptions, norms, and artefacts it becomes possible to generate valuable insights about a field (Hine 2015).

During one of my fieldwork visits a statistician suggested that I informally assist in setting up statistics webinars for college and university students, which I did haphazardly over the course of several weeks. Webinars were important to SN because they would allow the organization to strengthen collaboration with colleges and universities. Moreover, organizing webinars though platforms such as YouTube was considered prestigious in 2016; it was seen as characteristic of an innovative organization. But the following description of my participation in developing the webinars suggests webinars also served other ends:

A few months into the project, the statisticians decided that a YouTube livestream was preferable to the open source platform we were using previously because it offered the possibility to display the SN logo. Now we needed to figure out how to make a livestream possible from the SN lecture hall. The current video recording system would not work, as its use was regulated and could not be employed ad hoc. By contrast, a small off-the-shelf camera was used to organize a livestream that could be established quickly and on-demand, as one statistician stated: 'It needs to be professional, yet accessible for everybody'. We proceeded to test the system in an empty office. At *this point, I tried to blend in the background a bit more because I became instantly aware of my limited technical skills. However, I was egged along by the statisticians. It did not matter, as long as we all tried to make it work. Also, could I say something to the camera, so we can test it? By the end of our test, one of the statisticians pointed at the wires and duct tape we applied to the camera, exclaiming: 'Yes this is also innovation!'*

Developing the webinar not only served networking and educational purposes. The above suggests that it also performed a particular take on innovation. Through using a small camera and duct tape (see Figure 3.2), these statisticians demonstrated what they considered as elements of an innovative organizational culture: the inclusion of different skills sets and ideas, a focus on small 'do-it-yourself' projects, not saying no, and low-key improvements. By contrast, webinars had so far been organized top-down and access to the expensive equipment required was only possible on request.

To conclude, the example is about how screens are made operational in certain ways, and what this means for an organization and the culture associated with it. It indicates that the making of screen mediated work such as webinars can be a relevant site of research. As a methodological position, this suggests that the making and

Fig. 3.2 Testing a webinar system

application of screen-based practices can be studied as forms of digital work in their own right.

Conclusion

This chapter discussed research activities undertaken as part of an ethnography of official statistics. I set out to take a few steps towards clarifying issues regarding the role of screens in researching digital work. In doing so, I have primarily focused on screens as material devices (computer monitors) connected to larger technological configurations.

Conceptualizing the role of screens vis-à-vis other technologies and processes in digital work practices can be challenging. From previous conceptualizations of screen mediated work, we learn that it can have particular characteristics and effects. Among these are the ability of screens as 'scopic media' to introduce a temporal order by projecting streams of information; to captivate workers' attention to this temporal order; to connect geographically dispersed actors; and to mirror the actions taking by these actors. Knorr Cetina and Bruegger (2002a; 2014) contend that these capabilities can support the constitution of global social forms. Another capacity of screens is to enable the analysis of complex empirical phenomena through the display of inscriptions in ways that allow for embodied interaction (Goodwin 1995; Suchman 2000; Latour and Hermant 2006). Screens therefore take part in coordinating action, but also in bringing into being objects of study and intervention. Screen mediated work can furthermore be analysed through panoptic theories in which screens are parts of architectures of power. However, we also learn that coordination and communication through screens is an ongoing accomplishment best understood as always fragile and fragmentary. Finally, while screens make distributed forms of work possible, their exact role cannot be determined in advance as these are subject to meaning making and negotiation processes.

While some of these conceptualizations may correspond to particular methodological positions, there does not need to be a one-to-one relationship between how screens are conceptualized in a research project and particular fieldwork approaches. In the research project discussed in this chapter, the main theoretical starting points were performativity as conceptualized in ANT, and an ethnomethodological attention to embodied screenwork. This led to adopting a methodological position that takes into account that screen interfaces are constitutive of digital work and objects of knowledge such as populations. But I have also shown that fieldwork can be affected by unforeseen events, observations, and opportunities. As a consequence, at least five different 'small m' methodological positions in relation to screen mediated work emerged along the way. These included different research activities, among them passive and participant observation and screenwork demonstrations. This is not to say that these positions and research activities cover all possibilities or have always been successful. Rather, I presented them here to provide other researchers with material that can help to recognize opportunities and challenges. The practice I hope to promote is one that fosters reflexivity and analytical mobility to enrich our understanding, delineation, and constitution of a field site. For instance, being able to reflect on the presence of screens for teleconferencing in geographically dispersed government practices may enrich our understanding of the power relations shaping a field as in the example of the geographically dispersed offices of SN across The Hague, Heerlen and the Caribbean Netherlands.

These insights lead to four final considerations. First, understanding the role of screens as part of distributed work practices forces us to reconsider an often-mentioned research challenge in face-to-face ethnographies: we may not always be able to observe what happens on-screen. For instance, conversations previously observable at a conference may now take place in email lists. However, this chapter has shown that screen mediated work can be learned about through the relations developed as part of fieldwork. Participating in office chat, for example, offered contextualized and rich insights into the particularities of a digital knowledge infrastructure. An ethical issue is that it can be difficult to determine which parts of a conversation can and should be used as ethnographic data. Although participation in conversations can be experienced by ethnographers as a consensual mode of research, it is nevertheless relevant to ascertain informed consent before, during, and after fieldwork, through practices such as consent agreements and sharing drafts. Second, this chapter has focused on screens as an aspect of digital work. However, this does not mean that they always need to be central to our observations, as is illustrated by the methodological position of 'bracketing off' screenwork. In fact, similar considerations and challenges regarding the distributed nature and complexity of digital work practices may arise with regard to other devices and knowledge practices. For instance, ethnographers interested in automation need to make myriad decisions about where and how to include algorithms in their observations. An example of a theoretical question is whether we can consider algorithms apart from data, computer hardware, or even from the environments they intervene in. Methodologically, ethnographers will then need to make decisions about the centrality of algorithms in their observations of everyday automation, much like they need to when studying screen mediated work. Third, attending to screens inevitably risks excluding other aspects from our observations. Conceptualizations of screen mediated work are accompanied by visual metaphors that prioritize seeing over other senses. Being reflexive regarding our conceptualization and positioning of screens can contribute to decentring them in our research, while staying aware of their effects. Finally, the theories, methodologies, and examples discussed in this section suggest that screen mediated work is by no means a closed field of inquiry and that there is room to develop inventive ethnographic approaches that help to understand how social relations develop around digitalization.

Notes

1. Originally published in Het Vaderland. Retrieved from the Delpher database on 8 January 2021, http://resolver.kb.nl/resolve?urn=MMKB19:000856050:mpeg21:p00006.
2. See www.arithmus.eu. In this chapter I mostly draw on the fieldwork I conducted at Statistics Netherlands. For more about the collaborative aspects of the project, see Scheel et al. (2020). This chapter is indebted to ongoing conversations among team members, as well as conversations with participants to a workshop titled 'Screenwork ethnographies', conducted at Goldsmiths, University of London, on 2 June 2015. The research leading to this publication has received funding from the European Research Council under the European Union's Seventh Framework Programme (FP/2007–2013)/ERC Grant Agreement no. 615588 (Principal Investigator, Evelyn Ruppert, Goldsmiths, University of London). It was also supported by a BA-Leverhulme Small Grant (SRG\170291).
3. Co-location refers to fieldwork based on physical presence at the same site as informants, in contrast to co-presence (Beaulieu 2010).
4. The degree of openness that is practised varies. In many cases, as in ARITHMUS, several central themes and concepts are set up in advance to guide the project next to the research question(s).
5. Screens have been theorized in yet other ways in relation to, for instance, media and cultural production, see Turkle (1995, 2016).
6. Many of the the ARITHMUS project's theoretical premises with regard to the relevance of monitoring populations in modern government are directly or indirectly indebted to Foucault's writing. In particular to his (2009) work on governmentality, also see Scheel (2020).
7. The URLs in this fragment are fictional.
8. A significant amount of ethnographic work on digital practices 'brackets off' the role of screens in digital work. Take, for instance, Rosenblat's observations of Uber drivers' embodied interactions with screens (2018, 52). Yet, her primary (and relevant) interest is how drivers interact with algorithms

References

Armstrong, G. and Norris, C. 1999. *The Maximum Surveillance Society: The Rise of CCTV.* 1st edition. Oxford; New York: Berg Publishers.

Beaulieu, A. 2010. Research note: From co-location to co-presence: shifts in the use of ethnography for the study of knowledge. *Social Studies of Science*, 40(3): pp. 453–70.

Clifford, J. 1983. On ethnographic authority. *Representations*, 1(2): pp 118–146.

Clifford, J. 1988. *The Predicament of Culture*. Cambridge, MA: Harvard University Press.

Curtis, B. 2001. *The Politics of Population: State Formation, Statistics, and the Census of Canada, 1840–1875*. Toronto: University of Toronto Press.

Czarniawska, B. 2012. *Cyberfactories: How News Agencies Produce News*. Cheltenham: Edward Elgar Pub.

Daas, P., Roos, M., de Blois, C., Hoekstra, R., Ten Bosch, O., & Ma, Y. 2011. *New Data Sources for Statistics: Experiences at Statistics Netherlands* (Discussion paper 201109). The Hague/Heerlen: Statistics Netherlands.

Dubbeld, L. 2005. The role of technology in shaping CCTV surveillance practices. *Information,Communication & Society*, 8(1): pp. 84–100.

Foucault, M. 1995. *Discipline & Punish: The Birth of the Prison*. 2nd edition, 1995. New York: Vintage.

Foucault, M. 2009. *Security, Territory, Population: Lectures at the Collège de France, 1977–78*. Basingstoke: Palgrave Macmillan.

Garfinkel, H. 2002. *Ethnomethodology's Program: Working Out Durkheim's Aphorism*. Lanham, MD: Rowman & Littlefield Publishers.

Goodwin, C. 1994. Professional vision. *American Anthropologist*, 96(3): pp. 606–633.

Goodwin, C. 1995. Seeing in depth. *Social Studies of Science*, 25(2): pp. 237–74.

Grommé, F. Forthcoming. Thinking, seeing, and doing like a kingdom: the making of Caribbean Netherlands statistics and the "native Bonairian." In Guadeloupe, F. and Van der Pijl, Y. eds.), *Equaliberty in the Dutch Caribbean: Ways of Being Non/Sovereign*. New Brunswick, NJ: Rutgers University Press.

Haraway, D. J. 1988. Situated knowledges: The science question in feminism and the privilege of partial perspective. *Feminist Studies*, 14(3): pp. 575–99.

Hine, C., 2015. *Ethnography for the Internet: Embedded, Embodied and Everyday*. Abingdon: Taylor & Francis.

Isaacson, W. 2015. *The Innovators: How a Group of Hackers, Geniuses, and Geeks Created the Digital Revolution*. Reprint edition. New York: Simon & Schuster.

Knorr Cetina, K. 2014. Scopic media and global coordination: The mediatization of face-to-face encounters. In Lundby, K. (ed.), *Mediatization of Communication* (pp. 39–62). Berlin and Boston: de Gruyter.

Knorr Cetina, K. and Bruegger, U. 2002a. Global microstructures: The virtual societies of financial markets. *American Journal of Sociology*, 107(4): pp. 905–50.

Knorr Cetina, K. and Bruegger, U. 2002b. Traders' engagement with markets: A postsocial relationship. *Theory, Culture & Society*, 19(5–6): pp. 161–85.

Latour, B. 1993. *The Pasteurization of France*. Cambridge, MA: Harvard University Press.

Latour, B. 2012. *We Have Never Been Modern*. Cambridge, MA: Harvard University Press.

Latour, B. and Hermant, E. 2006. *Paris: Invisible City*. Online Project, Airs de Paris Exhibition, Centre Pompidou.

Latour, B. and Woolgar, S. 1986. *Laboratory Life: The Construction of Scientific Facts*. Princeton, NJ: Princeton University Press.

Law, J. 2004. *After Method: Mess in Social Science Research*. London and New York: Routledge.

Law, J. 2008. On sociology and STS. *Sociological Review*, 56(4): pp. 623–49.

Lyon, D. 2007. *Surveillance Studies: An Overview*. Cambridge: Polity Press.

Mann, S., Nolan, J., and Wellman, B. 2002. Sousveillance: Inventing and using wearable computing devices for data collection in surveillance environments. *Surveillance & Society*, 1(3): pp. 331–55.

Mody, C. C. M. 2005. The sounds of science: Listening to laboratory practice. *Science, Technology, & Human Values*, 30 (2): pp. 175–98.

Myers, N. 2008. Molecular embodiments and the body-work of modeling in protein crystallography. *Social Studies of Science*, 38(2): pp. 163–19.

Orlikowski, W. J. 2010. The sociomateriality of organisational life: Considering technology in management research. *Cambridge Journal of Economics*, 34(1): pp. 125–41.

Pols, J. 2011. Wonderful webcams: About active gazes and invisible technologies. *Science, Technology & Human Values*, 36(4): pp. 451–73.

Pritchard, K. and Symon, G. 2014. Picture perfect? Exploring the use of smartphone photography in a distributed work practice. *Management Learning*, 45(5): pp. 561–76.

Rosenblat, A. 2018. *Uberland: How Algorithms are Rewriting the Rules of Work*. Oakland, CA: University of California Press.

Ruppert, E. 2011. Population objects: Interpassive subjects. *Sociology*, 45(2): pp. 218–33.

Ruppert, E. and Scheel, S. 2019. The Politics of Method: Taming the New, Making Data Official. *International Political Sociology*, 13(3), 233–252.

Scheel, S. 2020. Biopolitical bordering: Enacting populations as intelligible objects of government. *European Journal of Social Theory*, 23(4): pp. 571–90.

Scheel, S., Grommé, F., Ruppert, E., Ustek-Spilda, F., Cakici, B., and Takala, V. 2020. Doing a transversal method: Developing an ethics of care in a collaborative research project. *Global Networks*, 20(3): pp. 522–43.

Suchman, L. 2000. Embodied practices of engineering work. Mind, *Culture, and Activity*, 7(1–2): pp. 4–18.

Timan, T. and Oudshoorn, N. 2012. Mobile cameras as new technologies of surveillance? How citizens experience the use of mobile cameras in public nightscapes. *Surveillance & Society*, 10(2): pp. 167–81.

Turkle, S. 1995. *Life on the Screen*. New York: Simon and Schuster.

Turkle, S. 2016. *Reclaiming Conversation: The Power of Talk in a Digital Age*. New York: Penguin.

Vertesi, J. 2014. Seamful spaces: Heterogeneous infrastructures in interaction. *Science, Technology, & Human Values*, 39(2): pp. 264–84.

Winthereik, B. R., Lutz, P. A., Suchman, L., and Verran, H. 2011. Attending to screens and screenness: Guest editorial for special issue of encounters. *STS Encounters*, 4(2): pp. 1–6.

Ziewitz, M., 2011. How to attend to screens? Technology, ontology and precarious enactments. *STS Encounters*, 4(2): pp. 203–28.

4

Me, Myself, and iPhone

Sociomaterial Reflections on the Smartphone as Methodological Instrument in London's Gig-Economy

Adam Badger

Introduction

With specific reference to organizations, smartphones have had three profound effects. They have changed the way in which day-to-day organizing takes place in existing firms, they have led to the creation of completely new roles in some organizations (mobile developers, for example) and finally they have precipitated whole new organizational forms based on the capabilities they offer. One such example of these new organizations are the gig economy platforms that have proliferated across the globe. According to Woodcock and Graham (2020), the gig economy is characterized by self-employed workers undertaking piecemeal 'gigs' through a labour platform. The labour platform is responsible for delivering an application and technical architectures for connecting customers with workers and mediating their interaction. In return for this service, they extract a fee from every transaction in the form of a 'commission'. In short, their most basic function is to organize multiple sides of a market (workers and clients) and facilitate an exchange. Woodcock and Graham (2020) note the gig economy is broadly split into two forms—'cloudwork' and 'geographically-tethered' work. Cloudwork is done remotely from anywhere that has an internet connection via platforms such as UpWork and Amazon Mechanical Turk. Geographically-tethered work must be done in a given locale, like delivering pizzas or providing taxi rides on platforms such as Deliveroo or Uber. This chapter focuses exclusively on research into this latter type of gig work.

Whilst these firms would like us to believe they offer freedom and flexibility to workers, it is becoming increasingly clear that their technologies also coerce and discipline workers in the undertaking of their labour (Gandini 2019). Although the organizational form may be new, it is our responsibility as management scholars to investigate and analyse the labour they facilitate. A key site of enquiry is the mobile

Adam Badger, *Me, Myself, and iPhone*. In: *Research Methods for Digital Work and Organization*.
Edited by Gillian Symon, Katrina Pritchard, and Christine Hine, Oxford University Press.
© Oxford University Press (2021). DOI: 10.1093/oso/9780198860679.003.0004

phone. For workers in the geographically-tethered gig economy their phone is a central organizing and labour distribution device, becoming the site where jobs are received, accepted, and monitored. As such, the mobile phone becomes a crucial site of enquiry for researchers. This chapter emerges from work following the broader spatial turn in organization studies (Dale and Burell 2008) in attempting to understand the spaces and materialities of gig work. It does so by focusing on the use of my smartphone in the process of studying the lived experiences of work for 'The Platform'.[1] First, I introduce my research and the ethical decisions made in research design before exploring my philosophical approach to the mobile phone. The remainder of the chapter will focus directly on how its capabilities were tailored to record and synthesize empirical data.

The Research in Brief

My smartphone was used as part of a covert (auto)ethnography of London's gig economy. I worked for 'The Platform' with varying intensity over the course of nine months, picking up and delivering meals from restaurants to offices and homes, mostly in East London. Whilst my methodologies were tailored specifically to The Platform, it represents a fairly typical gig-economy firm (Srnicek 2017). However, it should be noted that it administers a three-sided market place[2] through mobile devices and applications. The first side is the customer, who uses their own device to order food through a different application. The second is the restaurant, which receives a tablet computer with the proprietary Platform app pre-installed. Finally, the delivery worker uses a different application that is not publicly available and must be installed on their personal device. Workers are then free to log in and out when they choose and accept jobs as they are offered to them, being paid on a piece-rate basis for the discrete units of labour they provide.

Given its covert nature, it is important to reflect on the ethical considerations across my research project. Emerging from the long and hotly contested debate regarding the ethics of covert activity, I follow Spicker's (2011, 119) assertion that research is covert when 'not disclosed to the subject—where the researcher does not reveal that research is taking place'. This is more common than many would assume; for example, any participant observation where subjects are not made explicitly aware they are being observed for research is covert. As such, it is essential to clarify that the 'subject' of my autoethnographic inquiry was The Platform itself. Realistically, The Platform's secrecy would likely have resulted in my being denied access if operating overtly, ending the research before it had even started. Where I engaged with workers I did so overtly; informing them of my motives and arranging to interview them (in a separate stage of the research process). Where I observed workers, I sought to inform them whenever possible, however I came to accept this isn't always achievable given the fleeting interactions made with people in the process of food delivery; this is the same in most public settings (Spicker 2011). In practical terms,

I underwent a six-month ethical review process and regular check-ins throughout, both self-reflexively and in discussion with my supervisors.[3] Whilst this chapter's focus on the phone limits the space for a discussion of covert ethics in hard to reach workplaces, I have explored these debates elsewhere in direct relation to this research (Badger and Woodcock 2019).

To give a sense of scale, in the nine months I was in the field I captured 3000 images and generated over 100,000 words of ethnographic diary entries. Beyond the remit of this chapter, I also conducted 35 hours of semi-structured interviews and follow-up interviews with 10 participants.

Mobile Phone as 'Interface'

Before advancing to discuss the mobile phone as an interface, it is essential that some key lexical differences are outlined to aid comprehension of the chapter. First, 'The Platform' is a pseudonym for the organization being researched, and does not refer to platform companies in general. Second, is the differentiation between field*site* and field*work*. Field*site* refers to The Platform's technologies and the work of food delivery. Field*work* refers to the methodologies I used and academic labour of investigation. Elements of both the field*site* and field*work* became manifest through my phone (an iPhone 6, then an iPhone SE1). Any theoretical positioning of the phone in relation to the field*site* had implications for approaches to the mobile phone during field*work*, and vice-versa. Accordingly, it must be positioned theoretically ahead of discussions of the phone's use.

I build-upon the broader spatial turn in organization studies (see for example, Dale and Burrell 2008) and contemporary discussions from across the humanities that engage with Massey (2005) and Lefebvre (1991) in understanding space as socially produced and experienced; never static but forever 'in process'. More specifically I echo the work of Kinsley (2014, 365) in his efforts to 'find the matter in the virtual' and breakdown the 'separation between the physical, often referred to as 'real', world and the abstract or mental, 'virtual', world. This requires the digital not be reified as intrinsically separate from space, but rather as something (re)produced in and *through* space. In an organizational context, Orlikowski's (2007, 1435) sociomaterial approach posits 'materiality as constitutive of everyday life', taking the smartphone as a leading example wherein its performativity 'is sociomaterial, shaped by the particular contingent way in which the BlackBerry service is *designed, configured, and engaged in practice*' (Orlikowksi 2007, 1444, emphasis added). Put simply, Orlikowski is arguing that there are co-constitutive relationships between object, designer, and user that, taken together, in a given context generate lived realities.

This research understands the phone as an assemblage of technical objects (apps, GPS tracking, 4G networks, customer and restaurant applications, The Platform's labour distribution algorithm, cameras, etc.) in constellation with the communications that occur between them. Accordingly, the phone opens up my body to the experience of work and my empirical recordings of it in very particular ways. I have agency over it, and it has agency over me. Returning to Orlikowski (2007), the way that the phone and the applications I use are designed, configured and engaged in practice to create the possibilities for research. This meant being able to take pictures and edit them, recording my screen, tracking my movements, taking notes, and recording audio. All of this was then synthesized thanks to the smartphone's ability to bring multiple formats together in one place (using *Notes*). The phone provides my access to both field*site* and field*work* and the possibilities for each are shaped by interactions with the phone's capabilities. The remainder of this chapter will explore the role of the mobile phone as collaborator and interlocutor in the research process.

Dual Purpose of the Phone

I had initially hoped to use one device for the field*work* and a separate device for access to the field*site*, creating a distance between the two. However, due to financial limitations I could not afford a single device for my research, so had to use my personal mobile for both, which naturally presented challenges and opportunities. It encouraged me to follow the long tradition in ethnographic work of utilizing the materialities of the field*site* under scrutiny—such as Crang's (1994) use of the order pad for jotting notes whilst working as a waiter in his study of restaurant labour. In my case, this was further necessitated by the need to carefully manage my identity as a covert researcher (van Maanen 1991). By using only one device, it smoothed over the social relations of taking field notes,[4] echoing Emerson et al.'s (1995, n.p.) assertion that 'producing jottings is a social and interactional process'.

However, only having one device which was already enrolled in my personal life posed multiple security vulnerabilities. First, it exposed me to the physical vulnerabilities of loss or theft (to which I became victim in a mugging six-months into the research), as I was carrying my research around with me practically all the time and everywhere I went. Similarly, the material vulnerabilities of the phone had to be carefully considered. Phones and water famously disagree and working outdoors through a UK winter made getting wet inevitable. Whilst these vulnerabilities could be managed, a less identifiable, therefore more difficult to mitigate, security threat was posed by the work itself. In order to access The Platform, I needed to download and install an application direct from The Platform company that is not publicly available. Even opening it required manually over-riding the permissions and security measures Apple puts in place to grant it wide-ranging access across my phone. What they wanted access to was not transparent and I am still unclear how much access The Platform have. As such, I had to be doubly careful not to compromise my position as a researcher. As the research went on, I needed to speculatively perform to The Platform's surveillance architecture to try to appear as a typical worker, and not as an investigator. In a reflexive sense, this drew me naturally into the behaviours of a typical worker—having to satisfy The Platform sufficiently to retain continued access to future work opportunities—and brought my role as researcher into sharp relief. Here, my position as a researcher is precariously entwined with my position as a worker able to satisfactorily respond to the speculatively unknown surveillance capacities of The Platform. In essence, I needed to be a good worker before I could consider being a good researcher.

Installing The Platform's app alongside other mainstream apps brought the field*site* and field*work* into close proximity, as these technical objects (apps, 4G, GPS tracking, etc.) shared the same material home and thus became intertwined. Some may consider this a disadvantage as the 'academic distance' between the subject and the object of study was reduced to being housed in the same device. However, I do not stake a claim to such distance in any analysis, and actively disregard the possibility of academic objectivity in this pluralistic setting. In short, this means acknowledging that we all experience this work differently, and as such, overarching truth claims are difficult. Furthermore, this proximity allowed me to follow the rhythmic contours of the work; seizing opportune moments in between jobs to capture data and expanding upon this when I had the time. Not having to swap between devices liberated me from the distraction of trying to record *everything* and instead allowed me to concentrate directly on the work for as long as possible, reducing time spent pulling-out of 'authentic' experiences to take notes.

During the early stages I found this elision of -*site* and -*work* too close, each interfering with the other in unhelpful ways on a phone that was becoming difficult to navigate. In response, I 'mapped' the phone by spatially arranging and segmenting apps dependent on their function between field*site* and field*work* (see Figure 4.1).

Fig. 4.1 The layout of my iPhone, with two folders in the bottom right of the screen in an easy-to-reach location. Fieldwork and fieldsite, housed the relevant apps in each. The Platform's work app has been redacted to maintain anonymity

Whilst the taxonomic decisions were often clear, there were apps that transgressed this boundary for which I had to make decisions informed by my research practice. For example, *Strava* is used by couriers and researchers alike to track movements and fitted comfortably into both the -site and -work sections. As my primary use for it was as a research tool, it fell into the field*work* folder—Waze and Google Maps were used solely for navigation at work and remained in the field*site*. An added benefit of siloing apps like this on a personal device is the better achievement of work–life balance through the segregation of my research from any personal space on the phone (Gregg 2011).

However, one app did oscillate between these folders and the general population of the phone: *WhatsApp*. I used this in a personal capacity to communicate with loved ones and in research to communicate with other couriers and the broader workplace community. At the start of the working week I would move it to field*work* but at the end I would put it back in the personal area of my phone temporarily muting work 'chats'.

Once mapped, I could return to the 'home' screen and select relevant apps from field*site* or -*work*. I found this would often go through cycles of using particular apps depending on the task or time of day. For example in the early mornings, I frequently narrated voice notes, before switching to written notes over lunch. On an iPhone, these apps co-locate next to each other in the 'multi-tasking manager' that could be accessed with two presses of the home button; switching without having to close and re-start them. The reduction of 'friction' (see Ash et al. 2018) when traversing the interface encourages seamless movement, allowing quick jottings when necessary without withdrawing from the experience of work. Some applications, such as Strava, would fall naturally to the background whilst other apps ran in the foreground. Eventually, this settled into an efficient system of 'front' and 'back' of house. Drawing on Goffman's (1990 [1959]) work on the presentation of the self, the front of house generally consisted of the field*site*'s apps, especially The Platform's app, which continually surveilled my activity and analysed performance. Performing poorly risked my contract being terminated and abruptly ending fieldwork so, to them, I performed the role of diligent food courier. Meanwhile back of house I performed the role of researcher, taking notes discussing the behaviour happening out front. During busy times, I would fleetingly turn to the field*work* applications to take notes, focusing most of my attention and appearance at the field*site*. During the quiet periods of the day, this would pivot as I logged out of The Platform and ventured back of house to take notes.

Continuing to hold-up both of these working and researching 'selves' is physically and mentally tiring. Most of the time, the mobile made this easier by reducing the friction of moving between the two; in contrast it also made it more difficult at times as I carefully managed my presentation towards each in a confined space. A smartphone is a two-way device and, with the surveillance capabilities of The Platform largely unknown, I felt a constant sense of precarity and immense pressure to keep up the 'act' of being a cycle courier and not a researcher.

Table 4.1 Overview of applications used and the purpose of their deployment

Application	Purpose
Notes	Textual notation and transcription.
Voice Memos	Audio recording soundscapes, dictating observations.
Camera & Photos	Taking pictures, editing images, recording footage.
Screengrabs	Capturing still and moving images of my screen and accompanying soundscapes.
Strava	Mapping my movements.
Bluetooth	Connecting to other devices (GoPro).

Practice in the Field

This section will outline the various ways in which my mobile phone was used as a methodological tool, in addition to a reflexive analysis of these uses. The section will end with a discussion of how these materials were synthesized to create a multi-modal ethnographic field diary that became the core empirics of the study. Each sub-section is organized by the application used; listed in Table 4.1 for quick reference.

Notes: Textual notation and transcription

Field notes formed the basis of this ethnographic recording practice; the skeleton onto which other multi-modal findings were hung. As Clifford (1990, 52) suggests, they constitute 'a raw, or partly cooked, descriptive database for later generalisation, synthesis, and theoretical elaboration …' the process of which is outlined below.

As a food delivery rider, my labour was tied to the culinary desires of customers and the opening times of restaurants. This meant lunch and dinner were busy, with very little time to record field notes, whilst the start and middle of the day were quiet; often spent sitting on a bench catching-up on lunch. This posed the danger that reflections would focus disproportionately on the ennuyeux of 1.30pm to 5pm, whilst the details of intense moments of work may be lost. To combat this I developed a set of practices that fit writing around the 'contours and constraints of the work' (Emerson et al. 1995, n.p.) using notes differently at different times. In addressing Hammersley and Atkinson's (2007, 156) assertion that 'memory alone is an inadequate basis for subsequent analysis', I was able to record as little as a 'single word … enough to "trip off" a string of images that afford substantial reconstruction of the observed scene' (Schatzman and Strauss 1973, 95). This built on Crang's (1994, 676) development of 'scratch notes' to incorporate and mitigate the effects of busy work periods in his study of restaurant work. In this, he would jot 'single word "scratch-notes" and elaborate on them at the end of the shift'. The key difference for me, was that the order pad was replaced by the *Notes* app. An example from my field diary (3 October 2018) shows this process of scratch notation and write-up:

Scratch Notes (recorded between 12.13pm and 12.27pm):
  'Poké Chai
  Changing guard
  New PU
  Late
  13 lunch
  Cleaner
  Solidarity'

Elaborated notes: (4pm, same day):
'I arrived late to my next job, Poké Chai—the changing of the guard outside Buck-
ingham Palace meant I was stuck waiting. Plus, it was the first time I'd picked-up
from that restaurant, so I was even later trying to find somewhere to lock my bike
and locate the restaurant inside the shopping centre (shopping centres are always
THE WORST). I loaded up a particularly large order from a particularly distressed
manager as quickly and considerately as possible—not two things that naturally
go together—before getting back on the bike and riding to the drop off. Right and
right again onto Bressenden Place, arriving sweaty and gross, but just ahead of
lunch and hopefully early enough to pick-up another order before the rush ends.
No-one notices me more than they have to; looking away to hide the delight in their
eyes that the food is here, tempered by disgust and embarrassment at my appearance and the gap between us. I find my own way to the kitchen and begin laying
out the food. The only help I get is from the cleaner in what feels like solidarity as
we communicate in our respective Spanglish. I count 13 lunches including drinks
and sides'.

This demonstrates how seven jottings became the 'trip off' for a larger narrative reflection, made possible by the ease with which I could switch from The Platform's app
to my *Notes* app and the omnipresence of my phone on my handlebars. Additionally,
phone use blends in far easier than a pen and paper (see van Doorn 2013); disguising
note taking as checking my phone for updates on a job or simply idly passing time
on social media while waiting for an order. However, taking notes on the phone are
not without their moments of friction. Just like Burns (2000, 22), I 'developed a system of short-hand notation and abbreviations for commonly used terms' such as PU
(pick-up). Initially, my phone auto-corrected these to 'Put', 'Oh', or 'Or', leading to
much confusion when it came to subsequent elaboration. However, when I was able
to add these to the phone's dictionary it stopped. In this sense, the lexis my phone
permitted as 'good' English changed, following specific practices in the field.

Reflecting critically, it is clear that things can and do get lost in the account. I've
forgotten the office's name, failed to record the traffic conditions, or the feeling of
pulling out directly into traffic. Trying to completely render enormously complex
environments into a textual record is simply not possible and even if it were, the
accounts would be so dense they would be bereft of *feeling*. Furthermore, some detail

is lost as the method becomes unsafe—even the briefest of notes can cause enough distraction to end in a fatal crash when jostling with London's traffic. But this is only a small fragment of the notes I made, and when viewed as a corpus of reportage, these complexities are evident. Whilst silences do exist in the record these are not always negative—they give space to other details and connect to the other forms of data gathering I was able to undertake.

Voice Memos: Audio recording soundscapes and dictation

Audio recorders are a familiar instrument in the ethnographer's tool-kit (Hammersley and Atkinson 2007; Garrett and Hawkins 2014); most commonly as a device for recording interviews but increasingly alongside diary methods with remote participants (Crozier and Cassell 2016). I used *Voice Memos* to verbally inscribe my thoughts, feelings, and reflections in the field and as a personal diary (Mazanderani 2017). The particular materialities of the phone (including headphones with an in-line mic) and its enrolment into the labour process make it preferable to a traditional recorder in this context. Not only is it immediately proximate to the field*site*, it is also able to run back of house whilst The Platform's app continues front of house, or whilst reviewing other empirical data in periods of rest.

Voice Memos fulfilled two primary functions. First, 'in situ' either between jobs, or during the natural lull in the working day, they became a way to reflect substantially on a thought, verbally allowing more exploration than I could typing onto a small screen. They also captured (intentionally or otherwise) aural data from where I would rest and reflect. Any study of work in the city naturally becomes enrolled in its rhythms and sounds (Lyon 2016; Nash 2018) which if recorded can provide 'sonic data' (Yelmi 2016, 310) with visceral links and strong emotive responses to the site being studied. These sounds *pull* me back into the places I recorded them in, rooting me in the rich complexities that may have escaped the remit of textual accounts. When listening back even now I remember being stood in Hatton Garden, Shoreditch, or The City, all with their own distinctive soundscapes. The danger here is that I mis-remember them; so bringing them into concert with other forms of notation are essential.

Second, I used *Voice Memos* when on the job and on the move, recording audio on quiet patches of road or waiting at red lights (again, two presses of the home button, one tap of the screen to select the app, and a tap to record are all it takes—much simpler than pulling out a recorder, setting it up, testing it, and recording). Of course, this comes with an increased risk of having an accident that **I do not encourage** others to take. For me, this was measured against my proficiency as an urban cyclist and the benefits it brought which were two-fold. First, it meant recordings followed the flow of the work; speaking at length during easy bits and drifting off into silence mid-sentence when concentration was necessary. Although frustrating at times these silences highlight the various demands the work presents. Again it captured soundscapes of the workplace (Droumeva 2017), but this time in transit. This included the roaring of lorry engines as they raced between traffic lights, the sound of sirens reaching a crescendo and fading away, of winds funnelled through the gap between buses I would also share in my races across the city, of building sites, of shoes clipping into pedals, and of offensive remarks uttered by cabbies. As Niels van Doorn (2013) suggests, these recordings do not simply recreate sound, but activate multi-sensory memories of their making.

In a broader sense, voice notes engage the researching self with understandings that ethnographers cannot write themselves out of their data and that scientific objectivity or 'absolute truth' represent false horizons (see Oakley 1981; Denzin 1989). Dictation encourages a form of feminist research practice argued for in these accounts through the generation of 'situated knowledges' that Harraway (1988, 583) defines as 'embodied knowledges and an argument against various forms of unlocatable, and so irresponsible, knowledge claims'. By privileging my voice, spoken and captured within the work context, the very medium and approach applied decentre traditional research forms that come with the authority of the written word. These recordings present deeply situated knowledges, forever rooting personalized experience in place. I return to them regularly, as they 'speak-back' and continue to elucidate the 'conscious and unconscious, self-censorship we impose when relying solely on a textual rendering of experience' (Mazanderani 2017, 80). We continue to move away from these textual renderings of experiences through the other methods deployed in this chapter.

Visual Methods I, Camera & Photos: Taking pictures, editing images, and recording myself

Similarly, visual methods are excellent at capturing large amounts of information. However, whilst the adage 'a picture paints a thousand words' *may* be true, the notion that 'the camera never lies' must be considered more critically. As ethnographers, whether subconsciously or otherwise, we compose images to capture the experience we are aiming to convey. With an iPhone, much of the technical labour is now automated and digitized—such as setting the exposure, shutter speed, etc. but the moment of capture, and the angles chosen, are just one option picked by the ethnographer from an infinite number of possibilities. This theorizing has been done substantially elsewhere (Barthes 2000; Pink 2011; Sontag 2019 [1971], for example) so here I will discuss my own use of the iPhone, taking these critical texts as a common base.

The first use of the camera app was to record video diary entries. At the end of a shift I was often too tired to type and wanted to capture the exhaustion I was feeling audio-visually. Whilst not particularly attractive, and with none of the videos being published, I would review the footage as it re-ignited the sense of exhaustion—vividly reminding me of the feeling the work engenders. Similarly, using an iPhone's front facing, or 'selfie', camera, encouraged reflexivity as the technical affordance of relaying myself live whilst recording made me both object and subject of the video entry as I reflected on my own appearance.

I also used the camera to take photographs, most often using the rear-camera instead of the front. This was primarily to document what was happening when I was unable to take notes or felt they would not capture what I was trying to illustrate. An additional key feature was the ability to instantly edit. This does not refer to the use of filters, as per Kardashian (2016), but rather the potential to annotate the image as if it were a surface to be illustrated upon. The iPhone's interface allows images to be treated as an artefact for inscribing other notes and information, such as lines and words. Returning to Schatzman and Strauss (1973) this meant I could add contextual information when analysing the image.

Without the annotations, Figure 4.2 would just be a picture of some scaffolding on a nondescript London street. However, immediately after taking the photograph I marked it up to illustrate to my future self what was intended. When it came to reviewing this the circle served as a 'trip-off'—in this case, as evidence of hostile

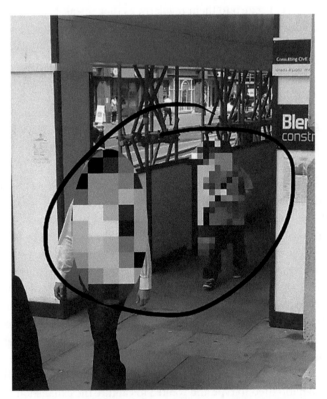

Fig. 4.2 This shows the image marked-up with a black circle to indicate the meaning behind the image when it came to subsequent write-up

architecture—to focus attention on the blocks around the scaffolding preventing anyone from locking-up their bike close to the restaurant. Without this, I would likely have forgotten what I was trying to capture when writing up my field diary entry at the end of the day. By giving instant recall to the images in an editable format the affordance of the iPhone re-shaped my capacity to capture and formulate empirical material 'on-the-fly' rather than taking the risk of remembering its relevance later on.

Visual methods II—Screengrabs/Screen Recordings: Capturing still and moving images of my screen

Whilst the iPhone's cameras are used to capture images 'outside' the phone, screen grabs are used to capture what is shown on-screen, preserving the otherwise ephemeral moments and interactions with The Platform's app. Requiring only one gesture (a simultaneous press of two buttons) images are saved directly in *Photos* without disturbing the app currently in use. This meant that workflow continued un-interrupted by moments of data capture, featuring as a digital shorthand that could be edited later—similarly to the camera images described above.

Video screen recordings were also used to expand this focus to The Platform's user interface. This facilitated reflection on two key features. First, how the app changed and updated whilst I was working and cycling through the city—as I had to keep my eyes on the road, and not on the app most of the time. In turn this pointed out the data I was missing whilst traversing the city at work. Just as field*work* apps are used in the background throughout research, screen recording operated to capture exactly what was happening in the foreground of the phone. This led to its second function, facilitating critical reflection on my own methods, as navigation between field*site* and field*work* was made visible. Here I could witness the interruptions between working for the platform and inscribing research matter. Finally, I chose to turn sound on for all screen recordings to capture the complex realities of the work. This audio-visual artefact, whilst only displaying the screen, highlights the multi-faceted realities of the work that play out beyond it. Attempts to capture these elements de-centre the role of technology, putting it into relief against the rest of the work through soundscapes of the city, traffic, restaurants, and more.

Strava: Mapping movements

Just as screen grabs lend permanency to the ephemeral traces of gig-work, so too does the use of location tracking services. Whilst The Platform continually tracked and stored my movements, I had no access to this dataset. Given that movement through space is an integral feature of the job, I sought to ensure I would have a copy. I chose *Strava* for the task, repurposing it from its target market of fitness tracking, and harnessing its geolocational systems to keep a record of my movements.

This crystallized my movement into a 'route' and I returned to this log when writing-up diary entries and subsequent analysis. *Strava's* interactive map allowed me to retrace my steps, 'tripping-off' thoughts and memories along the way. These 2D maps inspired 3D memories of my working day that clung to my tired limbs after the work was done. Even returning to them two years on to write this chapter, some things remain vividly alive in my mind, the maps acting as the gatekeeper to my memories.

Beyond the scale of the individual shift, maps offer a 'zoomed-out' point of comparison for the work. By looking at them as a corpus of collected labour delivered over time, patterns emerged that were not tangibly perceptible on a day-to-day basis; such as the effect of seasonality and climatic conditions. With these benefits in mind, it is critical to share a word of caution. *Strava* is a social media and by default all of these records are publicly available. This was not appropriate for covert research, and thus I had to manually enhance privacy settings to ensure they were not visible to others.

Bluetooth: Connecting to other devices (*GoPro*) and transferring files

Greenfield (2017) finds one of the smartphone's defining features is the way it can be personalized through interaction with the digital ecosystem of which it is a part. It is this proclivity towards hybridization that makes it such a powerful research tool. But beyond that which can be downloaded and installed on the phone, Bluetooth facilitates connection to other devices, allowing the iPhone to become one node in an assemblage of other sensors.

I used Bluetooth to connect mine to a *GoPro*—a small, rugged camera often used for filming in situations where traditional cameras would be inappropriate. These cameras also offer the ability to capture very personal and interesting perspectives (see Evers 2015; Vannini and Stewart 2016). For cycle messengers who record their rides, they have become a staple; taking over from the improvised heavy and cumbersome helmet camera set-ups used in the likes of Brunelle and Zenga's (2012) classic movie *Line of Sight*. Following Brown and Spinney (2010) I used the already present cultures of head-cam video to form the basis of this element of my ethnography (blending in with other workers who use them for insurance purposes, or to make films of their work). As Crang (1996) suggests, video should not only be seen as recording an event, but as part of the event itself. As such, I used the *GoPro* and phone in two distinct ways to capture what Pink et al. (2017) term 'empathetic accounts'. First, I used the camera to get different perspectives from my body and my bike, exploring the material assemblages of the work, and how differing points of view may elucidate these further. The connection to the mobile phone allowed me to check on the camera whilst cycling, and ensure that it was still capturing an interesting shot; as images were being beamed live from my camera to my phone in real time. The *GoPro* also allowed covert filming in other areas where capturing images on my iPhone would have been more difficult since contorting my body and phone to take an image is a revealing act, and difficult to disguise.

Secondly, the *GoPro* encouraged a reflexive review of the ways I was interacting with my phone during the process of work. Whilst some apps, such as *Strava*, or *Voice Memos* can run in the background, the iPhone's native camera app cannot. Another camera was needed to film my own interactions with the phone during the course of the work. To do this, I mounted the *GoPro* on my chest or handlebars, facing directly up at my own face and the sky. Whilst not a flattering angle, it allowed me to see how and when I interacted with my phone during the course of a job, switching my attention regularly between app and city and casting the other sociomaterial elements of the work into sharp relief. Finally, the phone allowed me to review and edit recently captured footage directly on the phone rather than the camera, meaning that findings could be incorporated into my notes and elsewhere without having to move between multiple devices.

It is also worth noting that whilst I only used a *GoPro* as an extension of my iPhone, any number of devices can be used depending on context and requirement. This accessibility opens-up the internet of things available and the interesting metrics, data, and empirical material they generate. These include GPS trackers, bike computers, *Fitbits*, heart rate monitors, and more, and can be tailored to your own research.

Data Synthesis

The methodologies explored in this chapter highlight the rich opportunities smartphones present researchers in the field. However, this is balanced against the risk of multi-faceted data streams becoming unmanageable and disjointed if not properly attended to. Whilst recordings may all be made at a similar time, on a singular device, unless they are brought together at a later stage they remain detached and spread across the phone and cloud storage, linked only by the chronology of their timestamps. To harness their full potential, multi-modal datasets like these must be synthesised together to create a whole picture, rather than a loose assemblage of objects and text. This follows Latour's (1999) reflection on the process of knowledge making in academic research, identifying quantity alongside the quality of resources and their curation. In essence, the aim of research is not simply to recreate the field in full, but to make it manageable and knowable by inscribing it in such a way that makes it fit for future analysis. By synthesizing datasets together they are 'transformed' (Latour 1999, 70) into this useful arrangement.

This reduction gives way to amplification as resources are brought together in harmony with one another. In so doing, they become greater than the sum of their parts in a new form, the ethnographic field diary. Here, it is not simply that more data, and more data sources are better, but rather the latent value of these data is only achieved through a process of synthesis. The presence and role of the researcher in this process renders objectivity or un-biased research impossible. Therefore, instead of trying to eliminate our presence in the research material, we should expend our efforts on reflexivity—understanding how we have shaped it and the impacts this might have. As this process of reduction and amplification is undertaken by the researcher, it naturally includes elements of choice and selection regarding what stays in and what is left behind. Accordingly, we must remember our earlier discussion of 'situated knowledges' (Harraway 1988) by acknowledging that the decisions made in what we capture and then re-produce in our field diaries are the result of our own set of circumstances.

To elucidate how this process took place in this work, we must return to *Notes*, where synthesis (or the reduction-curation-amplification of data) took place. Figure 4.3, is a segment of my own diary entry of the shift we first met above, trying to find Poké Chai.

This fragment makes clear how I, as researcher, have curated and composed these findings in the construction of a narrative that reports the day's events. Getting lost

Fig. 4.3 A screen grab of a section of completed diary entry (author's field diary, 7 September 2018)

is explored in the text and then supplemented by a screen grab from the day's *Strava* map. My lost body feels more tangibly present in these combined notes than in either the text or map alone. Elsewhere these notes were informed by other pictures and video, creating an account that is comprehensible and can be put into discussion with other notes from different shifts.

This forms part of a broader, ongoing approach in long-term ethnography whereby 'this process of inscribing, of writing field notes, helps the field researcher to understand what he has been observing in the first place and, thus, *enables him to participate in new ways, to hear with greater acuteness, and to observe with new eyes*' (Emerson et al. 1995, n.p., emphasis added). As such, this process of notation not only renders the past experience as legible, but also better calibrates us as researchers to the environments we are studying. Furthermore, my synthesized field diary entries began to change over time as I became more familiar with the environment I was studying. As my ideas developed, so too did the notes I was taking as they came to reflect, and be shaped by, my developing theorizations. This occurs naturally as researchers near 'saturation' (wherein findings appear to repeat and corroborate each other) and familiarity with the field and the ongoing research increases over time. In the latter half of my ethnographic research, the 'new eyes' with which I could greet the fieldsite opened-up possibilities for further, more nuanced observations and findings.

Reflexively, I must remain aware of the silences my data may hide, and how my own bodily realities may have produced a very specific set of data and reflections in the first place. For example, as a white man with no dependants and British citizenship, my relationship to work in the gig economy differed to those who may be sole wage earners in their family, or have insecure visa statuses. These reflexive concerns take into account intersectional scholarship that highlights the diversity and inequalities of individuals' experiences through the course of their day-to-day life (hooks 2000). In order to combat this, and include a diverse array of voices and experiences, I have deployed other methodologies in the remainder of my research, such as semi-structured interviews. Although beyond the remit of this chapter, these sensitivities are borne out in the analytical work that has resulted from this study, and can be seen elsewhere, such as in van Doorn and Badger (2020) where we discuss the racialized and expropriated labour that takes place in the gig economy in addition to our own experiences and theorizations.

Conclusion

In summary, it is clear that the iPhone is an immensely powerful tool when deployed in a research setting. Furthermore, by using it to investigate the spatial turn in organization studies in concert with understandings of sociomateriality, we are better placed than ever to engage the contemporary organization and forge new understandings into working lives. By robustly theorizing our research tools, we open ourselves up to their potential and possible deployments in the field. Furthermore, we open ourselves to a reflexive mode of research informed by feminist theory that flattens the ontological separation of researcher, research tool, and researched; particularly in light of blending this with other research avenues. This makes way for nuanced understandings of the material we generate.

In this particular example, the competing and complimentary politics of field*site* and field*work* provide fertile opportunities for engaged research, wherein the empirics are borne out of the realities presented by the workplace. However, this brings challenges in equal measure. Most notably it involves the continued negotiation of the self to multiple audiences (employer, future analytical self, and academic audience). Whilst this chapter shows just one constellation of the iPhone's technical affordances deployed in the field, smartphones are undoubtedly a Swiss Army knife in the qualitative researcher's toolkit. However, any prospective future investigations that use this tool should *not* feel tightly bound by the methodologies laid out here, but rather feel free to iterate and deploy them when and where they are appropriate. This research happened in a specific time and place, and any research done subsequently will be different. Even if I were to return to the field two years on, I would adapt these methods as the organization and the nature of the labour have changed in the intervening time.

Notes

1. 'The Platform' has been anonymized to protect the identity of the company under investigation in line with university ethics guidance.
2. This is typical in food delivery sectors of the gig economy as the worker must be in sync with the preparation of the food. In ride hail, the market only has two sides, the customer and worker.
3. The research project described was the author's PhD research.
4. Although many couriers use two phones—separating personal and work devices, the majority only use one. If people have two phones that they appear to be 'working' on, the assumption is that they are using multiple accounts and stealing the work of others—a reputation I was desperate to avoid.

References

Ash, J., Anderson, B., Gordon, R., and Langley, P. 2018. Unit, vibration, tone: a postphenomenological method for researching digital interfaces. *Cultural Geographies*, 25(1): pp. 165–81.

Badger, A. and Woodcock, J. 2019. Ethnographic methods with limited access: Assessing quality of work in hard to reach jobs, in Wheatley, D. (ed.), *Handbook Of Research Methods on the Quality of Working Lives* (pp. 135–146). Cheltenham: Edward Elgar.

Barthes, R. 2000. *Camera Lucida*. London: Vintage.

Brown, K. and Spinney, J. 2010. Catching a glimpse: The value of video in evoking, understanding and representing the practice of cycling, in Fincham, B., McGuinness, M., and Murray, L. (eds), *Mobile Methodologies*, London: Palgrave Macmillan.

Brunelle, L. and Zenga, B. 2012. Line of Sight [Film] Available At: https://lucasbrunelle.com/line-of-sight/

Burns, S. 2000. *Making Settlement Work: An Examination of the Work of Judicial Mediators*. Burlington: Ashgate.

Clifford, J. 1990. Notes on (field)notes, in Sanjeck, R. (ed.), *Fieldnotes: The Making of Anthropology* 1st edition (pp. 47–70). New York: Cornell University Press.

Crang, P. 1994. It's Showtime: on the workplace geographies of display in a restaurant in southeast England. *Environment and Planning D: Society and Space*, 12(6): pp. 675–704.

Crang, M. 1996. Watching the city: video, surveillance, and resistance. *Environment and Planning A*, 28(12): pp. 2099–104.

Crozier, S. and Cassell, C. 2016. Methodological considerations in the use of audio diaries in work psychology: Adding to the qualitative toolkit. *Journal of Occupational and Organizational Psychology*, 89(2): pp. 396–419.

Dale, K. and Burrell, G. 2008. *The Spaces of Organisation and the Organisation of Space: Power, Identity and Materiality at Work*. Basingstoke: Palgrave Macmillan.

Denzin, N. 1989. *Interpretive Biography*. California: Sage.

Droumeva, M. 2017. The coffee-office: Urban soundscapes for creative productivity. *BC Studies: The British Columbian Quarterly*, 195: pp. 119–27.

Emerson, R., Fretz, R., and Shaw, L. 1995. *Writing Ethnographic Fieldnotes*. Chicago: The University of Chicago Press.

Evers, C. 2015. Researching action sport with a GoPro™ Camera: An embodied and emotional mobile video tale of the sea, masculinity, and men-who-surf in Willard, I. (ed.), *Researching Embodied Sport Exploring Movement Cultures* (pp. 145–162). Oxford: Routledge.

Gandini, A. 2019. Labour process theory and the gig economy. *Human Relations*, 72(6): pp. 1039–56.

Garrett, B. and Hawkins, H. 2014. Creative video ethnographies: Video methodologies of urban exploration. in Bates, C. (ed.), *Video Methods: Social Science Research in Action* (pp. 152–174). London: Routledge.

Goffman, E. 1990 [1959]. *The Presentation of Self in Everyday Life*, London: Penguin.

Greenfield, A. 2017. *Radical Technologies: The Design of Everyday Life*. London: Verso.

Gregg, M. 2011. *Work's Intimacy*. Cambridge: Polity.

Hammersley, M. and Atkinson, P. 2007. *Ethnography: Principles in Practice*. 3rd edition. New York: Routledge.

Harraway, D. 1988. Situated knowledges: The science question in feminism and the privilege of partial perspective. *Feminist Studies*, 14(3): pp. 575–99.

hooks, b. 2000. *Feminist Theory from Margin to Centre*, Pluto Press: London.

Kardashian, K. 2016. *Selfish*. New York: Rizzoli.

Kinsley, S. 2014. The matter of virtual geographies. *Progress in Human Geography*, 38(3): pp. 364–84.

Latour, B. 1999. *Pandora's Hope*. Cambridge, MA: Harvard University Press.

Lefebvre, H. 1991. *The Production of Space*. Nicholson-Smith, D. [Trans]. Oxford: Blackwell.

Lyon, D. 2016. Doing Audio-visual montage to explore time and space: The everyday rhythms of Billingsgate Fish Market. *Sociological Research Online*, 21(3): pp. 1–12.

Massey, D. 2005. *For Space*. London: Sage.

Mazanderani, F. 2017. 'Speaking Back' to the self: A call for 'Voice Notes' as reflexive practice for feminist ethnographers. *Journal of International Women's Studies*, 18(3): pp. 80–94.

Nash, L. 2018. Performing place: A rhythmanalysis of the City of London. *Organization Studies*, 41(3): pp. 301–21.

Oakley, A. 1981. Interviewing women, a contradiction in terms. In Roberts, H. (ed.), *Doing Feminist Research* (pp. 30–61). London: Routledge.

Orlikowski, W. 2007. Sociomaterial practices: Exploring technology at work. *Organization Studies*, 28: pp. 1435–48.

Pink, S. 2011. Sensory digital photography: re-thinking 'moving' and the image. *Visual Studies*, 26(1): pp. 4–13.

Pink, S., Sumartojo, S., Lupton, D., and LaBond, C. 2017. Empathetic technologies: Digital materiality and video ethnography. *Visual Studies*, 32(4): pp. 371–81.

Schatzman, L., and Strauss, A. 1973. *Field Research: Strategies for a Natural Sociology*. New Jersey: Prentice Hall.

Sontag, S. 2019 [1971]. *On Photography*, London: Penguin.

Spicker, P. 2011. Ethical Covert Research. *Sociology*, 45(1): pp. 118–33.

Srnicek, N. 2017. *Platform Capitalism*. Cambridge: Polity.

Van Doorn, N. 2013. Assembling the affective field: How smartphone technology impacts ethnographic research practice. *Qualitative Inquiry*, 19(5): pp. 385–96.

Van Doorn, N. and Badger, A. 2020. Platform capitalism's hidden abode: Producing data assets in the gig economy. *Antipode*, 52(5): pp. 1475–95.

Van Maanen, J. 1991. Playing back the tape: early days in the field, in Shaffir, W. and Stebbins, R. (eds.), *Experiencing Fieldwork: An Inside View of Qualitative Research* (pp. 31–42). California: Sage.

Vannini, P. and Stewart, L. 2016. The GoPro gaze *Cultural Geographies*, 24(1): pp. 149–55.

Woodcock, J. and Graham, M. 2020. *The Gig Economy: A Critical Introduction*. Cambridge: Polity.

Yelmi, P. 2016. Protecting contemporary cultural soundscapes as intangible cultural heritage: sounds of Istanbul. *International Journal of Heritage Studies*, 22(4): pp. 302–11.

5

The Heartbeat of Fieldwork

On Doing Ethnography in Traffic Control Rooms

Claudio Coletta

Introduction

The development of smart urbanism, urban informatics, and the worldwide adoption of software and sensing networks to manage urban services offer an important source of knowledge for the study of digitally mediated work and organizational processes. At the same time, the re-distribution of agency through the networked and real-time nature of urban management challenges our research practice. How do we maintain coherent approaches and methods within an increasingly complex setting? This chapter directs attention towards the temporal aspects of such a dilemma and specifically focuses on time and temporality in ethnographic practice in relation to the temporality of the fieldsite.

In particular, I will discuss how heterogeneous temporalities scale up and down; how they resonate into algorithms, management, and working practices; and how ethnographers can engage with such dynamics. In other words, I am going to explore how an apparently tiny phenomenon—such as the time-frequency of a traffic related sensing device—connects to an apparently large phenomenon, such as networked mobility management in cities, and to discuss the role of ethnography in accounting for that connection. The chapter describes a case of a Traffic Control Room (TCR) as an emblematic site where ethnographic practice and socio-technical processes meet temporal complexity. I offer an account of the mutual engagement between research and fieldwork, aiming to escape the native–observer dichotomy and bring to the fore the rhythms as collectively produced by interferences, interruptions, and repetitions.

I am looking at TCRs as specific instances of *oligoptika* (Latour and Hermant 1998), that is, software enabled centres of calculation through which the urban space is scaled down to obtain screen size representations and make the city describable and manipulated. In this sense, TCRs represents an *oligoptikon* which allows tracing of the invisible texture of mediators that compose cities. Yet, TCRs are nodes connected to large networked infrastructures, where calculation is *dispersed* (Czarniawska 2004) and data sourced from different networked devices. Therefore, TCRs represent a crucial case to study what I would call 'networked management', that is,

Claudio Coletta, *The Heartbeat of Fieldwork*. In: *Research Methods for Digital Work and Organization.*
Edited by Gillian Symon, Katrina Pritchard, and Christine Hine, Oxford University Press.
© Oxford University Press (2021). DOI: 10.1093/oso/9780198860679.003.0005

the distributed management happening through dispersed calculation and software, adopted to manage digitally networked infrastructures like those related to mobility.

(Urban) control rooms have largely been observed to allow us to understand the interplay of software, work, and management, exploring how this affects life in cities and shapes urban space. However, the same attention has not been paid to the temporality of algorithms and working practices, especially in relation to the temporalities enacted through research practice itself. I argue that acknowledging the temporalization of research methods is most needed, especially when temporal aspects are materially embedded into and distributed across working practices and software. My approach draws on the ethnography of infrastructure (Bowker and Star 1999; Star 2002) and the temporal dimension of this approach. As Star and Ruhleder (1996, 111–12) point out, 'what is an infrastructure?' is a misleading question because infrastructures are not static, transparent, and ready-to-hand entities. We should better ask—they continue—'When is an infrastructure?', because infrastructures come into being in relation to heterogeneous and materially organized practices. As the becoming of an infrastructure happens in time, it also performs time: rather than accelerating the circulation of things, infrastructures produce intervals and interruptions and represent an *apparatus of delay*, 'out of which the present extracts wealth from the future' (Mitchell 2020).

The concept of 'heartbeat' will help me to describe the temporal entanglements in networked management of networked infrastructure. The word *heartbeat* recurred at various times during fieldwork, when interviewing city managers and practitioners. My research investigating the construction of Dublin as a smart city was part of a five-year research project, 'The Programmable City', focused on the translation of space into software and the transduction of software into space. The participants interviewed stressed the co-existence of many different timelines within Dublin: those produced in real-time urban management, whose *beats* are calculated in fractions of a second; and those that are produced by the deeper time of the city and its historical cycles, whose pulse rate is measured in decades and more. The *heartbeat of the city*—as one of the participants called it—coalesces as a complex timescape including many mutable urban rhythms acting at different and interfering frequencies. Algorithmic calculations and real-time management interact with the lived experience of people coping with parking, lighting, cars, public transportation, and the possibility to be informed in real-time and 'at the touch of a button' on traffic conditions. In turn, the data produced and the devices used in these measurements and calculations affect long-term decisions on mobility, environment, and other areas, and ultimately influence strategic planning and positioning with respect to other cities. All these aspects point to the complexity and heterogeneity of urban timescapes and to the issue of integrating different temporalities in management processes, especially in an age of desynchronization with 'a greatly increased variation of different people's times' (Urry 1994, 141). Given the interconnected and multifarious kind of rhythms and measures, management needs to combine different *tempos* in order to be effective. On the one hand, organizing the overlapping, concatenated, multiple rhythms of everyday life allows the generation of predictable models which are used to manage systems that mediate urban life; on the other hand, setting up the frequency and choosing the right measures requires continuous adjustments and balances, which depend on historical and contemporary city life. Thus, setting a rhythm requires making an important distinction between what is relevant for management and what is not, what is predictable and counts and what is not. Understanding how things become relevant through the lens of time has an important implication for research methods and their ability to tune in with the fieldwork, to study its tempos and their connections, and ultimately re-temporalize the research accounts.

Addressing the 'when' question, the chapter examines the activities taking place in a specific TCR across three connected issues. The first section describes the peculiarity of urban automated management in the digital age, and the shift from a clock-time (Adam 1990) to a real-time based society where big amounts of data circulate through digital and networked infrastructure, and thus inform automated decision making. More precisely, real-time processes can be considered as *realtimeness* (Weltevrede et al. 2014; Kitchin 2018), namely a contingent and relational product of working practices, software calculations, and other socio-technical arrangements, each of them with a specific real-time culture. The second section explores rhythms and rhythm-making, how the realtimeness is maintained and performed and how different temporalities coexist in it. Both sections aim to offer an analytical toolkit through a descriptive interplay of theoretical issues and empirical findings, to understand how the heartbeats of fieldwork are produced. The third section addresses the ethnographic methods and techniques, the way they enter into the particular real-time culture of a TCR, how they adapt to the complex rhythms of the fieldwork, and how the heartbeat of fieldwork is made 'audible' through research. I will introduce the concept of 'halfway ethnography' to describe the capacity of ethnographic practice to look in between beats and thus account for the interferences and changes of pace in complex settings. I will conclude the chapter proposing the concept of heartbeat as a way to redefine the analytical categories related to time and to engage with an increasingly temporally entangled fieldwork.

Synchronization, Rhythm-making, and Urban Management

In theoretical terms, time has been a crucial issue for social theory, especially in terms of its relations with social action (Nowotny 1992), the different ways through which it is articulated by social practices, and how it contributes to the human experience. With this purpose, Ballard (2007) introduces the concept of *chronemics* to describe the mechanism that allows the production of cyclical time (rhythm), synchronization of cycles (mesh), temporal patterns (tempos), time variations (paces), and the interactions among them. While Ballard's focus is on human agency and on the empirical aspects of the workplace, my attempt will be to adapt the temporal toolkit to emphasize the role of technologies and the methodological implications of a temporally, socially, and materially heterogeneous fieldwork. Taking the cue from Felt (2015), my aim is to account for a 'temporal choreography' that specifically addresses infrastructures, work, management, and ethnographic practices.

In methodological terms, while the issue of 'where the ethnography takes place' and 'where the action is' has been largely addressed, the issue of *when* the ethnography takes place and how it is synchronized with the fieldwork seems to have been less explored. As Dalsgaard and Nielsen (2013, 8) point out, what is required is to acknowledge the time dimension of fieldwork 'both in relation to concrete ethnographic work and as an anthropological representation … identifying the precise juncture at which new insights are constructed from the relationship between research questions and ethnographic data'. Synchronization affects ethnographic practice as well as the temporality of settings where ethnography takes place, the ethnographic account depending on the way the heartbeat of the fieldwork is set.

When approaching the Traffic Control Room, I did not start my fieldwork with the idea of rhythms and temporalities. The TCR was in fact one of the cases featuring Dublin smart city development, following the Smart Dublin initiative:[1] my job, together with my colleagues, was to map all the smart city related projects undertaken in the city, including traffic management. The research enabled me to undertake extensive interviews with researchers, entrepreneurs, associations, and city managers, who talked about different cases of smart city related services. The rhythm idea came to me on a rainy Irish afternoon, when I was interviewing a researcher in engineering, working on sensing devices for air pollution monitoring. In the interview, quite a few exciting 'boring things' came out, as Star (2002) called things hidden in plain sight that, once noticed, allow us to unravel the entanglements around them. What initially emerged as a side story of my research activity led me to look back to previous interviews and focus the analysis on temporal aspects; those that bind together digital technology and management. This episode made me reflect on a primary issue related to ethnographic practice: how do you decide that the things you are investigating through ethnography are concerns? And to whom? Doing qualitative research on (and in) cities seems especially indicative of the serendipitous character in the exploration of urban phenomena (Sonda et al. 2010). As Van Maanen (2011, 220) has pointed out, 'learning in and out of the field is uneven, usually unforeseen and rests more on a logic of discovery and happenstance than a logic of verification and plan'. Taken in a temporal perspective, the 'in and out' of ethnographic practice allows a serendipitous movement backwards and forward across the data collection routine, reflexivity, and writing. At a certain point, moving in and out of time, back and forth through a number of notes, conversations, materials, a change of pace happens: the ethnographic routine requires a new attunement, a new rhythm to cope with the one of the fieldwork, a new *beat*; that is when ethnography produces a drift from boredom to surprise, which forces you to differently re-articulate the entanglement in a possible, meaningful way. The conversation below, which took place in February 2016 at the middle stage of my fieldwork, was precisely the initial spark for my interest in temporality:

INTERVIEWEE: It takes time to understand whether sensors work or not. You need to choose the interval in which you retrieve the data. Because if you retrieve them every second, you have plenty of information, but there also can be much noise. If you retrieve them every hour it is more normal but you can lose information, so you need to find a compromise, the right balance.

INTERVIEWER: Also in relation with the times of the city: morning, peak hours, evening …

INTERVIEWEE: Exactly. Then the higher the resolution, the higher the consumption of battery; the more you keep data in the flashcard, the more you have to transmit them. There is a whole series of compromises you need to deal with. (Engineer, University)

The interview surprised me because it accounts for epistemological and ontological issues in a very pragmatic manner: epistemological, because it is the time intervals that decide what is signal and what is noise, what is relevant and what is not; ontological, because time-frequency has a material dimension and depends on the durability of the battery and the memory of the flashcard. Moreover, both epistemological and ontological aspects appear as contingencies of a practical 'compromise': how to adjust the time in order to listen to the 'heartbeat of the city'?

Once granted access, my research colleagues and I started to follow the development of the Smart Dublin initiative and we began facilitating workshops. We mapped ongoing initiatives connected with the Smart Dublin strategy, contacted related people, and arranged interviews. Basically, the pattern was quite straightforward: meet the interviewees, get their signed consent, ask questions, listen, record, encrypt, transcribe, repeat. We created a spreadsheet with the cases classified according to respective areas (Smart Mobility, Environment, Living, etc.), type of service provided (e.g. tourism, waste management, etc.), technology adopted (e.g. sensor network, web platform, mobile app), scale (e.g. local authority, city region, national, etc.), organizations involved, and so on. The spreadsheet allowed us to monitor the progress of research, recording contacts, the status of the interview (done/to do), the status of the related information sheet we were supposed to write (done/to do). Similar to a palimpsest, the spreadsheet was reworked and adapted several times as the team added and amended categories and the number of interviews grew. It also acted as a shared rhythm-making tool, setting up the pace and keeping track of the teamwork. The surprise came with repetition and routine: the rhythm of interviews and analysis and the resonance between the two added more questions and categories, which in turn were translated into new rows and columns. After a number of weeks of fieldwork, the Principal Investigator asked for a meeting to tune up our categories of analysis: 'Let's bring one transcribed interview each and code them together'. We started at noon with the first bit of transcript:

Well I suppose it's in common with most large cities we have had a traffic control centre for a number of years. So our first traffic control centre was built around 1987 or even 1986 and it has gone through several different iterations and expansions and so on. The latest version of it was considerably changed in 2013. The traffic management centre itself is a 24 hours, 7 day a week operation, it is staffed by our own control room operators. At peak times it has people from AA Roadwatch which is the motoring organisation here. We have facilities for the police and the public transport service to be here as well, so at the moment during the run up to the Christmas busy time they are in there every day. So we have somebody from the police and somebody from the public transport operators. We also have our own dedicated radio station which broadcasts six hours a day, 7:00 to 10:00 and 4:00 to 7:00. And the idea of that is it provides very detailed traffic information to people in very much a real time fashion using all the cameras and the technology that we have in the traffic control centre. (Senior executive manager, Local Authority)

Initiation year, peak times, continuous 24/7 time, evolutionary times, cyclic times, real-time, Christmas time, broadcast times—and it was just the first paragraph. A couple of transcripts, 40 pages and three hours later, we were pretty convinced that time and temporality were important categories to understand smart city development in Dublin. The temporality of texts analysed interacted with the temporality of our research practice: we tuned up our own categories and 'at the same time' shaped the rhythm for future analyses and fieldwork. During the following interviews, time and temporality were resonating at the back of my head until coming to the forefront one rainy afternoon in February 2016, when I met the engineer who was working on sensing devices for air pollution monitoring: time, indeed. No, wait, more than time: frequency, rhythm, 'algorhythms'![2]

As I addressed the literature, I acknowledged that the idea was not new, but embedded in a multifarious and rich debate, starting with the notion of algorhythm (Miyazaki 2012). At the same time, the 'scientific debate' did not exactly pre-exist the idea, rather it has been actualized in a specific, situated version. Being immersed in the literature pushed me to negotiate a position and angle the phenomena so to emplot the literature and the fieldwork in a story, a polyphonic one, where STS, software studies, and organization theory resonate and interfere with the concepts of rhythms and refrains.

From Rhythmanalysis and Temporal Work to Rhythm-Making and Productive Repetitions

According to Lefebvre (2004), rhythms are interactions between a place, a time, and an expenditure of energy. They are brought into existence as interferences of linear and cyclical processes through measure, calculation, and repetition to make things familiar, maintained, manageable. Yet 'there is no identical absolute repetition, indefinitely. Whence the relation between repetition and difference ... always something new and unforeseen that introduces itself into the repetitive: difference' (Lefebvre 2004, 6). As Elden (2004, 195) explained, Lefebvre's interest concerned the 'interdynamics' of rhythm which materializes in everyday life, namely 'how various rhythms relate to one another (in, say, polyrhythmic, isorhythmic, eurhythmic, or arrhythmic forms)'. As noted by Borch and colleagues (2015, 1082–84) in their account of high-frequency trading, while rhythmanalysis provides a rich repertoire to empirically study bodily practices, it needs to be re-actualized to grasp how rhythms are translated into software algorithms. Such approaches include a recent thread of research which adapted rhythmanalysis to study the technological and algorithmic aspects of environmental processes (Palmer and Jones, 2014; Walker, 2014) and traffic management (Coletta and Kitchin 2017).

The actualized version of rhythmanalysis suggests (1) looking at algorithms as part of a bigger assemblage (Dourish 2016), which is also time related; (2) looking at how rhythms embedded in bodily practices interfere with material and digital rhythms at a different scale; (3) focusing on the way the rhythms and temporality of software and networked infrastructure encounter those of networked management and working practices.

The temporal aspects of management, organizational, and institutional processes have been investigated by organization theory since the late 1980s (Dubinskas et al. 1988; Gherardi and Strati 1988). The focus was originally on the multiplicity of temporal ordering (evolutionary, mythical, historical, metahistorical, forward/backwards-looking) and on the embeddedness of organizational times into different media (speech, writing, narrative accounts, etc.). The idea of time and organizational life as both shaping and shaped by each other leads towards a qualitative understanding of temporal phenomena. Rather than the content of the fieldwork, the contributions in the field show a dialogue between the temporal aspects of the ethnographic method and the temporal work of organizational life. Scholars have emphasized the greater relevance of kairotic over chronological time (Whipp et al. 2002; Czarniawska 2004; Rämö 2004), where the qualitative and entangled features of time that define events are more interesting than its measurable and linear aspects. Roe (2009) proposed a pragmatist approach to measured time and experienced time in organizational research, which would help to overcome the opposition between positivist and interpretive perspectives. Studies of the temporal dimension of management explored time in the social practices of organizational and institutional actors. Ancona and Chong (1996) introduced the notion of *entrainement* as 'the adjustment of the pace or cycle of one activity to match or synchronize with that of another' (1996, 251). Orlikowski and Yates (2002) proposed the concept of temporal structuring to describe the multiple temporalities enacted by people in everyday practices, who coordinate distributed activities bridging linear and cyclic, objective and subjective time, Kairos and Chronos. More recently, Granqvist and Gustafsson (2016) introduced the concept of temporal institutional work to describe how 'actors formulate new temporally constructed understandings' (2016, 1010). Reinecke and Ansari (2015) showed how organizations at the intersection of temporally incongruent worlds engage in 'temporal brokerage' to negotiate conflicts between the timelines of different corporate actors engaged in market and development: these actors leverage on *ambitemporality*, namely they mediate temporal conflicts by switching from and to different temporal constructs, such as clock-time and process time. These contributions provide rich empirical accounts of temporal work for the synchronization and coordination of activities. Here rhythms and cycles result from the interaction of (multiple) temporal structures on the one hand, and structuring practices that adjust and maintain them on the other.

Following the kairotic sensitivity in qualitative research, I use concepts to describe temporal work (entrainment, ambitemporality, temporal brokerage, and so on) to reflect symmetrically on the temporal work of the ethnographer in relation to the temporal work of the fieldsite. The interplay creates an expanded time infrastructure where ethnographic practice co-exists and co-evolves with the temporality of participants. Such a perspective presents a number of productive features to keep in mind in order to engage with fieldwork.

First of all, it redistributes the agency of ethnographer in time. As we already know that the position of the ethnographer is spatially situated and multi-sited (Marcus 1998; Hine 2000), decentralized and proximal, we are now able to add temporal features to that condition. Situated in time, ethnographic practice participates in a series of rhythms and tempos which compose the heartbeat of the fieldwork. We could even consider that there could be rhythms without external time-givers or *Zeitgeber* (Ancona and Chong 1996; Bluedorn 2002) just as there is 'organizing without knowledge' (Luhmann 1998, 98 cited in Czarniawska 2009). What we have is rather a heterogeneous 'Zeitvermittlung', that is, a specific timescape internally infrastructured and mediated by human, technological, and organizational factors, as well as—ethnographically speaking—*methodological* tempos. Time-giving is thus a collective endeavour involving humans and 'more than human' actors (i.e. a software program, a specific organization of work, etc.), to which we add the timeline of ethnographic activity. During fieldwork, the ethnographers broker time with participants, for example to get their attention or to follow them in relevant activities, in order to entrain, adjust, and mesh each other's timeline. The entrainment also yields to ambitemporality, for example when 'stepping out' from the fieldwork activities to write personal notes and pinpoint analytical or theoretical insights which could be promising to contribute to the project team, to the scientific debate, to the career. Or simply to take a break and temporarily leave the studied activities, tuning up with their rhythm once back. Once considering the action of algorithm and digital tools as participants in the fieldwork, a temporally situated ethnography allows us to understand (1) how the experience and measure of time actually interact with (and are affected by) the temporalities measured by such devices; (2) how time is materialized, configured, and calibrated according to specific knowledge and practices; (3) how tiny technological devices generate new fieldwork relations and how they relate to a larger assemblage. The spreadsheet mentioned above represents one of the tools that guide the temporal work of ethnographers and allows time brokering among other researchers and participants, but also—as we are going to see below—the technical devices that compose the fieldwork have an effect on the collective temporal experience, creating displaced forms of ambitemporality.

Taking rhythms as constitutive of temporalities of networked management in cities is to shift the focus on translation processes from the linear and chronological ones to the kairotic 'productive repetition', synchronization, and interferences of beats in different settings. In fact, as Deleuze and Guattari (1987) point out, repetition does not entail mere reproduction of timing norms and institutionalized temporal routines: repetition is *productive*, that is, it creates a difference, thus generating territorial *refrains* with peculiar regimes of action. Refrains are rhythmic, repeated vibrations, such as the song of the bird which marks its territory or the humming of people in unknown places which establish a feeling of familiarity. In terms of the present analysis, we can consider the refrains as produced by a work of rhythm-making, which is in turn composed by different beats, pulses whose vibrations and interferences produce a familiar space-time arrangement: '[t]ime is not an a priori form; rather, the refrain is the a priori form of time, which in each case fabricates different times' (Deleuze and Guattari 1987, 349). The fieldsite, in this case the TCR, can thus be studied as a specific arrangement produced by rhythm-making, whose beats create refrains. The refrains maintain and combine multiple time patterns, and also allow the passage from one pace to another. This way, beats and rhythms can be used to describe the co-existence, maintenance, and the overlapping of different activities in the same place, and explore how the superposition of polyphonic flows of action—including ethnographic ones—are turned into a refrain, and vice versa how these refrains have their beats reshuffled to produce a new pace.

Halfway Ethnographies in a Traffic Control Room

The Dublin City Council Traffic and Incident Management Centre (TIMC) is a TCR where car traffic is managed remotely by means of operators, software, CCTV, and other tools. TIMC is a liminal place of informal and formal conversations, on-air transmissions and phone calls, automation and human management, a place which hosts dispersed temporalities shaped by multiple rhythms. That is why to grasp its temporal complexity, the ethnography must be liminal itself, both entrained and ambitemporal, acting in between to mesh with the rhythm-making of the field. I would call this kind of ethnographic condition *halfway ethnography*. The term halfway ethnography echoes the work of Karen Barad (2007) on quantum physics and agential realism. It rejects, as Barad does, '[the] attempt to find some "middle ground" between social constructivism and scientific realism' (2007, ivi, 408) and refers in this case to methodological aspects, looking at the concrescence of space, time, and matter (*spacetimemattering*) in doing research. In this sense, halfway ethnography represents an invitation for researchers to emphasize the temporal aspects of spacetimemattering and focus on beats as well as pauses which participate in the rhythm-making of the fieldwork.

At the centre of Dublin TIMC is the adaptive traffic management system, SCATS (Sydney Coordinated Adaptive Traffic System). SCATS is a software infrastructure that manages in real-time the traffic lights at junctions based on inductive loops installed on the street which count and detect vehicle presence in each lane and the time intervals between them, as well as demand for pedestrian crossings. The system interacts with operators in the TCR who can adapt and adjust SCATS timing based on CCTV monitoring—whose data are not stored—and feedback from drivers. Every 20 seconds, a GPS feed coming from the 1000 or so buses circulating in Dublin is integrated with the data coming from the inductive loops. As you enter the control room you can likely hear radio music coming from the speakers on the walls, and realize that a radio station is inside the room: three smaller desks located in the back-left corner host Dublin City FM's live broadcast of traffic news and music between 7–10am and 4–7pm, Monday to Friday. At the end of each song, the presenter goes on air updating drivers on the traffic situation, supported by an assistant and a producer. Meanwhile, operators continue to type on their CCTV controller, switching from camera to camera and monitoring the flow, also providing an additional layer of beats to the music and the voices inside the room. I would call it a rhythmically—as well as technologically (Bruni et al. 2014)—dense environment, where rhythms engage different human and non-human 'players', and slow down and accelerate according to the events:

> It's the end of yet another interview with A., the supervisor of the traffic control room, I am asking the last questions. Suddenly, the tail of his eye captures something on the CCTV screen that I (being in front of it) did not even notice: a Dublin LUAS tram is stuck in the middle of a busy junction blocking traffic on both ways. He addresses the operator on the other side of the room 'D.? Camera number ***' D. types the number on the CCTV controller, evaluating the possibility to override the SCATS in order to ease the flow which is around the congestion. Few seconds later the radio presenter starts to give the situation on traffic, but he is into another rhythm: he knows that there is something going on, but did not take the last event in the list of updates and skips the info. They call the LUAS control centre to have (or give) updates. Everything lasts a very long five minutes, then the tram moves and frees the street.
>
> **(Ethnographic note, 11th of November 2016)**

The CCTV controller catches the attention of the operator and changes the pace of the interview, a silence interval in a blink of an eye produces a difference through which the setting of the interview is transduced into the setting of traffic management. The beats of traffic management start to pulse differently, from the supervisor to the operator on the other side of the room, as a sort of duet, then to the SCATS system to change the phases. These abrupt changes of pace are part of the work inside the room and in turn, they interfere with the organizational refrains: the coffee breaks and lunch breaks, the temporal organization of the work of radio operators (two shifts of 3 hours per day excluding weekends), the work of traffic operators, 24/7 divided into shifts of six hours. The latter generates a further element of interference: the extended presence of operators through the whole day makes them able to provide assistance phone calls on water infrastructure faults and interruptions, providing information and redirecting the call in case of emergencies and repurposing the traffic centre management to a sort of call centre for plumbing issues. Finally, regular meetings of senior managers take place every two weeks to see if the configuration of the system continues to be effective or not and a situation room is available for major events, with desks reserved for police and other authorities during special events or emergencies. It was to observe what happens during one of these special events that I visited the TCR one Saturday afternoon in July.

> A very quiet Saturday afternoon, despite Beyoncé being announced as having a big concert in the evening. One operator in the silent room, with the radio station not airing during the weekend. It's a very different atmosphere with respect to the weekdays. The telephone rings, a taxi driver is stuck in the traffic and requires remote assistance to ease the flow. He reports that work in progress barriers have been removed in Stephen Green [one of the busiest junctions in Dublin, where in addition there are construction works for the new LUAS line]. This is probably due to some pedestrians that moved the barriers to create a shortcut for crossing the road, J. says. She checks in one of the displays a document with the updated shifts and contacts of workers in the street and make a call. There is no answer, she takes a memo in a notebook to call later. She says with a smile that she recognised the taxi driver on the phone: 'He's not new to call, he was talking hands-off with the speakers on because he wants to bully with the passenger that he can have the way cleared from the traffic management centre'
>
> **(Ethnographic note, 9th of July 2016)**

In the atmosphere of a Saturday afternoon, J.'s observation teleports me into the taxi so that I am sitting close to the passenger. I can watch myself in the traffic jam monitored in the CCTV camera controlled by J. in the control room, where she indicated to me precisely the taxi among the other cars, while the driver calls. I am halfway and simultaneously 'there', taking notes about the request and attitude of the taxi driver, and 'here', listening to the operator's account and comments. Then the pace changes again and J. switches to another programme of actions calling the workers on the street. Consider the scene just described in comparison with the following vignette from Boersma (2013) referring to his account of an 'Unofficial St. Patrick Day' local event, monitored from a police surveillance room:

> Late at night we had dinner in the operations center. The social media footage, the projected images of CCTV, and local television news reports fused into a long, cluttered image that we eventually experienced as cinema-like. It was as if we—present in the operations center—were watching a movie: eating pizza, drinking soda and staring at fragments of camera images from an event far away without a clear plot, but fascinating enough to hold our attention because we were, in one way or another, involved in the action, like the prison guard at the Panopticon. Halfway through the evening, a student, clearly in a state of drunkenness, yelled at the camera of the local television station: 'And the police gave us a lot of trouble today!' causing general laughter in the operating room.
>
> **(Boersma, 2013: 115–16)**

The surveillance room suggests a similar halfway mechanism, although with an emphasis on space, where the watchers are part of what is being watched: the activity of surveillance, in fact, prescribes a sharp distance between the law enforcement and potential infringements which generates sarcastic laughter. A halfway mechanism based on time sheds light on the interference of infrastructurally mediated pathways of action, such as those of the TCR in Dublin, meshing the schedules of road maintenance, drivers, and pop stars' concerts. In the meantime, the beats (and digital bits) of traffic users' tempos—car drivers, public transport, pedestrians, etc.—are silently gathered by the software and used to regulate traffic conditions. The encounter of such human and digital tempos could work eurhythmically or require a change of pace in traffic management workflow, and could also produce a switch from boredom to surprise in the ethnographic work. The point of suspension and micro-hesitation from the creation of one rhythm to another is where the halfway ethnography stands: it allows appreciation of the kairotic temporality where the ethnographic (in this case myself), technological (the calculation apparatus), organizational (the TIMC operator), and everyday (the taxi driver) activities converge or co-exist in the respective complexity and infrastructural loudness. In fact, with respect to the seminal accounts of control rooms (Suchman 1987; Heath and Luff 1992), the Dublin TIMC could appear much more silent: most of the communications have been delegated to automated management and the core staff is composed of five people (four operators and the supervisor) who alternate along the day and night shifts, the radio being in operation only six hours during weekdays. There is little running commentary or 'self-talk' (Heath and Luff 1992, 80) whether that be public and short conversations or jokes inside the room (face to face, by phone or by social media) while operators work. The informal spaces devoted to breaks—such as the legendary 'coffee machine' (which in this case is the kitchen)—are used in a lonely way for quick breaks. At the same time, in another sense, it is much louder: everybody talks (on the phone, on the radio), but not (directly) to each other. Radio staff act as traffic controllers and vice versa, they inform each other about the respective activities:

> What is good about the radio station is that is a live commentary, they get so much information using tweets, or people texting them. You can back a colleague to say what's happening, but the radio station is actually telling you what it's like as well. It's really helping to do your job. (Traffic controller #1)

As soon as he tells me this, the operator moves to the software that manages billboards on the street, and inserts the ad with the radio and the respective frequency:

> It's good way. It's free publicity. We want people [drivers] to listen to radio, as much as possible. (Traffic controller #1)

The CCTV on the operator screen is now showing the sign '103.2 DUBLIN CITY FM RADIO'. The situation is again estranging, halfway: I am in the room, listening to the radio and having an interview. The radio starts to give information to drivers, the operator tells me about the importance of the radio and immediately after activates the electronic billboard somewhere in Dublin, showing it to me with the CCTV management software. Where am I? When am I? Where and when are the operators when doing their work? In this view, halfway ethnography is a way to practise rhythm-making by moving in between beats, ready to grasp whether the last heard beat continues a refrain or rather represents a change of pace, or again is part of a bigger refrain that operates at a larger scale of a living entity. Ultimately, the heartbeat of fieldwork corresponds to the account that the ethnography is able to offer about what is studied. The condition of liminality between being inside the control room and inside the taxi is one example, as well as the condition of boredom and reflexivity that at some stage produces the surprise. Indeed, being halfway is not a privilege of the ethnographer, since as illustrated above traffic management is just one of the activities carried out by the staff, and different monitoring technologies, expertise, and settings are transduced into each other. Such forms of rhythm-making in between the beats reflect and interact with the silences and breaks within phenomena that change the pace of the situation, such as in the case of the LUAS or in the case of switching from the task of traffic operator to the one of support on infrastructure failure, from cameras to SCATS monitor, from certain cycles and phases to overriding them for easing the traffic. The organizing routines interfere with technical rhythms, which in turn interfere with the rhythms of fieldwork. Rhythms are more or less automated and more or less human, with different time ranges, either related to everyday management or to special events, either planned or unplanned. They involve theoretical, methodological and empirical aspects as well as GPS transponders, induction loops, visualizations, working practices, radio stations, large digital and material infrastructure, the whole city.

Conclusion: Heartbeats of Cities, Heartbeats of Ethnography

The chapter has illustrated a time-based ethnographic approach to the study of infrastructure in a case of networked urban management in a TCR. The study addressed the challenge posed by Star and Ruhleder to reflect on 'when is an infrastructure?' in empirical, methodological, and epistemological terms. While Gieryn (2006) described cities as a 'truth-spot' for urban studies, both the *where* and the *what*—the object and venue of the study—I argue that the focus on urban infrastructure could offer for urban studies a 'becoming-spot', whose scientific accountability refers to the *when* and the *how* the heartbeat of fieldwork is produced. Whereas literature on (smart) cities and urban management has given an emphasis to space, I propose to adopt a more symmetrical approach called halfway ethnography, emphasizing the time dimension. Just as the delays and intervals produced by infrastructure could offer sites to extract wealth, in Mitchell's (2020) terms, the same intervals or 'time-spots' offer opportunities to create knowledge value, in methodological and epistemological terms. This value depends on the ability of researchers to participate in rhythm-making and make sense of the rhythms, cycles, refrains, changes of pace, that compose and contribute to the heartbeat of the fieldwork. The TCR is a networked infrastructure made of different entities acting and interacting at a different time scale: its temporal flows participate in shaping the heartbeat of the city itself, which has an institutional, infrastructural, and historical 'pulse rate' measured in days, decades, and centuries, not immediately synchronized with the needs of real-time management (not to talk of the deep time of the Earth). The polyrhythmia and complexity of real-time cities, the superposition of human and non-human rhythms, seem to create a collective 'algorhythmic trance' without any centre of calculation or pace-setter. Automation by software algorithms produces a sort of obliteration of time and knowledge: work happens 'live', with the real-time videos from the 380 cameras all over the city not being stored, SCATS collects the data from counting the cars and automatically generates statistics to adjust timings without human oversight. Rather than temporal 'feed-back' from a specific and human pacesetter, we have a rhythmic 'feed-around' and time mediation from multiple beats and tempos, whose interferences contribute to phenomena of accidental urbanism (Coletta et al. 2019), that is, a temporally and spatially dispersed set of experimental smart initiatives that develop autonomously around the city. Knowledge dissolves in repetition and time is manufactured, embedded in technical devices showing the materialized aspects of temporality, the acts of configuring and calibrating time for others, and the heartbeat of larger assemblages.

Whereas the problem of temporality in management processes has been addressed by the scientific literature, either through the dualisms of agency/structure or subjective/objective time, this chapter shows that rhythm-making is based on productive repetition which creates transductions from one setting to another, creating the effect of a slow routine and a sudden change of pace. I believe that embracing a rhythm-making and halfway perspective offers various advantages to the study of organizing temporality and change. First, it allows us to take into account the agency of non-human entities in the construction of temporality. Second, bypassing the dualist approach to agency-structure allows us to focus on the 'making without structure' of temporality from a relational perspective. The same goes for the dualism of tense, subjective time (flowing, kairotic) and tenseless, objective time (discrete, chronologic): they are the (temporary) product of rhythm-making, as well as the evolutionary, episodic, cyclic and emergent characters of organizational change (Dawson 2014) and become a way to cut the interference of different (algo)rhythm-making. Finally, rhythm-making allows ethnographic and research time to be approached as both a concern and a way to frame how things happen, looking at how ethnography participates in and copes with the construction of multiple rhythms and temporalities. It also involves the issue of how long ethnography needs to last. Especially when doing research in organizational and networked settings, '[time] is condensed, and it is counted at many places concurrently. It is not only coeval, but also multiple. And it runs fast. The journalists I studied could not understand why I needed so much time to write my report. They believed as well that it would become obsolete in a year' (Czarniawska 2012, 133).

'As our world at reach has widened'—Czarniawska continues—'there is a problem in trying to record and interpret it. Zapping is one solution; a bird's-eye view another; but they hardly solve the difficulty of contemporary fieldwork: how to study the same object in different places at the same time?'. Halfway ethnography represents one possible way to study the different temporalities in the same place, or even different temporalities in different places, one possible way to deal with dispersed time-space and calculation and connect the time-boundedness of computational cultures, the time-boundedness of management cultures, and the time-boundedness of ethnography.

Acknowledgements

Thanks to Rob Kitchin and the whole Programmable City team in Maynooth University where the ideas in this chapter were initially developed. I am grateful to Christine Hine, Katrina Pritchard, and Gillian Symon for their generous editorial guidance and precious comments, which have helped me to write a more thoughtful contribution.

Funding

This work was supported by the 'Programmable City' project, funded by a European Research Council Advanced Investigator award (ERC-2012- AdG-323636-SOFTCITY) and by the 'INFRATIME' project, funded by the European Union's

Horizon 2020 research and innovation programme under the Marie Skłodowska-Curie grant agreement No. 892522.

Notes

1. The initiative (www.smartdublin.ie) involves the four Dublin Local Authorities: Dublin City Council, Dun Laoghaire-Rathdown City Council, Fingal City Council, South Dublin City Council. It consists of a mix of data-driven, networked infrastructure to foster economic growth, entrepreneurship, and citizen-centric initiatives (Coletta et al. 2019). The source material of the chapter is drawn from a set of 25 interviews and explicit participant observation conducted by three researchers between October 2015 and December 2016. All participants agreed to the use of their interviews after informed consent.
2. The notion of "algorhythm" has been introduced by Miyazaki (2012), as a computational model of "a machine that makes time itself logically controllable and, while operating, produces measurable time effects and rhythms" (p. 5)

References

Adam, B. 1990. *Time and Social Theory*. Cambridge: Polity Press.

Ancona, D., and Chong, C.-L. 1996. Entrainment: pace, cycle, and rhythm in organizational behavior. *Research in Organizational Behavior*, 18: pp. 251–84.

Ballard, D. 2007. Chronemics at work: Using socio-historical accounts to illuminate contemporary workplace temporality. *Research in the Sociology of Work*, 17: pp. 29–54.

Barad, K. 2007. *Meeting the Universe Halfway: Quantum Physics and the Entanglement of Matter and Meaning*. Durham: Duke University Press.

Bluedorn, A. C. 2002. *The human organization of time: Temporal realities and experience*. Stanford: Stanford Business Books.

Boersma, K. 2013. 'Liminal surveillance: An ethnographic control room study during a local event. *Surveillance & Society*, 11(1/2): pp. 106–20.

Borch, C., Hansen, K. B., and Lange, A.-C. 2015. Markets, bodies, and rhythms: A rhythmanalysis of financial markets from open-outcry trading to high-frequency trading. *Environment and Planning D: Society and Space*, 33(6): pp. 1080–97.

Bowker, G. C., and Star, S.L. 1999. *Sorting Things Out: Classification and Its Consequences*. Cambridge, MA: MIT Press.

Bruni, A., Pinch, T., and Schubert, C.2014. Technologically dense environments: What for? What Next? *Tecnoscienza: Italian Journal of Science & Technology Studies*, 4(2): pp. 51–72.

Coletta, C., and Kitchin, R. 2017. Algorhythmic governance: Regulating the 'heartbeat'of a city using the Internet of Things. *Big Data & Society*, 4(2): pp. 1–16.

Coletta, C., Heaphy, L., and Kitchin, R. 2019. From the accidental to articulated smart city: The creation and work of 'Smart Dublin'. *European Urban and Regional Studies*, 26(4):pp. 349–64.

Czarniawska, B. 2004. On time, space, and action nets. *Organization*, 11(6): pp. 773–91.

Czarniawska, B. 2009. Gabriel Tarde and organization theory. In Adler, P. (ed.), *The Oxford Handbook of Sociology and Organization Studies: Classical Foundations* (pp. 246–267). Oxford: Oxford University Press.

Czarniawska, B. 2012. Organization theory meets anthropology: A story of an encounter. *Journal of Business Anthropology*, 1(1): pp. 118–40.

Dalsgaard, S., and Nielsen, M. 2013. Time and the Field. *Social Analysis*, 57: pp. 1–19.

Dawson, P. 2014. Reflections: On time, temporality and change in organizations. *Journal of Change Management*, 14(3): pp. 285–308.

Deleuze, G., and Guattari, F. 1987. *A Thousand Plateaus: Capitalism and Schizophrenia*. Minneapolis: University of Minnesota Press.

Dourish, P. 2016. Algorithms and their others: Algorithmic culture in context. *Big Data & Society*, 3(2): pp. 1–11.

Dubinskas F.A. (ed.). 1988. *Making Time: Ethnographies of High-technology Organizations*. Philadelphia: Temple University Press.

Elden S (2004) Rhythmanalysis: An introduction. In Lefebvre H., *Rhythmanalysis: Space, Time and Everyday Life* (pp. vii–xv). London: Continuum.

Felt, U. 2015. The Temporal Choreographies of Participation: Thinking Innovation and Society from a Time-Sensitive Perspective. In Chilvers, J. and Kearnes, M. (eds), *Remaking Participation. Science, Environment and Emergent Publics* (pp. 178–198). London: Routledge.

Gherardi, S., and Strati, A. 1988. The temporal dimension in organizational studies. *Organization Studies*, 9(2): pp. 149–64.

Gieryn, T.F. 2006. City as Truth-Spot: Laboratories and Field-Sites in Urban Studies. *Social Studies of Science* 36: pp. 5–38.

Granqvist, N., and Gustafsson, R. 2016. Temporal Institutional Work. *Academy of Management Journal*, 59(3): pp. 1009–35.

Heath, C., and Luff, P. 1992. Collaboration and control: Crisis management and multimedia technology in London underground line control rooms. *Computer Supported Cooperative Work (CSCW)*, 1(1/2): pp. 69–94.

Hine, C. 2000. *Virtual Ethnography*. London: Sage.

Kitchin, R. 2018. The realtimeness of smart cities. *Tecnoscienza: Italian Journal of Science & Technology Studies*, 8, pp. 19–42.

Latour, B., and Hermant, E. 1998. *Paris: Ville Invisible*. Paris: La Decouverte.

Lefebvre, H. 2004. *Rhythmanalysis: Space, Time and Everyday Life*. London: A&C Black.

Marcus, G. E. 1998. *Ethnography through Thick and Thin*. Princeton, NJ: Princeton University Press.

Mitchell, T. 2020. Infrastructures work on time. E-flux. https://www.e-flux.com/architecture/newsilk-roads/312596/infrastructures-work-on-time/

Miyazaki, S. 2012. Algorhythmics: Understanding micro-temporality in computational cultures. *Computational Culture 2*.

Nowotny, H. 1992. Time and social theory: Towards a social theory of time. *Time and Society* 1(3): pp. 421–54.

Orlikowski, W.J., and Yates, J. 2002. It's About Time: Temporal Structuring in Organizations. *Organization Science* 13, 684–700.

Palmer, M., and Jones, O. 2014. On breathing and geography: Explorations of data sonifications of timespace processes with illustrating examples from a tidally dynamic landscape (Severn Estuary, UK). *Environment and Planning A*, 46(1): pp. 222–40.

Rämö, H. 2004. Spatio-temporal notions and organized environmental issues: An axiology of action. *Organization* 11(6): pp. 849–872.

Reinecke, J., and Ansari, S. 2015. When Times Collide: Temporal Brokerage at the Intersection of Markets and Developments. *Academy of Management Journal* 58: pp. 618–648.

Roe, R. A., Waller, M. J., and Clegg, S. R. (eds) 2009. *Time in Organizational Research*. London: Routledge.

Sonda, G., Coletta, C., and Gabbi, F. (eds) 2010. *Urban Plots, Organizing Cities*. Farnham: Ashgate.

Star, S. L. 2002. Infrastructure and ethnographic practice: Working on the fringes. *Scandinavian Journal of Information Systems* 14(2): pp. 107–22.

Star, S. L., and Ruhleder, K. 1996. Steps toward an ecology of infrastructure: Design and access for large information spaces. *Information System Research*, 7(1): pp. 111–34.

Suchman, L. 1987. *Plans and Situated Actions*. Cambridge: Cambridge University Press.

Urry, J. 1994. Time, leisure and social identity. *Time & Society*, 3(2): pp. 131–49.

Van Maanen, J. 2011. Ethnography as work: Some rules of engagement. *Journal of Management Studies*, 48(1): pp. 218–34.

Walker, G. 2014. The dynamics of energy demand: Change, rhythm and synchronicity. *Energy Research & Social Science*, 1: pp. 49–55.

Weltevrede, E., Helmond, A., and Gerlitz, C. 2014. The politics of real-time: A device perspective on social media platforms and search engines. *Theory, Culture & Society*, 31(6): pp. 125–50.

Whipp, R., Adam, B., and Sabelis, I. (eds) 2002. *Making Time: Time and Management in Modern Organizations*. Oxford: Oxford University Press.

PART II
DIGITAL WORKING PRACTICES

6

Digital Diaries as a Research Method for Capturing Practices in Situ

Mohammad Hossein Jarrahi, Cami Goray, Stephanie Zirker, and Yinglong Zhang

Introduction

Qualitative methods have helped researchers study the way social activities unfold in real-world contexts. However, methods such as interviews are often criticized for recall bias and for inadequately accounting for situated practices (Warner et al. 2005). Ethnographic methods, such as shadowing, have been more effective in helping researchers observe participants and their situated practices in the context of work or personal life (Quinlan 2008). However, there are limits to how and where methods involving direct observation can be used. In particular, direct observation methods are less effective when the observation may need to span multiple contexts (e.g. research foci that span home and work). In such situations, following and observing the participant through direct and traditional means tends to be unfeasible.

Diary studies are commonly used in computing-centred disciplines (such as human–computer interaction and information retrieval) and can be a pragmatic solution to this limitation. Diary studies are known for their high ecological value (Czerwinski et al. 2004), affording the collection of data in the context of participants' natural environment (Elsweiler et al. 2010), and giving insights into habits, behaviours, and situational decisions over time (Bolger et al. 2003).

Diary studies offer three commonly acknowledged affordances: 'in situity', context specificity, and longitudinality (Flaherty 2016). In situity refers to the quality of being in individuals' daily practices and focuses on understanding what workers actually do in practice to accomplish work (Brandt et al. 2007). Context specificity emcompasses information on habits, practices, attitudes, and motivations that is collected within the context in which they unfold; and these contexts come with unique institutional and social dynamics (Janssens et al. 2018). The diary study brings subtle observations to light by encouraging participants to reflect on many elements of their environment as events occur. Longitudinality means that the diary study approach typically evaluates a research phenomenon over a period of time (Church et al. 2014).

Mohammad Hossein Jarrahi, et al., *Digital Diaries as a Research Method for Capturing Practices in Situ.* In: *Research Methods for Digital Work and Organization.* Edited by Gillian Symon, Katrina Pritchard, and Christine Hine, Oxford University Press.
© Oxford University Press (2021). DOI: 10.1093/oso/9780198860679.003.0006

In this chapter, we review affordances of diary studies from various research traditions and describe how we incorporated the diary study method into our research projects. In outlining opportunities and challenges of diary studies, we reflect on our combined empirical projects, within which we used a major diary study component to study multiple research contexts: nomadic workers' use of technologies, users' response to digital distractions produced from mobile technology, remote work context, and users' information search behaviours for creative tasks. To provide a more detailed case study in the context of work and organizing, we specifically build on the use of the method for capturing mobile work practices of nomadic workers. In the project described here, we specifically focused on the ways nomadic workers engage in on-the-go solutions that enable them to anticipate or respond to situational contingencies and the challenges of mobile work. Our premise is that the digital diary method provides a useful means to capture some of these situated strategies.

Traditionally, organizational research has relied on a narrow set of diary study research methods. Many diaries have incorporated quantitative data collection, such as surveys, that workers complete in their work settings (Ohly et al. 2010). These studies have often been used for testing causal relationships among variables, particularly in relation to the psychological state of employees (e.g. Peiró et al. 2019; Stollberger and Debus 2019). However, in our application of diary studies, we integrated both multiple-choice and open-ended questions to explore the work context. This chapter offers a much-needed practical guide on conducting diary studies. Few writings in the past have focused on the 'utility' of diary studies, including benefits and lessons learned (Janssens et al. 2018).

Nomadic Work

The ubiquity of digital infrastructures and changing norms of work has contributed to the rise of nomadic work (Sørensen 2011). One of the key dimensions of this flexible work environment is spatial flexibility through which workers are enabled to untether themselves from fixed office spaces and work across various locations (Spinuzzi 2015). As a result, the number of nomadic workers (as both independent workers and organizational members) is expanding rapidly and mobile, remote work manifests itself as a defining element of emerging knowledge-intensive work (IDC 2013). Many workers are increasingly becoming 'nomadic' (Ciolfi and de Carvalho 2014), travelling long distances, sometimes lacking a stable workplace or organization to which they are tied, and having the responsibility to manage and carry their resources as they move about (Jarrahi and Thomson 2017).

In our case study, we examined the ways through which digital infrastructures shape different types of nomadic work. Such work involves the unpredictability of working in unfamiliar territories; nomadic workers have to constantly navigate and adopt strategies to overcome spatial challenges such as lack of access to work-related information resources or internet connections in different locales (Costas 2013; Jarrahi and Thomson 2017). Due to the fluid nature of these practices, with frequently altering social and environmental factors (Ciolfi and de Carvalho 2014), conventional and widely used (qualitative) research methods are less applicable and useful (Merriman 2014). For example, mobility and shifting work environments constrain researchers' ability to follow and observe nomadic workers over an extended period of time. Diary studies partly address the challenge of capturing nomadic practices by allowing research participants to self-report on their activities almost immediately after occurrence, helping them to provide a more accurate perspective on their situated activity.

Methods of Diary Collection

There have been many attempts to formalize diary data collection for research purposes. For example, as a systematic method of diary collection, the Experience Sampling Method (ESM) enables participants to respond to repeated assessments at random times during their everyday lives (Scollon et al. 2009). ESMs are systematic reports and are useful for exploring person-situation interactions (Larson and Csikszentmihalyi 2014; Roig-Maimó et al. 2018). ESM questions about participants' emotional states usually come in a structured quantitative form, such as a Likert scale.

Multiple modes have been used to record and collect diary entries. For example, in the field of human–computer interaction (HCI), different approaches and tools have been explored to log users' activities. Table 6.1 summarizes some of these methods and highlights useful examples of their application.

It is important to note that these approaches are not necessarily mutually exclusive, and participants can be provided with multiple channels to share their diaries (Brandt et al. 2007). In addition, many forms of diary studies have enabled participants to share multiple forms of data (Chen et al. 2019). For example, Sun et al. (2011) enabled participants to enter notes, take photographs, make annotations on the photographs, or record and share video clips or voice recordings depending on the experience they wanted to capture. The pervasive use of smart mobile devices enables 'digital diary' studies, recording and integrating different forms of digital data across various platforms (Sun et al. 2013; Liao et al. 2014). Table 6.2 lists the key features of digital diaries that distinguish them from non-digital formats. Digital diary studies provide researchers with new opportunities to elicit, manipulate, and store data during the data collection and data analysis phases. Because the diaries can generate real-time feedback of participant activity, the digital format lends itself to better collaboration between research team members and between researchers and participants.

Table 6.1 Modes of data collection in digital diary studies

Form of data collection and example study	Pros	Cons
Spreadsheet (see for example, Czerwinski et al. 2004)	• Efficient for logging detailed information • Automatically organizes responses	Limited ability to capture multi-modal snippets
Text messaging/email (see for example, Brandt et al. 2007)	• Convenient for participants to fill out in the moment • Do not require as much effort as voicemail or video diaries • Texts and emails can be automatically distributed	• Participants cannot see their diary history • The messages have to be formatted and re-posted so participants can review responses later • Responses are not stored in a central location like a spreadsheet
Voicemail (see for example, Palen and Salzman 2002)	• Natural way for participant to record observations	• Does not work well for unstructured responses • Can become tedious for the participant to record • Lack of privacy for the participant depending on their location
Photo diary (see for example, Shankar et al. 2018)	• Photos provide rich information about the user's environment ('a picture is worth a thousand words') • Photos are useful for stimulating recall from post-diary interviews because they provide a tangible prompt • Can be used more clandestinely than audio	• Photos lead to inconsistency of responses in the data analysis phase. Researchers need to label and organize content
Video diary (see for example, Iivari et al. 2014)	• Captures naturally occurring, real-time events and activities as well as tacit or unacknowledged actions that would not be recalled in videos or interviews	• Like the photo diary, captures the symbolic and tacit aspects of the experience through visual framing

Continued

Table 6.1 *Continued*

Form of data collection and example study	Pros	Cons
	• Video diaries are a more natural way of capturing participant expressions and emotions • By rewatching the video, the participant or researcher can 'revisit the field' • Participant acts as the narrator. Diaries give participants a voice to express themselves and promote reflection • Participants have more control over the data collection process. They can retake the video	• More difficult to analyse. It can be time consuming for both participants and researchers to review video content. Unlike a spreadsheet, researchers cannot conduct a query search in a video • Videos can be an intrusive technology

Table 6.2 Key features of digital diaries

Data collection	Data analysis
• Affords richness of data through multimedia/multisensory data collection (photo, video diary studies) • Immediacy and convenience of recording data (text/email, photo, video studies) • Editorial power—participants can re-record responses • Remote data collection—researchers can more easily monitor participants' responses online	• Data can be automatically structured and organized • Data can be searched consistently • Data can be organized based on metadata such as timestamps or other digital data points • Given its digital nature, data can be transferred more easily among members of the research team

An Interposed Approach to Diary Study

Depending on the research objective, a diary study can be an element that complements other data collection approaches within a larger research project. We specifically used an interposed approach, through which the diary study was preceded and succeeded by interviews with the same participants (see Figure 6.1). In other words, the research participants took part in the first interview, participated in a diary study, and were then interviewed again after the diary data were analysed.

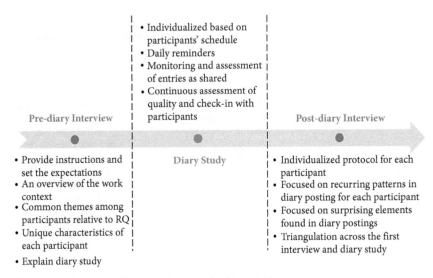

Fig. 6.1 An interposed approach towards diary study

The first interview (lasting one hour on average) helped us elicit (1) a detailed picture of the professional's fields, responsibilities, arrangements, and workspaces; (2) general patterns of spatial mobility; (3) each participant's interaction with various digital infrastructures and tools; and (4) challenges and opportunities affiliated with a nomadic lifestyle and the way these may shape adoption of digital technology. After the analysis of diary entries (more details are provided below), we conducted the second round of interviews, which were typically shorter, more targeted, and individualized. Like the first interviews, the post-diary interviews were semi-structured; but the observations from the analysis of the diary study served as starting points for probing questions. The participants were occasionally asked to clarify their notes or give specific details. The questions for the second interviews were more specific in that we examined (1) complementary elements: things that were observed in the diary study and were not mentioned in the first interview, and (2) contradictory elements: things that may have looked somewhat different from the general themes of the interview (a thematic analysis). Together, the two interviews and the interposed diary study provided a rich foray into the mobile work practices of each participant.

Procedure

Our initial interview sample consisted of 37 nomadic workers, selected based on their extensive mobile work style (people who were mobile for a good share of their week). The first set of interviews with these participants were in-depth and semi-structured. This was followed by a digital diary study with 12 of the participants, selected from the larger pool of interview participants based on our interest in their specific types of mobility (e.g. regular mobility between states in the USA versus constant mobility across several buildings on a daily basis), unique work practices (e.g. the habit of working on the move), unique technology uses (e.g. interesting patterns of public infrastructure utilization) as well as their willingness to partake in an extended diary study.

The protocol for the diary study was designed based on a holistic analysis of the first round of interviews as well as prior work on nomadic work practices (e.g. Costas 2013; Jarrahi et al. 2019). Our thematic analysis of the interviews resulted in general themes that defined the relationship between digital infrastructures and mobile work practices but also issues that required further verification; for example, a list of places frequented by nomadic workers or core technological infrastructures that undergird mobile work. Consequently, for diary entries we used a questionnaire about work activities and specific uses of digital technologies; participants were able to share relevant photos of their work environment, power sources and digital devices (see the Appendix 6.1 for more details). These questions covered what work had been occupying our participants' time and what technologies they had been using.

The questionnaire was a mix of multiple-choice and open-ended questions, and took, on average, 10 minutes to complete. A member of the research team emailed a link to the diary study participants twice a day for 7–10 days. Reminders were sent if the participants failed to submit diaries. The diary study was hosted on Qualtrics (https://www.qualtrics.com/), which allowed the participants to complete it on their computers or mobile devices. Participants were asked to complete both diary entries per day during the duration of the study. Participants were compensated $3 per entry, given by gift card after the completion of the diary collection (e.g. 2 entries per day for 7 days = $42 gift card). They were also compensated $30 for participating in the second interview. Overall, the participants found this approach reasonable and aligned with their busy schedule. Multiple questions were easy to handle and sending photos was easily done through the application. Reminders and other forms of communication with participants facilitated their participation by keeping them on track. We did not encounter any attrition among participants in the digital diary study as expectations were made clear before the study started.

Analysis of diary entries

Mintzberg (2019) speaks to the challenges associated with analysing and managing data obtained in a diary study. The diary study provides the benefit of flexibility in responses; however, the variation in participants' experiences can lead to challenges in categorizing the responses accurately and in deriving meaningful conclusions. In standalone diary studies, categories are often developed as observation takes place; Mintzberg argues in his structured observation approach that this can enable researchers to have adaptability in their analysis to accommodate new themes and categories.

In the study outlined here, analysis of diary entries revolved around two objectives: (1) contributing to the overall analysis of the use and affordances of digital infrastructures in the nomadic context, and (2) illuminating situated perspectives of each individual participant. Both objectives were tied to the role of diary studies as a complementary method of data collection. Pursuing the first objective, we used themes emerging from the diary entries to complement and validate findings from the first set of interviews. In addition, analysis of diary studies helped develop new, targeted questions for the second round of interviews (post-diary interviews), which were focused on individual habits, practices, and technology uses.

What the diary revealed

Use of digital diaries provided opportunities to collect data about participants' situated practices in naturalistic settings and over an extended period of time (Grinter and Eldridge 2001). The data collected through the diary study were closer to the actual unfolding of events that were of interest to us. For example, participants were enabled to report on infrastructural breakdown in their volatile work environments (e.g. when digital infrastructure stopped working or connecting to other infrastructures), and they could inform us about strategies they used to handle these moments. In practice theory, which informed this project, moments of breakdowns are often considered some of the most effective ways of observing how work practices are enacted and transformed; these are often referred to as instances of 'practice making' (Nicolini et al. 2004).

In particular, in this study, the diary study extended findings from interviews by providing more details on situated technology practices. The diary study also enabled us to contextualize these practices across different spaces, examining how participants mobilize their work practices beyond their home or corporate offices, and various technological and non-technological strategies to deal with spatial constraints. For example, one of the diary entries provided a detailed perspective on space-driven technological constraints and how the participant worked around them: '*I wanted to use my VPN (called Witopia) while I connected to the public WiFi at Starbucks, but it made the connection so slow it was basically unusable. I needed to do some sensitive stuff online (logging into PayPal and Xero to take care of some invoicing and accounting), so I decided to use the hotspot from my cell phone's data plan instead, which I understand is more secure than public WiFi. Then, to avoid using too much data, I switched back to using the Starbucks public WiFi once I was done with the more sensitive stuff*'.

In her diary posting, one of the participants provided an interesting perspective on a slice of her work context, detailing temporal challenges of working across two countries remotely: '*Today was just really busy with a lot of different requests and things to tend to. Being in a different time zone from what I'm used to, it can be hard to balance life here and non-work things with work as I shut down before a lot of the people in RTP [Research Triangle Park, North Carolina] do*'. In another diary posting, she went on to describe the infrastructural challenge and practices affiliated with this form of hypermobility: '*I have one phone that I am using with an international SIM card and my regular phone that I can use on WiFi. In Ireland, there are some places that don't have readily available public WiFi, which makes it difficult to connect at times. However, they are very far ahead technology wise in other aspects; the public buses have WiFi which allows me to message and do work on my phone while in transit*'.

In addition, the diary study helped us to establish a more holistic perspective on the inventory of diverse devices and technologies utilized by each participant. We built on and contributed to the concept of 'artefact ecologies' from the research on activity-centric computing to conceptualize the way participants brought together various tools and technologies in the form of an ecology of various artefacts to support their different work activities (for more details see Jarrahi et al. 2017).

Serendipitous findings

The English language adage 'a picture is worth a thousand words' has some truth here. As the next two examples demonstrate, important elements of situated practices can be captured in the form of photos submitted from workplaces and work activities. Such richness is often absent in traditional in-depth interviews. In addition, given that following certain participants in a nomadic work setting is not possible given their high level of mobility, photos can substitute direct observation to some degree.

As previously noted, interviews are susceptible to recall bias; furthermore, participants may not reveal things that could be considered salient by the investigators for two reasons (1) these interesting points could be driven by situated, tacit practices of the participants, and they may hence be less aware of the occurrences, and (2) the participant could be well aware of them but does not find them necessarily as important or central to their work. Our use of diaries provided some serendipitous findings that later resulted in interesting conversations with the participants in the second interviews. For example, one of the participants submitted the image shown in Figure 6.2 as part of one of his diary postings from a coffee shop. The device plugged into his laptop grabbed our attention, even though he had not brought it up when describing his technology practices in public places in the first interview. The second interview enabled us to enquire about it; he described it as a USB-powered firewall that provides a secure use of WiFi in public places and protection from intruders who may intercept his traffic in these locations.

Diary Study Opportunities and Best Practices

Even in our own work, we experimented with different uses of diary study as a research instrument. In order to mitigate gaps in certain approaches and to reveal various benefits and challenges of diary studies, we dedicate the following section to common opportunities and challenges discussed in the current literature or observed across our different research projects.

Fig. 6.2 A photo of artefact ecology in a coffee shop

Capturing shifting context

For research contexts that are not location-bound and that stretch beyond a specific or single time/place, a diary study can provide a pragmatic (and more affordable) alternative to more well-known ethnographic approaches (Gillham 2005). Here, the nomadic work involves frequently shifting social and spatial contexts (Ciolfi and de Carvalho 2014), making direct observations hard. In this context, the diary study offered a different lens into the workday of these workers, enabling us to capture how they may accomplish work across different locations and times.

Balance between open-ended and simple questions

For qualitative research, a mix of open-ended and simple questions can provide both rich insight and ease of participation. Multiple-choice questions help capture the information that is central to the study (e.g. list of central places from which nomadic work is accomplished). Multiple-choice questions help ensure the documentation of experiences and events that seem 'trivial' or may not be intuitive to participants (Brandt et al. 2007). At the same time, the diary can provide avenues for sharing thoughts and observations that cannot be captured in multiple-choice questions, but that the participant finds interesting and helpful. Open-ended questions lend that flexibility. An example of an open-ended question is: 'Please elaborate on any technological problems selected in the previous question' (see the appendix for more details).

Mitigating recall bias

As noted, one of the key challenges of interviews is the recall bias. Holistic analysis of diaries or specific examples from the diary postings (e.g. a photo or note about a problem) can help alleviate recall bias (Shankar et al. 2018; Barriage and Hicks 2020). In the second interview, the concrete findings from the diary study can help participants to refresh their memory and focus on instances of events or issues that were missed in the first interview. In our research project, when we asked participants to recount important things such as search behaviours in their creative projects, high-level diary data (e.g. summaries of what had been done each day, and challenges reported each day) helped participants recall what they did in their daily projects. In future studies, data visualizations could also be considered helpful in facilitating conversation with the participant in the second interview.

The snippet technique

Prevalence of mobile technologies is a catalyst for increased use of diary studies (Nelson et al. 2017; Janssens et al. 2018). However, in mobile contexts, participants may be more likely to view the process as a hassle and can struggle with remembering to provide information on the go (Brandt et al., 2007). In this context, the 'snippet technique' can serve as a useful strategy. The technique was first introduced by Brandt et al. (2007) as a way to optimize the benefits of diary studies in a mobile setting and to alleviate the burden on participants. In this approach, participants only submit small 'snippets' of information at the time they occur; an event-contingent protocol in which entries are triggered by the occurrence of an event (Bolger et al. 2003). Entries are compiled, entered, and stored on a website or in a database. Participants have the opportunity to later review the entries at a time that is convenient to them and provide additional clarifying information or details if needed. As an example, the snippet technique was used by Church et al. (2014) in their 'Large-Scale Study of Daily Information Needs Captured In Situ' and provided the basis for analysis of over 12,000 text messages.

In another of our own research projects on remote working, we used the 'snippet technique' to maximize participation because these workers had a busy schedule which required frequent movement. In this project, to adapt to varying remote work schedules and habits, participants had the option of sending 'snippets' in their chosen manner throughout the day by text, voicemail, a phone conversation, email, or another method suggested by the participant (individual participants were able to select their own method). A manual approach was used in that diary entries were maintained locally in a spreadsheet as information was received. Participants were then given the option to add more detail to their entries at a later time.

Piloting diary approach

Running a full diary study can be challenging and can involve a significant element of unpredictability. Therefore, finding the right fit between the specific methods, the nature of the research questions/focus, and the participants' specific context is pivotal. A small-scale, controlled pilot study can reveal specific unforeseen drawbacks and provide an opportunity to fine-tune the research protocol. For example, to test our specific diary approach, we conducted a pilot with two people in order to verify the questions and ensure clarity of expectations. We requested that participants undergo a trial run of the study and inform us if there was confusion about any of the instructions or tasks. Essentially, our objective was to ascertain if we were going to receive the kind of feedback that we needed in order to conduct the full diary study. Clarity is a central requirement for event-based studies like diary studies as participants must understand the kinds of situations that should trigger entries (Bolger et al. 2003). The pilot also confirmed the study length and design. Specifically, a pilot study can help check whether participants have trouble using tools designed for logging diary entries. The feedback collected from the pilot study can help improve the onboarding process and workflow of a diary study. Additionally, running a pilot study can test the viability of diary questions. It is important to make sure that these questions can realistically capture events or practices that are central to the research question during a diary session.

Diary Study Challenges

Hawthorne effect

Like many other research methods, diary studies are susceptible to the 'Hawthorne effect' (Havens and Schervish 2001). The Hawthorne effect refers to peoples' tendency to change their behaviours when they know or feel they are being observed (McCambridge et al. 2014). The participants' awareness about the research purposes and the mere fact that they are being observed may render them self-conscious and influence their behaviour and how they self-report. Participants may be selective in what they share and intentionally leave out interesting or relevant details in their diary postings. Therefore, they may omit information they do not feel comfortable sharing and may 'over rationalize', presenting information that is inconsistent with their normal behaviour. Likewise, participants may perform the reverse, where they over-observe based on what they believe is appropriate behaviour. Redmiles et al. (2019) recommended a solution to this problem: give participants some flexibility in the number of times they report but still compensate them the same amount. We believe our interposed approach towards the diary study alleviates some of these problems, where the first and second interviews provide opportunities to further converse with the participants and clarify researchers' confusion.

Interrupted temporality

Longitudinality affords an understanding of events and practices over time but it often requires some nontrivial commitment from the participants. According to the principle of longitudinality, the time frame for the study should be based on the expected amount of time needed for the phenomenon under study to occur. As such, selecting the time frame is a careful balance between minimizing effort for participants and maximizing results. Another primary challenge with diary studies is interrupting the participants' workflows. For example, journaling might add to the interruption of the flow of daily events (Czerwinski et al. 2004). This is often more pronounced in the case of 'in-situ logging', which requires participants to report extensive and exact details right after they engage in an activity of interest (Flaherty 2016). A partial solution here is the use of the snippet technique, which tends to be less disruptive of workflows.

Another temporal challenge of diary study is tied to punctuated observation, which may inevitably lack important consideration of transition in work rhythm and practices. That is, diary studies seem to lack a sense of movement or action. For example, shared photos show various things that participants use. But what cannot be gathered from the still photos is an understanding of how people move in relation to their environment; how they physically engage with objects and if there are things (e.g. coffee or music) that move in and out of their space throughout the day. As such, we tend not to see diary studies as a standalone method, as it may not offer a holistic perspective. For instance, supplementing the diary study by incorporating participant video or by conducting additional in-depth interviews could help provide an understanding of physical movement as well.

Fatigue and continuous participation

Diary studies typically span multiple days, and participants are required to frequently report events or information that they see and encounter. So participants could be overburdened easily when the number of reported events is too large (Brandt et al. 2007). One simple strategy we built on that helped mitigate this problem was asking participants to rapidly capture prompts that are comparatively easy to record (e.g. photograph), and then providing opportunities to describe them at a later time.

A detailed guide can facilitate continuous participation. The first interview can be used as an onboarding opportunity, helping those who participate in the diary study understand what is expected of them and gain a clear understanding about the way diary posting will be collected. Depending on the goals of the research project and what information about the participant has already been collected, the first interview may only serve as an initial briefing rather than an intensive research 'interview'. Additionally, it is important to share a digital copy of the diary study guide with participants. Participants might not remember all the details that have been discussed in the first interviews.

Finally, a check-in procedure helps to remind participants about diary postings. This requires continuous monitoring of each participant's postings during the study period to ensure their postings are consistent. The check-in procedure can be initiated automatically by the survey platform or by the researcher. Some survey platforms will send the participant a follow-up email if a lack of activity has been detected. However, it is also important for the researcher to manually review the responses early in the diary study period to make sure that the participant has correctly interpreted the instructions. The researcher may implement a check-in procedure on a weekly basis to provide more structure to the study or to promote a recurring dialogue between researcher and participant (Garcia and Cifor 2019). The researcher should consider whether the study reminders will be consistent or varied. In a study of mobile search behaviours, Church et al. (2012) chose to vary the times that participants received daily reminders to collect information about a more diverse range of experiences. In any case, in digital diary studies in which participants share entries immediately, the research team has to constantly monitor and evaluate the diary entries as they come in, and make sure to encourage continuous and consistent participation by staying in touch with the participants.

Incentives can be an effective strategy to encourage active and continuous participation. We used a contingency approach towards incentivization in which we offered monetary incentives proportional to participation level. In effect, the incentive should align with the amount of commitment needed on the part of the participants (Flaherty 2016). Researchers will need to compensate participants for their time appropriately. Researchers can learn from a pilot test the average time it takes for a person to fill out the diary. Getting time estimates correct is especially crucial because of the frequency of reporting demanded of participants (Williamson et al. 2015). Incentives and reminders help; the first interview can also clarify the goals and pragmatics of diary-based data collection. Automatic (or manual) reminders help the participants to establish a habit of filling out the form, encouraging sustained participation.

Under-reporting

Previous research indicates that a pervasive challenge of the diary study method is that a lack of responses can impact upon the validity of the research (Roig-Maimó et al. 2018). In many cases, participants hide information or do not record all necessary data. This could be due to a lack of trust between the participant and the research team. Establishing trust in a short period of time can be difficult. However, Larson and Csikszentmihalyi (2014) stress the importance of the *research alliance*, that is, the mutual understanding between participants and researchers about the procedure and ends of the study. Participants have to be invested and interested to some extent in the purpose of the study and its outputs to encourage participation. While this mutual trust is true for many forms of research, it particularly holds for such a time-intensive study like a diary study. For this reason, researchers should consider using a screener survey so that they recruit a sample that can effectively help demonstrate the research problem and to ensure that the participants are well aware of the time commitment (Hillman et al. 2016).

Usability of diary

The digital diary method builds heavily on the use of smart devices and digital applications. As such, the participants have to be comfortable with the data collection interfaces. A more usable diary application and a more individualized data collection approach are conducive to greater participation. For example, not only should participants have a clear understanding of what data are being collected, but they should also have control of when and how the data are being collected (Sun et al 2013).

Pilot studies are helpful for revealing the usability issues with the data collection channels or more broadly, other logistical issues. For example Chen et al. (2019) developed an exclusive mobile application to support modal commenting during a live streaming; however, the pilot study indicated the system was not stable enough for live streaming. As such, the research team decided to resort to a combination of Facebook Live and Facebook Messenger systems to offer reliable possibilities for live streaming as well as observing the modalities under investigation.

Researchers can also use a pilot study to assess if the duration of the study or frequency of reporting needs to be adjusted, which would impact how the researchers set the incentive amount. The pilot should be conducted with a small sample. Feedback from participants (through cognitive testing or an actual trial run) may reveal if there is any confusing terminology.

Ethical considerations

The ethical considerations of diary studies have often been neglected in past research (Waddington 2012). With any of the data collection forms of diary studies discussed above, it is important to have the participants' informed consent. Researchers should explain to participants exactly what data they are collecting and why, as well as how the data will be anonymized. Even after the diary study has concluded, participants should be able to request that any of the quotations, video recordings, videos, or images they submitted not be stored in the researchers' database or published in an academic paper. Participants may also be at risk of over-exposure, especially with unstructured diary study formats; they may share too much information in the diary (Bartlett and Milligan 2015). Furthermore, researchers should be aware of the vulnerability of not just the participants but also the people who interact with the participants. For example, a participant recording a video diary may accidentally capture the voices or videos of people who are unaware that they are being filmed (Williamson et al. 2015). Due to the complexity of informed consent, we recommend researchers take sufficient time to create their study protocol and review pilot tests.

Reflecting on the use of the digital diary method, we believe a line of honest and continuous communication with our participants about the goals and procedure before, during, and after the diary study enhanced their participation experiences. The method provides some unique affordances that complement and enrich other methods of data collection, but it does come with nontrivial challenges for the participants. We found that our participants approached the diary study with potentially different motivations. Recognizing and capitalizing on these motivations helped us encourage prolonged engagements. For example, even though the gift card as a token of appreciation was important to some participants, others were motivated by the broader impacts of the research. We were able to discuss how the findings from this work can provide grounded implications for more effective design and management of information systems that support nomadic work. Several participants expressed an interest in seeing the outcome of their contribution. By sharing the outcome of our study in the form of the final report, participants could see how their work was made meaningful. Others were motivated because they found the study a means to reveal and recognize their invisible work practices as nomadic workers. The diary study helped discover patterns of 'articulation work' that are often invisible to outsiders but are key defining aspects of a non-traditional work arrangement (Jarrahi and Nelson 2018). Several participants took an interest in learning these work patterns.

Finally, as a digital method, diary studies are hindered by technical issues. In the project on digital distractions, we made an effort to identify potential technical glitches early on by testing the diary application on multiple types of phones. This in turn led us to add a question about smartphone type in the initial questionnaire. Even before the pilot test, we were able to evaluate our own survey in the field. This is similar to the industry concept of dogfooding, in which product designers test their own beta product. We recommend research teams test the digital diary application on multiple operating systems and formats, including mobile and desktop, before the study starts.

Conclusion

Diary studies offer the means to get a situated perspective on participants' daily practices and routines. The qualitative methodology positions participants as the data collectors in which they document activities and experiences in a particular domain over a specified time span.

In the future, diary studies will continue to evolve and enable more natural data collection options; specifically, there will be a greater focus on accessibility. An emerging direction that can enrich diary studies is integrating passive data collection. For example, the diary study data are supported by sensor or GPS-location data that can be collected on participants' mobile phones (Elevelt et al. 2019). In addition, researchers are improving the timing and mode of notifications, with the desire to find ways to motivate continuous participation. For example, participants may receive daily SMS reminders to fill out the diary study (Rigby et al. 2018). The goal is to craft customizable reminders that succeed in engaging the participant without annoying them.

In this chapter we described the use of a digital diary approach to capture the mobile work practices of nomadic workers; nomadic workers' frequent movement can make them a difficult research population for direct observation. Moreover, data collection methods such as interviews typically require the participant to step away from their day-to-day work and to make time and space for the interview process. As indicated, diary studies provide a viable alternative and open up the potential to research nomadic work.

References

Barriage, S., and Hicks, A. 2020. Mobile apps for visual research: Affordances and challenges for participant-generated photography. *Library & Information Science Research*, 42(3): p. 101033.

Bartlett, R., and Milligan, C. 2015. *What is Diary Method?* Bloomsbury Publishing.

Bolger, N., Davis, A., and Rafaeli, E. 2003. Diary methods: capturing life as it is lived. *Annual Review of Psychology*, 54: pp. 579–616.

Brandt, J., Weiss, N., and Klemmer, S. R. 2007. txt 4 l8r: Lowering the burden for diary studies under mobile conditions. *CHI'07 Extended Abstracts on Human Factors in Computing Systems*, (pp. 2303–08), NY: ACM.

Chen, D., Freeman, D., and Balakrishnan, R. 2019. Integrating multimedia tools to enrich interactions in live streaming for language learning. *Proceedings of the 2019 CHI Conference on Human Factors in Computing Systems*, (pp. 1–14), NY: ACM.

Church, K., Cousin, A., and Oliver, N. 2012. I wanted to settle a bet! Understanding why and how people use mobile search in social settings. *Proceedings of the 14th International Conference on Human-Computer Interaction with Mobile Devices and Services*, (pp. 393–402), NY: ACM.

Church, K., Cherubini, M., and Oliver, N. 2014. A large-scale study of daily information needs captured in situ. *ACM Transactions on Computer-Human Interaction: A Publication of the Association for Computing Machinery*, 21(2): pp. 1–46.

Ciolfi, L., and de Carvalho, A. 2014. Work practices, nomadicity and the mediational role of technology. *Computer Supported Cooperative Work: CSCW: An International Journal*, 23(2): pp. 119–36.

Costas, J. 2013. Problematizing mobility: A metaphor of stickiness, non-places and the kinetic elite. *Organization Studies*, 34(10): pp. 1467–85.

Czerwinski, M., Horvitz, E., and Wilhite, S. 2004. A diary study of task switching and interruptions. *Proceedings of the 2004 CHI Conference on Human Factors in Computing Systems*, pp. 175–82, NY: ACM.

Elevelt, A., Bernasco, W., Lugtig, P., Ruiter, S., and Toepoel, V. 2019. Where You at? Using GPS locations in an electronic time use diary study to derive functional locations. *Social Science Computer Review*, 39(4): pp 509–526

Elsweiler, D., Mandl, S., and Kirkegaard Lunn, B. 2010. Understanding casual-leisure information needs: A diary study in the context of television viewing. *Proceedings of the Third Symposium on Information Interaction in Context*, (pp. 25–34), NY: ACM.

Flaherty, K. 2016. *Understanding Long-Term User Behavior and Experience*. Nielsen Norman Group. https://www.nngroup.com/articles/diary-studies

Garcia, P., and Cifor, M. 2019. Expanding our reflexive toolbox: Collaborative possibilities for examining socio-technical systems using duoethnography. *Proc. ACM Hum.-Comput. Interact.*, 3(CSCW), (pp. 1–23), NY: ACM.

Gillham, R. 2005. Diary studies as a tool for efficient cross-cultural design. *International Workshop on Internationalisation of Products and Systems (IWIPS)*, (pp. 57–65).

Grinter, R. E., and Eldridge, M. A. 2001. y do tngrs luv 2 txt msg? In *ECSCW 2001*, (pp. 219–38). Springer Netherlands.

Havens, J. J., and Schervish, P. G. 2001. The methods and metrics of the Boston area diary study. *Nonprofit and Voluntary Sector Quarterly*, 30(3): pp. 527–50.

Hillman, S., Stach, T., Procyk, J., and Zammitto, V. 2016. Diary methods in AAA games user research. *Proceedings of the 2016 CHI Conference Extended Abstracts on Human Factors in Computing Systems*, (pp. 1879–85), NY: ACM.

IDC. 2013. The rise of mobility. http://cdn.idc.asia/files/5a8911ab-4c6d-47b3-8a04-01147c3ce06d.pdf

Iivari, N., Kinnula, M., Kuure, L., and Molin-Juustila, T. (2014). Video diary as a means for data gathering with children—Encountering identities in the making. *International Journal of Human-Computer Studies*, 72(5): pp. 507–21.

Janssens, K. A. M., Bos, E. H., Rosmalen, J. G. M., Wichers, M. C., and Riese, H. 2018. A qualitative approach to guide choices for designing a diary study. *BMC Medical Research Methodology*, 18(1): pp. 140.

Jarrahi, M. H., and Nelson, S. B. 2018. Agency, sociomateriality, and configuration work. *The Information Society*, 34(4): pp. 244–60.

Jarrahi, M. H., and Thomson, L. 2017. The interplay between information practices and information context: The case of mobile knowledge workers. *Journal of the Association for Information Science and Technology*, 68(5): pp. 1073–89.

Jarrahi, M. H., Nelson, S. B., and Thomson, L. 2017. Personal artifact ecologies in the context of mobile knowledge workers. *Computers in Human Behavior*, 75: pp. 469–83.

Jarrahi, M. H., Philips, G., Sutherland, W., Sawyer, S., and Erickson, I. 2019. Personalization of knowledge, personal knowledge ecology, and digital nomadism. *Journal of the Association for Information Science and Technology*, 70(4): pp. 313–24.

Larson, R., and Csikszentmihalyi, M. 2014. The experience sampling method. In Csikszentmihalyi, M. (ed.), Flow *and the Foundations of Positive Psychology: The Collected Works of Mihaly Csikszentmihalyi* (pp. 21–34). Springer Netherlands.

Liao, J., Wang, Z., Wan, L., Cao, Q. C., and Qi, H. 2014. Smart diary: A smartphone-based framework for sensing, inferring, and logging users' daily life. *IEEE Sensors Journal*, 15(5): pp. 2761–73.

McCambridge, J., Witton, J., and Elbourne, D. R. 2014. Systematic review of the Hawthorne effect: New concepts are needed to study research participation effects. *Journal of Clinical Epidemiology*, 67(3): pp. 267–77.

Merriman, P. 2014. Rethinking mobile methods. *Mobilities*, 9(2): pp. 167–87.

Mintzberg, H. 2019. Structured observation as a method to study managerial work. In Stewart, R. (ed.), *Managerial Work*. Routledge.

Nelson, S. B., Jarrahi, M. H., and Thomson, L. 2017. Mobility of knowledge work and affordances of digital technologies. *International Journal of Information Management*, 37(2): pp. 54–62.

Nicolini, D., Gherardi, S., and Yanow, D. 2004. Introduction: Toward a practice-based view of knowledge and learning in organization. In Nicolini, D., Gherardi, S., and Yanow, D. (eds), *Knowing in Organizations: A Practice-based Approach*. ME Sharpe.

Ohly, S., Sonnentag, S., Niessen, C., and Zapf, D. 2010. Diary studies in organizational research. *Journal of Personnel Psychology*, 9(2): pp. 79–93.

Palen, L., and Salzman, M. 2002. Voice-mail diary studies for naturalistic data capture under mobile conditions. *Proceedings of the 2002 ACM Conference on Computer Supported Cooperative Work*, (pp. 87–95).

Peiró, J. M., Kozusznik, M. W., and Soriano, A. 2019. From Happiness Orientations to Work Performance: The mediating role of hedonic and eudaimonic experiences. *International Journal of Environmental Research and Public Health*, 16(24). https://doi.org/10.3390/ijerph16245002

Quinlan, E. 2008. Conspicuous invisibility: Shadowing as a data collection strategy. qualitative inquiry *QI*, 14(8): pp. 1480–99.

Redmiles, E. M., Bodford, J., and Blackwell, L. 2019. 'I just want to feel safe': A diary study of safety perceptions on social media. *Proceedings of the International AAAI Conference on Web and Social Media*, 13: pp. 405–16.

Rigby, J. M., Brumby, D. P., Gould, S. J. J., and Cox, A. L. 2018. 'I Can Watch What I Want'" In *Proceedings of the 2018 ACM International Conference on Interactive Experiences for TV and Online Video - TVX'18,*. NY: ACM. https://doi.org/10.1145/3210825.3210832

Roig-Maimó, M. F., Varona, J., and Manresa-Yee, C. 2018. Reflections on ESM in the wild: The case of a mobile head-gesture game. *Proceedings of the XIX International Conference on Human Computer Interaction*, (pp. 1–4), NY: ACM.

Scollon, C. N., Prieto, C.-K., and Diener, E. 2009. Experience sampling: promises and pitfalls, strength and weaknesses. In *Assessing Well-Being* (pp. 157–80). Springer. https://doi.org/10.1007/978-90-481-2354-4_8

Shankar, S., O'Brien, H. L., and Absar, R. 2018. Rhythms of everyday life in mobile information seeking: Reflections on a photo-diary study. *Library Trends*, 66(4): pp. 535–67.

Sørensen, C. 2011. *Enterprise Mobility: Tiny Technology with Global Impact on Work (Technology, Work, and Globalization)*. Palgrave.

Spinuzzi, C. 2015. *All Edge: Inside the New Workplace Networks*. University of Chicago Press.

Stollberger, J., and Debus, M. E. 2019. Go with the flow, but keep it stable? The role of flow variability in the context of daily flow experiences and daily creative performance. *Work & Stress*, 34(4): pp. 1–17.

Sun, X., Sharples, S., and Makri, S. 2011. A user-centred mobile diary study approach to understanding serendipity in information research. *Information Research*, 16(3): pp. 16–13.

Sun, X., Golightly, D., Cranwell, J., Bedwell, B., and Sharples, S. 2013. Participant experiences of mobile device-based diary studies. *International Journal of Mobile Human Computer Interaction (IJMHCI)*, 5(2): pp. 62–83.

Waddington, K. 2012. Using qualitative diary research to understand emotion at work. In Bakker, A. B., and Daniels, K. (eds), *A Day in the Life of a Happy Worker* (pp. 140–157). Psychology Press.

Warner, M., Schenker, N., Heinen, M. A., and Fingerhut, L. A. 2005. The effects of recall on reporting injury and poisoning episodes in the National Health Interview Survey. *Injury Prevention: Journal of the International Society for Child and Adolescent Injury Prevention*, 11(5): pp. 282–7.

Williamson, I., Leeming, D., Lyttle, S., and Johnson, S. 2015. Evaluating the audio-diary method in qualitative research. *Qualitative Research Journal*, 15(1): pp. 20–34.

Digital Diary Questions

Tell us about where you have worked so far today (or since the last diary entry). Select all that apply.

- ☐ familiar public place
- ☐ unfamiliar public place
- ☐ in transit
- ☐ home office

- ☐ work office
- ☐ coffee shop
- ☐ coworking space
- ☐ other (please fill in)
  _____

Take a picture of the three to four most important things about the environment you're currently in (or have been in). For example, those things that help you to be productive, or prevent you from being productive.

> Drop files or click here to upload

Another picture from your environment.

> Drop files or click here to upload

Another picture from your environment.

> Drop files or click here to upload

Another picture from your environment.

> Drop files or click here to upload

Please tell us what tasks/activities you have been engaged in during the last two to three hours.

How have you been connected to the Internet? Select all that apply.

☐ mobile data plan

☐ public WiFi

☐ private WiFi

☐ portable WiFi router

☐ computer tethered to phone's network connection

☐ other (please fill in)

Tell us about three important apps or softwares you have used for work so far today (or since the last diary entry).

What devices have you used for work in the last two to three hours? Select all that apply.

☐ laptop

☐ desktop computer

☐ cell phone

☐ tablet

☐ other (please fill in)

If relevant, take a photo of the power source you're using to charge one or more of your devices.

Drop files or click here to upload

What cloud services in the past two to three hours? Select all that apply.

☐ Dropbox

☐ Google Drive

☐ iCloud

☐ OneDrive

☐ other (please fill in)

☐ None

Have you worked offline? If so, what activity were you engaged in?

Have you faced any technological problems? Select all that apply.

☐ getting online

☐ accessing your work information

☐ syncing and connecting tools and applications

☐ other (please fill in)

☐ None

Please elaborate on any technological problems selected in the previous question.

Whom have you met today (or since the last diary entry) for work purposes?

☐ clients

☐ colleagues

☐ other (please fill in)

What was your reason for talking with/meeting the people mentioned in the previous question?

In what medium did you conduct your most recent conversation? Select all that apply

☐ face-to-face

☐ phone

☐ video conference

☐ social Media

☐ chat

☐ other (please fill in)

What has been your biggest work-related challenge so far and how did you handle it?

7

Using Netnography to Investigate Travel Blogging as Digital Work

Nina Willment

Introduction

Netnography is a specific method of qualitative online research, which draws upon and adapts ethnographic research techniques, such as online observation, photographic methods, and interviews, to explore the online communities and cultures which materialize as a result of the computer-mediated contingencies of the online world (Kozinets 2015). At the heart of the netnography method is a cultural focus on understanding social media and online data. It is this interpreting and understanding of cultural experiences through online data, by the researcher, which makes netnography distinctive as a method. Netnography is therefore an important method in developing our understanding of digital work. This is because netnography as a method allows researchers to think about and analyse how individuals work across (and beyond) a diverse array of digital platforms. Unlike other online methods, netnography allows researchers to analyse cross platform inter-relationships, online dynamics, and means of online communication. In particular, the netnography method enables researchers to understand these digital practices and their importance in the context of a wider set of work tasks. At the same time, netnography allows the researcher to consider the offline spaces and subjectivities of digital work in conjunction with the online. As a result, using netnography as a method stops us simply fetishizing the online and allows us, as researchers, to acknowledge the various ways in which digital work becomes entwined with offline work practices.

Turning to my own use of netnography as method, this chapter will highlight how netnography can be useful for studying particular examples of digital work and digital workers. In particular, through this chapter, I wish to show how netnography can be used as a method for understanding travel blogging as digital work. Travel blogging presents as a form of digital working which can seemingly be undertaken anywhere. This inherently nomadic quality poses various methodological challenges to those wanting to explore this multi-modal digital work. Netnography is useful as a method in this case, as it allows us to unpick and analyse this nomadic quality. First, netnography as a method allows us to explore digital labour as a form of work

Nina Willment, *Using Netnography to Investigate Travel Blogging as Digital Work*. In: *Research Methods for Digital Work and Organization*. Edited by Gillian Symon, Katrina Pritchard, and Christine Hine, Oxford University Press.

which occurs in spaces and times beyond the territorialized workplace. Netnography also allows us to explore the multi-platform and varied digital labour, which identifies travel blogging as a distinct kind of digital work activity. This chapter will begin with a discussion of the emergence of travel blogging as a form of digital work which possesses these nomadic qualities. It will then move to a short discussion of the emergence of the method of netnography and its current developments. Following this, the chapter will outline how the netnography method was used within my own research to investigate travel blogging, discussing the ethical issues that were taken into consideration. The chapter will then critically reflect on the advantages and challenges of the netnography method, both more widely and in relation to my own research. Finally, the conclusion of the chapter attempts to outline possible directions for future use of the method.

Travel Blogging as Digital Work

In 2002, the word blog was first included in the *Oxford English Dictionary* (Walker-Rettberg 2013). Since that time, there has been much commentary on the true definition of a 'blog'. As van Nuenen (2016) argues, due to their continual procedural mutation and variation (from social media profiles to video blogs) it is hard to formally define what actually constitutes a 'blog'. However, Hookway (2008, 91) describes blogs as 'a revolutionary form of bottom-up news production and a new way of constructing self and doing community in late modern times'. Blogs allow individuals to provide online commentary on any subject matter of the blogger's choice. This has meant that blogs can vary widely in content and function; from personal diaries to providing commentary on a diverse range of events to functioning as sources of advice (Nardi et al. 2004). The entire network of blogs, which is commonly referred to as 'the blogosphere', has grown exponentially over the last 20 years. In 2002, Technorati.com was launched. Technorati.com became one of the most comprehensive and popular blog search engines. It allowed individuals to search for any blog and to see which other blogs may be linking back to a specific blog. In 2008, after indexing close to 100 million blogs, Technorati.com refocused its outputs away from indexing the blogosphere to marketing and advertising. Since Technorati.com closed, it has been impossible to truly estimate how many blogs there are within the blogosphere, as there is no longer a central registry for blogs (Walker-Rettberg 2013). However, on WordPress (the world's most popular website/blog builder), there are roughly 70 million new blog posts each month (WordPress 2021). Moreover, the number of bloggers in the USA is set to reach 31.7 million sometime in 2020 (Statistica 2020).

One particularly large subsection of blogs are travel blogs. Bosangit et al. (2012) found that travel blogs make up on average 28 per cent of the total blogging market. Puhringer and Taylor (2008, 179) define travel blogs as 'the equivalent of personal online diaries and are made up from one or more individual entries strung together by a common theme (for example, a trip itinerary)'. Travel blogs fulfil a variety of functions from the exchange of travel experiences to identity construction to social networking. The labour of travel bloggers' is centred around the continual creation and dissemination of digital travel content, which ultimately facilitates one or more of these functions (van Nuenen 2016). Therefore, travel bloggers are (unsurprisingly) under pressure to travel; to move around producing diverse travel content from across the world, and to simultaneously share this content with their online audience.

As a result of the rapidly growing travel blogging industry, individuals are increasingly seeing travel blogging as a viable form of digital work. Travel bloggers can attempt to monetize their blogs through means such as paid partnerships, guest posts, sponsored posts, advertising, and affiliate links. Thirty per cent of UK travel bloggers stated that they had received between £101–£250 in compensation for a blog post, with 8 per cent stating they had received over £501 (Vuelio 2019). The ability to access these revenue streams is predominantly dependent on the travel bloggers 'traffic' or the amount of views on their blog. The popularity of the travel blog in terms of audience engagement (e.g. through the amount of comments or likes), also plays a key role in the selection of a particular travel blog for certain revenue streams, such as sponsored posts and/or paid partnerships (Müller et al. 2011). As a result of this desire to drive traffic to their blog, travel bloggers work across many diverse digital platforms. These include the virtual space of the blog itself but also social media platforms, through which the blog content can be viewed and shared. Travel bloggers may also undertake short-term freelance work (typically in the form of writing or copy-writing tasks) in order to supplement the income they make from blogging related activities. Sourcing these jobs may require the travel blogger to work across additional digital platforms including freelancer platforms such as UpWork (Walker-Rettberg 2013). As researchers, we therefore need a method which enables us to capture this liveliness of travel blogger's digital work practices. Netnography is one such method which proves useful in allowing researchers to capture both the embodied and digitally nomadic nature of this example of digital work.

Netnography as Method

During his studies of online discussions within fan cultures during the 1990s, Robert Kozinets (1998 2002) became aware of a lack of a well-defined research method for dealing with large online communities and the associated online data these communities generated. As a result, Kozinets (2002, 62) developed the concept of netnography, as a means to 'study cultures and communities emerging through electronic networks'. The word 'netnography' itself is a portmanteau, combining the words 'network', 'Internet', and 'ethnography', with the development of the concept being influenced by work in media anthropology (such as Baym 1993; Jenkins 1995) and digital anthropology (such as Turkle 1995; Walther 1995). In 2010, Kozinets (2010, 60) released the first book on the concept of netnography, redefining the method as one which relies predominantly on online participant observation to 'arrive at the ethnographic understanding and representation of a cultural or communal phenomenon'. Since the late 1990s the growth of Web 2.0, and particularly the development of social media, has facilitated a dramatic rise in the number and scope of online communities. Moreover, since the mid 2000s, social media has experienced even more unprecedented growth, morphing into a complex and unique social system which can reveal much about human life. As a result, in 2019, Kozinets (2019, 13) again revised his definition of netnography to 'a form of qualitative research that seeks to understand the cultural experiences that encompass and are reflected within the traces, practices, networks and systems of social media'.

However, since the introduction of the method, there has been much debate around what makes netnography distinctive from other online research methods. Wiles et al. (2013, 20) argue that netnography 'sits within a broader methodological context of online or virtual ethnography, which comprise approaches for conducting ethnographic studies of online communities and groups'. Various approaches to web-based ethnography have therefore been developed, including but not limited to; virtual ethnography (Hine 2000) or ethnography for the Internet (Hine 2015), Internet ethnography (Miller and Slater 2001), netnography (Kozinets 2015; 2019), digital ethnography (Garcia-Rapp 2018), mobile virtual ethnography (Germann Molz 2015), and ethnography of the virtual world (Boellstorff et al. 2012). Although these have been described as synonymous terms by some researchers such as Grincheva (2014), others have argued for finer methodological distinctions which recognize that each of these ethnographical styles is grounded within distinct theoretical and methodological ideas and guidelines (Caliandro 2014).

Netnography was specifically devised as a method to investigate consumer behaviours of cultures and communities present on the Internet (Kozinets, 1998). Having its methodological roots and background in consumerism may explain the development of the method to some extent, and this background further distinguishes netnography from similar approaches which may have different roots, such as those with methodological roots in anthropology. This methodological context may also somewhat explain the utility of the netnography method in applications to research, such as my own, which also seek to investigate issues of consumerism.

Digital ethnography, virtual ethnography, and cyber-ethnography are viewed as more general approaches to online research, as they are not characterized by any specific practices (Lugosi et al. 2012). Netnography, on the other hand, is distinctive as it offers a systematic approach to addressing the methodological issues of online research. In particular, the method provides clear direction and a set of detailed techniques for completing online and/or social media research (Kozinets 2019). Kozinets (2019, 7) describes netnography as a 'recipe' for conducting online research. In following the netnography 'recipe', the researcher is transformed into a 'chef' who is able to apply and adapt the netnography method to fit their own social media or online research agenda. However, Kozinets (2019) explains that there are particular research practices which should be carefully considered within the overall netnography recipe. There are six of these research practices: *initiation, investigation, immersion, interaction, integration,* and *incarnation.* Within the *initiation* step, researchers decide upon their own research focus and objectives. For *investigation,* the researcher is encouraged to map out their investigative area of interest. The *immersion* stage involves the researcher actively collecting data. The data are collected, examined, and described in reflexive notes, which are collated and stored as entries in an 'immersion journal' (the netnography term for a field diary). For many researchers, the *interaction* phase occurs next. This interaction phase involves engaging directly with online research participants. Interaction options include interviews, the use of digital diaries, or mobile ethnography techniques. *Integration* is the subsequent research stage. It involves an ongoing process of data analysis; including the collation, coding, and categorization of the netnography data. Within the integration stage, the researcher is undertaking processes of understanding, analysing, and interpreting their findings in relation to their research questions. The final stage, *incarnation,* is the process of writing, in which the method of netnography and netnographic research is made clear to the research audience.

The application of netnography has begun to develop across many fields. Wu and Pearce (2014) highlight how netnography is useful as it provides a powerful method for understanding how individuals, think, feel, and behave in the context of newly emerging phenomena (in their case, digital tourism practices). In tourism studies, the netnography method is becoming increasingly utilized as a means to investigate online tourist experiences and behaviours. For example, netnography is used by Vo Thanh and Kirova (2018) to uncover and analyse the experience of wine tourism, as it is discussed by users on TripAdviser. Similarly, in their investigations of female Chinese travellers' experiences, Zhang and Hitchcock (2017) use netnography to explore gendered views of travelling which Chinese women discuss in their blogs. Travel blogging is therefore an example of digital work where using the netnography method has proven valuable to researchers; however currently the method is underutilized.

Researchers are predominantly using other methods to study travel blogs at present, such as the use of content analysis to study travel blogs as textual artefacts (Wenger 2008). Similarly, while the use of the netnography method for studying bloggers is growing, very few studies focus on travel bloggers in particular. In her analysis of celebrity bloggers, Logan (2015) uses netnography as a means to investigate the varied self-presentation strategies used by online fashion bloggers. Turning to food blogging, Watson (2013) uses the netnography method to explore the online community of 'foodies', exploring their motivations for wanting to run and curate food blogs. Few studies have used netnography as a means to study the digital *work* practices and processes of bloggers. One exception to this is Mouratidis (2018) who uses netnography as one method to better understand the lives of 'digital nomads', that is individuals who have rejected conventional spaces of work and who are instead harnessing digital technologies in order to pursue globally nomadic working practices. Here, drawing on my own research, I seek to highlight how netnography can be a useful and productive method for investigating travel blogging as digital work.

Using Netnography to Understand the Digital Work of Travel Blogging

Following Kozinet's (2019) 'recipe', this section of the chapter will be dedicated to explaining how I used the netnography method within my own research. The first stage of netnography research is focused around *initiation* and requires the researcher to decide upon the research questions they wish to investigate. It is also important within this stage of the netnography to identify the online forums or platforms appropriate to these research questions (Kozinets 2019). The overall aim of my research was to provide an in-depth understanding of the working lives, spaces, and careers of British travel bloggers. Netnography allowed me to answer this research aim by providing me with a method that enabled me to capture the digitally mediated examples of a travel blogger's thoughts, feelings, and understandings of their creative work, as they emerged within the communities, cultures, and systems of their online world (Kozinets 2019). During this *initiation* stage, I also defined the data site of my netnography research as my participants' publicly accessible blogs and associated Twitter, Facebook, Instagram, and Pinterest accounts (Kulavuz-Onal and Vasquez 2013).

All participants within my overall research project were individuals who self-defined as travel bloggers and as British. This demographic of travel bloggers was chosen due to ease of linguistic communication with participants and their associated online outputs. Participants were recruited from a variety of travel blogger focused Facebook groups. Participants were also recruited through speculative, direct messages sent out via email or Twitter, to individuals whose contact details could be found from the first five pages of Google under the search term 'UK Travel Blogger' or under the 'UK Travel Blogger' hashtag on Twitter. Each participant was given a small token of thanks for their participation in the research, in the form of a small payment, charitable donation, or gift worth up to £20. Turning to the *investigation* step of the method, due to the sheer amount of netnography data available, the research has to focus on the amount and type of data to be captured (Kozinets 2010). I decided to limit the netnography part of my overall research design to the travel blog and social media of 7 of my 19 participants. For the netnography, one participant was chosen at random in order to complete a pilot netnography study. In addition to this pilot participant, one male and one female participant were selected at random from each of the hobbyist, professional, and transitioning blogger categories I had devised. 'Hobbyist' travel bloggers were defined as travel bloggers who actively did not seek to use their travel blogs as a source of economic income or form of work. 'Transitioning' travel bloggers were travel bloggers who were attempting to monetize their travel blog and who sought to position travel blogging as a key source of work and income.

'Professional' travel bloggers were travel bloggers who actively used travel blogging as one of their main sources of economic income and forms of work. Otherwise, the netnography participants were a mix of age, gender, ethnicity, and were originally from various locations across the UK.

At the *immersion* stage, I decided that within my netnography, I would attempt to comply with the unobtrusive nature of the method (Kozinets 2002) through resisting personal involvement in any of the observed online interactions. I felt adding my own voice would have been disruptive to the quality of the data collected (Kozinets 2015). I began my netnography data collection through 'scouting'. Scouting is the beginning of the filtering and selection process in the netnography, necessary to allow the researcher to locate specific platforms, sections of platforms, or conversations which will help them to best answer their research questions (Kozinets 2019). In the context of my own research, scouting involved looking explicitly across participants' blogs for pages which directly linked to their digital work. In particular, I looked for the presence of media kits or 'Work with Me' pages.

I captured my netnography data via screenshot, directly from the blog or social media for each participant, at the end of every week and saved this into a collated word document (Kozinets 2015). I supplemented this downloaded data in the word document with my own observational, ethnographic fieldnotes and therefore this document developed into my immersion journal. These fieldnotes aimed to elaborate upon the subtleties of the data which were not captured within the screenshot, that is, detailing the context within which interactions took place (Boellstorff et al. 2012). These immersion journal fieldnotes were important within the context of my own research because as Kozinets (2015, 192) argues: 'good fieldnotes help to make the links between online and other sites visible'. The netnography was conducted from August 2018 to June 2019.

I also undertook a process of *interaction* within my netnography. Following Garcia-Alvarez et al's (2015) use of netnography research to examine social media games, I did not want to limit myself to either the online or offline world, as this dichotomy is no longer viable within our current era, especially when we turn our focus to the digital work of travel bloggers. As a result, I sought to compliment my netnography, with two 'offline' interviews. I felt interviews were the most pertinent additional research method here, because as Kozinets (2015, 185) notes 'interviews can and often should be used to flesh out and amplify important topical areas that may not be explored in sufficient depth … to help interpret and probe the meanings behind difficult to decipher symbols and images'. All netnography research participants were interviewed twice, with each interview lasting 60 to 75 minutes. The first of these interviews was a semi-structured interview focused around participants' understandings of their working lives. The second of these interviews was a photo elicitation interview, in which participants discussed images they had taken which they felt expressed an element of their working lives, spaces, or career as a travel blogger. Extracts from my immersion journal were also shared with participants who had been involved in the netnography in this photo elicitation interview. Participants were explicitly questioned about this netnography data. In particular, they were asked to clarify any unclear details, for example why they may have posted cryptic messages. They were also asked questions which aimed to assist in providing additional information or context about specific online content or posts.

A period of *integration* or data analysis was also undertaken. Following Logan (2015), I analysed my netnography data using the same two-stage coding process I used to identify themes within my interview data. The first level of coding identified words and sentences, but also key aspects of images or overall social media compositions within the data (such as backgrounds, figures, interactions, objects, or colours) which were loaded with meaning relevant to my research aims. Reflecting on Logan's (2015) netnographic study of celebrity bloggers, Kozinets (2015, 12) discusses how Logan could have 'share[d] her self-reflections from reflexive fieldnotes and then reflect[ed] upon those reflexive reflections in deep data analysis'. As a result, following this first level of coding, I sought to follow Kozinet's (2015) suggestion, re-analysing my immersion diary fieldnotes to find additional key themes and patterns of meaning, using these additional themes to inform a secondary level of coding the data. I also returned to my interview data to find any additional themes which could additionally inform this secondary instance of coding.

Kozinets (2019) also describes how decisions must be made about how data are collected, analysed, and presented. He notes how netnography data must be presented in such a way that it provides a rich description of the embodied experience it captures, as well as being a useful example of the wider argument and claims that the research is making. In contemplating the *incarnation* of my own netnography data, I therefore used nethnographic writings and texts from my immersion diary to allow the research audience to become immersed in the lively experience of the realities of a travel blogger's digital work. These immersion diary extracts were also presented alongside screenshots of the netnography data, as shown in Figure 7.1.

> This is probably the second or third aeroplane tattoo that I've noticed already, and not just in the background but as the centrepiece of the image. A few of my bloggers seem to have them [the aeroplane tattoos] and use them as part of their brand image. It's like, look, travel is such as big part of my life, it means so much to me I've had it tattooed on my body. It's crazy really, I can't think of many other careers where people are happy to have a symbol of their job etched into their body forever
>
> **(Immersion Journal Fieldnotes 13/09/2018)**

Ethical Considerations of Netnography

It is also important to recognize the distinctive ethical considerations of netnography. One of the key ethical challenges within netnography relates to the concept of what

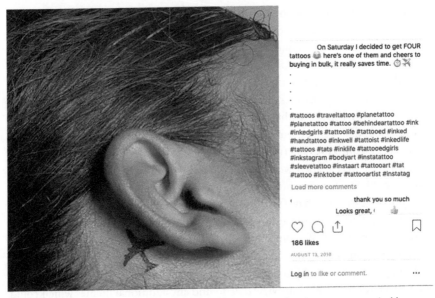

On Saturday I decided to get FOUR tattoos 😂 here's one of them and cheers to buying in bulk, it really saves time. ⏱️ 🎯

#tattoos #traveltattoo #planetattoo #planetattoo #tattoo #behindeartattoo #ink #inkedgirls #tattoolife #tattooed #inked #handtattoo #inkwell #tattoist #inkedlife #tattoos #tats #inklife #tattooedgirls #inkstagram #bodyart #instatattoo #sleevetattoo #instaart #tattooart #tat #tattoo #inktober #tattooartist #instatag

Load more comments

thank you so much

Looks great, 👍

186 likes

AUGUST 13, 2018

Log in to like or comment.

Fig. 7.1 An example of a screenshot from the netnography data accompanied by an extract from the immersion journal fieldnotes
Copyright acknowledgement Charlotte Louise.

is considered public or private within the online sphere. Kozinets (2019) discusses how research ethics should be applied to netnography, in relation to whether the research involves public and/or private sites. Public sites are defined as online platforms which have open access to the public, which are accessible via common search engines and which do not require registration or password login. For public sites, no special ethical considerations are required for netnography, as these public sites are presenting public data which has been voluntarily shared. In the context of my research, I understood the travel blogger's blogs and social media as examples of public sites. By individuals posting content onto these platforms, they are knowingly exposing their information to the public. Private sites are online platforms that require a password login or registration and that are not accessible via search engines. For private sites, extra levels of ethical consideration are required in netnographic research. These include reasonable compliance with platform policies, researcher disclosure, and permission on behalf of the moderator (Kozinets 2019). In order to ensure my netnography was as ethical as possible, I conducted my netnography overtly, gaining informed consent, and therefore permission, from all participants to observe their online outputs across their blog and social media. This is because, as Logan (2015) argues, bloggers may write to be read, but do not necessarily give permission to be part of a research project which will ultimately analyse, dissect, and cite their posts. I also fully disclosed my real identity, presence, affiliations, and intentions as a researcher to all participants during the netnography (Kozinets 2019).

Moreover, following the European Union's GDPR (General Data Protection Regulation) legislation, GDPR permits the collection of public data for research purposes, as long as the researcher is acting within the recognized standards for scientific research. In relation to the netnography method, public data can be used by social media researchers as long as appropriate research safeguards are in place (Kozinets 2019). One of the safeguards I put in place within my own research was the use of pseudonyms. All participants in the research were assigned a pseudonym alias of between 2 and 5 letters (Kozinets 2019). However, through the netnography, direct quotes and images from the blogger's blog and social media could be traceable and therefore could become linked to a specific blog or blogger. These social media/blog posts are already attributed and linked to a specific blogger within the public domain, so therefore the blogger is already aware and happy for this online content to be attributed to them. However, interview data could also potentially be cross-referenced against the netnography data and therefore attributed back to a specific blogger. As a result, I made each participant explicitly aware of a potential link between their interview and social media data. I then asked participants if they were happy for this link to be evident within the research. If a participant was not happy for this link to be evident, I offered the chance for the participant to withdraw from the research. However, all participants acknowledged this potential, identifiable link and still agreed to be involved. Again, following the existing UK GDPR framework at the time of the research, as a general guide gaining informed consent is not necessary for those who have knowingly published content in the public domain (Stainton and Iordanova 2017). As a result, I did not feel I needed to gain informed consent from everyone who interacted with a participant's blog or social media post, for example through liking or commenting (Markham 2005). However, to ensure the research was as ethical as possible, I treated all usernames as sensitive and therefore blanked these usernames out (Carter 2005).

Reflections on Netnography as a Method for Examining Travel Blogging as Digital Work

Within my research, netnography enabled me to uncover and detail the nomadic nature of travel bloggers' digital work and in doing so, better understand travel blogging as a *distinctive* form of mobile, digital work. In particular, the method allowed me to witness exactly how the work of travel bloggers moves across multiple online platforms. In demonstrating how travel bloggers are having to be both active and available on each of these platforms in turn, the netnography method allowed me to comment on the potential issues of burnout or overwork to which travel bloggers are susceptible. My netnography also allowed me to better understand the nuances of digital work, for example, in relation to the different levels of attentiveness to digital work displayed between those at different stages of their career, or between those who sought to monetize their blog and those who did not. Finally, the netnography also allowed me to acknowledge the importance of self-fashioning to travel bloggers. I could visually witness how work invested in the look of a particular travel blogger for example, flowed from the offline (in relation to the clothes they wear, or the spaces they are photographed in) to the online (in how these clothes or spaces are presented on social media in such a way that this distinctive look is continued).

Netnography can considerably reduce costs relative to traditional fieldwork methods, as the researcher does not have to travel to a specific community but can instead readily access communities online. The focus of netnography on investigating online communities within virtual spaces can therefore make the method particularly useful for exploring communities which may be difficult to access and therefore may not otherwise be included in research (Costello et al. 2017). Moreover, within more traditional methods such as overt participant observation and/or interviews, the presence of the researcher can affect and interrupt the natural practices of everyday life. Using netnography is therefore arguably more unobtrusive then these other research methods, as observations of participants are not occurring in a context which has been created by the researcher (Vo Thanh and Kirova 2018). Yet, the Internet and social media platforms also offer an additional stage for both the presentation of the self and of social dynamics. Netnography as a method therefore offers further opportunity to investigate the digital lives of participants, by enabling researchers to gain significant insight into how participants may present themselves online (Urbanik and Roks 2020). In relation to my own research, netnography allowed me to gain insights into the virtual communities that travel bloggers embed themselves in online, and the role of these communities in travel bloggers' everyday, digital working lives. One example of this was that netnography as a method allowed me to gain knowledge about (and also to visibly witness) the various tones of address which travel bloggers use to form affective relationships between themselves and other members of the blog community, such as their blog readers or other travel bloggers. However, one challenge of the netnography method is to recognize that the data you collect still presents a mediated view of how participants present their working lives online. In being critically reflexive on the netnography method, it is important to recognize and acknowledge that the Internet does not provide unmediated access to participants' values and beliefs, and therefore that your netnography data may ultimately reflect this mediated view.

It has been argued that one of the key limitations of netnography is its narrow focus on online communities and therefore it is unable to offer full, rich detail of lived experience (Kozinets 2002). Linked to this, it has been argued that within the method it is not possible for the researcher to guide discussions or to further probe for clarification on specific topics, decreasing the opportunity to explore in depth the social phenomena occurring within and beyond these online communities (Whalen 2017). I found it particularly challenging to wholly capture the lively experience of digital work solely through netnography. When I began the research, I wanted my immersion journal to be lively and inspired, giving the reader a sense of truly inhabiting the digital environments of work being crafted and created by the blogger. Yet, as the research continued, I began to reflect more on what netnography as a method allowed me to 'see', and therefore my immersion journal transformed as a result. My immersion journal developed into a more static and evidentiary artefact, visually showcasing the realities of travel blogging work as it is produced and performed online. The immersion journal also became a space in which I was able to reflect on the work bloggers invest in their self-presentation online. In reflecting on what netnography enabled me as a researcher to 'see' and to capture within my research, I subsequently recognized how netnography *alone* as a method would be insufficient to capture the full, lively experience of digital work. In complimenting my netnography with photo elicitation and semi-structured interviews, I was able to capture the fullest, lived experience of travel blogging as digital work. For example, these interviews offered elongated discussion around how the ubiquitous nature of digital technologies was resulting in issues of overwork (a theme which had not explicitly emerged through the netnography method itself). Importantly, the interviews also allowed me to discuss with participants how this issue of overwork was subsequently affecting their social relationships. As Kozinets (2019) argues, we can therefore attend to the limitations of netnography by supplementing the method with additional data collection methods, which allow researcher engagement with online participants. This phase, which Kozinets (2019) refers to as *interaction*, can bridge online and offline research and enable the researcher to probe further into the lived experience of participants.

Kozinets (2019) argues that one of the key advantages of netnography lies in the method comprising a specific, actionable research 'road map', which can be both followed but also adapted to suit the researcher's specific needs. Netnography is self-proclaimed as focused on studying online communities but within the case of my own research, I adapted the netnography method so that it allowed me to focus on specific individuals and their subjective experiences instead, as the means through which I explored the digital communities of travel blogging work. The ability to modify the methodological processes of netnography means the method can be continually adapted to suit new contingencies being mediated by the Internet, such as the development of distinct new Internet enabled collectives or groups (Morais et al. 2020). This is a distinct advantage of the method in the field of digital work, which is increasingly dynamic and constantly evolving to encompass new platforms, online communities, and practices of working. Relatedly, in areas of digital work which are still in their infancy, netnography as a method can enable the researcher to draw analytical conclusions on these new forms of digital working from limited online communities and discussions (Kozinets 2002). However, on a practical level, this ability to adapt the method may also represent a challenge to the novice method user. Novice users may feel concerned about how to best adapt the method to ensure that it still enables them to answer their research aims. In order to overcome this challenge within my own research, I undertook a pilot netnography. This pilot netnography allowed me to trial the method to see which modifications to the netnography 'recipe' were most beneficial within the context of my own research.

Within netnography, sampling issues may also be considered a limitation of the method. For example, individuals who post on social media are typically more extreme in their opinions than those who do not post (Kozinets 2019). Individuals may also have their own social or economic motivations for sharing their social media data publicly. As a result, participants who feel passionate about particular topics may dominate the research sample, with individuals who feel ambivalent about a topic being markedly absent. This issue is particularly stark when focusing only on public posts, as is the case with my own research. Yet, in the case of my own research, instead of being a limitation, the motivations behind the public sharing of data added another nuance to the discussion of digital work I sought to analyse. In reality, publicly sharing their data functioned *as* a form of digital work for my participants and therefore provided an additional subtlety to my understanding of how travel bloggers attempted to build and curate an audience. This issue of sampling bias also played a role in influencing my decision to provide each of my participants with a small, financial incentive for being involved in the research. Although small, this incentive helped to encourage individuals with less extreme views about digital work to be involved in my study. It is therefore important to recognize within netnography research that we rarely deal with a representative sample of the public, and therefore the analytical conclusions drawn from our netnography research should reflect this. Relatedly, within online spaces, we can never truly be sure who is posting on platforms (Kozinets 2019). Within his first writings on the subject, Kozinets (1998) warned about the prospect of spam or illegitimate posts within netnography. The presence of spam or illegitimate posts (for example, from someone who may have had an account hacked) may also influence the conclusions that can be drawn about an online community. However, again this limitation can be mitigated through the process of *interaction* as Kozinets (2019) discusses. Within my own research in order to combat these potentials of online ambiguity, the netnography data were discussed and validated within the second photo elicitation interview.

On a practical level, netnography is also arguably less cumbersome than other research methods, as data are already presented in written form, so transcription is not required (Mkono 2013). However, a real challenge that a novice user may face when using the netnography method is the sheer amount of data presented to them when they begin the research. Costello et al., (2017, 9) discuss the 'slog' involved in netnography and the sheer 'blood, sweat and tears' that the method requires. In particular, netnography involves researchers having to deal with the problem of information overload, as they are presented with large datasets to work through and make sense of (Kozinets 2019). This is a particular challenge I faced within my own research. Although documented, I was unprepared for the emotional, as well as physical, slog that the netnography entailed. The sheer amount of data which needs to be sifted through during the netnography may be a particularly stark issue when using netnography as a method to explore digital work. We would expect those who undertake digital work to be more active, both across online platforms and within online communities, than your typical Internet user. This is because these individuals use online platforms and online communities to source, promote, and/or discuss their digital work (Bosangit et al. 2012). To use my own research as an example, on just one day, one of my participants posted on Twitter 16 times. If we take this as an average, this gives you an idea of the sheer scale of the data which the researcher must engage with during the netnography. For me, this posed an emotional challenge as I felt overwhelmed by the amount of data I needed to engage with and sift through. In order to overcome this challenge, I ensured I was extremely strict in my scouting strategy, solely focusing on data directly related to my research objectives. As a result, the amount of data that needs to be gathered, in relation to the time and resources available to the researcher, should be considered when contemplating using netnography as a research method.

Conclusion

Within this chapter, I have demonstrated how netnography can be used to investigate travel blogging as digital work. In particular, I have provided a short introduction to both the digital work of travel blogging but also to the netnography method itself. I have aimed to demonstrate how I developed my own netnography 'recipe', detailing my decisions in relation to the method and its distinctive ethical considerations. I have also attempted to be critically reflexive in my considerations of the advantages and limitations of the method, particularly in relation to its application to research on digital work.

Netnography as a method can offer a window into the social, political, and economic happenings and understandings of digital work, as it is present and presented through the world of online communications and social media. Travel blogging is just one example. Digital work, as distributed, mobile and multi-modal, is only going to expand, as the pervasiveness of social and digital media continue to proliferate and infiltrate all aspects of our lives. Looking forward then, as a method, netnography could help researchers to further understand online communication and its effects on society, including the structural and cultural changes in labour markets which are increasingly facilitating a shift towards distributed digital work practices, subjectivities, and spaces. In turning to the digital gig economy for example, netnography could provide an insightful method for exploring how gig economy workers use social media as a place to discuss and debate themes such as discrimination and resilience (Graham et al. 2017). Another future use of the method could be to explore the resultant impacts of digitalization on work practices within traditional employment sectors such as healthcare or social work. For example, researchers could use the netnography method to better understand the attitude of a specific health-based online community towards new drugs. This insight could subsequently enable healthcare and social workers to better tailor their strategy for disseminating information about these drugs online (Del Fresno-Garcia and Lopez-Pelaez 2013). Future developments which use netnography to explore digital work are seemingly limitless, as the method and the researchers using it, can evolve and adapt to the contours and unpredictability endemic to digital work and its practices.

References

Baym, N. 1993. Interpreting Soap Operas and Creating Community: Inside a Computer-Mediated Fan Culture. *Journal of Folklore Research*, 30(2–3): pp. 143–76.

Boellstorff, T., Nardi, B., Pearce, C., and Taylor, T. L. 2012. *Ethnography and Virtual Worlds: A Handbook of Method*. Princeton University Press.

Bosangit, C., Dulnuan, J., and Mena, M. 2012. Using travel blogs to examine the postconsumption behaviour of tourists. *Journal of Vacation Marketing*, 18(3): pp. 207–219.

Caliandro, A. 2014. Ethnography in digital spaces: Ethnography of virtual worlds, netnography and digital ethnography. In Sunderland, P. and Denny, R. (eds), *Handbook of Business Anthropology*. (pp. 738–61). Left Coast Press.

Carter, D. 2005. Living in virtual communities: An ethnography of human relationships in cyberspace. *Information, Communication and Society*, 8(2): pp. 148–67.

Costello, L., McDermott, M., and Wallace, R. 2017. Netnography: Range of practices, misperceptions and missed opportunities . *International Journal of Qualitative Methods*, 16(1): pp.1–12.

Del Fresno-Garcia, M., and Lopez-Pelaez, A. 2013. Social work and netnography: The case of Spain and generic drugs. *Qualitative Social Work*, 13(1): pp. 85–107.

Garcia-Alvarez, E., Lopez-Sintas, J., and Samper-Martinez, A. 2015. The social network gamer's experience of play: A netnography of restaurant city on Facebook. *Games and Culture*, 12(7–8): pp. 650–70.

Garcia-Rapp, F. 2018. Trivial and normative? Online fieldwork within YouTube's beauty community. *Journal of Contemporary Ethnography*, 48(5): pp. 1–26.

Germann Molz, J. 2015. Giving Back, doing good, feeling global: The affective flows of family voluntourism', *Journal of Contemporary Ethnography*, 46(3): pp. 334–60.

Graham, M., Lehdonvirta, V., Wood, A., Barnard, H., Hjorth, I., and Simon, D. P. 2017. The risks and rewards of online gig work at the global margins. [Online]. Available at: https://www.oii.ox.ac.uk/publications/gigwork.pdf (accessed 21 January 2020).

Grincheva, N. 2014. The online museum: A 'placeless' space of the 'civic laboratory', *Museum Anthropology Review*, 8: pp. 1–21.

Hine, C. 2000. *Virtual Ethnography*. Sage Publishing.

Hine, C. 2015. *Ethnography for the Internet*. Bloomsbury.

Hookway, N. 2008. 'Entering the blogosphere': Some strategies for using blogs in social research, *Qualitative Research*, 8(1): pp. 91–113.

Jenkins, H. 1995. 'Do you enjoy making the rest of us feel stupid?: alt. tv. Twinpeaks, the trickster author, and the viewer mastery. In Lavery, D. (ed.), *Full of Secrets: Critical Approaches to Twin Peaks*. (pp. 51–69). Wayne State University Press.

Kozinets, R. V. 1998. On netnography: Initial reflections on consumer research investigations of cyberculture. *Advances in Consumer Research*, 25: pp. 366–71.

Kozinets, R. V. 2002. The field behind the screen: Using Netnography for Marketing Research in Online Communities. *Journal of Marketing Research*, 39(1): pp. 61–72.

Kozinets, R. V. 2010. *Netnography: Doing Ethnographic Research Online*. Sage Publishing.

Kozinets, R. V. 2015. *Netnography: Redefined*. 2nd edn. Sage Publishing.

Kozinets, R. V. 2019. *Netnography: The Essential Guide to Qualitative Social Media Research*. 3rd edn. Sage Publishing.

Kulavuz-Onal, D., and Vasquez, C. 2013. Reconceptualising fieldwork in a netnography of an online community of English language teachers. *Ethnography and Education*, 8(2): pp. 224–38.

Logan, A. 2015. Netnography: observing and interacting with celebrity in the digital world. *Celebrity Studies*, 6(3): pp. 378–81.

Lugosi, P., Janta, H., and Watson, P. 2012. Investigative management and consumer research on the Internet. *International Journal of Contemporary Hospitality Management*, 24(6): pp. 838–54.

Markham, A. 2005. The methods, politics and ethics of representation in online ethnography. In Denzin, N., and Lincoln, Y. (eds), *The Sage Handbook of Qualitative Research*. 3rd edn. (pp. 793–820) Sage Publishing.

Miller, D., and Slater, D. 2001. *The Internet: An Ethnographic Approach*. Berg.

Mkono, M. 2013. Using net-based ethnography (netnography) to understand the staging and marketing of 'authentic African' dining experiences to tourists at Victoria Falls. *Journal of Hospitality & Tourism Research*, 37(2): pp. 184–98.

Morais, G. M, Santos, V. F., and Gonçalves, C. A. 2020. Netnography: Origins, foundations, evolution and axiological and methodological developments and trends. *The Qualitative Report*, 25(2): pp. 441–55.

Mouratidis, G. 2018. Digital Nomadism. Travel, Remote Work and Alternative Lifestyles. MA thesis. Lund University.

Müller, S., Goswami, S., and Krcmar, H. 2011. Monetizing blogs: Revenue streams of individual blogs. *European Conference on Information Systems*. Helsinki, Finland, 9–11 June. Available at: https://pdfs.semanticscholar.org/0837/011f6ea57e8ff3a276bdb9ca604a525a4903.pdf?_ga=2.36150439.665269704.1590744745-498700283.1590574459 (accessed 27 May 2020).

Nardi, B. A., Schiano, D. J., and Gumbrecht, M. 2004. Blogging as social activity, or, would you let 900 million people read your diary? *Proceedings of Computer Supported Co-operative Work*, 6(3): pp. 222–30.

Puhringer, S., and Taylor, A. 2008. A practitioner's report on blogs as potential sources for destination marketing intelligence. *Journal of Vacation Marketing*, 14(2): pp. 177–87.

Stainton, H., and Iordanova, E. 2017. An ethical perspective for researchers using travel blog analysis as a method of data collection. *Methodological Innovations*, 10(3): pp. 1–7.

Statistica. 2020. Number of bloggers in the United States from 2014 to 2020. Available at: https://www.statista.com/statistics/187267/number-of-bloggers-in-usa/ (accessed 20 January 2020).

Turkle, S. 1995. *Life on the Screen: Identity in the Age of the Internet*. Simon and Schuster.

Urbanik, M., and Roks, R. A. 2020. GangstaLife: Fusing urban ethnography with netnography in gang studies. *Qualitative Sociology*, 43: pp. 213–33.

Van Nuenen, T. 2016. Here I am: Authenticity and self-branding on travel blogs. *Tourist Studies*, 16(2): pp. 192–212.

Vo Thanh, T., and Kirova, V. 2018. Wine tourism experience: a netnography study. *Journal of Business Research*, 83: pp. 30–37.

Vuelio. 2019. UK Bloggers Survey 2019. Available at: https://www.vuelio.com/uk/wp-content/uploads/2019/03/UK-Bloggers-Survey-2019.pdf (accessed 21 October 2020).

Walker-Rettberg, J. 2013. *Blogging*. Polity.

Walther, J. B. 1995. Relational aspects of computer-mediated communication: Experimental observations over time. *Organization Science*, 6(2): pp. 186–203.

Watson, P. J. 2013. Grab Your Fork: A Netnographic Study of a Foodie Blog and its Community. PhD thesis. Bournemouth University.

Wenger, A. 2008. Analysis of travel bloggers' characteristics and their communication about Austria as a tourism destination. *Journal of Vacation Marketing*, 14(2): pp. 169–76.

Whalen, E. 2017. A changing netnographic landscape: Is there a place for online ethnography in hospitality and tourism? Travel and Tourism Research Association International Conference, Quebec City, Canada. 20–22 June. Available at: https://scholarworks.umass.edu/cgi/viewcontent.cgi?article=2073&26context=ttra (accessed 27 May 2020).

Wiles, R., Bengry-Howell, A., Crow, G., and Nind, M. 2013. But is it innovation? The development of novel methodological approaches in qualitative research. *Methodological Innovations Online*, 8(1): pp. 18–33.

WordPress. 2021. A live look at activity across WordPress.com. Available at: https://wordpress. com/activity/ (accessed 4 June 2021).

Wu, M., and Pearce, P. 2014. Appraising netnography: Towards insights about new markets in the digital tourist era. *Current Issues in Tourism*, 17(5): pp. 463–74.

Zhang, Y., and Hitchcock, J. 2017. The Chinese female tourist gaze: A netnography of young women's blogs on Macao. *Current Issues in Tourism*, 20(3): pp. 315–30.

8

Autoethnography and the Digital Volunteer

Christine Hine

Introduction

This chapter argues that autoethnography offers a potent means to explore the experience of digital volunteering as a form of digital work. Digital work offers some challenges for research based on conventional forms of shadowing and participant observation. The digital worker may be physically quite alone for much of their working time, but they are tied into networks of co-workers, institutional structures of recognition and accountability and the competing demands of home and leisure. For a volunteer doing digital work in an unpaid capacity, institutional recognition and accountability structures may be more fluid than for paid employees and both paid work and family life may compete against volunteering priorities in unpredictable fashion. Digital workers may be engaging in a moment-by-moment flitting between various foci of attention and contexts of work and leisure. Digital forms of work are a challenge for the researcher wishing to observe the work 'in action' since these workers are, at the same time, isolated but also intensely social in their interconnections with and dependence on other physically distant co-workers. The solution to this methodological challenge put forward in this chapter is for the researcher to become the digital worker and to take an autoethnographic perspective to connect that personal experience with research questions focused on how work at a distance becomes meaningful.

The form of autoethnography employed here is built on the foundations of ethnography as a research method that uses sustained participant observation to explore how people make sense of their lives. Ethnography focuses on developing a micro-level understanding of experience delivered through evocative description but it does not ignore the macro-level structures that shape life opportunities. Instead, the ethnographer aims to recount how macro-level structures become real to participants within their lived experiences. This feature of ethnography is continued within autoethnography. In an autoethnographic study of the kind described here, the ethnographer is both participant in and observer of their own experience, simultaneously documenting daily activities and reflecting on the wider social, cultural, and political structures that impact on and become real within the personal expe-

Christine Hine, *Autoethnography and the Digital Volunteer*. In: *Research Methods for Digital Work and Organization*. Edited by Gillian Symon, Katrina Pritchard, and Christine Hine, Oxford University Press.

rience. The strengths of autoethnography are centred around its ability to explore tacit aspects of experience that might remain unspoken in interviews or unobservable in more conventional ethnography. Autoethnography offers us the possibility to home in on the emotional unfolding of moment-by-moment aspects of experience that might otherwise seem too small to observe, too obvious to mention or too banal to document. Autoethnography is also a highly flexible and adaptable method that can respond to a changing situation or to developing research priorities limited only by the autoethnographer's own lived constraints in time, space, and social connection.

First, this chapter unpacks the concept of digital volunteering and situates it within a wider framing of digital work and the kinds of research question that a qualitative sociologist might bring to digital work. The following section then introduces autoethnography as a research method and discusses the application of the method within a working context. Next, I present a fragment of autoethnographic writing about my own digital volunteering experience and highlight key research themes that transpire. These themes are then compared with findings from an interview-based study of digital volunteering, in order to highlight the strengths and limitations of the autoethnographic approach. Finally, in a concluding section the chapter looks beyond digital volunteering to reflect on the potential contribution of autoethnography to the understanding of a wider array of forms of digital work and considers the criteria we use to judge the success of an autoethnographic project.

Digital Volunteering as Digital Work

Work done voluntarily is an important contributor to the economy (Payne 2017) and to the wellbeing of both volunteers and the recipients of their voluntary efforts (Fujiwara et al. 2013; Haldane 2014). The numbers of people reporting that they do some voluntary work are consistently high, with two in five adults in the UK taking part according to a survey conducted in 2018 (McGarvey et al. 2019). For survey purposes, volunteering tends to be distinguished from other kinds of less formal 'helping out' or unpaid labour by virtue of being done in association with an organization, as this definition outlines:

> Volunteer work is distinguished from informal helping (e.g., mowing a neighbor's lawn) and caring (e.g., helping an elderly parent shop for groceries) by the fact that it takes place in or on behalf of an organization, such as a government agency, a non-profit organization, an advocacy group, a fund-raising campaign, a club, or a recreational association. Volunteer work is, above all, an organized experience. The principal difference between informal helping and volunteering is that the individual exchanges personal control over his or her resources (e.g., deciding

how to help an elderly neighbour) for the financial, physical and social resources provided by the organization.

(Musick and Wilson 2007, 420)

This distinction is very useful in highlighting some socially significant features of volunteering as an activity. In common with many forms of paid work, the volunteer gives up a certain amount of autonomy and is subject to various forms of management and surveillance that also come with norms, values, and expectations about performance. By virtue of association with an organization, the volunteer also gains access to a social environment that may offer the benefits of a support structure and friendship. Many volunteers are appointed through relatively formal application processes and subject to interview assessment, vetting, and training like paid employees, although smaller or informally constituted groups who are not part of a larger umbrella organization may lack such processes and appoint on a more ad hoc basis. Taking these factors into account, it is useful to think of volunteering as a form of work, albeit one where payment is not involved, and to expect that the experience of this work will be shaped by the relationship forged with the organization commissioning the work.

Among the forms of work undertaken by volunteers, a growing category has emerged of digital, online, or virtual volunteering (Amichai-Hamburger 2008; Cravens and Ellis 2014; Liu et al. 2016; Pritchard et al. 2016). These digital workers give their time for free to support organizations, clubs, and other kinds of group through activities conducted solely online—this might involve social media work, moderating online forums, providing chat room support or counselling, producing marketing materials, updating websites, or managing data. There is also a burgeoning field of digital activities where labour is given freely on a more sporadic basis including micro-volunteering (Jochum and Paylor 2013) and online disaster response volunteering (Roberts and Doyle 2017) but these activities are outside the remit of the current chapter. Here the focus is on regular and formal arrangements that involve a volunteer undertaking digital work for an organization on a sustained basis.

The digital forms of regular, formal volunteering that are the focus of this chapter are expanding. Cravens and Ellis (2014) termed their book the 'last' guidebook on virtual volunteering since they deemed that henceforth virtual forms of volunteering would become the norm, absorbed into the array of different forms of volunteering available. In a 2018 UK survey reported by McGarvey et al. (2019) 57 per cent of volunteers said that they do a mixture of online and offline activities with 6 per cent of volunteers saying that their volunteering is done exclusively online. Digital-only volunteering varies by demographic group, dropping to 3 per cent among the over 55s and rising to 10 per cent among those living with disabilities. According to the survey, online-only volunteering seems to be more common among recent volunteers and there is evidence of a growing trend.

The recruitment and retention of volunteers depends in large part on them finding the work meaningful and satisfying. It is therefore important to explore whether satisfaction looks the same for volunteers who may never or rarely spend time face-to-face with co-volunteers and volunteer managers and to consider whether they feel a sense of connection. There are some concerning figures in this regard among the survey results from McGarvey et al. (2019), with findings indicating that online volunteers are more likely to report tensions and conflicts and are more likely to report problems with feelings of belonging to the organization. A sense of the meaning of voluntary work is developed over time and articulated in contexts of social interaction: for example, Allahyari (2000, 3) explores the development of a moral community among volunteers that encompasses a diversity of meanings. It is of interest to ask, therefore, how the specific experiences and working contexts of a digital volunteer might affect the processes of meaning-making and attachment to a wider set of values and identities and whether digital volunteers draw on interactions with fellow volunteers to build their sense of meaning. Amichai-Hamburger (2008) attributes the success of online volunteering to the flexible and accessible opportunities for life-affirming and self-actualizing activity that it offers but this leaves it very much open to explore how 'self-actualization' works out in practice.

Digital volunteering can be viewed as home working, and as such we can expect that it may come with benefits in terms of flexibility but also costs, such as intrusion on home life (Redman et al. 2009). The locations of work matter in so far as they occasion shifts in the spatial and temporal proximity of co-workers and managers and thus have consequences for the social organization of work (Sewell and Taskin 2015). It is important therefore to consider how feedback is given and received, how monitoring is done and experienced, and how sociality among co-workers is enacted, creating a sense of a workplace. Various forms of direct communications are available to digital workers to tie them into the organizations commissioning their work, but there are also less direct indicators of the presence of others, in digital traces (Geiger and Ribes 2011). It is interesting to consider how digital volunteers gain a sense of themselves as workers among others and how they learn to read traces of the work of others who are physically distant. It is possible for home workers to feel at once more autonomous and more constrained, isolated from co-workers but over-crowded and distracted by domestic concerns (Sewell and Taskin 2015). For digital volunteers it is important to ask how they carve out time and space in their lives for their volunteering tasks and how they make this challenge meaningful to themselves and to those around them.

There are therefore a range of issues that are of interest to research in respect of volunteer experience and, while survey and interview studies may give us an effective overview of volunteer viewpoints, they do not necessarily show us how the volunteer experience develops over time and how it unfolds day-by-day. Researching this topic offers both a practical and an ethical research challenge. Practically speaking, each digital volunteer works in a different location, often drawing on a number of different technological platforms to carry out their work, using their own device or devices. Observing these different working locations and platforms would require considerable ingenuity and a solution tailored to the circumstance of each volunteer. Even then, capturing an appropriate level of detail for insight into moment-by-moment decision making and exploring the meanings attributed to everyday actions would be an immense burden on participants and have the potential fundamentally to impact the very experience that we seek to understand. Ethically, such an approach has the potential to intrude on aspects of the volunteer's life and that of their families and co-workers and spill out unpredictably beyond the confines of a conventional approach to informed consent. This is a situation that requires a flexible and adaptable approach to research and a real-time response to capturing whatever is practical, ethical, and of potential theoretical interest. With these criteria in mind, the next section turns to autoethnography as an approach to researching digital volunteering.

Autoethnography as a Method for Studying Digital Work

While the term autoethnography has been in use for some time to denote an account of a culture by an insider, autoethnography as a distinctive methodological genre has become acknowledged relatively recently. The contemporary formulation of autoethnography as an approach that uses personal experience as a stepping off point for exploring broader social cultural and political themes was articulated notably by Reed-Danahay (1997) and Ellis (2004). While the focus on personal experience is key to autoethnography, the boundaries of the genre are somewhat fluid and hard to define. All contemporary ethnography, after all, depends on a researcher being co-present with the setting and thus contains at least some element of reflection on the ethnographer's own experience within that setting. However, autoethnography is more than simply a reflexive or insider ethnography in that the focus is on interrogating the personal experience itself rather than the focus being on the access that being an insider offers to study the experience of others.

In autoethnography the researcher's own experience becomes the core of the work and provides the material that fuels theorizing. Autoethnography draws on the orientations of autobiography and ethnography (Chang 2016) to develop a genre that offers commentary on and critique of the conditions of contemporary existence, evoking personal experience to bring it to life for readers and interrogating what this tells us about culture more broadly. As an orientation to research it differs from a diary in the way that it interrogates personal experience for what it can tell us about the social, cultural, and political influences that structure and shape the prospects and practices of the individual. Among the different genres of autoethnography are some forms that are more focused on a theoretically oriented analysis and others that focus on an evocative form of writing designed to bring situations to life for readers and encourage them to reflect on their own positioning (Anderson 2006). There are critiques of autoethnography, focusing in on the very personal perspective that it provides, the corresponding lack of insight into diversity and difference and the potential to become mere self-indulgence rather than a theoretically valuable insight

(Sparkes 2002). This risk is somewhat averted in analytic autoethnography although the challenges of theorizing beyond individual experience without over-generalizing remain.

Autoethnography offers some distinctive and theoretically very fertile affordances for researchers interested in organizational culture, thanks to its ability to document and interrogate the nature of the experience of the organization from the perspective of the individual (Doloriert and Sambrook 2012). Sambrook and Herrmann (2018) note a burgeoning field of organizational autoethnography across a diverse array of settings. Boyle and Parry argue that organizational autoethnography can often involve an insight into the more tacit aspects of working within organizations including 'organizational processes such as emotional ambivalence, organizational deadlocks and roadblocks, and the variable and vicarious nature of organizational relationships' (Boyle and Parry 2007, 186). Sambrook and Herrmann (2018) note that conducting autoethnography as a complete member of an organization beyond academia can be practically challenging because of the demands it places on us fully to adopt the role and this therefore explains why so many autoethnographies focus on academia. Alternatives that Sambrook and Herrmann (2018) identify include co-produced autoethnography where an academic author teams up with a member of the organization in focus and together they interrogate the experience, or autoethnographies in which an academic reflects on past membership of a different organization. A further alternative, as exemplified in this chapter, is to acknowledge that many of us, academics included, are partial members of a number of organizations and that these partial memberships provide a basis for autoethnographic reflection. Partial and conflicting memberships can be the focus of an autoethnography in their own right: for example, Anderson (2011) writes about his experiences of combining academic work with family life and a serious leisure pursuit and Cohen et al. (2009) explore the complexities inherent within navigating work and home life priorities. In my own case, a volunteering role that I took on in my spare time provided the basis for developing an autoethnographic perspective on the relationship between the individual and the organization in digital volunteering but the focus, inevitably, included reflection on how I found time for the role amid other commitments.

Through its focus on interrogating the experience of the individual, autoethnography also offers some distinctive advantages for studying the uniquely digital qualities of digital work. The focus on the tacit aspects of organizational processes fits well with the qualities of digital communications in so far as these often involve uncertainties, ambiguities, and the need for pragmatic solutions rather than complete knowledge. The autoethnographer is able to home in on the processes that we use to make sense of getting work done in these conditions (Hine 2015). Markham's (1998) early study of life online employed a version of autoethnography to explore how digital communications make sense in terms of place, tools, and ways of being. Subsequently, Henning (2012) and Kruse (2013) have used autoethnography to interrogate the online learning experience, documenting the affective qualities of online learning and the experience of barriers and challenges alongside affordances. The autoethnographic perspective allows us to explore beyond the aspects of experience that people may be able to articulate in interviews. Autoethnography can examine the affective dimensions of experiences and explore the qualities of silences and uncertainties as much as what is explicitly known and possible to say (Hine 2020). The flexibility of autoethnography allows us to explore in a responsive way the tendency of our everyday experiences to meander across an array of digital platforms and devices in a fluid and unpredictable manner. As Winkler (2013) argues, identity in a working context is not a stable thing but is formulated and reformulated afresh across the working day. Autoethnography offers the flexibility to engage with this process rather than relying on the retrospective and stabilized accounts that an interviewee might offer.

O'Riordan (2014) argues for autoethnography in digital settings as a means for information systems researchers to interrogate digital ways of being. One key feature of distributed organizations is that workers are rarely co-present and thus may be unable to observe their co-workers on a regular basis. In such a situation it can potentially be challenging to develop a sense of oneself as a worker and develop an understanding of the rhythms and pace of the organization. The traces of themselves that digital workers leave on the platforms they use, through the edits that they make, the links that they code, the messages they send, and the documents that they create, offer traces of labour that digital workers can use to make sense of themselves and others (Beaulieu 2005; Beaulieu and Simakova 2006; Geiger and Ribes 2011). Making sense of these traces of labour is, however, coupled with making sense of emotions and silences (Hine 2020) and here autoethnography provides us a way to navigate the role both of what is explicit and what goes unrecorded within the experience of digital work. Webster and Randle (2016) argue that the virtual workers on whom they focus experience challenges emanating from spatial dispersion, precarity, and the dismantling of boundaries within their lives. While my own position is far more privileged and secure than these workers and my dependence on the digital volunteering role is very limited, there are some points here for reflection and comparison on the extent to which the role threatens my boundaries and feels at once intrusive and insecure.

The process of autoethnography is as much a process of reflecting through writing as it is of participant observation. An autoethnographic project often does not contain a clear division between a phase of data collection and a phase of writing up as would be typical of many research methods. Indeed, data collection is somewhat of a misnomer since, while an autoethnographer will often take notes and collect material that they encounter in the situation that they are writing about, these research materials are not considered as a stable and coherent dataset as much as they are resources to fuel reflection. This fluid approach to data feeds into an approach to writing that aims to be faithful to the experience that it wishes to evoke but without a reliance on evidencing specific claims with items of data. Autoethnographic writing takes a variety of forms that can encompass overtly fictional formats such as storytelling and poetry alongside more evidently academic styles of writing. In the example that forms the topic for this chapter, I reconstruct events in a narrative style. The materials that I draw upon are derived from over 10 years of experience in a digital volunteer role and include some fieldnotes and archived materials including email exchanges, training materials, and screenshots. There is no complete archive of my experiences. The keeping of fieldnotes is at best sporadic and occasioned when something specific draws my attention as potentially theoretically interesting such as when I want to closely interrogate a particular form of interaction or remember a key event.

Given the focus on personal experience, complex ethical issues arise in autoethnography and can potentially become intense (Sambrook and Herrmann 2018). We have a duty to stay on the right side of narrating an evocative and theoretically significant story without stepping into mere gossip or sensationalist commentary on the actions of others. It is rare for an autoethnographer to seek informed consent from all of those featured in their narratives, for these people are not active participants in a data collection process. The autoethnography is not about the characters who feature in it as much as it is about how we make sense of them as features of our own lived experience. This does not mean, however, that they may not read what we write and feel unfairly commented upon or exposed. Andrew (2017) suggests a systematic approach to evaluating the ethical challenges in autoethnography, identifying the parts of texts that offer potentially problematic exposure and then screening these according to the ideas that they develop and the duties of the autoethnographer to others. Without applying such a systematic approach, I have operated some sensitivity based on what I owe to my co-worker and the organization and have fictionalized and blurred some key details in the account that follows in order to make the theoretical point without an overly intrusive commentary. This is a personal judgement and potentially fallible. As Wall (2008) describes, we may come to a workable solution that navigates the demands of authenticity and respect, but thanks to the levels of self-disclosure involved in autoethnography, anxieties will often linger about how well we have discharged our responsibilities to those who feature in our stories.

Notes on the Experience of Digital Volunteering

As I sit at the desk in the corner of my living room typing this text, I am conscious, in a niggling, nagging, insistent way of various other things that I should be doing. Technically, my working hours are over for the day, but of course my chapter is long overdue and the notion of contracted hours is less significant than the apologies that I will owe my co-editors if I take even longer to get the chapter done. But still ... there is the uncleaned bathroom, the question of whether it's time I should check if the children have done their homework, my own unanswered emails, the growing heaps of filing and, if I really dig into my guilt list, there are the life projects (and the DIY projects) unfinished, the promises of self-improvement that are perpetually unfulfilled, the things I just never get round to. Life is a constant flow of micro-prioritizations, choosing this task over that one, leaving this undone for that, balancing my imposter syndrome against mother guilt and social embarrassment. And, along the way, often parking the bigger picture in the interests of momentary pleasure, choosing to do some things because they're fun, because they don't get me anywhere at all, because what harm could another game of solitaire do before I get down to work. Amidst all of these time pressures, why on earth did I choose to take on another role, not just a role but a responsibility and this time one that does not pay, does not garner me any thanks, does not contribute to my family or working life and is, in fact, largely unseen and unacknowledged? If I do this role effectively, nobody notices that I have done it, apart from one person that I have met face-to-face just once, in over 10 years of doing the role.

This role that I mysteriously have chosen to commit myself to is a digital volunteering role. I am one of two moderators for a local list that allows people to advertise items that they no longer need, with the aim of promoting re-use and reducing landfill. According to the rules of the parent organization, all items are to be freely given and must be legal and suitable for all ages. The group bans the advertising of live animals, for welfare reasons. My role is to act as moderator for this local group, assessing any advertisements that are flagged up by the automatic filtering system as potentially problematic and either approving them or rejecting them and notifying the member who made the post. Occasional emails come in as one member complains about another or about the length of time it has taken for their message to be approved. The work comes in as a steady trickle throughout the day and hence, as I sit at my desk typing this, one of the intrusive niggles that threatens to take me away from my current task is the thought that it is time I check if any new messages have come in for moderation.

There is no strict schedule for doing this checking work. There is no rota and my co-moderator and I do not have any clear sense of which of us is on duty at any one time. We correspond by email occasionally when there are policy decisions to be made and in those emails we are friendly and informal, we joke or tease one another a little but considering our decade of cooperation we talk very little about ourselves, our wider lives, or indeed how we fit this work into our day. We share little snippets of information, but we've never had what I would call a conversation. I have a very hazy memory even of what he looks like, having just the one brief encounter on my doorstep when he came to collect an item that I had offered on the site and we were briefly site users together rather than moderators. I have very little sense of him as a rounded social being but I know he has a good sense of humour and he has been compassionate a couple of times when I've had to tell him I'm having a tough time and need to step back for a bit. Our interactions are quite limited in terms of direct interaction but I do still have a sense of him as a co-worker, Sometimes I sense changes in the rhythm of his work: if I find myself checking in for the first time in the morning to a longer list of messages to vet than usual I wonder if he is on holiday or unwell and I pay heightened attention for the next few days until his working rhythm returns to normal. I wonder where he's been—but I don't ask. Sometimes, I confess, I accidentally on purpose leave a tricky decision for him, pretending to myself that I did not have time to deal with this complex issue just now and am delighted when I next check to find that he has in fact dealt with the vexed question of whether we should we allow baby milk or contact lens solution, whether to issue a warning about publishing a personal phone number. I wonder if he knows I do this. I think he probably does but he has never called me out on my sneaky behaviour in leaving him to do some of the tricky stuff.

We do this voluntary work as the lowliest members in a hierarchy that is topped off by a central coordinator based in another country and contains a network of national and area coordinators. Appointment is through an application to area coordinators, and acceptance leads to a programme of online training that must be completed satisfactorily before being appointed as moderator of a local group. The training covers practicalities of using the site and warnings about legal responsibilities that inform the acceptable usage of the site that we are to police. Once trained, we have largely been left to manage our own day-to-day work and make our own decisions, with a few notable occasions when we have been contacted by our area coordinators to instruct us to carry out a change deemed necessary by the central organization or to follow up on a complaint. We do our own thing, but we are conscious now, since being warned, that we are expected to be not too lenient and not too strict in what we let through. We do not receive any form of appraisal and nobody seems to monitor on a day-by-day or even month-by-month basis what we are doing. We only seem to get contact from our area administrators when there has been a complaint or when an edict comes down from the central coordinator that all moderators are to make a desired change. On the whole I do my volunteering work on a basis of trying not to get into trouble, making each moderating decision first and foremost to get it off the 'to do' list but, alongside that, trying to make the right decision according to my training.

I began this volunteering role without an intention for it to be research, but the urge to make sense of the experience increasingly called on my sociological sensitivities. Subsequently, my experiences as a moderator have been rendered as an autoethnography of the ways in which I make sense of myself as a worker and how this meaning-making is linked with the digital nature of the work. This is a form of work that connects me with an organization, but, in the form that it is conducted, much of the organization remains opaque to me, and I to it, and my relationship with a co-worker is built out of tiny fragments of interaction and traces of action. There is insufficient space here to explore findings in any depth, but in the interests of the methodological discussion it will be useful to highlight some key themes that become available to explore thanks to the micro-level of attention that autoethnography makes available. It becomes possible to focus on the socio-material embedding of the work, as I carve out the possibility of doing the work on the devices available to me and the temporal pressures I face. While most of my paid work is done on a desktop computer, I deliberately keep the moderation work on another device, usually a tablet that I grab as I move into a domestic or leisure frame of mind. I have a set of routinized practices that allow the volunteer work to fit into the interstices of the day—I have found ways of getting it done without consciously carving out the time to do it. As well as socio-material and temporal aspects of the work, autoethnography also allows me to attend to the various accountabilities that I experience, as I understand my practices being ordered through regulations and becoming accountable to diverse others. I am able to examine the ways in which others involved in the work become real to me, and I to them and where we remain oblivious to one another.

As autoethnographer I am able to switch my attention between the minutiae of individual moments of work and the broader biographical narrative of a volunteer within which they sit. My feelings about being a volunteer and my orientation to the organization have shifted and fluctuated. Through experiences of training and as a process of development from novice to relative expert, I have shifted from everything being notable and all decisions being difficult to a sense of routine and ease with the majority of the work. While once I might have wanted there to be someone around whose opinion I could ask, now I rarely feel that. There are still, however, occasional difficult decisions that disrupt the sense of routine, when I feel the stress levels rising and when I feel a heightened sense of accountability for whatever decision I choose to make. At those moments, again, I feel alone and I might call out to my co-worker, sending him an email in the hope that he'll reassure me and help me to navigate the difficult territory. We might both make the wrong decision but I will feel better to have some support.

Still, after all of these years, I experience ambiguities of belonging, feeling myself both an insider and an outsider to the organization. There is a mailing list that moderators can use to discuss issues that affect us all, but I find myself feeling like an observer rather than a participant, struggling to apply the issues they discuss to my own circumstances. In the day-to-day practice of the work I find myself more focused on not having anybody complain about me than the higher goal or sense of a moral communion with the organization as a whole. As Allahyari (2000) found, in the day-to-day business of voluntary work, moral community is a rather shifting and ambiguous thing. We can talk about it in sound bites and offer a version of 'why I volunteer' when asked, but in many instances it's not a passionate commitment but a more fluid conjunction of circumstances, life stages, a sense of needing a narrative of ourselves, and ebbs and flows across the other challenges of the working week and family life. I continue to do this volunteering because it has become a part of my daily life, because I would feel sad not to do it and because it feels like a good thing to do. When I draw conclusions about the nature of digital volunteering, I can concur with Amichai-Hamburger (2008) that digital volunteering provides flexible and accessible opportunities for life-affirming and self-actualizing activity but the autoethnographic insight gives me perspective on this as a set of socio-material practices and active and highly contextual meaning-making, rather than an outcome that proceeds from the technology itself nor indeed from the inherent rightness of the cause for which I volunteer.

Autoethnography as a Pre-cursor to Interviews

Autoethnography can by definition only give us insight into one set of experiences and, thus, it is inherently limited in its ability to generalize. I can make wider inferences from my own experiences, as I do in concluding that volunteering as a form of digital work relies on achieving a workable set of socio-material practices. From my own experiences I can suggest that this work makes sense through frames of reference that involve both the detail of how individual tasks are carried out satisfactorily according to various sets of accountabilities and the broader frame of reference that provides satisfaction in terms of living life well. These conclusions are an abstraction away from my everyday experience but leave open the question of how this might play out for other digital volunteers, doing different work and in other organizations. In order to address this question, I carried out a series of interviews aiming to explore themes raised in the autoethnography within the experience of other digital volunteers. Semi-structured interviews were chosen as the medium that would allow a focused conversation centred on key themes of theoretical interest from the ethnography and yet open enough that they could respond to the specific circumstances of digital volunteers working in quite different contexts. Fourteen interviewees were recruited via LinkedIn, searching for potential participants in the UK who mentioned digital, virtual, or social media volunteering in their profiles. Potential interviewees were sent private messages and those who responded positively were sent an information sheet and consent form and invited to choose their preferred medium for the interview. The majority were carried out on video conference via Skype. It is important to note that interviewees were selected because they self-described as volunteers on LinkedIn and we may therefore infer that this means of recruitment selectively targets those for whom their volunteering is seen as a salient part of their professional profile. It should be noted that I do not list myself in this way on my own LinkedIn profile and hence would not have featured as a participant in the interview study even though I am the focus of the autoethnography.

With interviewees, I explored a set of issues prompted by curiosity about how far my own experiences of digital volunteering and my abstracted conclusions about socio-material practices and meaning-making were shared by them. Interviews began with their biographies of volunteering, discussing how they were attracted to the opportunity in the first instance, what training they undertook, the forms of ongoing support and technical assistance available to them and how their commitment changed over time. We discussed the timing of their voluntary efforts, their routines and the competing demands on their time. We also explored their relations with line managers and co-workers and whether they felt part of a team. I asked about their experiences of any forms of monitoring, appraisal or feedback and the extent to which they knew and interacted with co-workers. I pursued open questions around whether the role worked out as they had expected it to and what were the key satisfactions and frustrations that they experienced in relation to the role.

In analysing the interview responses it became clear that my own experiences, taken as a detailed set of insights on how digital volunteering work is done, were not generalizable. A wide variety of forms of work were undertaken, with running a social media presence for an organization the most common but also website maintenance, technical support, content moderation in online forums, and content production for social media. Across interviewees and between interviewees and myself there were some very different spatial and temporal organizations of working and domestic lives. Some interviewees had children, some lived alone, and some were still students living partly in a parental home, and each of these came with different time constraints. The different forms of work came with expectations about when the work would be done and created their own rhythms. Online content moderation is quite reactive, for example, while social media work is accompanied by expectations about maintaining a stream of activity. Traces of other workers were available in different forms and to different timescales depending on the kind of organization and the work activities. Online content moderators could often see their co-workers in action decision-by-decision, while content producers often worked in relative isolation and delivered their work in batches. The different working arrangements constituted different power relations, just as Halford (2005) found for hybrid workspaces where people combined home working with some use of organizational spaces. I did not ask interviewees directly about power, but it became clear in interviews where they felt themselves to have agency and where the limits on that agency were experienced.

Making sense of oneself as a (digital voluntary) worker involved both the moment-by-moment and the broader picture and often was seen by the volunteers as a specific phase in one's life. As I worked my way through the various interviews I became aware of different timescapes within which volunteering became meaningful to interviewees. My own autoethnography is largely about immediate time pressure, with the volunteering something I manage in the present but also something I see as continuing indefinitely. By contrast, for many interviewees the frame within which volunteering became meaningful oriented towards a future in which they might gain a paid role that made use of these skills. Digital volunteering was commonly seen as a form of aspirational labour (Duffy 2016) or hope labour (Allan 2019), that might offer valuable experience leading to paid employment in future. This is not to suggest that the present was not meaningful or even sometimes problematic for volunteers nor that they were not committed to the cause of the organizations for whom they volunteered, but the different temporal framings cross-cut the experience and gave a different meaning to the day-to-day challenges in a way that was not the case for my own situation.

To some extent, different meanings of digital volunteering between interviewees and myself connected with life stage as, unlike me, many of my interviewees were currently in or recently graduated from university or were facing an enforced career change and this was strongly associated with an aspirational motivation for online volunteering. In terms of the specific characteristics of their volunteering experience, the digital volunteers that I interviewed were very different from myself.

However, the broader conclusions, about the importance of building a workable set of socio-material practices and about the interplay between multiple frames of reference that constitute a sense of meaning moment-by-moment and in terms of wider life narratives apply across the board. As Halford et al. (2015) outline, the third sector comprises hybrid work forces of paid workers and volunteers and takes forms highly responsive to place. This observation is offered as simultaneously an encouragement to study specificities of experience and an impetus to do comparative studies rather than extrapolating from a single site. This potentially applies as much to the particular configurations of organizational locations and communications infrastructure for digital volunteers as it does to the geographic locations of onsite volunteers. Each digital volunteer experience is highly responsive to the organizational form and the characteristics of the digital technologies through which it operates but also to the life circumstances of the volunteers themselves.

The interviews encouraged me to disaggregate the digital volunteer experience, to step back from assuming the universality of my own experience and instead suggested that, with more interviews to explore a wider array of experiences, I might be able to derive a typology of organizational forms and socio-material arrangements for digital volunteering into which I could insert myself. With this wider study, it might then be possible to explore in more depth how the various organizational forms and technological solutions feed into the tensions and conflicts experienced by digital volunteers and the problems with a sense of belonging (McGarvey et al. 2019). It may seem paradoxical that I begin this chapter as an autoethnographer and end by advocating a large-scale interview study. It is important to note, however, that the autoethnography framed the initial sociological puzzle about how digital volunteering makes sense and without the autoethnography there would have been a loss in terms of the questions to ask, the issues to delve into and the readings to place onto people's answers. While the autoethnography framed the interviews in this way, throughout the interviews I needed to beware of the risk of translating interviewees' concerns into my own. This required a very careful reading of interview transcripts to make sure that I grounded my analysis in what interviewees said and not what I thought they should say or had suggested to them that they should say. Making a shift from autoethnography to interview study involved being conscious to value the moments of surprise and difference as much as the moments of recognition.

Conclusion

In justifying autoethnography as a method for studying digital work, and digital volunteering in particular, I proposed it as a practical response to the difficulties of observing the minutiae of work done on a temporally and spatially unpredictable basis across an array of digital platforms. I have shown that an autoethnographic study of digital volunteering can help to unpack the ways in which minute digital traces of the work of others build into our sense of selves as co-engaged in meaningful endeavour (Amichai-Hamburger 2008), but at the same time can be lacking in the rich sense of co-presence that allows us to experience volunteering as being part of a moral community (Allahyari 2000), resulting in a risk of feeling the kind of disconnect from the organization that surveys hint at (McGarvey et al. 2019). While interviews allowed me to explore these issues in a more diverse array of settings than I could experience myself, the autoethnographic insights shaped the focus of those interviews and sensitized me to issues I might not otherwise have recognized as important.

This approach offers potential for research into other forms of digital work beyond volunteering. The flexibility of autoethnography allows engagement with the unpredictable nature of digital work and its shifting temporality and spatiality. The very personal focus of autoethnography allows us to interrogate how it feels to be a digital worker, to explore where the challenges, uncertainties, and satisfactions lie and to understand how a sense of meaning is assembled out of the uncertain traces that are available to show us our co-workers and build our sense of the organization. O'Riordan (2014) suggests that we should evaluate autoethnography according to the extent to which it delivers rich insights, resonates with an audience even if they are unfamiliar with the field, makes a contribution to our understanding, and is marked by sincerity (as more appropriate than verifiability). While space is too limited in this chapter fully to demonstrate these qualities, I hope that at least the potential to do so in the context of digital work has been demonstrated.

References

Allahyari, R. A. 2000. *Visions of Charity: Volunteer Workers and Moral Community*. University of California Press.

Allan, K. 2019. Volunteering as hope labour: The potential value of unpaid work experience for the un- and under-employed. *Culture, Theory and Critique*, 60(1): pp. 66–83.

Amichai-Hamburger, Y. 2008. Potential and promise of online volunteering. *Computers in Human Behavior*, 24(2): pp. 544–62.

Anderson, L. 2006. Analytic autoethnography. *Journal of Contemporary Ethnography*, 35(4): pp. 373–95.

Anderson, L. 2011. Time is of the essence: An analytic autoethnography of family, work, and serious leisure. *Symbolic Interaction*, 34(2): pp. 133–57.

Andrew, S. 2017. *Searching for an Autoethnographic Ethic*. Routledge.

Beaulieu, A. 2005. Sociable hyperlinks: An ethnographic approach to connectivity. In Hine, C. (ed.), *Virtual Methods: Issues in Social Research on the Internet* (pp. 183–98). Berg.

Beaulieu, A., and Simakova, E. 2006. Textured connectivity: An ethnographic approach to understanding the timescape of hyperlinks. *Cybermetrics: International Journal of Scientometrics, Informetrics and Bibliometrics*, 10(1). http://cybermetrics.cindoc.csic.es/articles/v10i1p5.html

Boyle, M., and Parry, K. 2007. *Telling the whole story: The case for organizational autoethnography*. Culture and Organization, 13(3): pp. 185–90.

Autoethnography and the Digital Volunteer

Chang, H. 2016. *Autoethnography as Method*. Taylor & Francis.

Cohen, L., Duberley, J., and Musson, G. 2009. Work–life balance? An autoethnographic exploration of everyday home–work dynamics. *Journal of Management Inquiry*, 18(3): pp. 229–41.

Cravens, J., and Ellis, S. J. 2014. *The LAST Virtual Volunteering Guidebook: Fully Integrating Online Service into Volunteer Involvement*. Energize Inc.

Doloriert, C., and Sambrook, S. 2012. Organizational autoethnography. *Journal of Organizational Ethnography*, 1(1): pp. 83–95.

Duffy, B. E. 2016. The romance of work: Gender and aspirational labour in the digital culture industries. *International Journal of Cultural Studies*, 19(4): pp. 441–57.

Ellis, C. 2004. *The Ethnographic I: A Methodological Novel about Autoethnography*. Alta Mira.

Fujiwara, D., Oroyemi, P., and McKinnon, E. 2013. Wellbeing and Civil Society. Estimating the Value of Volunteering using Subjective Wellbeing Data. Department for Work and Pensions Working Paper no 112. Cabinet Office/Department for Work and Pensions. https://www.gov.uk/government/uploads/system/uploads/attachment_data/file/221227/WP112.pdf.

Geiger, R. S., and Ribes, D. 2011. Trace ethnography: Following coordination through documentary practices. In *Proceedings of the 2011 44th Hawaii International Conference on System Sciences* (pp. 1–10). IEEE Computer Society.

Haldane, A. G. 2014. In Giving, how much do we receive? The social value of volunteering. Speech given by A. G. Haldane, Chief Economist, Bank of England. A Pro Bono Economics lecture to the Society of Business Economists, London. https://www.bankofengland.co.uk/-/media/boe/files/speech/2014/in-giving-how-much-do-we-receive-the-social-value-of-volunteering.

Halford, S. 2005. Hybrid workspace: Re-spatialisations of work, organisation and management. *New Technology, Work and Employment*, 20(1): pp. 19–33.

Halford, S., Leonard, P., and Bruce, K. 2015. Geographies of labour in the third sector: Making hybrid workforces in place. *Environment and Planning A*, 47(11): pp. 2355–72.

Henning, T. B. 2012. Writing professor as adult learner: An autoethnography of online professional development. *Journal of Asynchronous Learning Networks*, 16(2): pp. 9–26.

Hine, C. 2015. *Ethnography for the Internet: Embedded, Embodied and Everyday*. Bloomsbury Publishing.

Hine, C. 2020. Strategies for reflexive ethnography in the smart home: Autoethnography of silence and emotion. *Sociology*, 54(1): pp. 22–36.

Jochum, V., and Paylor, J. 2013. New ways of Giving Time: Opportunities and Challenges in Micro-volunteering. A Literature Review. http://www.ivr.org/image/stories/NESTA_literature_review_final_0502131.pdf

Kruse, N. B. 2013. Locating 'The Road to Lisdoonvarna' via autoethnography: Pathways, barriers and detours in self-directed online music learning . *Journal of Music, Technology & Education*, 5(3): pp. 293–308.

Liu, H. K., Harrison, Y. D., Lai, J. J. K., Chikoto, G. L., and Jones-Lungo, K. 2016. Online and Virtual Volunteering. In Horton Smith, D., Stebbins, R. A., and Grotz, J. (eds), *The*

Palgrave Handbook of Volunteering, Civic Participation, and Nonprofit Associations (pp. 290–310). Palgrave Macmillan.

Markham, A. N. 1998. *Life Online: Researching Real Experience in Virtual Space*. Altamira Press.

McGarvey, A., Jochum, V., Davies, J., Dobbs, J., and Hornung, L. 2019. Time well spent. A national survey on the volunteer experience. https://www.ncvo.org.uk/policy-and-research/volunteering-policy/research/time-well-spent .

Musick, M. A, and Wilson, J. 2007. *Volunteers: A Social Profile*. Indiana University Press.

O Riordan, N. 2014. Autoethnography: Proposing a new research method for information systems research. In ECIS 2014 22nd European Conference on Information Systems, Tel Aviv, Israel, 9–11 June 2014. https://aisel.aisnet.org/ecis2014/proceedings/track03/6/.

Payne, C. S. 2017. Changes in the value and division of unpaid volunteering in the UK: 2000 to 2015. Newport: Office for National Statistics. https://backup.ons.gov.uk/wp-content/uploads/sites/3/2017/03/Changes-in-the-value-and-division-of-unpaid-volunteering-in-the-UK-2000-to-2015.pdf.

Pritchard, K., Symon, G., Hine, C., and Mumford, C. 2016. Reconfiguring volunteering in the digital age. Paper presented at NCVO Voluntary Sector and Volunteering Research conference. Nottingham, UK.

Redman, T., Snape, E., and Ashurst, C. 2009. Location, Location, Location: Does Place of Work Really Matter?. *British Journal of Management*, 20: pp. S171–S81.

Reed-Danahay, D. (ed.) 1997. *Auto/ethnography: Rewriting the Self and the Social*. Berg.

Roberts, S., and Doyle, T. 2017. Understanding crowdsourcing and volunteer engagement: Case studies for hurricanes, data processing, and floods. In Molinari, D., Menoni, S., and Ballio, F. (eds), *Flood Damage Survey and Assessment: New Insights from Research and Practice* (pp. 121–34). American Geophysical Union.

Sambrook, S., and Herrmann, A. F. 2018. Organisational autoethnography: Possibilities, politics and pitfalls. *Journal of Organizational Ethnography*, 7(3): pp. 222–34.

Sewell, G., and Taskin, L. 2015. Out of sight, out of mind in a new world of work? Autonomy, control, and spatiotemporal scaling in telework. *Organization Studies*, 36(11): pp. 1507–29.

Sparkes, A. C. 2002. Autoethnography: Self-indulgence or something more? In Bochner, A. P. and Ellis, C., (eds), *Ethnographically Speaking: Autoethnography, Literature, and Aesthetics* (pp. 209–32). AltaMira.

Wall, S. 2008. Easier said than done: Writing an autoethnography. *International Journal of Qualitative Methods*, 7(1): pp. 38–53.

Webster, J., and Randle, K. 2016. Positioning Virtual workers within space, time, and social dynamics. In Webster, J., and Randle, K. (eds), *Virtual Workers and the Global Labour Market* (pp. 3–34). Springer.

Winkler, I. 2013. Moments of identity formation and reformation: A day in the working life of an academic. *Journal of Organizational Ethnography*, 2(2): pp. 191–209.

9

Research Methods to Study and Empower Crowd Workers

Saiph Savage, Carlos Toxtli, and Eber Betanzos-Torres

Introduction

Individuals are beginning to discover that digital platforms offer work opportunities and to find that they can earn a living from this work (Kuhn and Maleki 2017). Pew Research Center reported that by mid-2016 around 20 million Americans said that they had earned money through labour they completed on digital platforms in the previous year (Smith 2016). Jobs on digital platforms are expected to add $2.7 trillion to the global GDP by 2025. These digital platforms are typically coined 'crowd marketplaces' because employers offer temporary jobs in crowdsourcing platforms to workers on the platform (who are thus coined 'crowd workers'). For a growing number of individuals, crowd markets have become an important new source of income (Abraham et al. 2018). An especially popular crowd market is Amazon Mechanical Turk (MTurk) (Amazon 2020). The labour that is posted on crowd markets like MTurk is usually known as 'human-intelligence-tasks' (Eickhoff and de Vries 2011). These tasks are tasks that artificial intelligence (AI) by itself cannot do and hence human intelligence is necessary. Together, crowd markets not only help to power our AI industry, but these markets also inject millions of new jobs into the economy (Smith 2019).

The new jobs that the AI industry has created on crowd markets are essential to enable the real-world deployment of intelligent systems. Part of these new jobs typically focuses on labelling data for machine learning models (Sorokin and Forsyth 2008). For instance, a number of tasks on MTurk focus on having human workers label where pedestrians appear in blurry videos (Hall and Perona 2015), which can be difficult for machines to do on their own. The labelled videos are then fed into machine learning models that use the data to learn to detect pedestrians from non-pedestrians. These machine learning models can then be inserted into autonomous vehicles. Indeed, the human labour behind our AI has powered self-driving cars, voice-based virtual assistants and search results with minimum hate speech (Young et al. 2018). However, the crowd workers powering the AI industry are often invisible to end-users. Their invisibility has exacerbated power imbalances where workers

Saiph Savage, Carlos Toxtli, and Eber Betanzos-Torres, *Research Methods to Study and Empower Crowd Workers.*
In: *Research Methods for Digital Work and Organization.* Edited by Gillian Symon, Katrina Pritchard, and Christine Hine,
Oxford University Press. © Oxford University Press (2021). DOI: 10.1093/oso/9780198860679.003.0009

are often paid below the minimum wage (Hara et al. 2019) and have limited career growth (Deng and Joshi 2013). Part of the problem emerges because much of the algorithmic designs and platform choices of these crowd markets have focused on privileging employers and have not considered how they might harm workers. These types of designs can lead to unintended consequences that involve cruelty towards workers that is perpetrated by algorithms (henceforth referred to as 'algorithmic cruelty') for example platforms that automatically terminate workers (Jagabathula et al. 2014), resulting in workers losing their livelihoods and experiencing stress (Gray and Suri 2019).

In this chapter, we outline how human–computer interaction can re-envision the reality of crowd workers to improve their labour conditions. In particular, we present design criteria for tools that can serve to transform crowd markets and drive positive social change. Our design criteria are based on social theory that highlights how humans flourish when connected with the social essence of work (Yeoman 2014). For this purpose, we develop systems and computational methods that create on-demand 'professional leagues' for crowd workers. Our leagues focus on orchestrating workers to produce collective action while having social conversations. This collective social action enables: (1) increasing workers' wages (Savage et al. 2020); (2) enabling workers' skill development (Chiang et al. 2018b; Toxtli and Savage 2020; Hanrahan et al. 2020); and (3) driving justice in employers' evaluations of workers (Gaikwad et al. 2015). Unlike prior work that concentrated on primarily providing better communication and transparency (Huang and Fu 2013), the design criteria we present here open a new area of research focused on computationally orchestrating crowd workers to actively drive positive change in their professional lives.

Prior Research Methods to Investigate Crowd Work

Prior methods used for investigating crowd work can be broadly divided into two main strands: (1) qualitative studies for understanding crowd work (Hilton and Azzam 2019); (2) tools and platforms for improving crowd work (Kaplan et al. 2018). In the following section we present an overview of these methods and discuss where our research methods fall within this schema.

Qualitative studies for understanding crowd work

To understand the new work dynamics that are emerging in these crowd markets, some research has focused on conducting surveys and interviews with crowd workers and their employers to start to understand: how these crowd markets are functioning (Berg 2015; Hara et al. 2019; Kasunic et al. 2019); the type of dynamics that are emerging between the stakeholders of these markets (workers, employers, and platform owners) (Toxtli et al. 2019); and the challenges and opportunities that emerge in these markets (Slivkins and Vaughan 2014). Several of these qualitative research studies have been critical to understanding the precarious conditions in which crowd workers operate as well as helping researchers and practitioners to understand the unjust power dynamics and algorithmic cruelty that takes place within crowd markets (Gray and Suri 2019, Toxtli et al. 2021). We build on these previous studies to influence and improve crowd work. Additionally, the studies serve to identify critical points we can improve through systems design.

However, it is important to note that these qualitative studies based on self-reports from workers, while they are rich in information about workers' direct experiences in crowd markets, generally lack quantitative data based on direct measurement of crowd markets. Data from direct measurement or observation are important because they can help us to understand crowd markets from another perspective. For instance, crowd workers might state via surveys or interviews that they have low wages, and that the tasks they do within the crowd market do not facilitate their career growth. Without explicit log data, it can be difficult to understand just how low wages are. It is also difficult to understand the exact characteristics of the labour that crowd workers are exposed to, and that might not help their growth. This limited view makes it difficult to design adequate technologies and socio-technical interventions that can create and provide transformative change within crowd markets.

Tools and platforms for improving crowd work

Other research has focused on designing tools and platforms that aim to directly improve crowd work (Jarrahi and Sutherland 2019). The vast majority of research in this space has focused on studying the platform and system designs that are most appropriate for producing higher quality labour in these crowd markets while reducing costs (time, wages, etc.) (Allahbakhsh et al. 2013). These investigations are very much focused on the interests of employers and the owners of crowd markets (Singer and Mittal 2013). Crowd workers under these settings are sometimes viewed as 'clogs' in a pipeline whose operation needs to be optimized (Bernstein et al. 2012). These designs have led to circumstances where workers are earning less than minimum wage and have little opportunity to develop themselves (Saito et al. 2019b).

In part inspired by the qualitative research methods that identified the difficult living situations of crowd workers, a portion of investigations have also focused on devising tools and platforms that are more worker-centric. Part of the narrative around the worker-centric research is that crowd markets entail algorithmic cruelty in part because these markets have not been designed to provide transparency to workers. Economists consider that a market is transparent when all actors can access information about the market, such as products, services, or capital assets (Strathern 2000). The problem is that crowd markets have, for the most part, limited the amount of information that workers have about employers. Usually, employers (the individuals who post the labour they want workers to do) are granted access to information concerning the events in the marketplace, while workers have a much more limited perspective (Irani and Silberman 2013, 2016). For example, Amazon Mechanical Turk allows employers to view the previous performances and interactions that workers have had on the platform (Hara et al. 2018); while workers can discern very little about what employers have done previously (e.g. it is not possible to easily gauge whether a certain employer is paying unfair wages to workers, or whether the employer is actually a fraud looking to steal workers' data or obtain free labour; Irani and Silberman 2013; Gadiraju and Demartini 2019). This lack of transparency for workers can lead them to invest significant time in completing certain labour but receive anywhere from inadequate to no compensation. Six Silberman discusses how the lack of transparency on crowd markets affects workers earnings: 'A wide range of processes that shape platform-based workers' ability to find work and receive payment for work completed are, on many platforms, opaque' (Metall 2016).

To begin addressing the issue of transparency, Irani and colleagues (Irani and Silberman 2013) explored creating computational tools and forums through which workers could share information about crowd markets. Practitioners also started following similar efforts with the goal of empowering workers to share concrete and useful information about the crowd markets in which they worked (ChrisTurk 2018). The goal was that this information could help workers better navigate the crowd market and ultimately lead workers to have better working conditions. These tools and forums provide crowd workers with otherwise unavailable information about the employers, tasks, and expected payments within a crowd market. For instance, the computational tool of Turkopticon[1] (a popular tool used to bring workers transparency) allows workers to obtain an overview of the expected hourly wage they would receive if they worked for a particular employer. This value is calculated based on what other workers have reported receiving when completing tasks for that employer.

However, while an ever-increasing number of workers are using these tools for transparency (Kaplan et al. 2018), only a fraction of workers' earnings are well above the minimum wage (Hara et al. 2018). Additionally, despite the tools, crowd workers are still stuck without clear ways to develop themselves and grow within the marketplace. Perhaps part of the problem is that utilizing transparency tools to grow professionally is not straightforward? Each tool displays several different metrics that provide workers with transparency information about different aspects of the market (e.g. how much is a given employer expected to pay? How often does the employer reject workers' labour?). This leaves it unclear which metrics a worker could use to help them to build a career pathway within a crowd market. This complexity has likely led most workers to employ transparency tools ineffectively (Kaplan et al. 2018; Saito et al. 2019b).

For workers alone, it can be hard to learn how to navigate crowd markets to ensure fair wages and professional skill development. The design criteria that we present build on the prior work described above to present computational mechanisms and tools that create 'on-demand leagues' that inform workers on how to effectively and collectively use transparency information to grow professionally in crowd markets. The leagues focus on helping workers to use transparency information effectively through directed social conversations in order to construct career pathways on crowd markets. We showcase how we can use these types of design criteria to: (1) increase workers' wages (Kasunic et al. 2019; Savage et al. 2020); (2) enable workers' skill development (Chiang 2018b; Toxtli and Savage 2020); and (3) drive justice in employers' evaluations on workers (Toxtli et al. 2020). Unlike prior work that concentrated on providing more transparency for crowd workers (Huang and Fu 2013), the design criteria that we present here open a new area of research focused on computationally orchestrating workers to actively drive positive change in their professional lives through the use of transparency.

Research Framework: Computational Worker Leagues

In this chapter, we present our overarching research framework for studying crowd workers: 'Computational Worker Leagues'. Our Computational Worker Leagues are sets of tools that allow crowd workers to collaborate with other workers in an on-demand manner, to address and pursue any professional goals they set forward. These tools also offer the additional benefit of collecting quantitative log information about the conditions of the crowd market and present researchers with detailed information about workers' current markets and the challenges they face. Through this quantitative log data, researchers are empowered to design improved tools for crowd workers. Prior work had to infer the conditions from survey studies or interviews. Our framework, in contrast, offers ways for researchers to be able to study crowd markets 'in the wild' from a quantitative perspective.

Our Computational Worker Leagues tool uses a crowdsourcing technique called 'data brokers'. Our approach draws on the assistance of crowd workers who have become efficient in interpreting the information embedded in crowd markets to pursue professional goals. For instance, they may have become very effective at identifying what information to use to earn higher wages. We recruit workers ('data brokers') that have been able to achieve particular professional goals and enable them to share advice with other workers. Our approach also incorporates techniques from machine learning to learn the type of advice from the data brokers that is the most effective for enabling workers to achieve their desired goals. The result is that workers can define a specific professional goal (e.g. raising one's wages or developing skills) and locate concrete guidelines on how to navigate the crowd market to reach this goal.

We offer the data brokers different incentives for participating. For example, workers can be paid to provide the advice. Workers use our tool to provide the advice and then, at the end of the day, our tool measures how much advice a worker provided and pays the worker accordingly directly into the worker's bank account (just as if they were doing any other job on the platform). Another incentive we use is offering workers new career opportunities by becoming brokers. You can imagine that workers who provide the advice are in a way acting as managers for new workers. Workers who want to earn experience of becoming managers can participate and use our tool to gain that much needed expertise of guiding others to succeed. Workers acting as data brokers also do this based on their intrinsic motivation, with the purpose of helping their fellow workers have a better experience on the marketplace and to improve labour conditions for everyone. Our Computational Worker Leagues are composed of a group of data brokers who support workers to go after their goals with the help of the collective of workers. Figure 9.1 presents an overview of our Computational Worker Leagues.

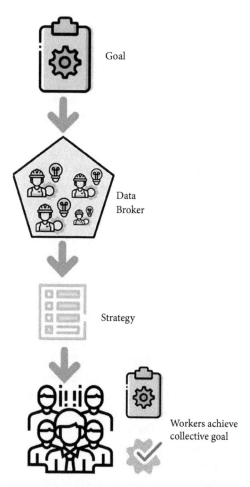

Fig. 9.1 Overview of a computational worker league

Design principles of the Computational Worker Leagues

While there are many ways in which we could computationally organize workers to create these leagues, we focus on collective help while on the job. In our design, we took into account that it was critical to reduce the amount of time that crowd workers spent outside crowd markets, as this was a time when they would not be receiving wages. Consequently, we utilized a web plug-in that would enable them to continue working on the crowd market and earning money at the same time as participating in the league. Web plug-ins are pieces of software that act as an add-on to a web browser and gives the browser additional functionality. Plug-ins can allow a web browser to display additional content that it was not originally designed to display. Most crowd markets allow for web plug-ins. This means we do not have to depend on crowd market owners (usually large technology companies, such as Amazon) for support. Through the plug-ins, we can add the functionality we desire to any crowd market. By being directly embedded where workers are working, it makes it easier for workers to participate in providing and following advice. Web plug-ins allow us to add three main functionalities into crowd markets: (1) an interface through which workers can act as 'data brokers' and provide advice on how to pursue a wide range of professional goals; (2) a means of directly displaying on the crowd market the advice that the data brokers are providing; (3) mechanisms through which researchers can collect information about the crowd market to conduct quantitative analysis.

Additionally, as stated above, it was important for us to design solutions that would allow for the data brokers to operate in a manner that would not distract them from their main job. Our design is based on ideas from 'Micro-Volunteering''' Savage et al. 2016), where people do micro-tasks as a side activity that does not disturb their main task. For this purpose, we frame the design of our intervention around: (1) *availability*: workers should be able to engage in collectively helping each other with a click; (2) *low cognitive load*: workers should be able to collectively help each other without the task being a distraction from the main work; (3) *paid training*: given the economically harsh labour conditions that crowd workers face, our design focuses on enabling workers to receive advice from the data brokers while they are earning money.

To enable these points, our data brokers utilize three components:
Peer Help Collector. The collector lives as a plug-in that connects with the given crowd market in which the worker is operating. In contrast to prior work where workers have to provide lengthy assistance to others (Doroudi et al. 2016), we focus on asking workers to provide micro-assistance. Our data brokers' interface has a small 'provide tip' button. Upon clicking the button, workers see a small pop-up window where they can provide their micro-advice that will help other workers navigate a crowd market to reach a particular goal. We allow workers to input advice anywhere they are within the crowd market. We store the context so as to display the information to other workers at the same point.

This setup enables our design principle of 'availability'. To limit the cognitive load, we limited the length of the micro-assistance that workers gave to each other to 100 characters (length established through trial and error). In the pop-up window, workers just have to select the type of goals for which their micro-advice is relevant (other workers first input the different professional goals they have and for which they would appreciate having assistance from others who have been able to work out how to achieve this goal). Workers select the goal and then type their advice. This allows us to match the advice to the particular goals for which advice is relevant in a simple and direct manner. Figure 9.2 presents how workers can provide advice to others to help them achieve certain goals.

Intelligent Selector. For each of the different tasks that workers have on crowd markets, the Peer Help Collector returns a long list of micro-advice. However, not all of this advice will necessarily be helpful for workers to achieve their particular goal. To overcome this issue, we have an Intelligent Selector that focuses on learning what type of advice is best for reaching a given professional goal.

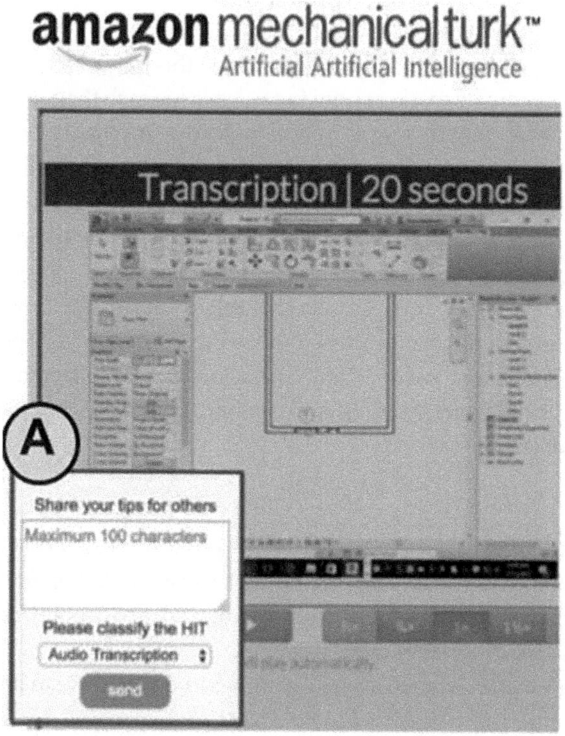

Fig. 9.2 Worker leagues use plug-ins in order to be directly embedded in crowdsourcing markets to ease collaborations

We use a reinforcement learning algorithm which focuses on maximizing the number of workers who consider that the micro-advice that is presented to them is useful. For this purpose, we first ask workers to micro-assess a particular piece of micro-advice for a given goal via upvotes or downvotes. These assessments are fed into our reinforcement learning algorithm that aims to maximize the number of upvotes it obtains from workers. Through this process, our data brokers start to learn the most suitable micro-advice.

Collective Help Display. This component focuses on presenting the micro-advice. The Collective Help Display presents workers with four different examples of micro-advice that the reinforcement learning algorithm ranked highest on the list. If workers want to read more advice, they can click the left or right button to view more. To ensure that new advice has a chance of being evaluated, our tool intermixes new advice that needs micro-assessments into the list of high-ranking advice.

Quantitative data collection

Given that our Computational Worker Leagues offer ways in which crowd workers can pursue goals, we had to establish mechanisms through which we could measure and study whether crowd workers were indeed able to reach their goals. For instance, if the goal was to earn higher wages, we had to develop mechanisms that would show whether we were actually able to increase workers' wages. Specifically, we needed methods for: (1) collecting and quantifying workers' behaviours and the labour they performed on the crowd market (this is necessary to start identifying how much the data brokers might help workers reach their desired goals); (2) flagging when workers followed the strategies from the data brokers; (3) measuring how much workers' behaviour and outcomes changed when following the strategies from the data broker. For this purpose, we developed tools that allowed us to collect information about crowd workers' behaviour, as well as information about the crowd market itself. The tool we built collected:

- Labour information, such as the title of the task posted on the crowd market, how much the task paid, timestamps (when a worker accepted to do the labour/when a worker submitted the labour/when a worker returned a task), employer IDs, and IDs of tasks.
- Worker information, such as daily earnings, tools they use to help their labour, approval rate (how much of their labour gets approved by employers), and worker IDs.
- Employer reputation information: this is part of the transparency information we collected from previous tools that focused on bringing more transparency to the crowd market. Such information can come from tools such as Turkopticon.

We use this information to study the effectiveness of our leagues. For instance, we have used our tools to identify the hourly wage of workers on Amazon Mechanical Turk (Saito et al. 2019b), as well as average wages (Hara et al. 2018). In this way, we offer researchers a more in-depth perspective on the marketplace and allow them to measure the quality of labour conditions for workers. Knowing the exact conditions facilitates taking action to be able to change and improve (Whiting et al. 2019). We believe it is especially valuable to connect these types of quantitative tools with interviews and surveys to have a much richer understanding of the reality of crowd markets. For readers interested in learning more about our tools, from the computational side, please refer to our research papers, Hara et al. (2018); Saito et al. (2019b).

Application of Our Research Framework

In this section, we present an overview of how our Framework has been used to help crowd workers attain two important professional goals: earning higher wages and developing their skills. We present how we deployed our tools in the wild and offer insights about how researchers could benefit from the quantitative data we collected.

Computational Worker Leagues for increasing wages

We conducted a field experiment to investigate how the hourly wage of workers changed when using our Computational Worker Leagues. It was not a simple task. Most crowd markets do not provide any information about the hourly wage for a particular task nor how much time it would take workers to complete the actual labour. It is, therefore, not straightforward to calculate the change in workers' wages over time (Hara et al. 2018). To overcome this challenge, we utilized the quantitative tools within our Computational Worker Leagues. These tools calculate how much time workers spend on each task and estimate each worker's hourly wage per task based on this. We are thus able to estimate how workers' wages varied over time.

Equipped with our Computational Worker Leagues and the associated tools for quantifying worker behaviour, we ran a two-week field experiment. We had real-world novice workers from Amazon Mechanical Turk complete over 25,000 tasks posted from 1,394 employers, with the experimental group of workers utilizing our Computational Worker Leagues and the control group operating as normal without being exposed to our Worker Leagues. Details about how we recruited workers for the study and how much we paid them for their participation can be found in our research papers (Saito et al. 2019a; Savage and Jarrahi 2020; Savage et al. 2020; Hanrahan et al. 2021). Our study concluded that having workers utilize the Computational Worker Leagues empowered them to increase their income.

Computational Worker Leagues for skill development

In our second application of our Computational Worker Leagues, we hypothesized that receiving advice from data brokers can help workers to build their skills in particular areas. Similar to Doroudi et al. (2016), we measured skills growth in terms of an increase in workers' speed and labour quality. To test this hypothesis and to understand the type of work that is well or poorly supported by the Computational Worker Leagues in the wild, we conducted: (1) a controlled field experiment; and a (2) real-world deployment of our design.

Controlled field experiment

The goal of our field experiment was to compare our Computational Worker Leagues with other approaches to evaluate the effectiveness of our proposed framework in helping workers develop their own skills. We considered three conditions: (1) workers do tasks without receiving any type of advice from the data brokers (control condition); (2) workers do tasks while receiving random advice from data brokers (random condition); (3) workers do tasks while receiving advice from data brokers that our machine learning models have identified are the best for helping workers to develop their skills (Computational Worker Leagues condition).

Given that we needed to measure participants' work quality, we focused on skill development for labour that was not open-ended and whose quality we could more easily measure. We focused on audio transcription tasks whose quality can be directly measured by transcription accuracy. It is important to note that audio transcription tasks are not only a popular task on crowd markets (Difallah et al. 2015) but, in addition, becoming proficient at audio transcription can substantially increase a person's wages. Transcribers typically earn US$0.01–0.02 per sentence (Novotney and Callison-Burch 2010), which could potentially translate to high wages if a worker is fast (and accurate) enough. Specializing in audio transcription can allow crowd workers to command higher wages as audio transcription is in high demand. Written records of court proceedings and captions for live television events, such as the news, sports, and political speeches, all require real-time audio transcription. Audio transcription skills are thereby highly specialized, highly valued, and well paid, earning up to $300 per hour outside MTurk. Building audio transcription skills on MTurk could thereby help crowd workers expand their horizons and increase their earnings.

We considered that novices were the ones who could benefit the most from our tool as it can be difficult to learn the ropes of a crowd market while also developing new skills. Novice workers were defined as both workers who were new to Amazon Mechanical Turk (i.e. to a particular crowd market) and those inexperienced in audio transcription tasks. Our field experiment therefore focused on investigating whether our design helps novice crowd workers improve their audio transcription skills.

We studied novices' completion time and work quality for three different audio transcription tasks under one of our three study conditions. We recruited a total of 90 novice MTurk workers and randomly divided them into three experimental conditions (30 in each condition). Participants in each condition were assigned the same audio transcription tasks with the same order. Tasks were sourced from real-world audio transcription tasks on MTurk and had similar difficulty: participants had to transcribe around 28 seconds of audio with similar levels of background noise, and with an average speaking rate of 165 words-per-second. We designed a tool that recorded workers' retention rate, completion time, and accuracy for each task. To calculate the time to complete a task, we measured the time when a worker first accessed the task as the start time and the time when workers submitted their labour (transcription) as their finish time. To study accuracy, we calculated the word error rate (WER) produced by each worker for each transcription, a commonly used metric to assess performance in audio transcription (Bigham et al. 2017). During the study period, novice workers completed a total of 253 tasks across all three conditions. Overall, our field experiment indicated that workers exposed to the Computational Worker Leagues were faster without sacrificing accuracy than workers without the advice from our data brokers. See our research paper Chiang et al. (2018b) for more details on this study.

Real-world deployment

We launched our Computational Worker Leagues for skill development and studied their use by real-world workers on Amazon Mechanical Turk. Our tool was installed by 179 workers; 86 per cent of these were active users of the system (i.e. they either became data brokers or used the advice from the data brokers to develop their skills); the rest used our system more passively (i.e. they just installed our tool). A total of 96 workers provided 363 snippets of advice while they acted as data brokers, and 146 workers provided 1401 micro-assessments of the advice from the data brokers.

From our real-world deployment, we found that workers who decided to become data brokers tended to create different types of advice each time. This is important, as it was unclear whether there would be an infinite set of advice that the data brokers could provide or whether there might be a vast but bounded set of advice that could be constantly shared to improve the experiences of workers. Our study highlights that a flow of advice can be constantly arriving from the data brokers. Crowd work is continuously evolving (Hara et al. 2018). We, therefore, believe that data brokers will likely always have new advice to provide. The popular worker tool of Turkopticon was published in 2013, and it is still active with new reviews of requesters (Irani and Silberman 2016). Therefore, we do see our data brokers being used long term. Through our real-world deployment, we identified that workers used our tool for all of the different types of tasks that are available on Amazon Mechanical Turk. This thus also highlights the viability of our tool. Our approach was able to get workers to act as data brokers for all of the different types of labour available on the platform. This is promising as there were no tasks where workers did not feel they could not help other workers become more efficient and develop their skills.

Broader Challenges

The research methods we present here focused on evaluating how our Computational Worker Leagues help workers to achieve the professional goals they set forward. This entails conducting real-world experiments. However, this is not simple given the variability and randomness that can exist around tasks that are available on the crowd market—it might be that in any one week some tasks that could help a worker achieve certain goals are not available and hence it is not so much that the Computational Worker Leagues were not effective, but rather what was available on the crowd market did not facilitate the achievement of the goal (Hara et al. 2018).

Another potential problem is that to recruit participants for our studies, we usually post tasks on crowd markets and use that platform for recruitment. But this means that we only reach workers who are willing to engage with our tasks in the first place. Future work could explore other ways of recruiting workers and eliciting information from them (e.g. via video recordings or interviews). Such studies could explore how using different mechanisms for eliciting information from workers shapes the type of information that is obtained. In other words, we believe there is significant value in exploring different setups of our data brokers. Additionally, we presented our systems primarily within the context of Amazon Mechanical Turk. Future work could also explore how our data brokers might operate in other crowd platforms (e.g. Uber, Upwork, or Citizen Science platforms). Nonetheless, given that our goal was to start to understand how our computational methods played out in the wild, we consider our approach to be appropriate and representative.

We also believe there are technical and educational challenges that need to be addressed. In particular, we think there is a gap between qualitative and quantitative researchers who are investigating crowd work. Qualitative researchers might not feel as comfortable deploying our Computational Worker Leagues to conduct studies, perhaps because significant technical knowledge is required to do such investigations in the wild. For instance, researchers need to have knowledge about databases to instal a database that can collect the worker data to conduct the quantitative data analysis; researchers also need to know some javascript in order to configure the plug-in and connect the plug-in to their database. Additionally, researchers need to have some data science skills in order to take the data collected from the plug-in and start to find patterns. However, despite these challenges, we have seen that qualitative researchers can make use of the quantitative data our studies collect (notice that this step involves simply having more data science skills). Our hope is that through the data collection that our systems offer, we can encourage and enable more qualitative researchers to study other aspects of crowd work that they might not have had access to in the past.

Ethical challenges

Our research approach involves collecting quantitative data about workers and the crowd market (including information about employers). While the data are used to benefit workers, ethical questions can emerge about close monitoring of workers even if it is for their benefit. Our research has always anonymized worker data, as well as conducting group analysis instead of studying individual behaviour. However, there are questions to ask about the best strategy for managing the data that are collected. Should it be data that are owned by the companies or universities which run the studies with our Computational Worker Leagues? Or should they always be data that are owned by a collective of workers? We believe that the best option is to develop approaches that involve all stakeholders, and especially include populations that are typically ignored and not given power over their data (e.g. workers). There is also value in exploring approaches that have been utilized in opensource collaboration projects to enable all stakeholders of the crowd market to use the anonymized data for the different goals they might have. For instance, employers might be interested in utilizing the data to improve the quality of the work that they obtain on the crowd market; however, workers might benefit from using the data to identify the best strategies for developing their skills; while researchers, on the other hand, might want to use the data to better understand the crowd market.

However, part of the problem is that state of the art tools that collect crowd market information are limited and tend to be focused on particular tasks. For instance, Turkopticon (as above) focuses primarily on collecting data about requesters' ratings (Irani and Silberman 2013). To address these challenges, we propose 'The Opensource Storehouse For Multiple Stakeholders'. The storehouse would function in the same way as a traditional repository that, for a given crowd market, collects different types of information related to the market. However, the storehouse would also request that metadata are uploaded that can help the different stakeholders to achieve their desired goals, for example:

- *Stakeholder and goals*: information about the goal for which the data were collected, and the stakeholder who was interested in the goal;
- *Data collected*: This relates to all the crowd market information that is collected, such as worker characteristics, types of tasks, employer information, etc.
- *General crowd market characteristics*: There is value in understanding the nature of the crowd market in which the data were collected. Was it location-based crowd work? Was it volunteer labour? Paid labour? In what national context(s) was the work carried out?
- *Feedback*: A space for the different stakeholders to provide input on the data that were collected for a particular crowd market and a particular goal.
- *List of to-dos*: List of things that can be done to enhance the data collection (e.g. perhaps data from more populations are needed).

Workers were paid to participate in using our Computational Worker Leagues. We believe there is value in considering setups where workers are paid to participate in research, especially given the harsh labour conditions they face. We also believe there is value in identifying the best setups to make tools, such as our Computational Worker Leagues, into something that is sustainable long term. Research has identified that the emergence of private tools to help crowd workers is creating further social divisions among workers (Williams et al. 2019). It is, therefore, important to find ways in which these types of tools could be accessible for all. Turkopticon has recently turned from a space that was primarily run by academics, into a space run by workers.[2] To continue its operation, Turkopticon has become a type of NGO that can receive funding from different parties. A similar setup could be explored with our tools. However, a committee that analyses from which parties it is acceptable to receive funding would also be required, in particular to ensure the tools remain appropriate for all of the different stakeholders.

Conclusion

Crowd markets offer a wide range of readily available labour (Alkhatib et al. 2017). Unfortunately, it is often difficult for workers to know how best to navigate these crowd markets in order to find labour that pays well and might actually be useful for workers' career growth. A number of tools have emerged to help workers better navigate crowd markets by bringing transparency (Irani and Silberman 2013). We argue that transparency is not enough. We need to provide workers with effective tools for using transparency for the different professional goals that workers might have. In this chapter, we presented a brief overview of how these tools can be used to help workers aim for different professional goals, in particular developing their skills and increasing their wages. We began with an overview of the type of labour markets that are feeding our artificial intelligence industry. We explained the types of problems that workers in these platforms face and discussed how we might design tools to empower workers to address these problems and change their labour conditions. We also presented ways other researchers can use this approach to not only create interventions in crowd markets but also conduct quantitative analysis of what is happening inside such marketplaces.

Funding

This work was partially supported by NSF grant FW-HTF-19541.

Notes

1. Turkopticon is an online tool that helps workers to see the reputation of employers (requesters) on crowdsourcing markets to help workers decide if they should work with those employers based on how much they typically pay, if they reject work, as well as other metrics. Turkopticon is built as a plug-in to be directly embded inside the crowdsourcing market. The use of plug-ins facilitates repurposing crowdsourcing markets to better suit the needs of workers. For instance, in this case the crowdsourcing market of Amazon Mechanical Turk did not officially share any reputation information about the employers. The plug-in helps workers to now be able to access such information even without the official support of Amazon.

2. Turkopticon was created by academics Lilly Irani and Six Silberman while they were both PhD students at the University of California, Irvine. However, they decided to turn Turkopticon into a worker-owned NGO to provide workers with more agency in how they wanted the tool and future tools to evolve and the type of governance associated. You can read more about this decision here: https://blog.turkopticon.info/?page_id=474

References

Abraham, K. G., Haltiwanger, J. C., Sandusky, K., and Spletzer, J. R. 2018. *Measuring the Gig Economy: Current Knowledge and Open Issues, Technical Report*, National Bureau of Economic Research.

Alkhatib, A., Bernstein, M. S., and Levi, M. 2017. Examining crowd work and gig work through the historical lens of piecework. In *Proceedings of the 2017 CHI Conference on Human Factors in Computing Systems* (pp. 4599–616), ACM.

Allahbakhsh, M., Benatallah, B., Ignjatovic, A., Motahari-Nezhad, H. R., Bertino, E., and Dustdar, S. 2013. Quality control in crowdsourcing systems: Issues and directions, *IEEE Internet Computing*, 17(2): pp. 76–81.

Amazon. 2020. Amazon Mechanical Turk, Amazon, https://www.mturk.com/ (accessed 28 September 2020).

Berg, J. 2015. Income security in the on-demand economy: Findings and policy lessons from a survey of crowdworkers. *Comparative Labour Law and Policy Journal*, 37: p. 543.

Berg, J., Furrer, M., Harmon, E., Rani, U., and Silberman, M. S. 2018. Digital labour platforms and the future of work, *Towards Decent Work in the Online World. Rapport de l'OIT*, Vol. 1

Bernstein, M. S., Karger, D. R., Miller, R. C., and Brandt, J. 2012. Analytic methods for optimizing realtime crowdsourcing. *arXiv*: 1204.2995.

Bigham, J. P., Kushalnagar, R., Huang, T.-H. K., Flores, J. P., and Savage, S. 2017. On how deaf people might use speech to control devices. In *Proceedings of the 19th International ACM SIGACCESS Conference on Computers and Accessibility* (pp. 383–84), ACM.

Chiang, C.-W., Betanzos, E., and Savage, S. 2018a. Exploring blockchain for trustful collaborations between immigrants and governments. In *Extended Abstracts of the 2018 CHI Conference on Human Factors in Computing Systems* (p. LBW 531), ACM.

Chiang, C.-W., Kasunic, A., and Savage, S. 2018b. Crowd coach: Peer coaching for crowd workers' skill growth. In *Proceedings of the ACM on Human-Computer Interaction* 2(CSCW), 37.

ChrisTurk. 2018. TurkerView Worker Review Platform for Amazon Mechanical Turk, Turkerview, https://turkerview.com/ (accessed 28 September 2020).

Deng, X. N. and Joshi, K. 2013. Is crowdsourcing a source of worker empowerment or exploitation? Understanding crowd workers' perceptions of crowdsourcing career. In *International Conference on Information Systems*. Association for Information Systems.

Difallah, D. E., Catasta, M., Demartini, G., Ipeirotis, P. G., and Cudr´e-mauroux, P. 2015. The dynamics of micro-task crowdsourcing: The case of Amazon MTurk. In *Proceedings of the 24th International Conference on World Wide Web* (pp. 238–47). International World Wide Web Conferences Steering Committee.

Doroudi, S., Kamar, E., Brunskill, E., and Horvitz, E. 2016. Toward a learning science for complex crowdsourcing tasks. In *Proceedings of the 2016 CHI Conference on Human Factors in Computing Systems* (pp. 2623–34). ACM.

Eickhoff, C., and de Vries, A. 2011. How crowdsourcable is your task. In *Proceedings of the workshop on crowdsourcing for search and data mining (CSDM)* (pp. 11–14) at the fourth ACM international conference on web search and data mining (WSDM).

Gadiraju, U., and Demartini, G. 2019. Understanding worker moods and reactions to rejection in crowdsourcing. In *Proceedings of the 30th ACM Conference on Hypertext and Social Media*, (pp. 211–20). ACM.

Gaikwad, S., Morina, D., Nistala, R., Agarwal, M., Cossette, A., Bhanu, R., Savage, S., Narwal, V., Rajpal, K., Regino, J., and Mithal, A. 2015, November. Daemo: A self-governed crowdsourcing marketplace. In *Adjunct proceedings of the 28th annual ACM symposium on user interface software & technology* (pp. 101–2). ACM.

Gray, M., and Suri, S. 2019. *Ghost work: How to stop Silicon Valley from building a new global underclass.* Eamon Dolan Books.

Hall, D., and Perona, P. 2015. Fine-grained classification of pedestrians in video: Benchmark and state of the art. In *Proceedings of the IEEE Conference on Computer Vision and Pattern Recognition* (pp. 5482–91). IEEE Computer Society.

Hanrahan, B. V., Ma, N. F., Betanzos, E., and Savage, S. 2020. Reciprocal research: Providing value in design research from the outset in the rural United States. In *Proceedings of the 2020 International Conference on Information and Communication Technologies and Development* (pp. 1–5). ACM.

Hanrahan, B. V., Chen, A., Ma, J., Ma, N. F., Squicciarini, A., & Savage, S. (2021). The Expertise Involved in Deciding which HITs are Worth Doing on Amazon Mechanical Turk. *Proceedings of the ACM on Human-Computer Interaction*, 5(CSCW1), 1–23.

Hara, K., Adams, A., Milland, K., Savage, S., Callison-Burch, C., and Bigham, J. P. 2018. A data-driven analysis of workers' earnings on Amazon Mechanical Turk. In *Proceedings of the 2018 CHI Conference on Human Factors in Computing Systems*, (p. 449). ACM.

Hara, K., Adams, A., Milland, K., Savage, S., Hanrahan, B. V., Bigham, J. P., and CallisonBurch, C. 2019. Worker demographics and earnings on Amazon Mechanical Turk: An exploratory analysis. In *Extended Abstracts of the 2019 CHI Conference on Human Factors in Computing Systems*, (pp. 1–6). ACM.

Hilton, L. G., and Azzam, T. 2019. Crowdsourcing qualitative thematic analysis. *American Journal of Evaluation*, 40(4): pp. 575–89.

Huang, S.-W., and Fu, W.-T. 2013. Don't hide in the crowd! Increasing social transparency between peer workers improves crowdsourcing outcomes. In *Proceedings of the SIGCHI Conference on Human Factors in Computing Systems*, (pp. 621–30). ACM.

Irani, L. C., and Silberman, M. 2013. Turkopticon: Interrupting worker invisibility in Amazon Mechanical Turk. In *Proceedings of the SIGCHI conference on human factors in computing systems* (pp. 611–20). ACM.

Irani, L. C., and Silberman, M. 2016. Stories we tell about labour: Turkopticon and the trouble with design. In *Proceedings of the 2016 CHI conference on human factors in computing systems* (pp. 4573–86). ACM.

Jagabathula, S., Subramanian, L., and Venkataraman, A. 2014. Reputation-based worker filtering in crowdsourcing. In *Advances in Neural Information Processing Systems*: Proceedings of the 2014 Conference (Vol. 27), (pp. 2492–500). MIT Press.

Jarrahi, M. H., and Sutherland, W. 2019. Algorithmic management and algorithmic competencies: Understanding and appropriating algorithms in gig work. In *International Conference on Information*, (pp. 578–89). Springer.

Kaplan, T., Saito, S., Hara, K., and Bigham, J. P. 2018. Striving to earn more: A survey of work strategies and tool use among crowd workers. In *Proceedings of the AAAI Conference on Human Computation and Crowdsourcing* (Vol. 6, No. 1, pp. 70–78). PKP.

Kasunic, A., Chiang, C.-W., Kaufman, G., and Savage, S. 2019. Crowd work on a CV? Understanding how AMT fits into turkers' career goals and professional profiles, arXiv: 1902.05361.

Kuhn, K. M., and Maleki, A. 2017. Micro-entrepreneurs, dependent contractors, and instaserfs: Understanding online labour platform workforces, *Academy of Management Perspectives*, 31(3): pp. 183–200.

Lampinen, A., and Cheshire, C. 2016. Hosting via Airbnb: Motivations and financial assurances in monetized network hospitality. In *Proceedings of the 2016 CHI conference on human factors in computing systems* (pp. 1669–80). ACM.

Li, T., Luther, K., and North, C. 2018. Crowdia: Solving mysteries with crowdsourced sensemaking. In *Proceedings of the ACM on Human-Computer Interaction 2(CSCW)*, (pp. 1–29). ACM.

Metall, I., 2016. *Frankfurt paper on platform-based work—proposals for platform operators, clients, policy makers, workers, and worker organizations*, IG Metall, Frankfurt.

Novotney, S. and Callison-Burch, C., 2010. Cheap, fast and good enough: Automatic speech recognition with non-expert transcription. In *Human Language Technologies*:

The 2010 Annual Conference of the North American Chapter of the Association for Computational Linguistics (pp. 207–15). Association for Computational Linguistics.

Radford, J., Pilny, A., Reichelmann, A., Keegan, B., Foucault Welles, B., Hoye, J., Ognyanova, K., Meleis, W., and Lazer, D. 2016. Volunteer science as an online platform for experiments in organizations. In *Academy of Management Proceedings*, Vol. 2016 (p. 17008). Academy of Management.

Saito, S., Chiang, C.-W., Savage, S., Nakano, T., Kobayashi, T., and Bigham, J. 2019a. Predicting the working time of microtasks based on workers' perception of prediction errors. *Human Computation*, 6(1): pp. 192–219.

Saito, S., Chiang, C.-W., Savage, S., Nakano, T., Kobayashi, T. and Bigham, J. 2019b. Turkscanner: Predicting the hourly wage of microtasks. arXiv:1903.07032.

Savage, S., and Jarrahi, M. H. 2020. Solidarity and AI for transitioning to crowd work during covid-19. In *The New Future of Work Symposium 2020*. Microsoft.

Savage, S., Monroy-Hernandez, A., and Höllerer, T. 2016. Botivist: Calling volunteers to action using online bots. In *Proceedings of the 19th ACM Conference on Computer Supported Cooperative Work & Social Computing* (pp. 813–822). ACM.

Savage, S., Chiang, C., Susumu, S., Toxtli, C., and Bigham, J. 2020. Becoming the super turker: Increasing wages via a strategy from high earning workers. In *Proceedings of the 29th International Conference on World Wide Web, WWW '20*, International World Wide Web Conferences Steering Committee.

Singer, Y., and Mittal, M., 2013. Pricing mechanisms for crowdsourcing markets. In *Proceedings of the 22nd International Conference on World Wide Web* (pp. 1157–66). ACM.

Slivkins, A., and Vaughan, J. W. 2014. Online decision making in crowdsourcing markets: Theoretical challenges, *ACM SIGecom Exchanges*, 12(2): pp. 4–23.

Smith, A. 2016. Gig work, online selling and home sharing, *Pew Research Center* 17.

Sorokin, A., and Forsyth, D. 2008. Utility data annotation with Amazon Mechanical Turk. In *2008 IEEE Computer Society Conference on Computer Vision and Pattern Recognition Workshops* (pp. 1–8). IEEE.

Strathern, M. 2000. The tyranny of transparency, *British Educational Research Journal*, 26(3), pp. 309–21.

Toxtli, C., and Savage, S. 2020. Enabling expert critique at scale with chatbots and micro-guidance, *13th International Conference on Advances in Computer-Human Interactions, ACHI 2020*. International Academy, Research, and Industry Association IARIA.

Toxtli, C., Hara, K., Callison-Burch, C., and Kristy, M. 2019. Understanding the crowd markets that workers and requesters imagine. In *Proceedings of the 7th ACM Collective Intelligence (CI) Conference*. ACM.

Toxtli, C., Richmond-Fuller, A., and Savage, S. 2020. Reputation agent: Prompting fair reviews in gig markets. In *Proceedings of the 29th International Conference on World Wide Web, WWW '20*, International World Wide Web Conferences Steering Committee.

Toxtli, C., Suri S., & Savage, S. (2021). Quantifying the Invisible Labor of Crowd Work. *Proceedings of the ACM on Human-Computer Interaction*, 5 (CSCW1), 1–23.

Whiting, M. E., Hugh, G., and Bernstein, M. S. 2019. Fair work: Crowd work minimum wage with one line of code. In *Proceedings of the AAAI Conference on Human Computation and Crowdsourcing*, Vol. 7, (pp. 197–206). PKP.

Williams, A. C., Mark, G., Milland, K., Lank, E., and Law, E. 2019. The perpetual work life of crowdworkers: How tooling practices increase fragmentation in crowdwork. In *Proceedings of the ACM on Human-Computer Interaction 3(CSCW)*, (pp. 1–28). ACM.

Yeoman, R. 2014. Conceptualising meaningful work as a fundamental human need, *Journal of Business Ethics*, 125(2), pp. 235–51.

Young, J., Swamy, P., and Danks, D. 2018. *Beyond AI: Responses to hate speech and disinformation.* Unpublished paper presented at Carnegie Mellon University. Retrieved from http://jessica-young.com/research/Beyond-AI-Responses-to-Hate-Speech-and-Disinformation.pdf.

PART III
DISTRIBUTED WORK AND ORGANIZING

10

Exploring Organization through Contributions

Using Activity Theory for the Study of Contemporary Digital Labour Practices

David Rozas and Steven Huckle

Introduction

Contemporary working practices and the organizational forms that sustain them are changing. Distributed and crowdsourced forms of labour are becoming increasingly important, and major corporations are becoming involved in the digital labour space (Gray and Suri 2019). Documenting and analysing the new organizational forms and practices that are dependent on distributed digital labour has become an urgent task for researchers.

Research on the organizational practices of Free/Libre and Open Source Software (FLOSS) communities provides valuable use-cases for academics interested in studying emergent forms of distributed digital labour. FLOSS features non-discriminatory behaviour and non-restrictive licences, a practice that requires applications (and associated source code) to be freely redistributed (Gnu.org 2001). The result is that FLOSS software inhabits a space referred to as a *digital commons* (Stadler 2010), which is a freely available and collectively produced repository of code, information, and knowledge.

Commoning practices, however, are not exclusive to software. The extension of these commoning practices has resulted in what Benkler (2002; 2006) describes as an emergent mode of production: Commons-Based Peer Production (CBPP), which represents an alternative to the traditional hierarchical modes. Collaborative work in the commons is present in a diverse range of areas (Fuster Morell et al. 2014), including open science, urban commons, peer funding, and open design, to name but a few. Hence, whereas capitalism uses the economics of commodification to transform goods into commodities that can be bought and sold on the market, CBPP communities enable counter-commodification. They revolve around an *economy of contribution*, where 'people contribute to a project because they want it to succeed'

David Rozas and Steven Huckle, *Exploring Organization through Contributions*. In: *Research Methods for Digital Work and Organization*. Edited by Gillian Symon, Katrina Pritchard, and Christine Hine, Oxford University Press.
© Oxford University Press (2021). DOI: 10.1093/oso/9780198860679.003.0010

(Siefkes 2008, 9). The digital commons is inhabited by *digital commoners*, who are a self-determining, politically independent voluntary collective of skilled enthusiasts who cooperate with often ethnically and geographically diverse peers (Kelty 2008). It is a mode of practice which represents an alternative to the traditional hierarchical styles of production that feature within capitalist culture. Often, *digital commoners* become more involved with CBPP projects as they gain trust and, with greater trust, gain greater access to governance processes. Thus, the practices of CBPP create a self-reinforcing loop (Bollier 2003).

Because of their governance and economic models, CBPP communities present significant differences to wider forms of platform[1] digital labour, such as Amazon Mechanical Turk (MTurk) and Universal Human Relevance System (Microsoft), labour marketplaces that outsource projects to globally diverse workers. However they also present similar characteristics and challenges for researchers interested in studying them. First, the researcher must adopt different types of methodological approaches that combine diverse datasets drawn from online and offline media (Hine 2015) in order to explore organizational forms that can be highly complex and difficult to capture in a conventional model of hierarchies and sub-divisions. Second, it can be difficult to distinguish work from recreation because blurred organizational boundaries result in flexible work-lives that reduce the distinction between the private and the professional. Finally, it is challenging to draw conclusions from globally disparate groups, especially when the platforms that mediate these groups are not necessarily open to scrutiny.

We have employed Activity Theory (AT) to explore perceptions of contribution in CBPP (Rozas et al. 2021), a setting in which activities considered as 'work' and individual contributions to that work are particularly blurred as a result of being increasingly created by crowds and communities of diverse participants (Arvidsson and Peitersen 2013). As stated above, CBPP communities focused on digital commons, such as Drupal, typically rely on an economy of contribution (Wittel 2013) that gives value and recognition to various forms of activity as contributions to the organization. Consequently an important focus for our AT analysis was 'What does it mean to contribute in a community such as Drupal?' We also used AT to identify how two intertwined dynamics of formalization and decentralization of decision-making operate in this type of community (Rozas and Huckle 2021). In this chapter, we use examples from Drupal, however researchers focused on other forms of distributed digital labour can benefit from the use of AT as an organizing framework for their research.

First, we introduce our research site, Drupal, then we provide an overview of AT and the main concepts of the analytical framework applied during these studies. Subsequently, we describe the application of AT to Drupal. Finally, we reflect on the benefits and limitations of applying AT to the study of organizational practices in broader forms of digital labour.

An Overview of Drupal

Drupal is a FLOSS content management system that provides a framework for the development of websites. The history of the Drupal project began in 1998 at the University of Antwerp (Dolin 2011, 822), when two undergraduate students decided to establish a wireless bridge to share their Internet connection and develop a simple content management framework for exchanging messages and news between students. The system was publicly released as FLOSS in 2001 and it has since gone on to power approximately 1.5 per cent of websites worldwide.[2] The main motto of the project,—'come for the software, stay for the community'—reflects the idea that Drupal cannot be understood without considering its community. The community has experienced significant growth: regular Drupal communitarian events are held all over the world, and more than 1.3 million people have registered some interest in the system at its central mediating platform, drupal.org (Rozas 2017, 85–95), becoming a notable example of the phenomenon of CBPP. Our selection of Drupal as a case study was driven by our interest in understanding how a large and global CBPP community self-organizes (Rozas 2017, 99). Our studies (Rozas et al. 2021; Rozas and Huckle 2021) of the Drupal community explored two key types of activities in the community: *the development of source code* and *the organization of events*.

For the development of source code, we explored the organizational aspects of three types of projects within Drupal. The first type is Drupal's *core projects*. These are the projects that form part of a default installation of Drupal, presenting the basic set of functionalities to develop a website. The second type is *contributed projects*: those that form part of the main collaboration platform, drupal.org, and provide additional features. Core and contributed projects require communitarian peer-reviewing practices in order to become part of the platform. Drupal.org provides tools for the coordination of the development, maintenance, and decision-making for these digital commons. The final type of project is *custom projects*, which are projects that have been freely shared and developed in external platforms such as github.com but have not been subject to the required peer-reviewing to include them in drupal.org. In this chapter, we focus particularly on *contributed projects*.

For the organization of events, we explored the three main types of events present in the community. The first is *DrupalCons*, which are annual conferences attended by thousands of participants. They have a global scope and last almost a week. The second is *DrupalCamps*, which are two-day events organized regionally or nationally by local Drupal communities. Hundreds typically attend them. The final type includes a wide range of *local events*, such as presentations or social gatherings with other Drupal members. Between 10 and 30 participants typically attend local events. While the events are face-to-face, the coordination to organize them is facilitated through online platforms These include drupal.org, Drupal websites specifically developed to coordinate each event, or external sites, such as meetup.com. Online platforms are essential to coordinate organization. For example, they enable peer-reviewing practices in the selection of presentations at events. Other online tools, such as Telegram and WhatsApp groups, are also key to sustaining the coordination of Drupal face-to-face events.

Activity Theory

AT is the main theoretical framework which we employed to explore the organizational processes and dynamics of Drupal and which enabled us to study the digital labour practices surrounding both the development of source code and the organization of events. Rather than a theory in the strictest sense, we used AT as an analytical tool: a lens that helped us to untangle the complexity behind the organization in large CBPP communities, such as Drupal. As we will further detail in Section "Results", we found the use of AT particularly useful: first, for its capacity to create cross-contextual comparisons by bringing together substantially different organizational processes within the same analytical umbrella. Second, AT is agnostic with respect to an a priori macro-/micro-level of analysis. It instead provides the researcher with a set of concepts which enable analyses at both levels and, if needed, link them. Third, AT incorporates the notion of tension, which is valuable to trace changes in fluid organizational settings, as is the case for CBPP communities. As such we argue that AT offers a useful framework for researchers interested in understanding the emerging organizational forms of distributed digital labour.

The first generation of Activity Theory

The capacity of AT to identify patterns and establish cross-contextual comparisons is built upon the idea of object-driven activities (Marx 1924, 143–5). Marxism has, therefore, a crucial influence in AT. Marx understood the processes of production and transformation as historical phenomena dependent on social practices, whereby the subject produces itself by producing the object and thereby, transforms the object's nature. Such processes might introduce several systemic inner contradictions and tensions, but these too may become a force for development (Hegel 1975). Hence, Marx (1924, 143–5) considered the relationship between objects and subjects as critical to understanding transformation. Subsequently, the first generation of AT was built on Vygotsky's (1978) notion of *mediated action*, whereby culturally meaningful artefacts condition the individual because when someone develops activities in collaboration with other humans, they internalize social norms and modes of behaviour. Leont'ev (1978) developed Vygotsky's ideas and established the concept of activity as a unit of analysis. As is the case with other socio-cultural perspectives (Kaptelinin 2012), Leont'ev assumed the social nature of the human mind, as well as its inseparability from the activity. For Leont'ev (1978), there was no activity without an object. Thus, activities influence an object's characteristics and vice versa. AT incorporates these notions of relationships between elements and tensions between them as conceptual elements for the study of activity systems.

The second generation of Activity Theory

In the 1980s, Leont'ev's ideas became known to a new generation of academic theorists, such as Engeström (1987). The first generation of AT did not present a conceptual model for the study of collective activities. Engeström (1987) proposed a new model which included them. Engeström's proposal became known as the second generation of AT (2GAT). Figure 10.1, the model of *human activity system*, represents the outcome of an activity through six interrelated elements that account for social relations:

1. *Subject*. The actors who perform the activity and who are subject to the internalization processes.
2. *Tools*. The mediating artefacts employed by the actors in the system. Cultural factors influence tools and they change according to the accumulated experience.
3. *Object*. The element towards which the activity is directed. It has social and cultural properties. The object is transformed as the activity progresses.

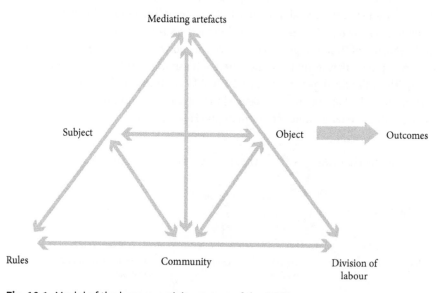

Fig. 10.1 Model of the human activity system of the 2GAT
Adapted from Figure 2.6 in Engeström (1987, 78).

4. *Rules*. The rules that regulate the subject's actions toward an object and their relations with other participants. They can be explicit or implicit.
5. *Community*. The totality of actors sharing an interest in the same object.
6. *Division of labour*. A representation of the distribution of processes between actors.

For example, imagine an activity that consists of the redesign of the User Interface (UI) of a particular software application. Here, the object of the activity is the current design of the computer interface (Kaptelinin 2012). A community forms to complete the action, which involves a division of labour, because the activity requires, for example, project managers, developers, and UI designers. A UI designer might use a set of artefacts to work on the transformation of the object, from hardware capable of rendering sophisticated graphics, to software for designing those graphics. Additionally, the UI designer might interact with the community through implicit and explicit rules; for instance, they may attend project meetings and receive a salary for their efforts. Overall, the coordinated work of the team produces a set of new outcomes—in this instance, a new user interface.

The third generation of Activity Theory and beyond

During the 1990s, researchers began to realize the necessity of developing the next generation of AT. Engeström (1999) proposed a new approach which captures the interactions between several human activity systems The minimal model, with two activities, is shown in Figure 10.2. The interactions between activity systems result in the sharing of (often fragmented) objects, enabling the researcher to study forces for development that result from the inherent tensions between systems (Engeström 2009). Thus, the third generation of AT (3GAT) continued to be inspired by Marx, who, as described above, also considered the development of potential of processes that introduce systemic inner contradictions (Hegel 1975).

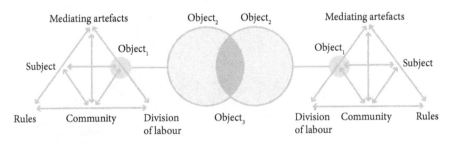

Fig. 10.2 The minimal model of the 3GAT
Adapted from Figure 3 in Engeström (2001, 136).

Consider the redesign of the UI, described above, and that the expected outcome (a new UI), is part of an effort to develop a new version of a much broader application. This requires the integration of the UI with outcomes from other activity systems, such as back-office databases. This introduces inherent tensions as the different systems attempt to provide their solution to the whole. However, that leads to a development dynamic that delivers a solution because the interaction between the UI designer and the database administrator results in software that meets requirements satisfying all parties.

In the last few decades the emergence of new forms of organization, such as CBPP, distributed work, or crowdsourcing, opened up a debate between activity theorists on the need to rethink the shape of these activity systems. Engeström (2006) contributed the concept of *runaway object* to the debate, which he later developed (Engeström 2009). Engeström (2009, 306) cites four prerequisites for such objects:

1. they must have intrinsic properties that transcend the utilitarian profit motive;
2. they must yield useful intermediate products, yet remain incomplete;
3. they must be visible, accessible, and cumulable so that participants return time and again;
4. there must be useful feedback from and exchange among the participants.

Engeström highlighted the notions of negotiation and peer review as key to understanding the coordination mechanisms and the new forms of organization that emerge in the constant development of these runaway objects. Figure 10.3 depicts this new model, which acknowledges and highlights that the boundaries and structures in these new forms of organization, such as those in CBPP, are not so clear: they are subsumed by the object, rather than the other way around.

Hence, for Engeström, the challenge for the future of AT involves integrating analytical tools that capture a multitude of issues of subjectivity and their multiple interconnected human activity systems which remain valuable to study the changes in more blurred and distributed forms of organization, such as those in Drupal.

Applying AT to the Study of Peer-production: The Case of Drupal

In this section, we discuss the application of AT in our study of Drupal. To investigate the digital labour practices of Drupal, we used an ethnographic approach combining: three years of participant observation; documentary analysis of an archive of 8613 documents;[3] and 15 semi-structured interviews (Rozas 2017, 125–58). The first author (Rozas 2017, 129–30) was as an 'insider researcher' (Brannick and Coghlan 2007):

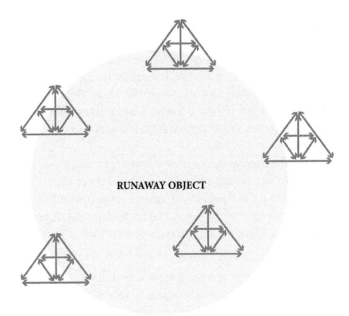

Fig. 10.3 A runaway object with several activity systems
Adapted from Figure 19.2 in Engeström (2009, 306).

the researcher-author describes a cultural setting to which s/he has a 'natural access', is an active participant, more or less on equal terms with other participants [and] then works and/or lives in the setting and then uses the experiences, knowledge and access to empirical material for research purposes

(Alvesson 2003, 174).

Due to the digital nature of the main object sustained by the community—software—and its size and global nature, a large amount of the day-to-day activity in Drupal is, unsurprisingly, carried out through online media. For that reason, the research initially drew on virtual ethnographic methods (Hine 2000). Nevertheless, the relevance that offline activities have in the community emerged during the course of the study and it was consequently concluded that this research required immersion and participation in both online and offline activities. requiring a breakdown of the traditional dualism (Orgad 2005). This approach was congruent with that already taken in similar studies, as in Coleman's (2013) study of FLOSS communities and hacker culture.

AT was employed to constantly inform the research methodologically. The online/offline distinction emerged as blurred and continuous, rather than binary (Rozas 2017, 127–8). However, conversely, the definition of 'contribution activity' as the main unit of analysis facilitated a clearer distinction with respect to immersion and participation in the communitarian activities. Furthermore, it led us to the question: 'What does it mean to contribute in a community such as Drupal?' We applied the 2GAT model for the study of such contributions. We explore this further in the next section. Additionally, AT does not consider an a priori micro-/macro-divide (Miettinen 1999), which allowed us to expand the level of analysis to the study of the organizational environments in which these activities were taking place. For that purpose, we drew on the concept of runaway object from the 3GAT, and this is illustrated in the following section.

Application of AT at a micro-level: writing code and organizing events

For the analysis at the micro-level, this study drew on the model of the human activity system from the 2GAT. Hence, during the first stage of the research it was necessary to study the notion of contribution within Drupal in detail and to include within that the less visible forms of contribution. Furthermore, to understand how a vast global community organizes, it was also necessary to include other elements and factors (e.g. processes, dynamics, and structures, among others) which surround such contributions.

Using the 2GAT model as a lens, we analysed some of these contribution activities in-depth, including the relationships between the artefacts employed for collaboration, the roles played by its members (division of labour), and the implicit and explicit rules. The use of the activity system as a unit of analysis enabled the incorporation of these notions as part of a dynamic phenomenon (Uden et al. 2007), avoiding simple monocausal explanations in the study of CBPP.

Figure 10.4 depicts an example of this application of the model of activity for the study of the development of contributed projects in Drupal, in which the elements of the activity were defined as follows:

1. *Subject.* The maintainers of the contributed project. In other words, the Drupal members responsible for coordinating development and maintenance.
2. *Tools.* The mediating artefacts used by the maintainers and the rest of the members of the community, such as issues lists. This is where users report bugs, tasks can be assigned, or new features are requested. Thus, issues lists are artefacts that function as a coordination tool for maintainers and enable technical discussions and decision-making about how to address issues. Other types of mediating artefacts are chat channels, email, social networks, such as Twitter, or Drupal discussion groups.[4]
3. *Object.* The contributed project.
4. *Rules.* Examples of explicit rules are community-agreed coding standards[5] and guidelines for contribution.[6] For example, if a project is to move from a custom project to a contributed project, developers must follow a peer-reviewing

process called the *Project Application Process* (Rozas and Huckle 2021, 212). Examples of implicit rules are those employed by maintainers for the evaluation of contributions by other Drupal members who do not have direct permission to make changes to the project.

5. *Community.* All the members of the Drupal community. Their involvement in an individual project often arises because they are users of it. They can make use of tools as mediated artefacts to provide feedback, supply patches to solve bugs or extend the project's features.

6. *Division of labour.* The different roles typically associated with contributed projects; for example, developers or UI designers. Again, tasks can be allocated by using the tools as mediating artefacts.

Similarly, we employed the model of the activity system for the study of a significantly different activity, the organization of events. For example, Figure 10.5 provides an example of the application of the model to study the organization of a DrupalCamp, a type of event organized by local communities consisting of a conference typically lasting two or three days:

1. *Subject.* The participants in the event.
2. *Tools.* The mediating artefacts used to coordinate the event. For example, the platforms employed to coordinate the event, mailing lists, and specific discussion groups for the event at groups.drupal.org.
3. *Object.* The DrupalCamp.

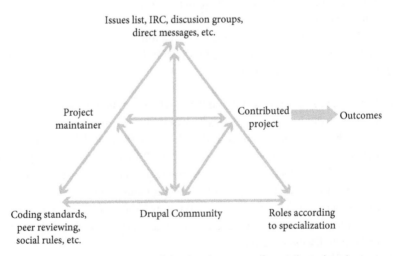

Fig. 10.4 Conceptualization of the development of contributed projects from an AT perspective

Adapted from Figure 3.7 in Rozas (2017, 119).

4. *Rules*. Examples of explicit rules are the selection criteria for any presentations made at a DrupalCamp,[7] as well as DrupalCamp codes of conduct, which outline the shared ideals and values of the community.[8] Examples of implicit rules are social norms related to the reputation of a subject in the community. For example, to be able to organize a DrupalCamp, community members require a significant degree of legitimacy.

5. *Community*. All the members of the Drupal community.

6. *Division of labour*. The different roles of the participants of the event; for example, session reviewers, presenters, and the DrupalCamp attendees themselves.

We draw on the previous two examples to illustrate the very different nature of these two activities: maintaining the source code of a contributed project; and organizing a DrupalCamp. The application of AT to both allows us to establish cross-contextual comparisons because all activities are categorized using consistent concepts. For instance, we could make comparisons between the emergence of peer-reviewing practices to assess quality and acceptance in the main platform of source code and the practices for accepting a presentation at a community event, which are both categorized as rules within AT. We can also draw comparisons between activities in which the focus is the same, but whose organizational characteristics differ; for example, between having code officially accepted in core projects and in contributed projects.

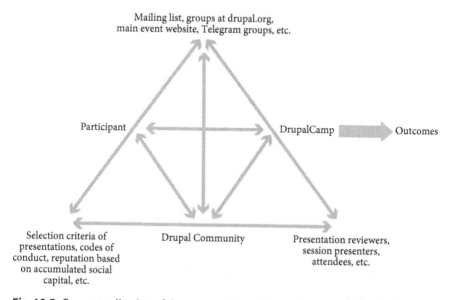

Fig. 10.5 Conceptualization of the organization of DrupalCamps from an AT perspective

Adapted from Figure 3.8 in Rozas (2017, 120).

To achieve this, we employed the previously described AT elements as initial analytical categories for each activity, and then explored the relationships between them. An example of the type of relationships explored are those between: the artefacts employed for collaboration (e.g. the issues list of a contributed project in Drupal.org or the website to coordinate the organization of a DrupalCamp); the division of labour (e.g. Drupal roles played by participants such as being a maintainer of a contributed project or being a member of the peer-reviewing team for presentations submitted at a DrupalCamp); and the implicit and explicit rules around such activities (e.g. coding standards for contributed projects, or codes of conduct for DrupalCamps). Establishing such cross-contextual comparisons between relationships led us, for example, to find similarities in the emergence of peer-reviewing practices to assess the quality of source code and the submission of presentations to communitarian events (Rozas and Huckle 2021). Subsequently, following these practices, we found similar organizational characteristics, such as degrees of specialization, legitimacy, and perceived value (see tables 3 and 4 in Rozas and Huckle 2021, 209–10), despite the different nature of the activities.

The employment of the 2GAT model also proved useful for incorporating findings from previous studies of Drupal. For instance, the tensions between designers and developers described by Zilouchian-Moghaddam et al. (2012) were incorporated initially as emerging from the division of labour. As a result, we could study their impact on other entities of the 2GAT model—for example, how contributions are represented or not in the collaboration artefacts, such as the official user profiles at drupal.org. For instance, one category was 'object-oriented' contributions, encompassing all activities whose main outcomes from an AT perspective are typically directed towards digital commons such as source code, documentation, and translations. The second category was 'community-oriented' contributions, in which the main outcomes from an AT perspective are directed towards the community. These categories helped us to identify significant differences between the indicators which measure and aggregate forms of value in CBPP (Rozas et al. 2021). These findings led us to argue (Rozas et al. 2021) for a need to broaden our understanding of contribution in CBPP communities, so that traditionally less visible forms of work are acknowledged as of value in the communities and visualized in the online platforms that support peer production.

Application of AT at a macro-level: Drupal as a 'runaway object'

AT does not establish an a priori micro-/macro-divide (Miettinen 1999). Instead, as above, AT provides researchers with a set of analytical concepts, such as the main elements of the 2GAT model, to foster conceptual connections in the context of their studies. In CBPP communities, such as Drupal, 'the boundaries and structures of activity systems seem to fade away' (Engeström 2009, 309). Because their simultaneous reciprocal processes are multidirectional and multilayered, their boundaries and structures are often difficult to distinguish and do not usually have a single stable centre. Instead, this mode of production requires and creates 'bounded hubs of concentrated coordination efforts' (Engeström 2009, 310). In order to connect the micro and macro aspects of this case study, this research explored these bounded hubs shedding light on how a large global CBPP community such as Drupal organizes itself (Rozas and Huckle 2021). To achieve this, we carried out a first step in the conceptualization by framing the whole of Drupal as a 'runaway object', as depicted in Figure 10.6.

We conceptualized Drupal (Rozas et al. 2015) in line with Engeström's (2009, 306) set of prerequisites for runaway objects, discussed earlier. As with any other FLOSS project, Drupal transcends utilitarian motives and bases its sustainability on collaborative production (requisites 1 and 4). The nature of the project is dynamic, and it is in a constant process of change (requisite 2). Additionally, the main production processes and project outcomes are also visible, cumulable, and accessible all of the time (requisite 3).

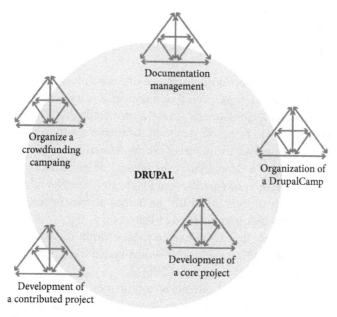

Fig. 10.6 Interconnecting Drupal activities result in Drupal as a runaway object

Adapted from Figure 1 in Rozas et al. (2015, 5).

However, while the concept of runaway object operates as a nexus allowing an initial connection between organizational micro and macro aspects, this study required a more precise definition of these 'bounded hubs of concentrated coordination efforts'. This reflects a critique of the 3GAT (Spinuzzi 2011). Spinuzzi (2011) proposes instead to corral the *runaway object* in ways which allow it to be enriched appropriately. In other words, to attune the definition of what the runaway object is in order to contextualize it to the case study. Overall, this need to provide a more accurate definition is in line with the ongoing efforts of activity theorists to rethink the 3GAT to accommodate the changes in newer forms of organization, characterized by a distributed workforce and the predominance of knowledge work, as is the case in peer-production.

Being aware of this conceptual issue as described by Spinuzzi in the application of the 3GAT, we attuned to it by providing a more accurate definition of what Engeström's (2009) bounded hubs of coordination were in the context of Drupal. As a result, we brought together the 3GAT's concept of a runaway object and the concept of socio-technical systems from organizational theory (Trist 1981). The result was the development of the concept of a '*socio-technical system of contribution*', in the context of peer-production, defining it as:

> A set of interacting parts, including people, software, hardware, procedures or rules among others, which form a complex whole that revolves around networks of human activity systems which are perceived contributions within the community and share a similar main focus of action.
>
> **(Rozas 2017, 122)**

For example, while we previously presented our conceptualization of the development of a contributed Drupal project as a human activity system from a 2GAT perspective, the network of thousands of contributed modules in Drupal.org can be conceptualized as a socio-technical system of contribution within the community. Similarly, while we employed the model of the human activity system for the analysis of the organization of a DrupalCamp, the network of DrupalCamps was framed as a socio-technical system of contribution. Figure 10.7 provides an illustration of the application of this concept, in which the human activity systems are grouped according to the socio-technical system they belong to.

Figure 10.7 also shows how the human activities within these groups are interconnected and displays the interactions between different socio-technical systems of contribution within the runaway object of Drupal.

The notion of socio-technical systems of contribution enabled them to be connected to the macro-levels at which they occur, as well as the tensions between different systems The result was to enable an analysis not exclusively focused on the workings of contribution activities themselves (micro-level), but also on the interactions between the networks they form as socio-technical systems of contribution (macro-level). This led us to study how these socio-technical systems of contribution

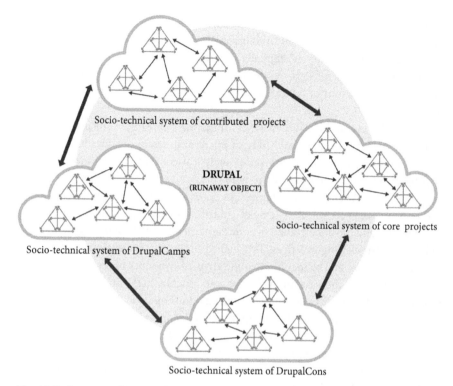

Fig. 10.7 Conceptualization of Drupal (runaway object) as a set of socio-technical systems of contribution

Adapted from Figure 3.9 in Rozas (2017, 123).

emerge, evolve, interact, with each other, and are shaped by different organizational dynamics (Rozas and Huckle 2021).

Reflections

In this section, we discuss the main insights concerning the application of AT to broader forms of digital labour beyond CBPP. We subsequently provide an evaluation of the general challenges tackled during the undertaking of this research and discuss specific limitations concerning the application of AT.

Insights from applying Activity Theory to digital work

We found three main benefits of the application of AT to the study of digital labour. First, AT facilitates the identification and deconstruction of activities into several components in ways that allow strategic and cross-contextual comparisons. This study used 2GAT to describe the elements of contribution activities within the development of source code and the organization of face-to-face communitarian events. Although they are substantially different organizational activities, the use of AT provided a useful lens to compare them. This capacity to facilitate cross-contextual comparisons of AT can also be useful when researching broader forms of digital labour.

Second, the use of AT as an analytical framework to explore collaboration was valuable in order to connect the study of micro and macro organizational aspects of peer-production practices. AT's set of analytical concepts and its tools' flexibility proved to be useful in this case study to connect actions at different levels, from carrying out a code commit or submitting a presentation for an event (micro-level), to the whole socio-technical systems of contribution for the development of software projects and the organization of communitarian events (macro-level) and their different peer-reviewing practices. This helped us to trace the evolution of organizational structures, and to identify two intertwined dynamics of formalization and decentralization in the case study (Rozas and Huckle 2021). In this respect, AT provides a useful lens to cope with complexity and untangle the dense and multidirectional dynamics which lie within a broader range of contemporary working practices which are increasingly mediated by digital platforms. Similarly to this case study, a researcher exploring a platform such as MTurk could employ AT to connect actions such as 'getting a task' with the socio-technical systems and the dynamics to distribute value which operate in such scenarios.

Third, the use of the model of activity as a unit of analysis also helped in reconsidering the notion of contribution in CBPP communities, leading to the exploration of certain contribution activities which have traditionally remained less visible in FLOSS and CBPP literature, such as the training and mentoring of community members (Rozas et al. 2021). These perceptions of what can be considered contribution contrast with those recognized in the main collaboration platform. This issue was identified while exploring a tension between the division of labour (the different roles present in the Drupal community) and the artefacts (in this case how drupal.org profiles record some of these contributions). The result was a call to broaden our understanding of the notion of contribution in CBPP communities, incorporating new kinds of contributions customarily left invisible (Rozas et al. 2021). In this respect, AT offers a powerful lens for the study of similar, increasingly blurred boundaries on a broader spectrum of digital labour for what is or is not considered work. Researchers interested in the study of such boundaries in crowdsourcing platforms, such as MTurk or Upwork, might similarly identify tensions and interactions from which to explore the practices behind more extensive forms of digital labour. Examples of these tensions and interactions could be those between the division of labour (e.g. owners and workers of the platform) and the rules (e.g. those embedded in the algorithms employed to allocate work). From these interactions between AT elements, researchers can trace the emergence of organizational structures associated with them, or perhaps experiment with a gradual shifting of the power of decision-making about the rules that determine the distribution of value to the members of such platforms.[9]

Challenges

An important source of challenges derived from the first author's position as a researcher, since he was already an active member of the Drupal community for over three and a half years before embarking on this research. This previous experience proved valuable for more rapid access to the community: from a faster understanding of the meanings around the software and the community to practicalities for entering the fieldsite and gaining access to certain activities. This previous experience came at the cost, however, of having to address challenges related to the dynamics of insider research, such as role duality and preunderstanding (Brannick and Coghlan 2007, 67–71). Regarding the latter, for example, the fact that the first author's previous experience within the Drupal community was mainly as a software developer was identified as a potential source of partiality. Consequently, an effort was made to have a wider understanding from the perspectives of Drupalistas with different roles (the division of labour from an AT perspective) during participant observation, the selection of interviewees, and the documentary analysis.

Another source of challenges derived from the ethical aspects arising from the use of ethnographic methods. Overall, this involved a constant assessment of the possibility of new ethical issues arising during its course. When new issues were discovered, actions were designed and implemented. For instance, with regards to the type of access while conducting participant observation, there was a constant effort to undertake it in the most overt way possible, but being aware of the limitations. Examples of these actions include for the first author to present himself at local events as 'a Drupalista who was currently studying the Drupal community for his PhD research' (Rozas 2017, 137–43, 153–7), and making his role as researcher visible in the digital platforms employed by the community.[10] Furthermore, efforts were made to expose his role as a researcher to the global community to the highest degree possible. Examples include: participation in a podcast and interviews in communitarian channels,[11] and dissemination of the research findings at local events, DrupalCamps, and a DrupalCon.[12] Notwithstanding, limitations existed: the role could not be qualified as that of a completely known observer, since some attendees were not aware of the first author's role, especially while participating in large international events, such as DrupalCons, with thousands of attendees.

Limitations from the application of AT

As with any other analytical lens, the application of AT is not free from limitations (Nardi 1996, 63–4). In the context of its application for this case study, we identified two limitations of particular relevance when reflecting on a more generic application to studies on digital labour.

First, defining human activity as the primary unit of analysis and observation has an impact, as any other choice would, on the emergence of relevant thematic areas explored during the overall processes of data collection and content analysis. For example, a deeper understanding of certain organizational aspects, such as the role of private companies to influence the direction of Drupal, emerged only tangentially. A different choice of unit of analysis would have highlighted this type of organizational aspect. The study could have focused on participants carrying out changes to contributed projects under company sponsorship. That may have helped uncover the role of companies in shaping the direction of large FLOSS projects (and CBPP projects in general), thereby framing Drupal as a *community of companies* (González-Barahona et al. 2013) rather than a community of individuals. Researchers drawing on AT for the study of other forms of digital labour should be carrying out a continuous process of review and self-reflection in order to identify the impact of the choice of unit of analysis and observation on their data to implement adaptations in the research design accordingly.

Second, the flexibility offered by AT as an analytical framework can, at times, be a 'double-edged sword'. As we have seen, the notion of runaway object can lead to a need for methodological and theoretical contractions of the object (Spinuzzi 2011). Researchers studying broader forms of digital labour might face similar challenges. Overall, this type of issue connects with the efforts (e.g. Spinuzzi 2020) of activity theorists who acknowledge that the ongoing changes in new forms of organization, such as CBPP and broader forms of digital labour, are so profound that they require a radical rethinking of the models. The identification of limitations, drawing on case studies of these novel forms of organization, is essential to sustain the path to an emerging fourth generation of AT (Spinuzzi and Guile 2019). The application of AT to more comprehensive cases of digital labour could contribute, in that respect, to better identifying such limitations which would be useful to reflect and refine a new generation of AT conceptually into the current context, as has happened in previous periods (e.g. Kuutti 1996).

Conclusion

In this chapter, we have found three benefits of particular relevance for the use of Activity Theory for research on digital labour. First, AT is useful to identify, deconstruct, and compare collaborative activities mediated by digital platforms. Second, AT possesses a high degree of flexibility for the study of organizational practices at different levels. Rather than imposing a predefined micro/macro divide, AT provides a series of concepts which researchers can adapt according to specific digitally-mediated contexts. Third, AT offers a suitable lens to deal with the blurred organizational characteristics present in emerging forms of digital labour. Key notions of AT, such as its models, entities, and tensions, provide useful categories from which to explore practices in digital labour.

Given the benefits we demonstrate, we hope other digital labour researchers employ AT, contribute to its development and identify its limitations. In this way, AT will continue to be an invaluable analytical lens for the study of organizational practices.

Acknowledgements

This work was partially supported by the project P2P Models (https://p2pmodels.eu) funded by the European Research Council ERC-2017-STG (grant no.: 759,207) and by the project Chain Community funded by the Spanish Ministry of Science, Innovation and Universities [grant no.: RTI2018-096820-A-100].

We would like to thank Christine Hine, Gillian Symon, and Juan Pavón for their helpful comments and suggestions. We also thank Elena Martínez Vicente for her help editing the diagrams. Finally, we would like to thank Tabitha Whittall for her help in copy-editing and proofreading this chapter.

Notes

1. See Gray and Suri (2019) for an in-depth account of the increasing 'under-the-hood' task-based and content-driven work which is mediated by platforms such as MTurk (Amazon), Universal Human Relevance System (Microsoft), and UpWork, among others.
2. Usage statistics and market share of Drupal— https://w3techs.com/technologies/details/cm-drupal/all/all, accessed on 19 October 2020. This percentage includes well-known websites with complex architectures and high loads of traffic, such as mtv.co.uk and economist.com.
3. The 8613 documents included a significant amount of material collected from an open Drupal archive. They were processed using scripts available at https://davidrozas.cc/lab/drupal_planet_archive.php.
4. Drupal discussion groups are available at https://groups.drupal.org/.
5. Drupal coding standards are available at https://drupal.org/coding-standards.
6. The guidelines for contribution are available at https://drupal.org/contribute/development.

7. For an example of speaker guidelines used at *DrupalCamp Spain 2012*, see http://2012. drupalcamp.es/en/node/23.html.

8. For an example of a code of conduct used at *DrupalCamp Brighton 2015*, see http://www. drupalcampbrighton.co.uk/content/code-conduct.

9. See https://p2pmodels.eu/exploring-models-for-a-more-cooperative-distribution-of-tasks/ for an example of these types of initiatives in the context of undergoing research with blockchain technologies.

10. For examples, see https://www.drupal.org/u/drozas (profile in Drupal's main platform), https://events.drupal.org/u/drozas (profile in platform that supports the organization of DrupalCons), and https://www.meetup.com/London-Drupal-Pub-Meet/members/122334662/(profile in platform employed to organize events in London).

11. For examples, see https://www.drupaleasy.com/podcast/2015/10/drupaleasy-podcast-163-drupal-potato-david-rozas-open-source-contributing (podcast) and https://www.youtube.com/watch? v=DrbJ9xwSstE (interview in DrupalCamp London 2016).

12. For examples for each type of event, see https://vimeo.com/131301737 (Drupal Show and Tell in London, May 2015), https://drupalcampnorth.org/session/keynote-talk-silver-code-gold-contribution-beyond-source-code-drupal (keynote in DrupalCamp North 2015), and https://www.youtube.com/watch? v=TdEVaOjL20s&t=15m37s (keynote in DrupalCon Barcelona 2015).

References

Alvesson, M. 2003. Methodology for close up studies—struggling with closeness and closure. *Higher Education*, 46(2): pp. 167–93. doi:10.1023/A:1024716513774

Arvidsson, A., and Peitersen, N. 2013. *The Ethical Economy: Rebuilding Value after the Crisis*. Columbia University Press.

Benkler, Y. 2002. Coase's Penguin, or, Linux and 'The Nature of the Firm'. *The Yale Law Journal*, 112(3): pp. 369–446.

Benkler, Y. 2006. *The Wealth of Networks: How Social Production Transforms Markets and Freedom*. Yale University Press.

Bollier, D. 2003. The rediscovery of the commons. *UPGRADE*, 4(3). Retrieved from http://dlc.dlib.indiana.edu/dlc/bitstream/handle/10535/4979/up4-3Bollier.pdf?sequence=1&isAllowed=y

Brannick, T. and Coghlan, D. 2007. In defense of being 'native': The case for insider academic research. *Organizational Research Methods*, 10(1): pp. 59–74. https://doi.org/10.1177/1094428106289253

Coleman, E. G. 2013. *Coding Freedom: The Ethics and Aesthetics of Hacking*. Princeton University Press.

Dolin, K. Q. 2011. Drupal's story: A chain of many unexpected events. In Melançon, B. (ed.), *The Definitive Guide to Drupal 7* (pp. 821–33). Apress.

Engeström, Y. 1987. *Learning by Expanding. An Activity-Theoretical Approach to Developmental Research.* Cambridge University Press.

Engeström, Y. 1999. Activity theory and individual and social transformation. In Engeström, Y., Miettinen, R., and Punamäki, R.-L. (eds), *Perspectives on Activity Theory* (pp. 19–38). Cambridge University Press.

Engeström, Y. 2001. Expansive learning at work: Toward an activity theoretical reconceptualization. *Journal of Education and Work*, 14(1): pp.331–56. https://doi.org/10.1080/13639080020028747

Engeström, Y. 2006. From Well-bounded ethnographies to intervening in mycorrhizae activities. *Organization Studies*, 27(12): pp. 1783–93. https://doi.org/10.1177/0170840606071898

Engeström, Y. 2009. The future of activity theory: A rough draft. In Sannino, A., Daniels, H., and Gutierrez, K. D. (eds), *Learning and Expanding with Activity Theory* (pp. 303–28). https://doi.org/10.1017/CBO9780511809989.020

Fuster Morell, M., Martínez, R., and Maldonado, J. 2014. Mapping the common based peer production: A crowd-sourcing experiment. Presented at "The internet, policy & politics conferences". http://blogs.oii.ox.ac.uk/ipp-conference/2014/papers.html

Gnu.org. 2001. What is free software? Retrieved 28 February 2020, from https://www.gnu.org/philosophy/free-sw.en.html

González-Barahona, J. M., Izquierdo-Cortázar, D., Maffulli, S., and Robles, G. 2013. Understanding how companies interact with free software communities. *IEEE Software*, 30(5): pp. 38–45. https://doi.org/10.1109/MS.2013.95

Gray, M. L., and Suri, S. 2019. *Ghost Work: How to Stop Silicon Valley from Building a New Global Underclass.* Eamon Dolan Books.

Hegel, G. W. F. 1975. *Lectures on the Philosophy of World History.* Cambridge University Press.

Hine, C. 2000. *Virtual Ethnography.* Sage.

Hine, C. M. 2015. Mixed methods and multimodal research and internet technologies. In Hesse-Biber, S. N., and Johnson, R. B. (eds), *The Oxford Handbook of Multimethod and Mixed Methods Research Inquiry.* Oxford University Press. https://doi.org/10.1093/oxfordhb/9780199933624.013.31

Kaptelinin, V. 2012. Activity theory. In Soegaard, M., and Dam, R. F. (eds), *The Encyclopedia of Human–Computer Interaction.* Retrieved from https://www.interaction-design.org/literature/book/the-encyclopedia-of-human-computer-interaction-2nd-ed/activity-theory

Kelty, C. M. 2008. Two bits: The cultural significance of free software. Retrieved from http://twobits.net/download/index.html

Kuutti, K. 1996. Activity theory as a potential framework for human–computer interaction research. In Nardi, B. A. (ed.), *Context and Consciousness: Activity Theory and Human-Computer Interaction* (pp. 17–45). MIT Press.

Leont'ev, A. N. 1978. *Activity, Consciousness, and Personality.* Prentice-Hall.

Marx, K. 1924. Theses on Feuerbach. In *Marx-Engels Archives* (Vol. 1). Marx-Engels Institute, Moscow.

Miettinen, R. 1999. The riddle of things: Activity theory and actor-network theory as approaches to studying innovations. *Mind, Culture, and Activity*, 6(3): pp. 170–95. https://doi.org/10.1080/10749039909524725

Nardi, B. A. 1996. Studying context: A comparison of activity theory, situated action models, and distributed cognition. In Nardi, B. A. (ed.), Context and Consciousness: Activity Theory and Human-Computer Interaction (pp. 69–102). MIT Press.

Orgad, S. 2005. From online to offline and back: Moving from online to offline relationships with research informants. In Hine, C. (ed.), *Virtual Methods* (ch. 4, pp. 51–66). Berg.

Rozas, D. 2017. Self-organisation in Commons-Based Peer Production. Drupal: 'The drop is always moving'. https://epubs.surrey.ac.uk/845121/ PhD. University of Surrey.

Rozas, D., Gilbert, N., Hodkinson, P., & Hassan, S. (2021). Talk is silver, code is gold? Beyond traditional notions of contribution in peer production: the case of Drupal. *Frontiers in Human Dynamics*, 3, 618207, 1–16. https://doi.org/10.3389/fhumd.2021.618207.

Rozas, D., and Huckle, S. 2021. Loosen control without losing control: Formalization and Decentralization within commons-based peer production. *Journal of the Association for Information Science and Technology*, 72(2), pp. 204–23. https://doi.org/10.1002/asi.24393.

Rozas, D., Gilbert, N., and Hodkinson, P. 2015. Drupal as a runaway object: Conceptualisation of peer production activities through activity theory. In *Proceedings of the European Group for Organizational Studies 2015. Subtheme 17: 'Activity theory and organizations'*, (pp. 1–17). Athens, Greece.

Siefkes, C., 2008. *From Exchange to Contributions. Generalizing Peer Production into the Physical World*. Ed. Siefkes.

Spinuzzi, C. 2011. Losing by expanding: Corralling the runaway object. *Journal of Business and Technical Communication*, 25(4): pp. 449–86. https://doi.org/10.1177/1050651911411040

Spinuzzi, C. 2020. 'Trying to predict the future': Third-generation activity theory's codesign orientation. *Mind, Culture, and Activity*, 27(1): pp4–18. https://doi.org/10.1080/10749039.2019.1660790

Spinuzzi, C., and Guile, D. 2019. Fourth-generation activity theory: An integrative literature review and implications for professional communication. In *2019 IEEE international professional communication conference (procomm)*, 37–45. https://doi.org/10.1109/ProComm.2019.00012

Stadler, F. (2010, April 22). Digital Commons: A dictionary entry. Retrieved 10 October 2017, from http://felix.openflows.com/node/137

Trist, E. 1981. The evolution of socio-technical systems: A conceptual framework and an action research program. In Joyce, W. F., and Van de Ven, A. H. (eds), *Perspectives on Organization Design and Behavior* (pp. 19–75). Wiley.

Uden, L., Damiani, E., Gianini, G., and Ceravolo, P. 2007. Activity Theory for OSS Ecosystems. *In Inaugural IEEE-IES Digital EcoSystems and Technologies Conference (Vol. 2007, pp. 223–228). Cairns, Australia: IEEE. https://doi.org/10.1109/DEST.2007 .371974*

Vygotsky, L. 1978. *Mind in Society: The Development of Higher Psychological Processes.* Harvard University Press.

Wittel, A. 2013. Counter-commodification: The economy of contribution in the digital commons. *Culture and Organization*, 19(4): pp. 314–31. https://doi.org/10.1080/ 14759551.2013.827422

Zilouchian-Moghaddam, R., Bailey, B., and Fu, W.-T. 2012. Consensus building in open source user interface design discussions. *In CHI '12* (pp. 1491–500). https://doi.org/ 10.1145/2207676.2208611

11

Thick Big Data

Development of Mixed Methods for Study of Wikipedia Working Practices

Dariusz Jemielniak and Agata Stasik

Introduction

Social life has largely transitioned into the digital world and there is no escaping it (Bauman 2007). While still a decade ago it was entirely viable to perform some form of social science research without a digital component, today it could typically lead to important omissions. Online and offline spheres have become intertwined, which makes it difficult to conceive of a social phenomenon that would not extend to the digital world and leave no digital traces. Thus, instead of perceiving these domains separately, we should assume that social life is 'virtual' and 'real' at the same time, and that the digital world is an extension of the non-digital one. That is, the nearly universal connectivity adds another layer to local realities and opens up new possibilities of action for long-established strategies. For example, the use of the internet changes the strategies of social movements, influencing the process of knowledge creation and distribution (Stasik 2018) and the mobilization of allies (Lis and Stasik 2018; Rodak 2019). The investigation of virtual activity alongside actions taken in the real world—and the better understanding of the relationship between them—emerges as a new challenge for social science, from sociology through anthropology to management.

The Big Data revolution challenged the social sciences (Lazer and Radford 2017) with what was famously called 'the data deluge' (Anderson 2008). As we witness a radical increase of the volume and variety of data, it should not come as a surprise that social sciences have become increasingly 'datafied' (Millington and Millington 2015). That is, as a result of the availability of new types of data and new analytical strategies, scholars in social science have discovered many new research questions, which were not possible to answer without the availability of Big Data. Analysing quantifiable information about phenomena is simply too tempting and also brings a lot of valuable context. Moreover, some well-studied topics have benefited from analysis through Big Data on digital behaviour: we learn how to seek new answers to old questions.

Dariusz Jemielniak and Agata Stasik, *Thick Big Data*. In: *Research Methods for Digital Work and Organization.*
Edited by Gillian Symon, Katrina Pritchard, and Christine Hine, Oxford University Press.
© Oxford University Press (2021). DOI: 10.1093/oso/9780198860679.003.0011

For instance, we know that declarative racism studies do not reflect the full scale of the phenomenon, according to the racist practices that become easily identifiable through, for example, dating websites' preferences (Hwang 2013). Using digital data and quantitative insight may help in better understanding topics such as attitudes towards technology (Przegalinska et al. 2019), organization of virtual work in open source software development (Chełkowski et al. 2016), sexual behaviour online (Morichetta et al. 2019), or health and medical knowledge in lay populations (Smith and Graham 2019). Additionally, the development of new technologies and tools of communication and cooperation has resulted in what some call the collaborative society revolution (Jemielniak and Przegalińska 2020): a growing trend of people collaborating together online. This trend is visible in phenomena such as citizen science, peer production, remix culture, or the Quantified Self movement. The vast growth of social networks has also resulted in entirely new and complex phenomena related to online identity, privacy, or intimacy (Hodkinson 2017).

The availability of Big Data creates a new situation for disciplines in which—traditionally—data gathering was expensive, time and resource intensive, and in most cases driven by preconceived research questions. That is, the formulation of the research question or hypothesis determined what kind of data were created in the research process, with the use of specific methods, such as surveys or interviews (Stasik and Gendźwiłł 2018). The new situation of Big Data abundance may lead to an overreliance on digital sources alone. Yet if one confines investigation to the digital dimension of reality, it is difficult to understand the relationship between online actions and their entanglement in local, material processes. For example, we can scrape data on the popularity of an anti-fracking documentary distributed online and claim that it shows unconventional gas production to be internationally controversial (Control Risks Group 2012). However, these results show just the beginning of the story; we need to broaden the investigation to understand in which circumstances the online-distributed documentary inspires local opposition against the extraction industry. That may be done by conducting field studies which demonstrate the role of online content and social networks in enabling the emergence of local cooperation and trans-local networks of resistance (Hopke 2015; Vasi et al. 2015; Lis and Stasik 2018; Stasik 2018).

The Thick Big Data approach offers a way to address this challenge, providing researchers with a set of tools to conduct quantitative analysis of the virtual dimension of the given activity and treat its results as a point of departure for in-depth qualitative investigation. Qualitative study, either conducted as digital or traditional ethnography, allows for deeper interpretation of phenomena spotted with Big Data analysis. While the traditional division into quantitative and qualitative methods of analysing social phenomena remains useful in many respects, the Thick Big Data approach offers a new way of bridging this division.

One of the consequences of the over-abundance of Big Data is that specialists trained in different disciplines have become interested in matters traditionally investigated by social scientists. As meaningful analysis of Big Data requires the support of new and complex computational methods, specialists who were trained to master the necessary technical skills—physicists, biologists, data scientists—have entered social sciences' traditional domains and topics. And yet, paradoxically, this invasion increases rather than decreases the need for experienced social scientists. Understanding different methodologies, existing traditions and schools of thought, as well as the need to emphasize the limitations of our methods, all become much more important in the face of far-reaching conclusions that some can draw from big datasets (Grätz 2018). Moreover, we believe that Big Data not only benefits from, but actually requires *thick data* (Wang 2013; Blok and Pedersen 2014), as data never speak for themselves. Not only in social science, but also in other disciplines the empirical material requires a broader framework to assure the meaningful interpretation able to advance the academic discussion. To believe that access to Big Data makes contextual or domain-specific knowledge irrelevant is rather naive (Kitchin 2013). Indeed, quantitative analysis of Big Data may benefit from an interpretative approach, usually associated with qualitative studies (Babones 2016), simply because without a deeper understanding of the studied phenomena it is easy to fall for spurious correlations, incidental results, as well as simply false conclusions.

In this chapter, we are going to describe a new approach to doing social studies online: the Thick Big Data paradigm, which postulates taking advantage of the available large repositories of quantitative data to inform qualitative research. Mixed methods are a particularly good match for digital studies (Hine 2015; Stasik and Wilczyńska 2018) as they allow researchers both to *explore* and to *explain* observed phenomena (Creswell 2009). Combining large datasets with deep interpretation sounds like a perfect approach (Charles and Gherman 2019), as it allows us to benefit from the unprecedented detail of quantitative granularity, while still keeping the advantages of understanding the meaning behind the data (Halavais 2015). The postulated approach is similar to the sequential explanatory strategy described by Creswell (2009), where collection and analysis of quantitative data is followed by the collection and analysis of qualitative data. However, in contrast to this approach, more weight is given to the second, qualitative stage of investigation. When Big Data allow us to observe behaviours and actions which leave digital traces, supplementing the study with thick data gives an opportunity to understand meanings, motivations, and subtle consequences of online actions. At the same time, the Thick Big Data approach goes beyond using the result of Big Data analysis as justification for the case selection for in-depth ethnographic study (Howard 2002). Rather, the results of Big Data analysis are used not only to identify the most intensive cases, but also to shed light on the digital dimension of the phenomena under study.

However, as usual, the devil is in the detail. One of the biggest challenges in making the Thick Big Data union work is the fact that those who are experienced in advanced methods of quantitative data analysis often lack qualitative training and the other way around. Even though data science skills appear to be difficult to obtain, we believe paradoxically that it is more time-consuming to acquire a proper understanding of ethnography than to learn how to obtain and analyse large datasets useful for digital social sciences. Introducing digital qualitative studies to data scientists is not particularly different from teaching qualitative methods in general: it typically requires extensive learning of theory, and then a longitudinal, laborious study of a selected population. It is difficult to make shortcuts in learning the lore of ethnography. It is, however, entirely possible to look for shortcuts in aggregating digital data, as the field is rapidly evolving and programming is often no longer necessary for many of the tasks previously requiring more advanced coding skills, as we demonstrate with the case presented in this chapter. An overview of the picture emerging from Big Data may be achieved today without a long training in coding and quantitative analysis. We assume that this trend of availability of tools enabling analysis of digital data without coding will increase in the coming years, opening up new possibilities for social researchers trained in qualitative methods. Still, highly trained data scientists remain able to use their advanced skills to perform analyses that overcome the limitations of ready-made analytical tools, such as the lack of customization of analytical algorithms, parameters of analysis, or the relative lack of control over the selection of data.

In this chapter, after introducing the specific features of Wikipedia which makes it a particularly good fit for the Thick Big Data approach, we demonstrate the merit of this approach as applied to this case. However, we do not conduct one full analysis by one tool, but take the opportunity to showcase several tools for data acquisition. Used as a proof-of-concept, the chapter is meant as a simple introduction to quantitative data acquisition methods that can be used as a starting point for further qualitative research, leading to a Thick Big Data analysis. We are not offering a fully-fledged Thick Big Data report—rather, we focus on possible sources and tools for the quantitative part of the analysis, assuming the reader's familiarity with qualitative ones. It is worth noting that the choice of tools that we have presented here is arbitrary and they could have been replaced by other ones. What is important, though, is that we postulate informing qualitative studies with Big Data research, and the other way around.

Wikipedia as an Object of Thick Big Data Research

Wikipedia communities emerged as a representative of a new kind of digital organization and peer production 20 years ago. Wikipedia is representative of a new kind of digital organization, typical of the collaborative society (Jemielniak and Przegalińska 2020). It relies on an open collaboration by a large number of people who do not know each other personally and cooperate with each other to create the largest encyclopedia of humankind (Jemielniak 2014). It involves tens of thousands of people developing and updating an online encyclopedia on a daily basis, relying on different forms of labour, with varying levels of visibility and quantifiability.

According to some authors, the new mode of collaboration represented by Wikipedia has the potential to revolutionize the capitalist system (Benkler 2004).

Even if its influence is not so far-reaching, Wikipedia is a fascinating example of new forms of social interaction and work. In free and open source software projects it is typically professionals who cooperate to develop code (Chełkowski et al. 2016), and this endeavour can therefore be perceived either as a CV building or professional networking exercise. In contrast, Wikipedia is largely developed by non-professionals. Including Wikipedia article writing on one's resume does not make any sense in most contexts, and also virtually no one is a professional encyclopedia writer. Nevertheless, Wikipedia is highly successful and its quality is considered on par with the traditional sources (Mesgari et al. 2015).

Wikipedia is worth studying not just because it is an example of a product of a new, specific form of digital labour (Scholz 2012). It is also a perfect object of analysis for at least two other reasons. First, it is an enormous repository of social interactions. The number of discussions is several times larger than the number of encyclopedic articles. Since all decisions on Wikipedia are made participatively, and all have to be carried on Wikipedia, which stores every single edit forever, Wikipedia is a project that is priceless for all scholars interested in qualitative studies of digital life. In contrast to other, commercial projects, Wikipedia not only promises to archive all discussions and keep them in public access, but also allows easy access to all of its pages. This practice leads us to the second reason that Wikipedia is a worthy object of study: Wikipedia is based on a philosophy of sharing and as a result it is fully scraping-friendly. That is, it supports automated retrieving of data into a local database for later analysis. Unlike websites such as Amazon or Quora, which not only do not appreciate scraping, but also make their website structures obscure on purpose to make it more difficult, Wikipedia welcomes the re-using all of its data, including very detailed statistics on user behaviour. Big Data studies of Wikipedia itself and the patterns of collaboration and editing therefore become possible in a way that cannot be done on proprietary platforms (Hill and Shaw 2020; Keegan and Gergle 2013).

At the same time one must be aware that while all Wikipedia data are open and accessible, it is only possible to quantify, calculate, and interpret the measures chosen by developers. Understanding these measures often requires a deeper understanding of what they manifest in Wikipedia culture. For instance, one easy and commonly used measure to describe Wikipedias is article count, and many language communities celebrate crossing important milestones in their local Wikipedia's growth, such as reaching their first 100,000 or 1 million articles. However, this measure is very misleading: the second largest Wikipedia in the world, after the English one, is in Cebuano.[1] Cebuano Wikipedia has a number of users two to three orders of magnitude smaller than that of other Wikipedias in the top ten. Observing this peculiarity immediately invokes the need for a qualitative follow up to understand the reasons behind it. And indeed, after talking to people well-versed in Wikipedia history and culture, we can learn that in 2006 Cebuano Wikipedia started growing rapidly, not as a result of people editing it, but thanks to automatically generated articles. We can discover that most of the articles created by bots are simple, short articles about villages and towns all over the world. We can also discuss the unintended consequences of such development, such as flooding the section 'Random Article' on the Cebuano Wikipedia main page with nearly exclusively geographical factoids. Simple numeric discovery can lead us to discovering a story of deep contention and disagreements between local Philippine-language Wikipedians, as well as leading us to larger international repercussions, or a debate from 2017 on whether Cebuano Wikipedia should be closed down.[2] These examples show why Wikipedia is an ideal example for demonstrating the merits of a Thick Big Data approach in which an initial quantitative analysis is followed up with qualitative research.

Investigating Wikipedia Impact with Twitter Data

In addition to the data held by the Wikipedia platform itself, one may also use other sources of digital data to understand the relationship between Wikipedia and its broader environment, such as its impact on public discourse and the emergence of different collective identities. For the purpose of this chapter, we are going to guide the reader through the basic steps of the process of Thick Big Data analysis: data retrieving, analysis, and identification of topic and themes which can then serve for a later, qualitative follow-up. That is, we show how to scrape tweets from Twitter, perform sentiment analysis on them, as well as perform a TribeFinder check on followers of selected accounts in order to explore affinities between users. Other possible combinations of quantitative analyses useful for Thick Big Data include, for example, social network analysis, culturomics (Bohannon 2011), using Google Trends or Ngram, as well as scraping any website with tools such as ParseHub or OctoParse. A summary is given in Table 11.1. We are not going to describe all of these approaches in detail, but a fuller description is available in Jemielniak (2020). There are also many other useful methodological books dedicated to specific tools and methods (e.g. Gloor 2006; Fielding et al. 2008; Mejova et al. 2015; Franklin and Ii 2016). It should be noted that this is a relatively volatile field and tools can rapidly emerge and become redundant since few have sustained financial support and all are dependent on features of the social media platforms themselves that may be changed without notice.

Using Twitter for digital social research is very popular and for a good reason: the data are easily available, public, and the whole system is not geared towards selecting the audience which is allowed to see the message, as is the case for other social networks such as Facebook or Instagram. This is important, as we know that the message is directed at the general public, while in other social networks we may not be aware of the filtering selections made by the author. At the same time, one must be aware of some limitations of Twitter data. First, it is not easy to retrieve a representative sample of tweets (Liang and Fu 2015). It is also difficult to access historical tweets. Second, most of the content on Twitter is generated by a relatively small number of users, whose demographic profile does not represent the whole of society (Lindgren and Lundström 2011). That is, Twitter is dominated

Table 11.1 An overview of tools for digital analysis for researchers without or with limited coding skills

Tool	Function	Purpose	Require coding
ParseHub, OctoParse	Data acquisition	Scraping data from websites, e.g. Wikipedia	no
Twitter Archiver	Data acquisition	Scraping data from Twitter	no
VADER, Textblob3	Data analysis	Sentiment analysis	Basic Python coding skills
Condor, Gephi, NodeXL	Data analysis	Social network analysis	No coding required, important to learn software functions
Tribe Finder	Data acquisition and analysis	Machine-learning categorizing of users	no
Google Trends	Data acquisition and analysis		no
Meaning Cloud	Data analysis	Sentiment analysis	no

by journalists, politicians, celebrities, campaigners, and other individuals seeking channels to influence public opinion. Thus, the investigation of Twitter exchanges should not be treated as a replacement for a representative opinion poll, but rather as an important addition to research on public discourse performed in traditional media outlets. Still, Twitter can prove useful in making unexpected discoveries. For instance, it turned out to be useful in crowd-sourced disaster management during a tsunami, although its effect was visible mainly through influencers and opinion leaders, and not so much official governmental accounts (Carley et al. 2016). It can be used for stock market predictions (Zhang et al. 2011), as well as in general information credibility judgements (Castillo et al. 2013).

Even though important elements of Twitter Inc's business model rely on the selling of data through the Gnip company, there are many tools allowing Twitter scraping which bypass this intermediary. Thus, even without access to the official Twitter 'firehose', those with even minimal experience in Python can find numerous libraries allowing for harvesting data, such as Tweepy or GetOldTweets3—with them, collecting several hundred thousand tweets with a given hashtag should not take more than one to two days and just a single line of commands. We strongly recommend researchers get a basic grasp of Python or R, as the plethora of available modules and libraries useful for gathering data is breathtaking.

For the purpose of this chapter, let us just acknowledge that there are also quite a few free, standalone scrapers. To demonstrate how easy the beginning of digital quantitative data exploration can be, we are going to rely only on tools that are

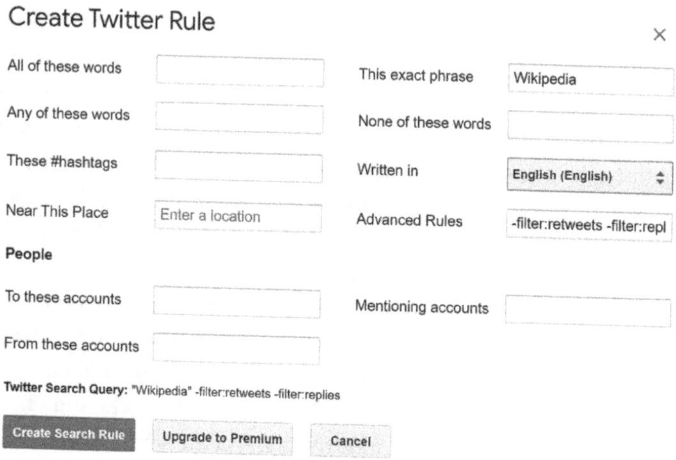

Create Twitter Rule

Fig. 11.1 Creation of Twitter rule in Tweet Archiver

extremely user-friendly, require no coding, and can be used by virtually anyone with some basic command of computer use. We are going to start with Tweet Archiver, a Google Sheet add-on, allowing for extremely easy archiving of tweets through configurable queries. It requires installing the add-on, and configuring it with a Twitter account (we recommend using a separate one than the one you normally use just in case the scraping behaviour affects your main account). A full walk-through tutorial is available on Youtube,[3] but the process is extremely straightforward and user-friendly.

We used available data from Twitter to investigate the current public debate on Wikipedia: we aimed to identify issues which raise public controversies, and understand how the reliability of Wikipedia as a source of knowledge is constructed, attracted, and defended.

For that purpose, in the period of 2–17 January 2020, we collected 31,095 tweets containing the word 'Wikipedia'. The number is so high because many people link to Wikipedia in their posts. We decided to start the analysis by studying a subset of 7445 tweets without any external links, so as to only focus on tweets that comment about Wikipedia itself, rather than discuss some other issue and only use Wikipedia as a source to confirm some point. It is worth mentioning that our 2-week scope would typically be longer—but for the purpose of method demonstration we decided to show that even a very quick, preliminary check done this way can already prove quite useful. In this way we obtained a snapshot of Twitter exchanges for the studied period.

The database that was generated directly in Google Sheets contains well-structured data on the tweets, including date, screen name, full name, tweet text, tweet ID (linking to the original tweet), link(s) from the tweet, media, location, the number of retweets, the number of likes, app used, the number of followers, or the number of accounts followed. Additionally, there is also a number of other cells with further information, such as whether the account is verified, what the user location and time-zone is, the date of registering on Twitter, a link to the user's homepage and a profile image. It is important to remember that just because tweets are public it does not necessarily mean that they all should be singled out for research. Just because someone posted something does not mean we are justified in using it. Some scholars even advocate treating tweets as private conversations (Jackson et al. 2020). Because of these considerations, in this chapter we are only using direct quotes of highly visible and already highly popular tweets.

A quick check based on just sorting the columns by the number of retweets shows that the two most popular tweets (with 1199 and 417 retweets respectively) relate to an incident on Wikipedia. Ahead of the release of the movie *Chhapaak*, someone vandalized a Wikipedia page about the victim of an acid attack, and changed the name of the aggressor.[4] This attempt to hide the name of the actual culprit was quickly picked up by social media and widely criticized. This type of discussion shows how the public opinion active in social media guards the reliability of Wikipedia, reacting robustly to acts of vandalism. The third most retweeted tweet comes from an account about Red Velvet, a South Korean girl group, taking pride in their single 'Psycho' reaching the top of the all-time chart in a TV show, *Show! Music Core*. The fourth is a comment about Wikipedia's quality, praising it as a great source for research: 'It's actually sad how many people think Wikipedia is not a decent source/starting point for research. Wikipedia provides citations so you can go check. That alone makes it better than 99% of OpEds from >major< publications'. A tweet from the official Wikipedia account, celebrating its 19th birthday is only number 12.

A total of 1010 tweets were retweeted three or more times. We decided to perform a sentiment analysis on these, that is, attempt to numerically analyse whether the tweets' content is positive, neutral, or negative, or whether it is written in a subjective or objective voice. It should be noted that sentiment analysis is still in its infancy, and especially when more complex contextual reading is required, such as in ironic tweets, the automated approach will not be very effective. It is typically an automated approach, depending on pre-defined dictionaries of sentiment-laden phrases. Still, in the Thick Big Data approach, we focus on pre-selecting certain subsets of material for further qualitative analysis, or to discover otherwise hidden phenomena, and there sentiment analysis can prove quite useful. For that purpose, we decided to use another Google Sheets add-on from Meaningcloud.com. The add-on allows a point-and-click sentiment analysis of text.

As a result of the check, 40 tweets were labelled as 'very negative', 233 were marked as 'negative', 99 as 'neutral', 214 as 'none', 358 as 'positive', 66 as 'very negative'. The clear dominance of positive tweets is interesting (42 per cent positive versus 27 per cent negative).

A closer look also confirms that positive perceptions are more popular as well, at least in terms of being 'favoured' (a heart symbol clicked by other users of Twitter to indicate support) and retweeted (cited and propagated further by other users, sometimes with a commentary). Reading the content of the top 20 most retweeted and

Fig. 11.2 MeaningCloud
Sentiment Analysis
selection

most favoured tweets, we find it surprising to see that Wikipedia is only described positively. However, to study the topic of Wikipedia's perceived reliability a little further, we used a query function in Google Sheets on the whole dataset of tweets to find all tweets with a string 'reliab' (to cover 'reliability', 'reliable', 'unreliable', etc.):

```
=QUERY(Wikipedia! A:U, 'select * where D contains "reliab"')
```

We found 152 tweets with this string. The most retweeted one was by Ann Coulter, criticizing Wikipedia for having an anti-conservative bias: 'Wikipedia, while usually reliable for basic, non-political facts, "functions as a libel factory" against conservatives and immigration patriots'. The tweet was illustrated by an image 'Wikifake do not trust what strangers are writing online' and a link to an article on vdare.com. The second most retweeted tweet was from Team Louis News, an account made to promote singer Louis Tomlinson, and stating 'We'd like to remind everyone that Genius isn't any better than Wikipedia in terms of reliability, as both can be edited by anyone and they don't run checks on whether the information being added is factual.

Don't trust anything you see unless it comes from official websites!' Apparently, some information appeared on Genius, a website gathering knowledge about music and musicians, and Team Louis criticized it by comparing it to Wikipedia. The third most retweeted tweet came from the Wikipedia Library, an initiative run by the Wikimedia Foundation, and promoting adding references to Wikipedia: 'Its time for @Lib1Ref! Come join us in making @Wikipedia more reliable by adding a citation. In the face of misinformation around the world, Wikipedia needs #libraries and #librarians even more!'

Now, clearly Ann Coulter and The Wikipedia Library have quite contradictory views on the reliability of Wikipedia. A simple way to use machine learning to compare their followers is employing TribeFinder, a very intuitive tool available at GalaxyAdvisors.com, and developed by Peter Gloor from MIT. TribeFinder allows creation of 'tribes' (Gloor et al. 2019), based on deep learning analysis of expressions of Twitter. An AI-based heuristic, trained on a large dataset of tweets, predicts similarity in vocabulary and syntax to four key distinct categories of digital personalities (Ciechanowski et al. 2020). TribeFinder assigns individuals to tribes through the analysis of their tweets and the comparison of their vocabulary. These tribal vocabularies are previously generated based on the vocabulary of tribal influencers and leaders selected using Tribecreator. Each tribe has certain characteristics, making it more or less similar to several core archetypes in five macro-categories: personality, ideology, lifestyle, alternative reality, and recreation. For instance (Figure 11.3), a sample of Ann Coulter followers are most commonly 'risk takers' (for a more detailed description of the available options, see Przegalinska et al. 2019).

Even more interestingly, one can compare two tribes to each other (Figure 11.4).

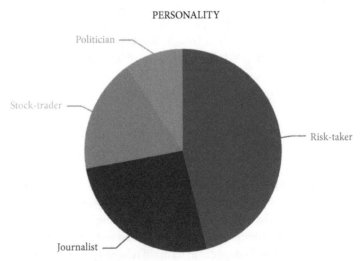

PERSONALITY

Politician

Stock-trader

Risk-taker

Journalist

Fig. 11.3 TribeFinder analysis of Ann Coulter followers

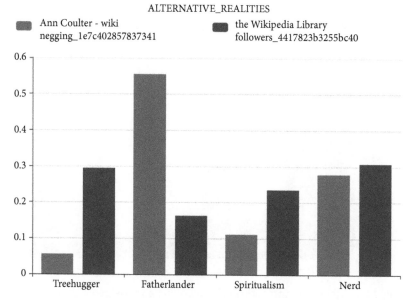

Fig. 11.4 TribeFinder comparison of Ann Coulter and Wikipedia Library followers: alternative realities

Wikipedia Library followers are much more ecology oriented than Ann Coulter followers. These are predominantly 'fatherlanders' (a group characterized by nationalism, reluctance to progress, anti-immigration sentiments, etc.) (Figure 11.5).

In terms of ideologies, Ann Coulter followers are more often 'complainers' (people who contest all ideologies). Surprisingly though, the Wikipedia Library tribe is much more often capitalism-supporting, as well as noticeably less socialism-supporting. This result clearly contradicts the common perception of Wikipedians as 'digital Maoists' (Lanier 2006). TribeFinder allows comparison against other characteristics as well. Using TribeFinder categorizations can prove useful for future interviews of the analysed individuals. It may also serve as a quantitative approach allowing specific people or tweets to be pre-selected for a more thorough qualitative content analysis.

One useful tool TribeFinder also offers is creating wordclouds of most common hashtags, as well as hashtag networks. For Ann Coulter followers it is shown in Figure 11.6.

A quick look shows immediately that this tribe is very political and contains a lot of Donald Trump supporters. Slogans such as #kag2020, #fourmoreyears, or #maga come from his campaign. In comparison, the hashtag network of Wikipedia Library is quite different, with Wikipedia dominant, but a lot of other scientific, political, and social topics visible. The wordcloud analysis may serve as a quick extraction of key topics and motives suited for a more thorough qualitative follow up. While relying on this analysis alone will likely not allow a deeper insight into the studied population, it is a good introductory snapshot.

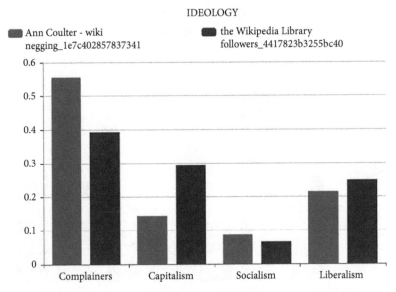

Fig. 11.5 TribeFinder comparison of Ann Coulter and Wikipedia Library followers: ideology

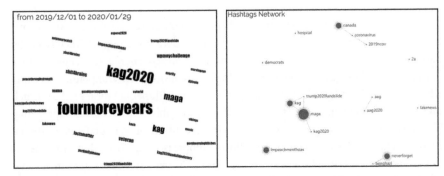

Fig. 11.6 TribeFinder wordclouds of most common hashtags and hashtag networks of Ann Coulter followers

Adding Thick Analysis to Big Data

Simple analysis of Big Data from Twitter allowed us to identify the topics and mechanisms important for an understanding of the online construction of Wikipedia's reliability which are worth in-depth qualitative investigation. Such a quick pilot study exposed what, actually, is an important topic for Wikipedia and Wikimedia communities: trust in the reliability of knowledge contained there is one of their defining notions, often contested and discussed within the communities, as well as outside of them, especially at the interface with the academic and educational worlds (Jemielniak and Aibar 2016; Konieczny 2016). Especially for those interested in the perception of the reliability of Wikipedia, the check we presented earlier could also be a really good start for a wider analysis of the issue. That may include investigations of how far arguments presented on different public arenas, such as Twitter exchanges, are internalized or rejected by the Wikipedia community and what is its impact on the Wikipedians' work practices. For example, to what extent is the possible Twitter influencers' line of attack taken into account while editing or creating new entries? How important is the task of defending the Wikipedia reliability on different social media platforms and who is engaging in this activity? Such questions are best answered through ethnographical participant observation within the Wikipedia community, which allows for the observation of both immediate reactions to the vivid public discussions and more subtle long-term changes influencing Wikipedians work practices.

The discussion about the vandalization of a Wikipedia article connected to the story about the *Chhapaak* movie, signalled that the discussion in social media served as an additional instance of quality control. That is, the widespread outrage against the attempt to hide the culprit's name secured the reliability of Wikipedia content. At the same time, the discussion of the incident shows just one dimension of the broader processes regarding gender, cyber and physical violence, propaganda, or cyberactivism—all discovered accidentally, through a brute force search. One may want to understand better how the online representation of violence, its survivors, and perpetrators, impact social norms and public attitudes. That may be done with the use of traditional research methods, such as interviews. Narrative interviews reflecting both online and offline life experience would be a particularly good choice.

Another question arises about the connection between the political orientation of Wikipedia-supporters and its foes. Clearly, the right-wing perceives Wikipedia as leftist, but machine learning text analysis indicates that the issue is more nuanced, and we already know that Wikipedia is often stereotyped (Jemielniak 2019). Is there a left-wing or right-wing bias? How do ideological differences influence the everyday functioning of Wikipedia and shape the content of the entries? How does it influence its credibility in different circles and contexts? To understand that better, one should conduct a qualitative study—for example, digital ethnography could allow us to give an account of how the Wikipedia community struggles with political biases, or how perceived politicization and polarization impacts Wikipedia's influence in different social groups. In fact, the political alignment of Wikipedias in different languages is a great topic to study, and connects well with the issues of equality, gender gap, or Internet colonization in Wikipedia communities (Jemielniak 2016; Couldry and Meijas 2019). A quantitative analysis here allows us to balance the loudest voices with the overall averaged out perception, available through large datasets, and makes a great segway into a qualitative study.

Yet another interesting issue that emerged through our analysis concerns the balance of positive and negative opinion and their amplification. Generally, even though Wikipedia seems to be often criticized, the sentiment analysis of a small sample of tweets shows that positive remarks about Twitter largely prevail. This may be a good starting point for a qualitative study, focusing on the loudness and reach of negative voices, even if in the minority. One may also compare different channels shaping public opinion, especially the relationship between social media to traditional media outlets. For instance, checking quantitatively the number of linked references to different media and listing the most popular ones often reveals interesting differences when two different tribes are compared.

In the case of each of the suggested themes, the successive qualitative analyses—either based on digital or traditional ethnography—should go back to the results of the quantitative part of study, to make sure that the two types of data are used together to deepen the understanding of the phenomena. It is worth noting that we should not expect that in all cases our analyses will be complementary. It is possible that the quantitative and qualitative results are contradictory. This is the reason why we propose using quantitative analysis as supplementary and supporting the qualitative results, which remain the leading ones.

Conclusion

In this chapter our aim was to show how easy it is to rely on large datasets to perform pilot studies informing qualitative research. We demonstrated how Big Data analysis opens up the possibility to identify interesting and important processes worth in-depth qualitative investigation. What is more, to conduct this type of analysis, it is no longer necessary to have the experience and skills of data scientists. Even a simple, several hour-long check of key topics and notions, analysed with free, non-coding tools, shows a large number of possible tropes and themes for the following qualitative analysis. Naturally, the reverse direction is also possible, that is, performing a deep, ethnographic study, and supplementing it with quantitative insight, based on Big Data gathered for the areas that the qualitative study indicated as important.

We believe that using a Thick Big Data approach allows us to avoid a typical pitfall of quantitative studies, which is providing a lot of data without a lot of context. However, it also makes qualitative studies more grounded in data, and makes starting a research project quicker: a reconnaissance by the means of data science is simply a quick way to highlight areas that are potentially worth examining through a more thorough qualitative project. Especially in ethnography, such initial insight is indispensable for at least two reasons. First, it allows the researcher to get a starting point for him- or herself. Second, equally importantly, it allows them to have a conversation starter for the fieldwork. Even straightforwardly showing our quantitative results to the interviewees can be a good beginning of a dialogue. Moreover, having some initial data makes it easier not to get distracted by the very first responses we gather, even before we can make our own opinion.

Our purpose was to show that even with limited coding skills it is entirely possible to harness machine learning tools, as well as do data scraping. We believe that one of the main reasons qualitative researchers avoid combining their research with digital large-scale data is mainly traditionalism, as well as fear of incompetence. This fear is justified to some extent, but we should remember that data scientists enter the social science domain without hesitation, even though on many occasions their lack of qualitative depth, as well as the lack of proper social sciences training, may lead to questionable conclusions.

Another source of qualitative researchers' unwillingness to incorporate Big Data analysis into their studies is uncertainty regarding incommensurability of different approaches. Here, we believe that as long as the researcher understands how data are generated and takes into account the biases caused by these mechanisms, they are able to use it to support the research conducted in an interpretative or constructivist paradigm. Trained ethnographers can, and in our view should, introduce elements of digital quantitative studies into their projects to build a solid background and justification for their research questions, helping to conceptualize key initial topics, as well as to problematize and challenge their findings. Similarly, data scientists should learn how to deepen their conclusions in qualitative studies although, as already stated, this approach is more difficult and goes beyond the scope of this chapter.

The age of Thick Big Data is coming. Let's embrace it.

Funding

Dariusz Jemielniak's contribution was supported by grant no. 2019/35/B/HS6/01056 from the Polish National Science Centre.

Notes

1. See: https://wikistats.wmflabs.org/display.php?t=wp
2. See: https://meta.wikimedia.org/wiki/Proposals_for_closing_projects/Closure_of_Cebuano_Wikipedia
3. https://youtu.be/MGU7azCYFpw
4. More context is available here: https://perma.cc/X5TK-2AQ4

References

Anderson, C. 2008. The End of Theory: The Data Deluge Makes the Scientific Method Obsolete. *WIRED*. Retrieved 17 February 2020, from <https://www.wired.com/2008/06/pb-theory/>

Babones, S. 2016. Interpretive quantitative methods for the social sciences. *Sociology*, 50(3): pp. 453–69.

Bauman, Z. 2007. *Liquid Times: Living in an Age of Uncertainty*. Polity Press.

Benkler, Y. 2004. Sharing nicely: On shareable goods and the emergence of sharing as a modality of economic production. *The Yale Law Journal*, 114(2004): pp. 273–358.

Blok, A., and Pedersen, M. A. 2014. Complementary social science? Quali-quantitative experiments in a Big Data world. *Big Data & Society*, 1(2): pp. 1–6.

Bohannon, J. 2011. Google Books, Wikipedia, and the future of culturomics, *Science*, 331(6014): p. 135.

Carley, K. M., Malik, M., Landwehr, P. M., Pfeffer, J., and Kowalchuck, M. 2016. Crowd sourcing disaster management: The complex nature of Twitter usage in Padang Indonesia. *Safety Science*, 90: pp. 48–61.

Castillo, C., Mendoza, M., and Poblete, B. 2013. Predicting information credibility in time-sensitive social media. *Internet Research*, 23(5): pp. 560–88.

Charles, V., and Gherman, T. 2019. Big Data analytics and ethnography: Together for the greater good'. In Emrouznejad A. and Charles V. (eds), *Big Data for the Greater Good* (pp. 19–33). Springer International Publishing.

Chełkowski, T., Gloor, P. A., and Jemielniak, D. 2016. Inequalities in open source software development: Analysis of contributor's commits in Apache Software foundation projects. *PloS one*, 11(4): e0152976.

Chmielewska-Szlajfer, H. 2018. Opinion dailies versus Facebook fan pages: The case of Poland's surprising 2015 presidential elections. *Media, Culture & Society*, 40(6): pp. 938–50.

Ciechanowski, L., Jemielniak, D., and Gloor, P. 2020. AI research without coding: The art of fighting without fighting: Data science for qualitative researchers. *Journal of Business Research*, 117: pp. 322–30.

Control Risks Group. 2012. *The Global Anti-Fracking Movement. What it wants, how it operates and what's next*. Control Risks Group.

Couldry, N., and Mejias, U. A. 2019. Data colonialism: Rethinking Big Data's relation to the contemporary subject. *Television & New Media*, 20(4): pp. 336–49.

Creswell, J. W. 2009. *Research Design: Qualitative, Quantitative, and Mixed Methods Approaches*. Sage.

Fielding, N. G., Lee, R. M., and Blank, G. 2008. *The SAGE Handbook of Online Research Methods*. SAGE.

Franklin, B., and Ii, S. E. 2016. *The Routledge Companion to Digital Journalism Studies*. Taylor & Francis.

Gloor, P. A. 2006. *Swarm Creativity: Competitive Advantage through Collaborative Innovation Networks*. Oxford University Press.

Gloor, P. A., Fronzetti Colladon, A., de Oliveira, J. M., and Rovelli, P. 2019. Put your money where your mouth is: Using deep learning to identify consumer tribes from word usage. *International Journal of Information Management*, 51: p. 101924.

Grätz, M. 2018. Gaydar and the fallacy of decontextualized measurement. *Sociological Science*, 5: pp. 270–80.

Halavais, A. 2015. Bigger sociological imaginations: Framing big social data theory and methods. *Information, Communication and Society*, 18(5): pp. 583–94.

Hill, B. M., and Shaw, A. 2020. The most important laboratory for social scientific and computing research in history. In J. M. Reagle and J. Koerner (eds), *Wikipedia @ 20: Stories of an Incomplete Revolution* (pp. 160–74). MIT Press.

Hine, C. 2015. *Ethnography for the Internet: Embedded, Embodied and Everyday*. Bloomsbury Publishing.

Hodkinson, P. 2017. Bedrooms and beyond: Youth, identity and privacy on social network sites. *New Media and Society*, 19(2): pp. 272–88.

Hopke, J. E. 2015. Hashtagging politics: Transnational anti-fracking movement twitter practices. *Social Media and Society*, 1(2): pp. 1–12.

Howard, P. N. 2002. Network ethnography and the hypermedia organization: New media, new organizations, new methods. *New Media and Society*, 4(4): pp. 550–74.

Hwang, W.-C. 2013. Who are people willing to date? Ethnic and gender patterns in online dating. *Race and Social Problems*, 5(1): pp. 28–40.

Jackson, S. J., Bailey M., and Welles, B. F. 2020. *# HashtagActivism: Networks of Race and Gender Justice*. MIT Press

Jemielniak, D. 2014. *Common knowledge? An Ethnography of Wikipedia*, Stanford University Press

Jemielniak, D. 2016. Breaking the glass ceiling on Wikipedia. *Feminist Review*, 113(1): pp. 103–8.

Jemielniak, D. 2019. Wikipedia: Why is the common knowledge resource still neglected by academics? *GigaScience*, 8(12): giz139.

Jemielniak, D. 2020. *Thick Big Data: Doing Digital Social Sciences*. Oxford University Press.

Jemielniak, D., and Aibar, E. 2016. Bridging the gap between wikipedia and academia. *Journal of the Association for Information Science and Technology*, 67(7): pp. 1773–76.

Jemielniak, D., and Przegalińska, A. 2020. *Collaborative Society*. MIT Press.

Keegan, B., and Gergle, D. 2013. Hot off the wiki: Structures and dynamics of Wikipedia's coverage of breaking news events. *American Behavioral Scientist*, 57(5): pp. 595–622.

Kitchin, R. 2013. Big data and human geography. *Dialogues in Human Geography*, 3(3): pp. 262–7.

Konieczny, P. 2016. Teaching with Wikipedia in a 21st-century classroom: Perceptions of Wikipedia and its educational benefits, *Journal of the Association for Information Science and Technology*, 67(7): pp. 1523–34.

Lanier, J. 2006. Digital Maoism. The hazards of the new online collectivism. *The Edge*. org, http://www.edge.org/3rd_culture/lanier06/lanier06_index.html: retrieved on 6 April 2012.

Lazer, D. M. J., and Radford, J. 2017. Data ex machina: Introduction to Big Data'. *Annual Review of Sociology*, 43: pp. 19–39.

Liang, H, and Fu, K.-W. 2015. Testing propositions derived from Twitter studies: Generalization and replication in computational social science. *PLoS ONE*, 10(8): pp. 1–14.

Lindgren, S., and Lundström, R. 2011. Pirate culture and hacktivist mobilization: The cultural and social protocols of #WikiLeaks on Twitter. *New Media & Society*, 13(6): pp. 999–1018.

Lis, A., and Stasik, A. 2018. Unlikely allies against fracking: Networks of resistance against shale gas development in Poland. In Whitton, J., Cotton, M., Charnley-Parry, I. M., and Brasier, K. (eds), *Governing Shale Gas* (pp. 117–29). Routledge.

Mejova, Y., Weber, I., and Macy, M. W. 2015. *Twitter: A Digital Socioscope*. Cambridge University Press.

Mesgari, M., Okoli, C., Mehdi, M., Nielsen, F. A., and Lanamäki, A. 2015. 'The sum of all human knowledge': A systematic review of scholarly research on the content of Wikipedia. *Journal of the Association for Information Science and Technology*, 66 (2): pp. 219–45.

Millington, B., and Millington, R. 2015. 'The datafication of everything': Toward a sociology of sport and Big Data. *Sociology of Sport*, 32(2): pp. 140–60.

Morichetta, A., Trevisan, M., and Vassio, L. 2019. Characterizing web pornography consumption from passive measurements. In Choffnes, D., and Barcellos, M. (eds), *Passive and Active Measurement. PAM 2019.* (pp. 304–16). Springer.

Przegalinska, A., Ciechanowski, L., Stroz, A., Gloor, P., and Mazurek, G. 2019. In bot we trust: A new methodology of chatbot performance measures. *Business Horizons*, 62(6): pp. 785–97.

Rodak, O. 2019. Hashtag hijacking and crowdsourcing transparency: social media affordances and the governance of farm animal protection. *Agriculture and Human Values*, 37: pp. 281–94.

Scholz, T. 2012. *Digital Labor: The Internet as Playground and Factory*. Routledge.

Smith, N., and Graham, T. 2019. Mapping the anti-vaccination movement on Facebook. *Information, Communication and Society*, 22(9): pp. 1310–27.

Stasik, A. 2018. Global controversies in local settings: Anti-fracking activism in the era of Web 2.0. *Journal of Risk Research*, 21(12): pp. 1562–78.

Stasik, A., and Gendźwiłł, A. 2018. Designing a qualitative research project. In Ciesielska, M. and Jemielniak, D. (eds), *Qualitative Methodologies in Organization Studies.* (pp. 223–44). Palgrave Macmillan.

Stasik, A., and Wilczyńska, E. 2018. How do we study crowdfunding? An overview of methods and introduction to new research agenda. *Journal of Management and Business Administration*, 26(1): pp. 49–78.

Vasi, I. B., Walker, E. T., Johnson, J. S., and Fen, H. 2015. 'No Fracking Way!' Documentary film, discursive opportunity, and local opposition against hydraulic fracturing in the United States, 2010 to 2013. *American Sociological Review*, 80(5): pp. 934–59.

Wang, T. 2013. Big data needs thick data. *Ethnography Matters*, 13.

Zhang, X., Fuehres, H., and Gloor, P. A. 2011. Predicting stock market indicators through Twitter 'I hope it is not as bad as I fear'. *Procedia—Social and Behavioral Sciences*, 26:pp. 55–62.

12

Images, Text, and Emotions

Multimodality Research on Emotion-Symbolic Work

Itziar Castelló, David Barberá-Tomás, and Frank G. A. de Bakker

Introduction

In light of current digital transformation, new forms of organization are emerging. These organizations require alternative ways of organizing and managing strategic alignment. Organizations with self-managed teams (Trist et al. 1963; Barker 1993), network organizations (Pratt 2000), online communities (O'Mahoney and Ferraro 2007), activist organizations (Van Laer and Van Aelst 2010; de Bakker 2015), or internet-based voluntary organizations (Wilde 2004; Bunderson and Thompson 2009) are examples of forms of organizing in which internet communication mediates how work is managed and strategy is communicated. Social media spaces such as Facebook and Twitter and new communication tools such as Zoom or Microsoft Teams are supplementing or replacing face-to-face conversations and meetings. However, despite the claimed decentralized and non-hierarchical nature of these forms of organization and the inclusive culture of these communication spaces (Hatten 1982; Barker 1993), managers still need to align members to their strategy and influence their activities. In this chapter, we explore how such online strategy alignment can be examined, paying attention to the interplay between images, text, and emotions in multimodal spaces.

Strategy alignment, through social media and online tools, requires new forms of understanding how meaning making is constituted and how emotions can be mobilized to facilitate action. Emotion-symbolic work (Barberá-Tomás et al. 2019), which consist of 'using visuals and words to elicit negative emotions through moral shock, and then transforming those emotions into emotional energy for enactment' (Barberá-Tomás et al. 2019, 1790) can help managers to align members to their strategy, even if the strategy is radically different, or difficult to implement.

In this chapter, we study emotion-symbolic work and, as a running example, examine the leaders of a social movement organization (SMO) that aims to create a new strategy to reduce plastic pollution that is focused on reducing plastic consumption instead of recycling plastic. First, we explain *why* it is important for managers and organizational leaders operating online to consider emotions and visual symbols in aligning organizational members with their strategy making. We

Itziar Castelló, David Barberá-Tomás, and Frank G.A. de Bakker, *Images, Text, and Emotions*. In: *Research Methods for Digital Work and Organization*. Edited by Gillian Symon, Katrina Pritchard, and Christine Hine, Oxford University Press.
© Oxford University Press (2021). DOI: 10.1093/oso/9780198860679.003.0012

discuss the notion of 'emotion-symbolic work' and examine how to understand the importance of interactions in creating emotional energy that can then lead to the enactment of the strategies. Second, we analyse the opportunities and challenges of doing research based on multimodal online data that includes the use of text and images and the interrelation between these two elements. We conclude this chapter by proposing several open questions and new avenues for research.

Theoretical Underpinnings of Emotion-Symbolic Work

In this section, we highlight the role of interactions, emotions, and symbols, which together configure the notion of emotion-symbolic work in strategic communication in multimodal spaces, such as social media and other online communication spaces.

Emotion-symbolic work (Barberá-Tomás et al. 2019) describes the work involved in the intertwined transformations of transient emotions into emotional energy, for one side, and ideas or objects into symbols, for the other. This involves, for example, using visuals and text to elicit negative emotions through moral shock, and then transforming those emotions into emotional energy for enactment. It operates in multimodal interactions consisting of three activities that help to embed stakeholders into organizational social structures and align them to the organization's strategy: *connecting stakeholders to the strategy or the collective cause*; *connecting stakeholders to a collective identity*; and *connecting stakeholders to the organization* in order to facilitate their emotional transformation and ongoing enactment of the strategy and goals of the organization.

To *connect stakeholders to the strategy or the collective cause*, managers work on anchoring and responsibilization of the stakeholders. Anchoring between verbal and visual modes refers to a process where 'verbal captions can narrow down the content of images and make it more specific' (van Leeuwen 2005, 77). Anchoring in emotion-symbolic work thus operates by using a symbol together with verbal interactions to educate stakeholders about the organization's cause or its strategy. Responsibilization refers to a 'process whereby subjects are rendered individually responsible for a task which previously would have been the duty of another ... or would not have been recognized as a responsibility at all' (Wakefield and Fleming 2009, 277). *Connecting those stakeholders to a collective identity* then involves promoting solidarity and hope in the efficacy of collective action. Promoting solidarity and hope gives relief to stakeholders from the moral shock evoked by the symbol and the guilt associated with being responsibilized for the problem, and thus helps to transform negative emotions into positive ones. Finally, *connecting the stakeholders to the organization* relates to the use of symbols to establish both the organization's legitimacy and the manager's influence as expert leader. Establishing legitimacy and influence are key, not only to develop engagement with the key stakeholder but also to have extensive influence in social media and therefore be able to promote the organization's campaigns and products in the longer run.

At the core of emotion-symbolic work is the transformation of the moral shock elicited by a symbol into enduring emotional energy. The main challenge managers face is to connect the (deliberate) moral shock provided by the symbol (or by any other symbols that might relate to the organization's strategy) with positive emotions that can lead to strategy alignment, especially if radical changes are needed. Stakeholders need to be shocked but also mobilized; their emotional energy needs to be unleashed. We found three elements of emotional energy in response to emotion-symbolic work: *energetic arousal, identification,* and *moral emotions* (Barberá-Tomás et al. 2019). *Energetic arousal* is the 'feeling that one is eager to act and capable of acting' (Quinn and Dutton 2005, 36), consisting of individual motivation and collective excitement. *Identification* relates the stakeholders with the organization's strategy and cause. *Moral emotions* are feelings associated with doing the right (or wrong) thing (Haidt 2003). These emotions are reflected in stakeholders showing they are internalizing the cause, or the new organizational strategy. In sum, emotion-symbolic work helps managers to connect with stakeholders via a constant interaction with the symbol and to create the necessary emotional energy that can then lead to the enactment of the strategies.

Key to understanding emotion-symbolic work and the use of emotions to drive strategic change is the examination of *how* interactions configure emotions and how these emotions are constituted by multimodal exchanges of symbols, images, and text. Emotions are 'passions and desires [that] are not reducible to the pursuit of rational interests' (Voronov and Vince 2012, 59). They are important because they are indicators of what is salient to people (Voronov and Vince 2012). Emotions connect people to social norms in a community (Lok et al. 2017) and in the organization where they work. Emotions reflect the negative or positive self-evaluation and evaluation by others (Creed et al. 2014). The resulting internalized unconscious representation of what is good and bad helps in managers' imposition of organizational norms but also induces self-imposed limitations on individuals' behaviour (Voronov and Vince 2012).

Sociologist Randal Collins (2004, 2014) developed the 'interaction ritual chains theory', which is relevant to the study of emotion-symbolic work. For Collins, successful interaction rituals should have at least two 'ingredients': first, 'transient emotions', such as grief or joy, and second, a shared 'mutual focus of attention' on specific 'objects or ideas' (Collins 2004, 33). Transient emotions are 'transformed' (Collins 2004, 107) during interactions into 'long-lasting, underlying tones or moods' (Collins 2004, 106), which Collins calls 'emotional energy'. The second ingredient of successful interaction rituals (that is, rituals generating a considerable amount of emotional energy to their participants) is a mutual focus of attention on objects or ideas. As an outcome of these rituals, objects or ideas are experienced as symbols by participants in the interactions. Symbols are cultural codes shared by a group of people. Managers of organizations maximize emotional energy through their chains of interactions around symbols, and gain from them a desire for action along what they consider a morally proper path. At the same time, they can transmit part of this energy to other participants in their interactions.

Although Collins' work provides us with a solid scaffolding, it also has two shortcomings. First, it lacks a specific understanding of how symbols are used by managers.

Collins does not clearly show how agency is executed by managers who need to ensure that their view and the new organizational norms are taken into consideration and introduced in everyday organizational activities. Second, Collins' assumption that any 'object or idea' could be transformed into a symbol through ritual interactions has also been criticized. Rivera (2015, 1343) affirmed that 'the content of what tends to produce or inhibit emotional energy in particular types of interaction rituals remains unclear', highlighting that differences between symbols matter. Indeed, increasingly, research acknowledges the different role of symbols and images in strategic work. Images, compared to verbal text, contain more vivid information and draw their persuasive power from this attribute (Meyer et al. 2013). Furthermore, visual symbols are often used metaphorically, communicating in a way that elicits emotional responses (Meyer et al. 2018).

In the next section we examine the details of conducting research into emotion-symbolic work, taking into consideration the analysis of interactions, the use of emotions to promote emotional energy to fuel interactions and symbols, together with text that conforms to the multimodal expressions of emotions. We focus on social media interactions, emotions, and multimodality because these communication spaces are gaining importance in the way organizations build, communicate, and maintain their strategy and yet have been understudied in research related to interaction-ritual chains.

Research Methods for Online Emotion-Symbolic Work

The study of emotion-symbolic work requires an understanding of three key elements: *interactions*, as central elements of research configuring action; *emotions*, as facilitators of interactions; and *multimodality*, as the element eliciting emotions. Drawing on the above explanation of these elements, we now develop their characteristics in social media and elaborate on the challenges and opportunities that they provide for new research.

Interactions and social media data

Social media have been considered inclusive spaces of communication since participation is free, easy, and, in principle, gives all stakeholders an equal opportunity to be heard (Papacharissi 2004). Social media have been defined as a venue to 'fight' against irresponsible business conduct (Lyon and Montgomery 2013); they act as a catalyst for social movement ideas (Bennett et al. 2014; van den Broek et al. 2017); and are a primary outlet for citizens wishing to express their concerns and voice their opinions (Russell Neuman et al. 2014; Barberá 2015). They are also important venues for organizations to express themselves and engage with other stakeholders (Castelló, Etter, and Nielsen 2016; Etter, Ravasi, and Colleoni 2019). Such interactions configure the content of social media.

Social media therefore provide a unique opportunity to study interactions as they unfold, without researcher intervention. Such so-called naturalistic observations have typically been related to ethnographic research but they may also apply to social media. While social media posts may subsequently be altered or modified by users, oftentimes such changes leave traces on the platform for a long time. Retrieving interactions is relatively easy with the use of the platform's API (the 'application programming interface' which is often publicly accessible), or by scraping data directly from the sites with specialized software tools. Interactions can then be stored and organized in a database, including not only the actors involved in the interactions and the exact images, texts and symbols, but also the exact timeline of these interactions. The digital traces thus offer a detailed overview of the interaction as it has unfolded over time.

In a previously published paper (Barberá-Tomás et al. 2019), we showed the interaction between leaders of a social movement organization (SMO) and their targets, and how, through emotion-symbolic work, they were able to convince thousands of people to join their cause *and* their organization. Through a qualitative analysis of social media interactions (mainly Facebook but also Twitter and Instagram) our research identified how SMO leaders of a plastic pollution movement used words and images to elicit reactions from their target audience, mostly users of social media. Showing the timeline of the interaction and displaying the conversations between leaders and targets, our research showed how leaders gradually created emotional energy to convert their targets. We explore this example further throughout the remainder of this chapter.

There are significant challenges in the study of online interactions and organizations' and managers' emotion-symbolic work, especially when large numbers of actors are involved. Here we discuss five of these challenges: big data, coding, timing and synchronicity, platform features and uses, and ethical issues.

First, *big data*. In general, big data is the availability of a huge volume (terabytes) of data that are moving at a high velocity as they are created in, or nearly in, real time. Big data are very diverse, being both structured and unstructured (Kitchin 2017). When organizations rely on a large group of stakeholders, many interactions take place via social media. Social media spaces such as Twitter or Facebook have millions of participants. The data potentially available to study therefore are beyond what a researcher can process through a traditional qualitative approach. Researchers in this area face the paradox of big data, that is, the amount and detail of data and opportunities to understand a phenomenon are significant but, at the same time, information overload makes processing the information costly, while a necessary aggregation of data reduces the possibility of understanding micro-phenomena such as emotion-symbolic work. To overcome this challenge, research on social media requires an important preparatory exercise that involves fundamental questions, such as:

- how can the phenomena be defined and limited;
- which actors are the focus of the study;
- how much data have these actors produced;

- what is the relationship between these actors;
- what are the social media spaces that the researcher should study to grasp actors' interactions in a holistic and meaningful way;
- and, very important in the case of big data, what data, and what amount of data is *not* useful to the researcher due to errors?

Since emotion-symbolic work is typically done by leaders or managers in an organization, these questions can be reformulated to explore how managers are defining their targets, their communicative relations with them, and the spaces they are using to communicate. In the example we use in this chapter, the phenomenon is limited to one leading SMO dedicated to denouncing and reducing the problem of plastic pollution in the USA. The phenomenon studied involves the strategy used to convince their targets to join their organization and reduce the problem of plastic pollution. In our own case, the 'targets' are people interested in the issue of plastic pollution but also other environmental organizations and entrepreneurs working on plastic related issues. The leader's aim is to make these targets join their organization to coordinate forces and establish a common frame. In our organization, the relationship between the leaders and other actors is not as strong as if they were working within the same organization. Oftentimes the SMO leaders did not know their targets upfront. The aim of the SMO leaders was to get to know these people in order to convince them to join the organization, embrace the organization's cause and engage with them in an online and offline relationship as volunteers so that the SMO could execute their strategy of organizing events, festivals, and other offline activities which required volunteer input. The social media spaces they used were Facebook, Twitter, and Instagram since their strategy was aimed at attracting as many people as possible to work towards the overarching organizational goal of reducing plastic pollution. These spaces often suffer from unproductive postings by 'trolls'. Trolls are users in social media that intentionally aim to upset other users by posting inflammatory, digressive, or off-topic messages. The challenge for leaders, and researchers alike, is to filter out these postings and avoid the negative comments by trolls to reduce the positive emotional energy created by them. We took all these challenges into consideration when we created our database to analyse emotion-symbolic work. Limiting the data to a single organization and its conversations with their stakeholders enabled us to approach the data in a qualitative way.

Despite the challenges of big data in social media research, combining big data analysis with more qualitative forms of research presents new opportunities for researchers. Big data analysis can not only help researchers to validate qualitative models at a larger scale, but the application of artificial intelligence techniques together with sophisticated forms of data coding can provide qualitative researchers with the capacity to analyse new phenomena that are difficult to grasp otherwise. Small and thick datasets can be combined with larger datasets. The human-based interpretation of symbols and keywords then can be complemented with dictionaries and combinatory analyses that provide good levels of semantic and categorical analysis (Young et al. 2018); these are useful to analyse and interpret, for instance, emotional appeals in large sets of (online) interactions. These combinations, using mixed methods, or qualitative and quantitative approaches, may represent a challenge for the researcher but they are also opening new avenues for understanding interactions and emotions in social media.

The combination of qualitative and quantitative methods to analyse an online community is explained in a second article by Castelló and Lopez-Berzosa (2021). Castelló and Lopez-Berzosa (2021) analysed an online community of 48 actors, including civil society organizations and corporations willing to engage on the issue of plastic pollution. Starting with 120k tweets, this research took a quantitative approach to reduce the database to constructive interactions. The degree of constructiveness was calculated through an algorithm. Constructive interactions included any form of interaction with a toxicity level below 0.65 on a scale from 0 to 1; the toxicity level is calculated by an artificial intelligence-based engine that analyses emotions using natural language processing (NLP) and that is trained to signal positive and negative words in text. Through the AI engine, the sample size was reduced to 26k. Qualitative coding was then conducted on the remaining sample to identify meaningful interactions and the emotions involved in the interactions. The NLP engine helped classify the data by type of emotions. Finally, a qualitative analysis of a random sample of 10 per cent of tweets was analysed to develop a model of emotional work that was then quantitatively verified by the algorithm.

A second challenge to studying emotion-symbolic work online relates to the linguistic and symbolic codes involved. Coding of textual and non-textual data requires a certain understanding of the semiotics shared by the group the researcher is studying. The symbols, the types of expressions and even the narratives of events differ per group and per platform. For example, Instagram, described by its creators as a 'fun and quirky way to share your life with friends through a series of pictures' (Instagram 2015) is being used by people and organizations to tell stories, mainly using visual images. Instagram is image-based; these images have developed an entire semiotic code (Mirsarraf et al. 2017), that is, a shared understanding of meanings created by Instagram users that are not universally shared or recognized by other people. For example, the light in the picture may define the mood of the users, or the mood style that people on Instagram use to tell a story. The sequence of images defines a storyline while the use of '#' (hashtags) signals topics and conversations already present on the platform (Giannoulakis and Tsapatsoulis 2016). Additionally, emoticons are used as expressions of emotions (Derks et al. 2007). Such codes may be specific to individual social media spaces, but also often specific to the different demographic groups that interact on a particular platform. Understanding such codes requires a 'netnographic exercise' (Kozinets 2002) of almost ethnographically analysing the platform, which involves looking at the composition, rules, and behaviours of the community through direct observation. This process can be complemented with the use of methods, for example interviews, that can more precisely define the different codes in each platform and their use for emotion-symbolic work. For example, Castelló and Lopez-Berzosa (2021) in their analysis of the use of Twitter by civil society organizations to engage with corporations looked at how the symbols @ and

are used by different actors in the plastic pollution community to create meaning around the problem of plastic pollution and to grow their community. The analysis highlighted the evolution of the key hashtags over time and how the actors' ways of creating and using them defined the interactions between them.

Third, the *timing* and *synchronicity* of online interactions are also different from face to face interactions and, again, differ per social media space. Interactions create conversations composed of verbal text and visual symbols. Conversations have a context and a relevance in a specific time. Beyond the socio-political context of the conversation, different spaces have a 'timespan context'. This is the time the interaction is visible in the feed page of a user. The timespan of the conversation is defined by the algorithms driving the social media spaces. Social media data provide the possibility to observe these conversations in real time, which makes it easier for the researcher to understand the context and therefore value and interpret the content. However, social media also store these conversations, which can then be accessed asynchronically at a later point in time. For example, in our running example of the leaders of an anti-plastic pollution organization, we analysed data from 2008 to 2019. The interactions analysed were conversations that usually took place within hours or days on Facebook, Twitter, and Instagram at the different times, whereas we conducted our analysis in 2019.

Fourth, *features* and *uses* of social media evolve rapidly. Remediated genres (e.g. selfies, retweets, spoof videos, and remixes) that emerge amongst groups of users define new forms of multimodal interactions. The different uses on each platform (e.g. number of characters of written text, the type of symbols that can be shared, or features such as stories on Instagram or retweets on Twitter) also influence how interactions are created and how they advance. Furthermore, social media spaces themselves also evolve rapidly and social customs evolve with them—partly defined by the features designed by platform owners but also influenced by platform users' interactions. Understanding how each community adopts these different features and defines social customs is also an important task for a researcher investigating emotion-symbolic work. In our case, our analysis of social media from 2008 to 2019 showed an evolution in the use of the different social media spaces. The first social media space widely used by the SMO leaders was Facebook. They employed Facebook to communicate their new messages but especially to connect with new target actors and build a network of followers. Facebook's multimodality allowed them to use the images of dead albatrosses and other images of animals suffering from the consequences of plastic pollution, and to have a conversation about these images. In 2008 Twitter was also used but, at that time, more as a space to amplify the reach of their messages rather than to develop one-to-one conversations. Later on, around 2017, Instagram started to play an important role in the SMO leaders' way of executing emotion-symbolic work. The use of Instagram was focused on the images and the evocation of transient emotions rather than on a more strategic process of conversion of the emotional energy. The SMO leaders posted the images of the dead albatrosses, evoking emotional shocks. The textual cues they provided below these images subsequently served to direct their followers' energy towards changing their behaviour with respect to plastic use. The combination of Instagram, Facebook, and Twitter helped SMO leaders to amplify their messages but also to consolidate the use of a multimodal communication that relied on pictures and the new message of the need to refuse plastic pollution.

Finally, *ethical issues* such as the definition of norms on the appropriate use of data and associated issues of privacy are important issues related to studying emotion-symbolic work. The ethical parameters and norms of data usage in social media spaces are still developing, although the literature increasingly offers helpful advice (e.g. Beninger 2017; Whiting and Pritchard 2017). Ethical research considerations usually involve certain abstract principles based on wide consensus within the scientific community (Webster et al. 2013): obtaining informed consent and maintaining anonymity and confidentiality. Following these principles in social media, however, poses serious challenges such as: how to obtain consent from every single participant on a particular platform, especially when the data are accessed asynchronously, sometimes years after the interaction took place? Do researchers need to ensure users of the social media spaces have accessed the information about the research and have agreed with the purpose and methods of the research? Regardless of the stance of individual researchers on this issue, obtaining users' consent can be difficult in practice, certainly retrospectively. Also, maintaining the anonymity of the data presents new challenges. Since there is a permanent record of most information posted in these spaces, direct quotations from participants can quite easily be traced back to the original sources through search engines or scraping methods. In this case, anonymity cannot be fully protected. This also relates to issues of copyright (Beninger 2017); anonymity requires researchers to exclude the names of the users but some users may explicitly want to be given credit for their information since they consider it part of their intellectual property. At this stage of the evolution of social media research, 'researchers seeking to embark on social media research should conduct a risk assessment to determine likely privacy infringement and potential user harm from publishing user content' (Williams et al. 2017, 28). Researchers thus might have to work through a set of context-specific decisions on a case-by-case basis and be guided by core ethical principles (Beninger 2017) and the guidelines of their particular institutions. To deal with the ethical issues of data collection in our research on plastic pollution SMO leaders, we used interviews, observational, and archival data as well as social media data to explain emotion-symbolic work. Through the interviews, we were able to obtain informed consent from the main actors, in their case the SMO leaders.Information about our research was also posted in the main social media spaces the SMO leaders used, thus informing part of the target actors that conversations were being studied. To further protect the informants, we made the data anonymous.

Analysing emotions and emotions work online

Social media also offer promising opportunities to develop research on the analysis of emotions. There are different approaches to analysing emotions online. On the one hand, there is automated sentiment analysis. Sentiment analysis is the use of computer programs to estimate some aspects of the sentiment(s) conveyed by a text (Liu 2012). As explained previously, sentiment analysis uses natural language processing techniques (NLP) and the creation of dictionaries to identify whether the emotion in a text is positive or negative. It then assigns a numerical score or category to the text. Research and commercial tools that analyse automated sentiment are increasingly becoming available and are applied in research in multiple disciplines from marketing (Rambocas and Pacheco 2018) to sociology (Evans and Aceves 2016), finance (Wang et al. 2020) to political science (Ceron et al. 2014). Sentiment analysis programs have been created for several different types of tasks. Some of the simplest tools decide whether a text is positive, negative, or neutral overall. Others identify the strength of the sentiments and through artificial intelligence applications increase their accuracy to understand jargon, humour, and other particularities of language that are more complex to typify. Sentiment analysis in general allows the processing of very large amounts of data and therefore an almost real time exploration of elements related to reputation (Etter et al. 2019) and the emotional perception of organizational activities or discourses. However, sentiment analysis also has its limitations since the type of outcome is usually limited to whether a text is in the range of the positive or negative but it does not provide further information about the concrete emotions (e.g. love, hate, rage, etc.) involved or their relation to emotion-symbolic work activities.

A second approach to studying emotions online is through direct observation of data and qualitative analysis of the conversations online. Mindful of our earlier review of ethical challenges, in principle observation online can happen in two ways: unobtrusive observation or participant observation. The unobtrusive form, also called external observation, allows researchers to collect data without interviews or involving themselves in the online community. Just as in naturalistic ethnographic research, the research would act as the proverbial 'fly on the wall' and observe without any direct interference. The observations of emotions are not mediated by the researcher and the emotions are genuinely generated by interactions in the group. Capturing the interaction and how they generate these emotions and analysing them can provide interesting insights into how managers or actors generate these emotions, what the mechanisms are that make the different emotions appear, and how these emotions are handled by actors in the process of emotion-symbolic work. In our case on the plastic pollution SMO leaders, we analysed the interaction between these leaders and the activists they targeted. We observed the emotional reactions of target actors to the SMO leaders' post. For example, when the SMO leaders were posting the image of the baby albatross, target activists often expressed emotions of rage and horror in messages such as: Clementine: 'So sad'; Graveyard lover: '"Liking" this just seems wrong, but you've captured something so heart-breaking but important'; Glimpse lady: 'so utterly sad'; Arrested development: 'This totally broke my heart last night' (Barberá-Tomás et al. 2019, 1801). Capturing these emotions in the interaction allowed us to understand how emotions were strategically evoked but also transformed into tangible support for the cause.

Emotions could also be observed in a mediated way, through participant observation. The researcher then actively engages with the discussion. In the same way as in ethnographic research, the researcher might join an organization or community and thereby observe in a fairly open manner (Fine 1993), revealing their role and their intentions. Such interventions, for instance by posting comments or prompting questions to forums or walls, can help the researcher to direct emotions and experiment with them. Yet, this form of interaction must be accounted for in the analysis of the data as data have been prompted by the researcher's intervention.

In between the purely quantitative orientation of sentiment analysis and the qualitative approach, there are a range of semi-automated techniques that are starting to be adopted by researchers and that seem helpful to overcome the shortcomings of both of the other approaches. They can capture the large volume of interactions and add more nuance to the analysis. Some of these techniques for instance detect a range of emotions such as love, rage, sadness, anger, joy, etc. through NLP techniques enriched with artificial intelligence techniques to achieve significant improvements in text classification tasks (Young et al. 2018). These approaches use human annotated datasets to integrate qualitative approaches of concrete and new codifications with quantitative analysis in larger datasets. For example, in our research about the use of Twitter by civil society organizations on the issue of plastic pollution (Castelló and Lopez-Berzosa 2021), we developed a semi-automated technique based on an NLP engine to analyse emotions on Twitter. We combined qualitative and quantitative methods to better understand the complex processes of deliberation online in which emotions play a crucial role. We first analysed the complete database of tweets using our NLP engine. Second, we took a sample of these tweets and performed a human coding round, defining themes that were more complex than the binary set of emotions that we had initially defined with the NLP engine. Adjusting the algorithm on the basis of the qualitative coding with other key signs such as '?, @', helped us to better define a set of codes to explain patterns of online deliberation. Our study of online debates on plastic pollution offers an understanding of the combination of transient emotions, such as grief or joy and emotions aiming to create a sense of collective identity amongst activists and corporations. We showed how the combination of these transient emotions helped the leaders of civil society groups dedicated to denounce plastic pollution to convince some corporations about the importance of reducing the production and usage of single-use plastic instead of just recycling.

Multimodality in emotion-symbolic work

Emotion-symbolic work is fundamentally multimodal, including both textual (written or spoken) and visual elements in a process that converts the moral shock elicited by visual images into emotional energy and through that, the strategy alignment of the stakeholders with the organization. Multimodality is important since visuals and verbal or written text together are key resources to give sense to audiences (Zamparini and Lurati 2017; Höllerer et al. 2018) as they enhance the representation, theorization, resonance, and perceived validity of narratives (Höllerer et al. 2018).

Multimodality enhances the power of emotion-symbolic work because, as argued by Meyer et al. (2018), visual versus verbal texts have different semiotic features, which provide different operational opportunities.

Despite the emerging research in organization studies looking at multimodality (Zamparini and Lurati 2017; Höllerer et al. 2018), studies of multimodality and strategy alignment are still scarce. Research on the process of strategy alignment using mainly online social media spaces and communication tools has either focused on the analysis of the power of images, drawing on the tradition of media studies (e.g. Carroll and McCombs 2003), or on the analysis of texts, narratives, and discursive strategies associated with them (Vaara 2002; Bartel and Garud 2009). Exploring multimodality requires a research agenda and methodology that combines the analysis of images, symbols, and text and the interrelation between these elements. Arguably this could even be broadened (as in ethnography) to encompass multisensoriality, involving different senses (Pink 2011) as this would allow accounting for other senses such as feelings (closely linked to emotions). In this chapter, though, we focus on images and their interaction with text.

Visuals in social media can take many forms and require a careful consideration of established approaches in visual culture studies (Hand 2017). Also, the circulation of visual data in social media destabilizes research objects in ways that challenge visual analysis of textual meaning (Hand 2017). Visuals help to make visible social interactions but they are also produced to construct social interactions in social media. The images and symbols shared on online spaces are not only a representation of the social interactions offline but also mediate offline interactions to conform to what is happening in social media spaces.

Users of social media spend time taking photographs not only for the sake of the image but also to construct a certain social image online. Images are therefore objects of the interaction but also construct the interaction. Most studies in social media seek to understand user behaviour within an explicitly visual social media platform (e.g. Facebook or Instagram). Researchers have studied, for example, how many pictures, and what types of pictures, are shared by different groups that might have different socio-characteristics. They tend to trace temporal and special patterns of events that are made visible through images (Brandtzaeg and Haugstveit 2014; Lillqvist and Louhiala-Salminen 2014). However, other studies seek to analyse the contextualization of visuals and the effects of the circulation and use of these visuals (Miller 2011; Barberá-Tomás et al. 2019). This approach focuses on the interaction between the visual, the social media space, and the practice the visual represents. Visuals have to be considered as a phenomenon in their own right, that is, as a means of visualizing social life, but also as a means of configuring social life, for example by creating modes of participation on social media such as Instagram.

For example, in our research on SMO leaders in the plastic pollution social movement (Barberá-Tomás et al. 2019), we analysed the use of the image of a baby albatross to convey a specific sequence of emotions against plastic pollution. The image of the albatross was strategically used by the leaders of an SMO to evoke a moral shock and then a certain sense of identification with both the cause and the organization.

Sharing the image of the albatross on Facebook, Twitter, and Instagram was, therefore, followed by talking about the organization's strategy in the context of the image. The image conveyed an inherent meaning of sadness and rage but it also provided a symbolic meaning of death, caused by the parents feeding their chicks with plastic. And ultimately, it helped the organization's leaders to make people understand their cause of combatting plastic pollution. The image was also used by these leaders to present themselves as knowledgeable, since they had been on the island when the picture had been taken, and as legitimate, since they could experience the pain firsthand. They knew what they were talking about, they made their target audience feel responsible and they offered solutions: refusing single-use plastics. The use of images, supplemented with well-chosen text, conveyed these messages and evoked the transient emotions able to create emotional energy. This was done through Facebook conversations in which SMO leaders were sharing the pictures and engaging in conversations with the target activist. Instagram posts and Twitter messages were also used. Key to the creation of emotion-symbolic work in our study was the combination of the emotions created by the picture of the baby albatross with the talk about that picture in the subsequent posts by the SMO leaders, responding to the emotional reactions of target activists and channelling these emotions towards strategy alignment.

Concluding Remarks

In this chapter, building on the notions of emotion work and the role of interactions, emotional energy, and symbols, we introduced and expanded the notion 'emotion-symbolic work', which involves efforts to manage the emotions and emotional energy of individual participants at the group level through the use of symbols. Emotion-symbolic work involves managers' work with symbols specifically designed to build emotional energy in order to fuel the enactment of an organizational strategy. In emotion-symbolic work, the symbol becomes a potent reminder for people of why they should continue to enact that strategy. Furthermore, it is a tool for members of the collective to build a collective identity and reinforce the sense of organizational identification.

We have discussed how symbols are used in multimodal interactions in social media spaces. While the production and broadcasting of symbols in more traditional media such as newspaper or television, have already been analysed in the environmental communication literature (Neilson 2018), the study of social media communications enables researchers to further understand the importance of the work done in these interactions. We argue that this work involves the creation of symbols (through images) and the use of these symbols in their conversations with others to achieve strategy alignment. In sum, emotion-symbolic work is a promising tool for managers, especially when enacting the moral principles proposed is difficult, requiring emotional energy. Social media provide unique spaces for managers to communicate new ideas and strategies using emotion-symbolic work. This context is unique because it allows for direct, non-mediated, fast, and multiple communications with stakeholders. It is also unique because these communications create interactions and dialogues that can help people make sense of a new strategy.

The role of visuals in aligning emotions through emotion-symbolic work also opens new avenues for research. We have claimed that visuals are a powerful tool in the arsenal of managers deserving of much more research attention. Questions such as: are particular types of visuals more powerful than others? Does the impact of visuals depend on audiences' epistemologies and cultural codes? Do social media enhance or reduce cultural codes and differences? Do social media impose or define different features so visuals can be used and developed by managers? Under what conditions are visuals more persuasive than other cultural elements? How do visuals work together with other cultural elements in social media and multimodal communications? While we only begin to address these questions, we join others (e.g. Meyer et al. 2018) in calling attention to this important, and mostly missing aspect of research in management. The methods are being developed, the questions are being asked, so there are plenty of research challenges ahead.

References

Barberá, P. (2015). Birds of the same feather tweet together: Bayesian ideal point estimation using Twitter data. *Political Analysis*, 23(1): pp. 76–91.

Barberá-Tomás, D., Castelló, I., de Bakker, F. G. A., Zietsma, C. 2019. Energizing through visuals: How social entrepreneurs use emotion-symbolic work for social change. *Academy of Management Journal*, 62(6): pp. 1789–817.

Barker, J. R. 1993. Tightening the iron cage: Concertive control in self-managing teams. *Administrative Science Quarterly*, 38(3): pp. 408–37.

Bartel, C. A., and Garud, R. 2009. The role of narratives in sustaining organizational innovation. *Organization Science*, 20(1): pp. 107–17.

Beninger, K. 2017. Social media user's views on the ethics of social media research. In Sloan, L., and Quan-Haase, A. (eds), *The Sage Handbook of Social Media Research Methods* (pp. 57–73). London, UK: Sage Publications Ltd.

Bennett, W. L., Segerberg, A., & Walker, S. (2014). Organization in the crowd: peer production in large-scale networked protests. *Information, Communication & Society*, 17(2), 232-260.

Brandtzaeg, P. B., and Haugstveit, I. M. 2014. Facebook likes: A study of liking practices for humanitarian causes. *International Journal of Web Based Communities*, 10(3): pp. 258–79.

Bunderson, J. S., and Thompson, J. A. 2009. The call of the wild: Zookeepers, callings, and the double-edged sword of deeply meaningful work. *Administrative Science Quarterly*, 54(1): pp. 32–57.

Carroll, C. E., and McCombs, M. E. 2003. Agenda-setting effects of business news on the public's images and opinions about major corporations. *Corporate Reputation Review*, 6(1): pp. 36–46.

Castelló, I., and Lopez-Berzosa, D. 2021.Affects in online stakeholder engagement: A dissensus perspective. Business Ethics Quarterly, Accepted.

Castelló, I., Etter, M., and Nielsen, F. A. 2016. Strategies of legitimacy through social media: The networked strategy. *Journal of Management Studies*, 53(3): pp. 402–32.

Ceron, A., Curini, L., Lacus, S. M., and Porro, G. 2014. Every tweet counts? How sentiment analysis of social media can improve our knowledge of citizens' political preferences with an application to Italy and France. *New Media & Society*, 16(2): pp. 340–58.

Collins, R. 2004. *Interaction Ritual Chains*. Princeton University Press.

Collins, R. 2014. Interaction ritual chains and collective effervescence. In Von Scheve, C., and Salmela, M. (eds), *Collective Emotions* (pp. 299–312). Oxford: Oxford University Press.

Creed, W. D. E., Hudson, B. A., Okhuysen, G. A., and Smith-Crowe, K. 2014. Swimming in a sea of shame: Incorporating emotion into explanations of institutional reproduction and change. *Academy of Management Review*, 39(3): pp. 275–301.

de Bakker, F. G. A. 2015. Online activism and institutional change for corporate social responsibility: A typology. In Uldam, J. and Vestergaard, A. (eds), *Civic Engagement and Social Media: Political Participation Beyond the Protest* (pp. 23–43). Basingstoke: Palgrave Macmillan.

Derks, D., Bos, A. E., and Von Grumbkow, J. 2007. Emoticons and social interaction on the Internet: The importance of social context. *Computers in Human Behavior*, 23(1): pp. 842–49.

Etter, M., Ravasi, D., and Colleoni, E. 2019. Social media and the formation of organizational reputation. *Academy of Management Review*, 44(1): pp. 28–52.

Evans, J. A., and Aceves, P. 2016. Machine translation: Mining text for social theory. *Annual Review of Sociology*, 42(1): pp. 21–50.

Fine, G. A. 1993. Ten lies of ethnography: Moral dilemmas of field research. *Journal of Contemporary Ethnography*, 22(3): pp. 267–94.

Giannoulakis, S., and Tsapatsoulis, N. 2016. Evaluating the descriptive power of Instagram hashtags. *Journal of Innovation in Digital Ecosystems*, 3(2): pp. 114–29.

Haidt, J. 2003. The moral emotions. In Davidson, R. J., Sherer, K. R., and Goldsmith, H. H. (eds), *Handbook of Affective Sciences* (pp. 852–70). Oxford: Oxford University Press.

Hand, M. 2017. Visuality in social media: Researching images, circulations and practices. In Sloan, L., and Quan-Haase, A. (eds), *The Sage Handbook of Social Media Research Methods*. London: Sage Publications Ltd.

Hatten, M. L. 1982. Strategic management in not-for-profit organizations. *Strategic Management Journal*, 3(2): pp. 89–104.

Höllerer, M. A., Jancsary, D., and Grafström, M. 2018. 'A picture is worth a thousand words': Multimodal sensemaking of the global financial crisis. *Organization Studies*, 39(5–6): pp. 617–44.

Instagram. 2015. FAQS.

Kitchin, R. 2017. Big Data—hype or revolution? In Sloan, L., and Quan-Haase, A. (eds), *The Sage Handbook of Social Media Research Methods*. Sage Publications Ltd.

Kozinets, R. 2002. The field behind the screen: Using netnography for marketing research in online communities. *Journal of Marketing Research*, 39(1): pp. 61–72.

Russell Neuman, W., Guggenheim, L., Mo Jang, S., & Bae, S. Y. (2014). The dynamics of public attention: Agenda-setting theory meets big data. *Journal of Communication*, 64(2), 193-214.

Lillqvist, E., and Louhiala-Salminen, L. 2014. Facing Facebook: Impression management strategies in company–consumer interactions. *Journal of Business and Technical Communication Theory*, 28(1): pp. 3–30.

Liu, B. 2012. *Sentiment Analysis and Opinion Mining*. New York: Morgan Claypool.

Lok, J., Creed, W. D., DeJordy, R., and Voronov, M. 2017. Living institutions: bringing emotions into organizational institutionalism. In Greenwood, R., Oliver, C., Lawrence, T. B., and Meyer, R. E. (eds), *The SAGE Handbook of Organizational Institutionalism*.Vol 2. Thousand Oaks, CA: Sage Publications Ltd.

Lyon, T. P., & Montgomery, A. W. (2013). Tweetjacked: The impact of social media on corporate greenwash. *Journal of Business Ethics*, 118(4): pp. 747-757.

Meyer, R. E., Höllerer, M. A., Jancsary, D., and Van Leeuwen, T. 2013. The visual dimension in organizing, organization, and organization research: Core ideas, current developments, and promising avenues. *Academy of Management Annals*, 7(1): pp. 487–553.

Meyer, R. E., Jancsary, D., Höllerer, M. A., and Boxenbaum, E. 2018. The role of verbal and visual text in the process of institutionalization. *Academy of Management Review*, 43(3): pp. 392–418.

Miller, D. 2011. *Tales from Facebook*. Cambridge: Polity.

Mirsarraf, M., Shairi, H., and Ahmadpanah, A. 2017. Social Semiotic Aspects of Instagram Social Network. Paper presented at the IEEE International Conference on INnovations in Intelligent SysTems and Applications(INISTA).

Neilson, A. 2018. Considering the importance of metaphors for marine conservation. *Marine Policy*, 97: pp. 239-43.

O'Mahoney, S., and Ferraro, F. 2007. The emergence of governance in an open source community. *Academy of Management Journal*, 50(5): pp. 1079–106.

Papacharissi, Z. 2004. Democracy online: Civility, politeness, and the democratic potential of online political discussion groups. *New Media and Society*, 6(2): pp. 259–83.

Pink, S. 2011. Multimodality, multisensoriality and ethnographic knowing: Social semiotics and the phenomenology of perception. *Qualitative Research*, 11(3): pp. 261–76.

Pratt, M. G. 2000. The good, the bad, and the ambivalent: Managing identification among Amway Distributors. *Administrative Science Quarterly*, 45(3): pp. 456–93.

Quinn, R. W., and Dutton, J. E. 2005. Coordination as energy-in-conversation. *Academy of Management Review*, 30(1): pp. 36–57.

Rambocas, M., and Pacheco, B. G. 2018. Online sentiment analysis in marketing research: A review. *Journal of Research in Interactive Marketing*, 12(2): 146–63.

Rivera, L. A. 2015. Go with your gut: Emotion and evaluation in job interviews. *American Journal of Sociology*, 120(5): pp. 1339–89.

Trist, E. L., Higgin, G., Murray, H., and Pollock, A. B. 1963. *Organizational Choice*. London: Tavistock.

Vaara, E. 2002. On the discursive construction of success/failure in narratives of post-merger integration. *Organization Studies*, 23(2): pp. 211–48.

van den Broek, T., Langley, D., & Hornig, T. (2017). The effect of online protests and firm responses on shareholder and consumer evaluation. *Journal of Business Ethics*, 146(2): pp. 279–294.

Van Laer, J., and Van Aelst, P. 2010. Internet and social movement action repertoires: Opportunities and limitations. information, *Communication & Society*, 13(8): pp. 1146–71.

Van Leeuwen, T. 2005. *Introducing Social Semiotics*. Abingdon: Routledge.

Voronov, M., and Vince, R. 2012. Integrating emotions into the analysis of institutional work. *Academy of Management Review*, 37(1): pp. 58–81.

Wakefield, A., and Fleming, J. 2009. *Responsibilization, The Sage Dictionary of Policing* (pp. 277–8). London: SAGE.

Wang, C., Wang, T., and Yuan, C. 2020. Does applying deep learning in financial sentiment analysis lead to better classification performance? *Economics Bulletin*, 40(2): pp. 1091–105.

Webster, S., Lewis, J., and Brown, A. 2013. Ethical considerations in qualitative research. In Ritchie, J., and Lewis, J. (eds), *Qualitative Research Practice: A Guide for Social Science Students and Researchers*. London: Sage Publications.

Whiting, R., and Pritchard, K. 2017. Digital ethics. In Cassell, C., Cunliffe, A., and Grandy, G. (eds), *SAGE Handbook of Qualitative Business and Management Research Methods*, Vol. 1. London: Sage Publications Ltd.

Wilde, M. J. 2004. How culture mattered at Vatican II: Collegiality trumps authority in the council's social movement organizations. *American Sociological Review*, 69(4): pp. 576–602.

Williams, M. L., Burnap, P., Sloan, L., Jessop, C., and Lepps, H. 2017. Users' views of ethics in social media research: Informed consent, anonymity, and harm. In Woodfield, K. (ed.), *The Ethics of Online Research. Advances in Research Ethics and Integrity*, Vol. 2 (pp. 27–52). Emerald Publishing Limited.

Young, T., Hazarika, D., Poria, S., and Cambria, E. 2018. Recent trends in deep learning based natural language processing. *ieee Computational intelligenCe magazine*, 13(3): pp. 55–75.

Zamparini, A., and Lurati, F. 2017. Being different and being the same: Multimodal image projection strategies for a legitimate distinctive identity. *Strategic Organization*, 15: pp. 6–39.

13

Structuring the Haystack

Studying Online Communities with Dictionary-Based Supervised Text Analysis and Network Visualization

*Eliane Bucher, Peter Kalum Schou, Matthias Waldkirch,
Eduard Grünwald, and David Antons*

Introduction

The study of communities has a long tradition in the social sciences (e.g. Whittaker 1970; Suttles and Suttles 1972), and with the advent of digital platforms, research into *online communities* has surged in the last decade—especially so at the intersection of organizational studies, information systems research, and computer-mediated communications (e.g. Autio et al. 2013; Hwang et al. 2015; Barrett et al. 2016; Faraj et al. 2016). Online communities may be particularly promising contexts to study digital and distributed work performed outside of organizational holding environments, as digital workers often turn to and self-organize within online communities (e.g. Curchod et al. 2020; Bucher et al. 2021).

Online communities are built on digital platforms which bring together large numbers of geographically dispersed individuals with common interests, identities, or activities (Malinen 2015; Faraj et al. 2016). Preece and Maloney-Krichmar (2005) define online communities as online spaces where *individuals* come together for a particular *purpose*, guided by *policies* (including implicit norms and rules) and supported by *software*. Online communities (1) facilitate interactions on an *unprecedented scale*; they generally entail (2) lower access thresholds than offline communities—as members can participate often anonymously and independently of their geographic location; and they (3) codify interactions in a way that persists over time and can thus be accessed both in real-time and in retrospect for research purposes (Faraj et al. 2016). Configurations of online communities may vary considerably in size, accessibility, anonymity, purpose, functionalities, structures, incentive schemes, and role distribution.

Large-scale online communities have emerged as a particularly promising research context as they offer insight into an unprecedented range of real-time user discourses. Such community data have the advantage of reflecting naturally occurring exchanges among individuals without researcher interaction, thus revealing

Eliane Bucher et al., *Structuring the Haystack*. In: *Research Methods for Digital Work and Organization*.
Edited by Gillian Symon, Katrina Pritchard, and Christine Hine, Oxford University Press.
© Oxford University Press (2021). DOI: 10.1093/oso/9780198860679.003.0013

practices and dynamics in their natural form (Schatzki 2001). One of the largest and most active of these communities is Reddit with roughly 430 million monthly users (Reddit 2019) and over 130,000 active sub-communities ('subreddits') dedicated to almost any conceivable area of interest or activity—both large-scale and niche— including for example *freelance work* (e.g. r/upwork), *politics* (e.g. r/politics), *cooking* (e.g. r/gifrecipes), *fringe ideas* (e.g. r/flatearth), or *pet care* (e.g. r/doggrooming). In our case example (Waldkirch et al., 2021), we wanted to understand how digital freelancers perceive the human resource management (HRM) practices (hiring, onboarding, development, etc.) performed by digital work platforms. To do so, we scraped data from a Reddit community of gig workers working through the digital platform Upwork (r/upwork).

Challenges in Researching Online Communities

Current scholarship striving to access, collect, and meaningfully process such large-scale conversation data faces a continuous trade-off between capturing breadth (structures, relationships) and depth (content, meaning) of the extensive corpus of community interactions (Table 13.1). Recent studies of online communities encompass three main approaches. The first—and most popular—structural approach seeks to unveil community *structures*, *relationships*, and *boundaries*, employing quantitative or mixed methods—often based on machine learning and automated text analysis—and building upon large datasets. In this approach, which is often based on testing hypotheses, community interactions are investigated on an aggregate level. For example, Faraj and Johnson (2011) study network exchange patterns in online communities where they scrutinize direct reciprocity, indirect reciprocity, and preferential attachment between community members. The second content-focused approach is most interested in understanding the *content and meaning* of community interactions, employing qualitative or mixed methods. Here, community interactions are investigated both at the aggregate level as well as at the level of single users. As an example, Barrett et al. (2016) combine interviews and qualitative analyses of strategy documents with a netnography to understand how value is created in online communities (Hine 2000; Kozinets 2010). Finally, the third combined approach strives to understand both *context* (structures and relationships) and *content* (meaning and motivations). For instance, Moser et al. (2013, 557) first carried out a network analysis to 'map out the topology of the network' (structure) and then performed a qualitative discourse analysis on the comments of one central actor in order to reach a deeper understanding of the community (meaning).

While much of the current work on online communities favours the structural approach, researchers caution that 'a strictly structural perspective may not reveal the full dynamics of online communities' (Faraj et al. 2016, 669). On the other hand, studies which focus primarily on content and meaning of community interactions

Table 13.1 Analytical approaches to study online communities

	Analytical approaches to online conversation data		
Approach	*Structural approach (how/where)*	*Content approach (what/why)*	*Combined approach (how/where/what/why)*
Primary purpose	Unveiling *structures, relationships,* and *boundaries* of the community space	Understanding *meaning* and *content* of community interactions	Understanding *structure* and *meaning*
Typical methodologies	Network analysis Survey	Content analysis Discourse analysis Ethnography/ Netnography Interviews	Multi-method
Exemplary outcomes	Networks Central actors (Directed) relationships Knowledge flows Exchange patterns	Themes Mechanisms Meanings Motivations, attitudes, intentions	Multi-outcome
Sample work	Faraj and Johnson, 2011 Hwang et al. 2015 Dahlander and Frederiksen 2012	Barrett et al. 2016 Jeppesen and Frederiksen 2006 Kozinets 2010 Kozinets et al. 2010	Moser et al. 2013 Autio et al. 2013

often rely on smaller datasets or excerpts and might overlook larger patterns. As digital work increasingly unfolds outside of the holding environments of traditional organizations (Petriglieri, Ashford and Wrzeszniewski 2019), combined approaches allow us to capture the content, dynamics, and various actors of digital work and thus enable researchers to ask a plethora of new questions. Typical queries could, for instance, investigate thematic clusters (e.g. what are the primary coping strategies of workers vis-à-vis algorithmic management?), changes over time, perhaps in relation to specific critical events (e.g. how do digital workers adapt to a design change over time?) or comparisons among actors (e.g. how do strategies of central versus non-central actors differ?).

The Scope of our Contribution

Just like finding the proverbial needle in a haystack, researchers of large-scale community data are challenged to identify a small amount of highly relevant data from an inconceivably large amount of irrelevant data. Here, our contribution adds to the 'toolbox' of combined research approaches, harnessing the advantages of both structural and content-focused methods to access, process, and interpret the 'haystack' of large-scale community data. The proposed digital method encompasses five steps (Figure 13.1). In the following, we will describe each step in detail and provide exemplary excerpts from a current data collection within a community of freelancers on Reddit (r/upwork) (Waldkirch et al. 2021). Conversations on Reddit are anonymous and unfold in an informal manner where one user posts their opinion, question, or observation and other users chime in to comment, support, or counter the original submission. Valuable comments are 'upvoted' by the community, so that the most useful contributions are shown first. While some forums have very strict guidelines with respect to language or allowed content and are consistently moderated, others are more permissible of 'trolling' or vulgar language.

Our approach comes with several advantages. In focusing our analysis on the entire dataset and not solely on the central actors—who often represent a small fraction of the entire community—we manage to capture interactions taking place among the vast majority of less prominent community members as well, thus providing a more complete picture of the community discourse. Further, by using a dictionary-based text-analysis to pre-structure the 'haystack' of community data, we provide a powerful way to reduce complexity, reveal patterns, and distinguish relevant from irrelevant comments in the data effectively and parsimoniously.

Accessing Data—Assembling the Haystack

The first step towards structuring and analysing large-scale conversation data consists of identifying a suitable online community as well as deciding on an appropriate strategy of accessing and collecting the conversation data (Table 13.2). Here, depending on the research goals, researchers should carefully evaluate different communities in terms of their thematic fit, their degree of activity as well as their members' expectations of privacy. Besides questions of fit and accessibility, there are also ethical questions to be considered when digital technologies are used to record 'the minutiae of individuals' everyday lives' (Marabelli and Markus 2017, 1). In particular, researchers should ensure that online community members cannot be 're-identified' with their personal identity, based on the research output (Marabelli and Markus 2017). In our case example, we wanted to understand how digital freelancers perceive HRM practices (hiring, onboarding, development, etc.) on digital work platforms. Here, we identified three potential communities which would grant us insight into freelancer conversations: the official forum of a freelancing platform, a freelancer community on Reddit, as well as a Facebook group of freelancers.

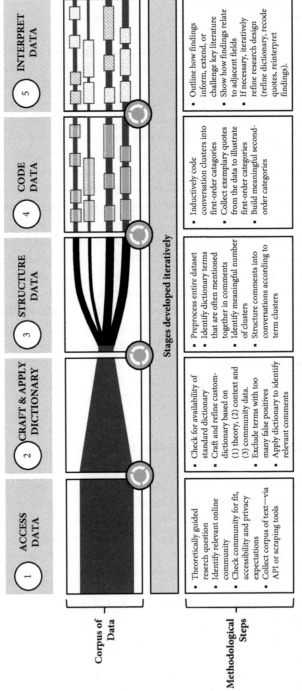

Fig. 13.1 Methodological Framework—step-by-step process of assembling, structuring, and interpreting community data

Table 13.2 Accessing data (Step 1)—Key questions and challenges

Potential issue	Challenges/Questions	Insight from current example
Research fit	How well does the chosen community fit the **research goals**? Are community members a **representative sample** of the target group? Are there **systematic constraints** (e.g. strict moderation of specific opinions) which hinder open conversation? Is there a conversation clearly centred on the **topic of interest**? How frequent are off-topic or 'spam' contributions?	The identified community is deemed suitable as it contains conversations between a large group of freelancers (target population) spanning several months. The community is freely accessible and, while moderated for vulgar language and off-topic contributions, does not systematically exclude a specific opinion.
Activity	How **active** is the community? (static delayed vs. dynamic real-time conversation) How many **members** are **online** at any given time? What is the **frequency of posts**? Which percentage of members is **positing frequently**?	The community provides a steady conversation with an average number of 23 posts per day with between 80 and 100 users being online at any given time.
Expectation of privacy	Which are the **access thresholds** to the community? How **anonymous** are users? How **sensitive** is the topic (e.g. community of cancer survivors vs. online gamers)? Do community members use their **real names**?	The identified community is publicly accessible and users assume pseudonyms/nicknames.
Data mining strategy	Which is the appropriate **data mining strategy**? Is there an **API** which can be accessed directly? (Reddit, Twitter, YouTube, etc.) Is the **size of the resulting corpus** large enough so as not to be distorted by single members or short-term issues?	Reddit provides an API which allows access to 1000 submissions with all their comments at a time. The accessed corpus of text spans several months which precludes short-term spikes from distorting the overall data.

Table 13.3 Excerpt from a self-developed dictionary 'HRM in the Gig Economy' (adopted from: Waldkirch et al., 2021)

Theoretical categories	Practices	Select dictionary terms
People flow	Staffing	*hire, fire, ban, recruit, select, suspend, …*
	Training	*develop, educate, help, teach, test, learn, …*
	Mobility	*advance, promote, progress, career, build, …*
	Job security	*replace, safe, turnover, sick, separate, …*
Appraisal and reward	Appraisal	*feedback, performance, score, rating, …*
	Rewards	*badge, earning, payment, punish, reward, …*
Employee relations	Job design	*JSS, monitoring, video, tracking, profile, …*
	Participation	*chat, forum, dialogue, community, …*

After observing all three communities for several weeks, we decided to study the Reddit community because it was *independent* from the platform provider (the official forum discourages critical contributions and thus inhibits some conversations); it was *sufficiently active* to facilitate an actual conversation with about 80–100 members being online at any given time; and it was *anonymous* as members used pseudonyms. Furthermore, unlike within the Facebook group where new members had to be accepted by a moderator, members on the Reddit forum *did not have a strong expectation of privacy* as conversations could be accessed publicly.

After settling on an appropriate community, we chose a suitable data mining technique. For communities such as Twitter or Reddit that provide a well-documented interface (API), we can directly access data, such as posts, usernames, time-stamps, or upvotes. For communities that do not provide such convenient access, web scraping or web-crawling tools or packages such as *beautifulsoup, scrapy,* or *selenium* have to be employed (e.g. Mitchell 2018; Munzert et al. 2014). In our case example, we used a self-developed script within the Python Reddit API Wrapper (PRAW[1]) to collect the 1000 most recent discussion threads from the online community, which returned 12,293 posts spanning six months from 22 October 2018 until 5 May 2019. The python package allows simple access to Reddit's API. These comments build a comprehensive dataset of the online community that includes *all contributions of all participating community members,* over an *extended period of time so as to avoid one 'hot topic' dominating the analysis.* Some of the posts (*n* = 202) only contained a thread-title without the text in the actual text section and were excluded from the following filtering and structuring. This resulted in a final record of 12,091 posts from a total of 1311 authors, with an average word count of 49.61 words> per post.

Crafting and Applying the Dictionary—Filtering the Haystack

The data gathered from the online community encompasses a large amount of comments. In our case, the 12,091 comments collected from the target community on Reddit translate into 1781 pages of singe-spaced text. However, not all of these comments are expected to be equally relevant to the research project at hand. While a subset of comments may indeed pertain to the investigated phenomenon, others may be off-topic; they may be simple utterances of agreement or disagreement with a previous speaker, or they may be non-specific 'social exchanges', such as jokes or banter between the participants. In our example, we are interested only in comments surrounding HRM practices. In order to identify such *relevant* comments within the 'haystack' of data, we apply a list of key terms ('dictionary') to the dataset, thus effectively dividing our data into a 'pile' of *likely relevant comments*, which contain at least one of the keywords and are thus used for further analysis, and another 'pile' of *likely irrelevant comments*, which contain none of the keywords and will be excluded from further analysis (Table 13.4).

There are several such dictionaries available from previous research, including dictionaries on linguistic dimensions and psychological processes (e.g. Pennebaker et al., 2015) or moral foundations (e.g. Graham et al. 2009). In the absence of a suitable standardized dictionary for our research topic, we developed a custom-dictionary, taking inspiration from Humphreys and Wang's (2018) suggested path towards theoretical dictionary development. However, instead of following either a fully theory-driven deductive approach or a solely data-driven inductive approach, we combined the two. First, we derived dictionary categories as well as an initial word-list from the literature (Sun et al. 2007) surrounding our research topic (which terms are mentioned in the *literature*?, see Table 13.3). Categories in our case example included '*people flow*', '*appraisal and rewards*', and '*employment relations*'.

Second, we complemented and validated the dictionary based on the context, including, in particular, technical terms which pertain to the industry, organization, or platform in focus (which technical terms can be derived from the *context*?). For instance, the digital work platform we researched used the term *JSS* as an abbreviation for *job success score*. Third, we contrasted the resulting dictionary with a random subset of the data to ensure that the chosen terms reflect the way community members speak (which terms and vernacular are used by *subjects*?). For example, community members who talked about being excluded from the platform did not just use the words *suspended* or *banned*, they also used more colloquial terms such as being *fired* or *booted*. In a final step, we iteratively tested the resulting dictionary against the data to see if each term was indeed identifying relevant comments. In particular, if one term yielded too many corresponding comments (>500 comments), we manually checked the respective sub-set of comments for 'false positives'—instances where a term is used in a way that is not helpful in meaningfully breaking down the data. This process yielded a final custom dictionary of 110 terms. In the following step, we only retained comments that contained at least one of the dictionary terms, effectively reducing the entire dataset of 12,091 by 59 per cent to 4981 comments. In the next step, we clustered the remaining data based on the dictionary terms (Table 13.4)

Structuring Data—Clustering the Remaining Haystack

To unveil underlying structures in the remaining comment-data, we conducted a supervised[2] document clustering analysis (combining text analysis, Louvain clustering, and network visualization) based on the dictionary (Table 13.5). Here, we are not just interested in (1) which dictionary terms were mentioned how often, but also in (2) the likelihood of specific dictionary terms appearing together in the same comments, and thus in (3) which meaningful clusters of keyterms (and thus comments) can be identified. The vast majority of the data collected through the Reddit-API is available in unstructured (textual) form. This is difficult for analytical software to interpret, mainly because it is unable to differentiate between significant and insignificant parts of text, for example it does not take account of punctuation and stop words. The next section is concerned with preparing the data material in such a way that it can be read and interpreted by the machine before being structured into dictionary-based clusters.

Pre-processing: Pre-process the text-data

This step is performed with the programming language R that relies on several established tools (libraries) and methods (Feinerer 2008), which are important for the following steps of reading and processing (Table 13.5). Here, Python and Java could also be conceivable alternatives since they offer the necessary tools for processing and evaluating text data internally or externally through additional packages and libraries (Vijayarani and Janani 2016; Stevens et al. 2015). For our application, the *cleaning* and *standardization* of text are particularly important (Vijayarani et al. 2015).

The cleaning is done by removing insignificant parts of the text, such as punctuation, redundant spaces, and stop words. Stop words are words that do not provide essential information (e.g. 'and', 'he', 'the', 'too', 'very', etc.) (*quanteda/stopwords* 2019). Depending on the field of application, these can also contain valuable information, but they do not represent any value for our analyses and are thus deleted from the text corpus.

The next step is standardization, during which words in various forms are converted to a root form so that the computer can interpret them. For the computer, for example, 'accept' and 'acceptance' are two different words, even if their content is identical for certain purposes and has the same meaning. The word-context-related standardization aims to take this fact into account and to reduce words back to their original form, that is, convert '*acceptance*' back into the original form '*accept*' (Jivani 2011; Silge and Robinson 2016).

Table 13.4 Crafting the dictionary (Step 2)—challenges and key questions

Potential issue	Challenges/Questions	Insight from current example
Choosing the right approach	Which **information** are we looking to extract from the data? Is there a **standard dictionary** which could help identify relevant comments?	We started the dictionary development with an interest in a concrete phenomenon (HR-practices on gig-platforms). In the absence of a standard-dictionary for either HR practices or the gig economy, we decided to create a theoretically informed custom dictionary.
Dictionary development	Which terms are mentioned in the **literature**? Which technical terms can be derived from the **context**? Which terms and vernacular are used by **subjects**? Which are further possible **synonyms**, antonyms? Are there **ambiguous terms** (homonyms) which have to be avoided?	Our dictionary development was initially guided by theory. Theoretical categories were enriched by technical terms and by specific vernacular and terminology of community members. While some ambiguous terms were avoided, others were retained due to their importance for the area of interest (e.g. monitor).
Iterative dictionary validation	How do we deal with '**false positives**' and remaining ambiguous terms? How can we qualitatively **validate** the dictionary? Are dictionary **categories well balanced**?	Several terms yielded too many false positives and were excluded from the dictionary development early on. Key terms which yielded a large amount of comments and could not be excluded were manually checked for 'false positives'. The three dictionary categories (see Table 13.3) each contained at least 21 terms. There is a slight imbalance in the category people flow which is larger than the other two. We decided to retain this as people flow (staffing, training, mobility, job security) is a particularly important dimension for this community and is captured in a very rich terminology.

Table 13.5 Structuring the data (Step 3)—challenges and key questions

Potential issue	Challenges/Questions	Insight from current example
Pre-processing	Which is a suitable tool for preprocessing? Do we lose any content or meaning through stemming? Are there phrases (word combinations) that we want to retain for the analysis?	In our example, we were not concerned with the basic cleaning of stopwords and punctuation as we didn't focus on these elements in our analysis. However, we checked all stems to ensure that their meaning was still intact.
Document term matrix	How do we deal with too many 'isolated' terms? How can we iteratively re-evaluate parts of the dictionary at this point?	If there are too many isolated terms, it is likely that either (1) there isn't a sufficiently active conversation surrounding the target phenomenon or (2) the dictionary doesn't sufficiently capture the phenomenon. In the latter case, the dictionary should be refined.
Louvain clustering	How many clusters are ideal? Does the resulting structure reveal weaknesses in the dictionary?	The number of clusters is defined through modularity optimization (Blondel et al., 2008) which yielded five clusters as an 'optimal' solution in our case example. Clusters were roughly of the same size, except for one cluster, which was slightly smaller.

Document term matrix: Identify co-occurring dictionary terms

After the cleaning and standardization, we convert the text into numerical data; this is a necessary step for the subsequent procedures. Specifically, it means that we convert the texts into a Document-Term-Matrix (DTM), where the document titles are at line level and our dictionary terms are at column level. In our case example, this process results in a 12,091 × 110 DTM that renders transparent which of the 12,091 comments contain which of the 110 dictionary terms If, for example, the dictionary term 'accept' occurs 5 times in comment 3, the entry of the matrix at line 3, column 17 (for 'accept') is provided with the entry 5. From this matrix, a relation of the words to the documents can be represented. If we want to examine the relationship between the words, we have to convert this DTM into a Term-Term-Matrix (TTM). This is done by transposing the DTMs and multiplying it with the DTM itself:

$$TTM = DTM^T * DTM$$

The TTM contains all terms that have occurred in the dictionary, listed in rows and columns. From this, we can draw conclusions about how often specific terms appear together in one comment. If there is the value 7 at line 17 ('accept') and column 5 ('rating'), this means that the two words 'accept' and 'rating' occur 7 times in the same comment across all comments. Mathematically, the TTM is an adjacency matrix, which forms the base for creating and visualizing a network object.

Louvain clustering: Grouping co-occurring dictionary terms

Networks are an excellent way to organize and visualize the relationship between individual features in a clear way (Csardi and Nepusz 2006). In our case, we use them to convert the relationship of the individual dictionary terms into clusters and then visually display them. In Figure 13.2, the dictionary terms are represented by the nodes, while the edges (connections between nodes in a network) represent the co-occurrence of a term in one comment. The more words appear together, the stronger the edge value is. We examine the resulting network object for statistical relationships using Louvain clustering, which is a common method of community detection (e.g. Held et al. 2016). If words occur frequently together and rarely with other words, they are grouped into one cluster. This process creates groups which are very homogeneous within the group and very heterogeneous between groups. In our case example, the Louvain clustering results in a network structure of five homogeneous clusters of dictionary terms which are often discussed together. Here, one cluster is termed 'training and development' as it contained terms such as *test, learn, train, educate,* and *develop*. Other clusters are termed 'scoring and feedback', 'access and mobility', 'appraisal and control', 'platform literacy and support'. Figure 13.2 provides an overview of the cluster.

Coding Data—Making Sense of the Clusters

In the next step, we conduct a qualitative content analysis of each identified cluster of comments to create theoretical categories from the material (Miles et al. 2014; see Table 13.6). At this point, we know which terms often appear conjointly in each of the clusters. However, we cannot make sense of this co-occurrence just yet as we do not

Cluster 2:
Training and
Development

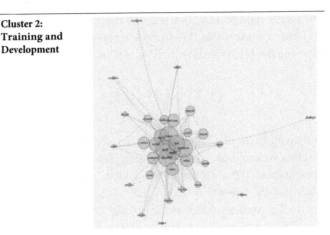

Fig. 13.2 Excerpt of term-cluster surrounding 'Training and Development'

know *how*, *why*, or in *which context* those terms are being used in the conversations among workers. Therefore, we qualitatively code the data to understand the meaning of the clusters.

Drawing on qualitative methods to understand the clusters

The strength of qualitative analysis is that it allows researchers to build theory inductively from data, while being informed about extant theoretical frames and previous knowledge(Glaser and Strauss 1967; Gioia et al. 2013; Gehman et al. 2018). Qualitative data analysis requires the researcher to structure data, identify patterns, and connect them to theoretical concepts. As online communities draw on discursive interactions, a more interpretivist stance (Berger and Luckmann 1967) is appropriate for the analysis. Here, researchers strive to gain an understanding of how members of the online community construct, interpret, and make sense of the community and interactions within it. To code the data, we drew on a coding process inherent in the grounded theory approach (Glaser and Strauss 1967; Corbin and Strauss 1990), which is commonly utilized in a plethora of research streams and has become the foundation for popular qualitative methodologies, such as the 'Gioia Method' (Gioia et al. 2013; see also Langley and Abdallah 2011). This approach is fitting as its focus is neither on testing nor confirming existing theories but instead on developing new concepts and 'understanding the essence of the organizational experience' (Gioia et al. 2013, 13). We thus propose this methodology for the qualitative coding due to its inductive nature, methodological rigour, and wide-spread use among qualitative researchers.

Table 13.6 Coding data (Step 4)—challenges and key questions

Potential issue	Challenges/Questions	Insight from current example
Are the codes and categories **consistent** *and the findings* **credible?**	Is there a **stable empirical basis** for the first-order codes? Do you find codes **across various community members** or are they driven by one key individual? Are the codes and patterns **affected by an external event,** such as a change in community guidelines?	We engaged in constant debriefings, in which we explained and compared our emerging themes and patterns and mutually challenged our interpretations. Further, we built the empirical evidence on a broad set of codes and quotations across various conversations within the community.
Are the second order categories **stable** *and* **confirmable?**	Are there **alternative explanations** for the findings? Can you combine second order codes into **broader categories?** How does the **researcher team's perspective** affect the findings?	In order to confirm the findings, the coding process was done by two researcher teams that consequently could challenge the interpretations. Further, the team engaged in reflexive discussions about the emerging findings to uncover how our perspective might have driven certain findings.
How do the findings relate to the **initial framing** *and the* **conversation clusters?**	To what extent do findings in the online community **challenge or confirm extant research?** How closely are the findings and codes **aligned to the initial frame?** Do the emerging codes **allow to explain the conversations?** To what extent do the codes **capture the conversation dynamics?**	In aligning the findings with the initial frame, we decided to drop several empirical concepts that were, ultimately, not related to HRM systems Our emerging codes highlight how workers themselves provide HR practices individually and as part of the crowd and thus challenge classic HR training literature.

Coding clusters through inductive qualitative methods

The coding process can be divided into three steps. The *first* step encompasses *open coding* (Corbin and Strauss 1990), in which researchers assign first-order codes to the data (Miles et al. 2014). These codes provide empirically-driven categories that can often result in many codes (<100). While the researcher may note down 'nuggets' in the statements, there should be no attempt to distil the data here. In this step, researchers engage in constant comparisons, noting down incidents in line with the research question and comparing them to other incidents to understand similarities and differences. Such first-order codes remain close to the data and are usually short and descriptive, rooted in the phrases of the informants. For each code, we selected at least one representative quote. Here, we retained grammatical errors, colloquialisms, and even swear words in the quotes in order to convey the tone and terminology of community members. For instance, our case-cluster 'training and development' contained first-order codes such as 'refining proposals', 'learning to talk to clients', and 'critiquing profile pictures'. Here, one of the representative quotes is from a freelancer who offers advice on a profile picture: 'You need a new profile picture. Your current picture says "keyboardist in 80's music video" more than "reliable IT professional"'.

In the second step, researchers engage in axial coding (Corbin and Strauss 1990), in which they compare first-order codes looking for similarities and differences. In this step, researchers combine, reduce, delete, or merge first-order codes and aggregate them into focused and more abstract second-order codes, resulting in a more manageable number of codes. It is at this point that a structure in the data should emerge and allow the researcher to see patterns. These patterns allow researchers to step into the theoretical realm and create emerging theory on the phenomenon under study (Locke and Golden-Biddle 1997). In our case example, we combined the aforementioned codes 'refining proposals', 'learning to talk to clients', and 'critiquing profile pictures' into the broader second-order category 'improving self-presentation', which contains the comments of freelancers who either seek help from the community or who are willing to spend time tutoring others in how they can improve their visibility on the platform (see Figure 13.3).

In the third step, researchers engage in selective coding (Corbin and Strauss 1990), in which they relate their codes around the central phenomenon of the study. Here, researchers aim to explain variations between categories, draw together second-order constructs to more abstract categories, and aim to uncover the main analytic finding of their work. This is often the hardest step in qualitative research, as it requires a conceptual leap between empirics and theory (Klag and Langley 2013) and sets the stage for interpreting the findings in line with extant theory. Following Gioia et al. (2013), it is important to conceptually develop how the clusters and their meaning relate to each other. This can be done in various ways, such as through practices that communities develop, a process model, propositions, taxonomies, discursive patterns, or types of narratives in the community. In our findings, the various second-order codes in the 'training and development' cluster allowed us to recognize a common pattern: all these training practices were initiated and conducted in a bottom-up manner by community members. Based on this systematic observation, we formulated the proposition that training and development on digital work platforms is predominantly 'crowd-created' by the crowd of workers, and further discussed implications of this proposition.

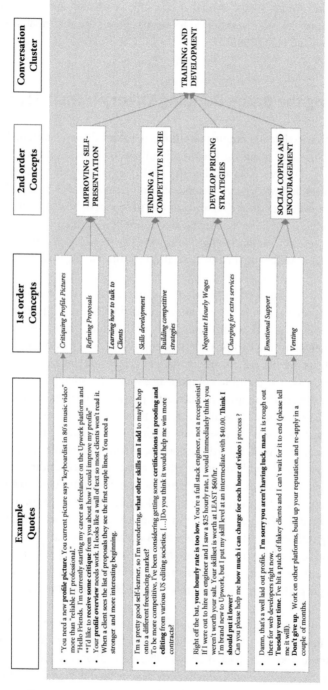

Fig. 13.3 Coded cluster 'Training and Development'

Finally, it is important to note that this qualitative approach is iterative, meaning that throughout the coding process, researchers move back and forth between these steps (Corbin and Strauss 1990). To further strengthen each step, authors should test their codes against the other authors' codes to strengthen the confirmability of the analysis (Lincoln and Guba 1985).

Interpreting the Data—Building Theory from Patterns

In this last step, we relate our empirical findings to extant theory, outlining how the unveiled structures and meanings extend, illuminate, or question existing scholarship (see Table 13.7). Here, Klag and Langley (2013) argue that this 'conceptual leap' requires creativity, knowledge, and serendipity to be successful (Klag and Langley 2013). While we will not repeat Klag and Langley's account of how to create conceptual leaps, we aim to provide a systematic account of how to interpret the empirical findings of our research method in light of the key literature (*challenging the deductive foundations*) as well as against the backdrop of adjacent fields (*following up on inductive leads*).

A *first* step towards interpreting the empirical findings is to demonstrate how they relate to current scholarship in the key literature stream. This step, therefore, relates directly to the research endeavour's main body of literature that makes up the deductive foundations of the dictionary's development. It is key to discuss how the empirical findings inform, enrich, and challenge current thinking. As part of the interpretation process, it is useful to compare and evaluate assumptions from extant theory with the research findings to problematize previous knowledge and create new understandings (Alvesson and Sandberg 2011). Relating the findings and emerging theory to a clear theoretical discussion allows for an easier framing of their novelty and boundary conditions. This further allows researchers to transfer their findings into other contexts and highlight under which conditions their findings might be applicable against the backdrop of the original body of literature (Lincoln and Guba 1985). In our case example, we relied on the well-established literature on HRM systems (Sun et al. 2007; Jiang et al. 2012) to build the dictionary; consequently, we dedicated a significant part of the interpretation towards this scholarly debate. As a result, our work contributes by drawing out how HRM practices transform in the gig economy and how digital platforms use a *hybrid* HRM system that combines elements of high-performance and control-oriented HRM philosophies (Waldkirch et al. 2021).

While the initial, deductive framing provides an important starting point for positioning the findings, the inductive nature of the qualitative coding might steer the findings toward another, related body of literature. Therefore, in a *second* step, it is important to follow up on 'inductive leads' generated during the coding process (Van de Ven 2007). Here, it is possible that unveiled structures and meanings

Table 13.7 Interpreting data (Step 5)—challenges and key questions

Potential issue	Challenges/Questions	Insight from current example
*How do our findings relate to **previous research?***	How do our findings challenge **underlying assumptions in the key literature** of the project? How do our findings relate to **adjacent fields** of scholarship? What can we surmise with respect to **future research**?	The key finding within training and development showcases how, in absence of organizational support, individual workers and the crowd itself develop bottom-up HR practices to support each other. We relate these findings to extant literature on HRM systems to challenge the assumption of HR practice provision occurring purely in a top-down manner.
*Do we need to **reframe the initial focus?***	Are the unveiled structures and meanings suitable to enrich/**challenge** the **key literature**? Do we need to **recode the data** in light of the emerging findings? Do we need to **refine the dictionary** in light of the findings?	Even though the finding that HR practices are co-created by workers was intriguing and initially unexpected, after carefully going through our dictionary development approach again we concluded that we had captured the most important terms.
*How do our findings **shape** future research?*	How should researchers interested in the phenomena of the study **think differently** about future projects? Which **novel methodological approaches** could enrich future studies? Which **practical implications** does the study derive for workers, communities, and policy makers?	Our findings cast light on the phenomenon of bottom-up HR practices. Such a perspective opens new areas of research regarding how decentralized training might be provided, under which conditions workers start engaging in proactive HR practices, and what such a trend might mean for the power relations inside organizations.

lead to adjacent scholarly debates. In our case example, the finding that freelancers themselves create instances of training and development has allowed us to link our findings further to adjacent scholarship in the field of HRM on how employees actively 'consume' HR practices and informally mentor each other (Ragins and Kram 2007; Meijerink et al. 2020).

Third, after mapping out challenges to the key literature as well as possible relationships to adjacent streams of literature, we detach ourselves from specific theoretical discussions (Klag and Langley 2013) in order to outline how our findings shape future research. Here, we encourage researchers to draw out bold implications, as this last stage represents the most fruitful ground for further research. It is at this stage that the entire methodology can be re-visited as well. For instance, now that we know that digital platforms seem to 'outsource' several traditional organizational functions to the freelancers—a pattern which emerged across several inductively coded categories—it would be interesting to retroactively extend the dictionary by this perspective and thus perhaps gain an even more nuanced picture of this unveiled phenomenon. While it is of course possible to emphasize this as a potential avenue for a future research project, it is also possible to understand the current methodology as a continuously iterative process which—based on a theory-driven initial dictionary—could be shaped and perfected over several iterations.

Conclusion and Limitations

Over the past decade, the interest in online communities has steadily grown and an increasing number of researchers from various areas and traditions have discovered the potential of online communities as research contexts. With this surge in interest, researchers have developed various methods, most of them either focusing on the *structure/relationships* or the *content/meaning* of online communities. Our suggested approach provides a novel way to combine a structure-driven approach (identify and cluster relevant data) with a content-driven approach (qualitative content analysis).

While our approach provides a novel way to investigate large online communities, it is not without its limitations. *First*, the comprehensibility and strength of the identified clusters depends strongly on the quality of the initially created dictionary. To mitigate this issue, we encourage researchers to carefully craft their dictionary in line with best practice (Humphreys and Wang 2018), while being conscious of the idiosyncrasies of the community context. Here, it might be necessary to iteratively revise the dictionary and clustering based on a first qualitative coding, as highlighted above. *Second*, in our personal view, planning and executing all five stages of this method is time consuming and requires not just specific technical skills, such as the use of R or Python, but also expertise in qualitative research methods. Here, multidisciplinary teams may be at an advantage. Third, in the automated reduction and structuring of large-scale data, some nuances and potentially relevant data may be lost. In our case, this pertains to social exchanges, banter or humour in particular, which may be important cues when it comes to interpreting and contextualizing specific conversations. Here, we recommend dedicating enough time to refine the dictionary iteratively so that as much community-specific language as possible can be captured. *Last*, it is important to consider potential ethical implications of this approach. While there is generally no expectation of privacy with respect to the content on digital platforms, such as Reddit, there is often an expectation of anonymity, especially if users rely on pseudonyms. However, given a particular username, it may still be possible to find identifying markers from their post history. To deal with these issues, we suggest that researchers anonymize usernames, refrain from publicizing complete posts and—if possible—strive to anonymize personal information that has no direct relevance to the study (e.g. omit references to a user's [hometown], [family status], or [health issues]).

Concluding, in line with the idea of 'communities', we encourage and invite researchers from various fields to draw on our methodological approach and to further refine the ideas presented in this chapter. In particular, we hope that future research will continue to explore and harness the possibilities of machine learning and automated text analysis to help access, structure, and interpret large-scale community data. At the same time, we would like to emphasize the crucial and critical role that human planning, intervention, and interpretation play during each step and iteration of such 'mechanized' analyses. In this light, our chapter should be read as a hopeful outlook towards a balanced research paradigm that harnesses both human insight and automated processing power.

Notes

1. https://github.com/praw-dev/praw
2. Supervised categorization relies on known categories and labels (the dictionary).

References

Alvesson, M., and Sandberg, J. 2011. Generating research questions through problematization. *Academy of Management Review*, 36(2): pp. 247–71.

Autio, E., Dahlander, L., and Frederiksen, L. 2013. Information exposure, opportunity evaluation, and entrepreneurial action: An investigation of an online user community. *Academy of Management Journal*, 56(5): pp. 1348–71.

Barrett, M., Oborn, E., and Orlikowski, W. 2016. Creating value in online communities: The sociomaterial configuring of strategy, platform, and stakeholder engagement. *Information Systems Research*, 27(4): pp. 704–23.

Berger, P. L., and Luckmann, T. 1967. *The Social Construction of Reality: A Treatise in the Sociology of Knowledge* (Repr.). Penguin.

Blondel, V. D., Guillaume, J.-L., Lambiotte, R., and Lefebvre, E. 2008. Fast unfolding of com-munities in large networks. *Journal of Statistical Mechanics: Theory and Experiment*, 2008(10): P10008.

Bucher, E. L., Schou, P. K., & Waldkirch, M. 2021. Pacifying the algorithm – Anticipatory compliance in the face of algorithmic management in the gig economy. *Organization*, 28(1): 44–67. doi:10.1177/1350508420961531

Corbin, J. M., and Strauss, A. 1990. Grounded theory research: Procedures, canons, and evaluative criteria. *Qualitative Sociology*, 13(1): pp. 3–21.

Csardi, G., and Nepusz, T. 2006. The igraph software package for complex network research. *Interjournal, Complex Systems*, 1695(5): pp. 1–9.

Curchod, C., Patriotta, G., Cohen, L., & Neysen, N. 2020. Working for an algorithm: Power asymmetries and agency in online work settings. *Administrative Science Quarterly*, 65(3): pp. 644–676.

Dahlander, L., and Frederiksen, L. 2012. The core and cosmopolitans: A relational view of innovation in user communities. *Organization Science*, 23(4): pp. 988–1007.

Faraj, S., and Johnson, S. L. 2011. Network exchange patterns in online communities. *Organization Science*, 22(6): pp. 1464–80.

Faraj, S., Von Krogh, G., Monteiro, E., and Lakhani, K. R. 2016. Special section introduction—Online community as space for knowledge flows. *Information Systems Research*, 27(4): pp. 668–84.

Feinerer, I. 2008. An introduction to text mining in R. *The Newsletter of the R Project*, 8/2, October 2008, 8, 19.

Gehman, J., Glaser, V. L., Eisenhardt, K. M., Gioia, D., Langley, A., and Corley, K. G. 2018. Finding theory–method fit: A comparison of three qualitative approaches to theory building. *Journal of Management Inquiry*, 27(3), pp. 284–300.

Gioia, D. A., Corley, K. G., and Hamilton, A. L. 2013. Seeking qualitative rigor in inductive research: Notes on the Gioia Methodology. *Organizational Research Methods*, 16(1): pp. 15–31.

Glaser, B. G., and Strauss, A. L. 1967. *The Discovery of Grounded Theory: Strategies for Qualitative Research*. Transaction Publishers.

Graham, J., Haidt, J., and Nosek, B. A. 2009. Liberals and conservatives rely on different sets of moral foundations. *Journal of Personality and Social Psychology*, 96(5): pp. 1029–46.

Held, P., Krause, B., and Kruse, R. 2016. Dynamic clustering in social networks using Louvain and Infomap Method. *Third European Network Intelligence Conference (ENIC)*, 61–68, Wroclaw, Poland: IEEE.

Hine, C. 2000. *Virtual Ethnography*. Sage Publications Ltd.

Humphreys, A., and Wang, R. J.-H. 2018. Automated text analysis for consumer research. *Journal of Consumer Research*, 44(6): pp. 1274–306.

Hwang, E. H., Singh, P. V., and Argote, L. 2015. Knowledge sharing in online communities: Learning to cross geographic and hierarchical boundaries. *Organization Science*, 26(6): pp. 1593–611.

Jeppesen, L. B., and Frederiksen, L. 2006. Why do users contribute to firm-hosted user communities? The case of computer-controlled music instruments. *Organization Science*, 17(1): pp. 45–63.

Jiang, K., Lepak, D. P., Han, K., Hong, Y., Kim, A., & Winkler, A.-L. 2012. Clarifying the construct of human resource systems: Relating human resource management to employee performance. *Human Resource Management Review*, 22: pp. 73–85.

Jivani, A. G. 2011. A comparative study of stemming algorithms. *International Journal of Computer Applications in Technology*, 2(6): pp. 1930–8.

Klag, M., and Langley, A. 2013. Approaching the conceptual leap in qualitative research. *International Journal of Management Reviews*, 15(2): pp. 149–66.

Kozinets, R. V. 2010. *Netnography: Doing Ethnographic Research Online*. Sage Publications.

Kozinets, R. V., de Valck, K., Wojnicki, A. C., and Wilner, S. J. 2010. Networked narratives: Understanding word-of-mouth marketing in online communities. *Journal of Marketing*, 74(2): pp. 71–89.

Langley, A., and Abdallah, C. 2011. Templates and turns in qualitative studies of strategy and management. In D. D. Bergh and D. J. Ketchen (eds), *Building Methodological Bridges* (Vol. 6, pp. 201–235). Emerald Group Publishing Limited.

Lincoln, Y. S., and Guba, E. G. 1985. *Naturalistic Inquiry*. SAGE Publications.

Locke, K., and Golden-Biddle, K. 1997. Constructing opportunities for contribution: Structuring intertextual coherence and "problematizing" in organizational studies. *The Academy of Management Journal*, 40(5): pp. 1023–62.

Malinen, S. 2015. Understanding user participation in online communities: A systematic literature review of empirical studies. *Computers in Human Behavior*, 46: pp. 228–38.

Marabelli M and Markus ML. 2017. Researching big data research: Ethical implications for IS scholars. In: *Proceedings of the 23rd Americas Conference on Information Systems*, Boston, MA, 10–12 August.

Meijerink, J., Bos-Nehles, A., and Leede, J.de. 2020. How employees' pro-activity translates high-commitment HRM systems into work engagement: The mediating role of job crafting. *The International Journal of Human Resource Management*, 31(22), pp. 2893–918.

Miles, M. B., Huberman, A. M., and Saldaña, J. 2014. *Qualitative Data Analysis: A Methods Sourcebook* (3.). SAGE Publications.

Mitchell, R. 2018. *Web Scraping with Python: Collecting more Data from the Modern Web*. O'Reilly Media, Inc.

Moser, C., Groenewegen, P., and Huysman, M. 2013. Extending social network analysis with discourse analysis: Combining relational with interpretive data. Özyer, T., Rokne, J., Wagner, G., & Reuser, A. H. *The Influence of Technology on Social Network Analysis and Mining*. Vienna: Springer.

Munzert, S., Rubba, C., Meißner, P., & Nyhuis, D. 2014. *Automated Data Collection With R: A Practical Guide to Web Scraping and Text Mining*. John Wiley & Sons.

Pennebaker, J.W., Boyd, R.L., Jordan, K., & Blackburn, K. 2015. *The Development and Psychometric Properties of LIWC2015*. Austin, TX: University of Texas at Austin

Petriglieri, G., Ashford, S. J., and Wrzesniewski, A. 2019. Agony and ecstasy in the gig economy: Cultivating holding environments for precarious and personalized work identities. *Administrative Science Quarterly*, 61(1): pp. 124–70.

Preece, J., & Maloney-Krichmar, D. 2005. Online communities: Design, theory, and practice. *Journal of Computer-mediated Communication*, 10(4). https://doi.org/10.1111/j.1083-6101.2005.tb00264.x

Ragins, B. R., and Kram, K. E. 2007. *The Handbook of Mentoring at Work: Theory, Research, and Practice*. SAGE Publications.

Reddit. 2019. Year in Review. Staff Announcement, 4 December 2019. Available at https://redditblog.com/2019/12/04/reddits-2019-year-in-review/

Schatzki, T. R. 2001. Introduction – practice theory. In T. R. Schatzki, K. D. Knorr-Cetina, & E. von Savigny (Eds.), *The Practice Turn in Contemporary Theory: 1–14*. London: Routledge.

Silge, J., and Robinson, D. 2016. tidytext: Text mining and analysis using tidy data principles in R. *Journal of Open Source Software*, 1(3), p. 37.

Stevens, Jean-Luc R., Rudiger, Philipp, and Bednar, James A.2015 "HoloViews: Building complex visualizations easily for reproducible science". In: *Proceedings of the 14th Python in Science Conference*. Ed. by Kathryn Huff and James Bergstra. pp. 61–69.

Sun, L.-Y., Aryee, S., and Law, K. S. 2007. High-performance human resource practices, citizenship behavior, and organizational performance: A relational perspective. *Academy of Management Journal*, 50(3): pp. 558–77.

Suttles, G. D., and Suttles, G. D. 1972. *The Social Construction of Communities* (Vol. 111). University of Chicago Press.

Van de Ven, A. H. (2007). *Engaged Scholarship: A Guide for Organizational and Social Research*. Oxford University Press.

Vijayarani, S., and Janani, R. 2016. Text mining: open source tokenization tools—an analysis. *Advanced Computational Intelligence: An International Journal (ACII)*, 3(1): pp. 37–47.

Vijayarani, S., Ilamathi, M. J., and Nithya, M. 2015. Preprocessing techniques for text mining-an overview. *International Journal of Computer Science and Communication Networks*, 5(1): pp. 7–16.

Waldkirch, M., Bucher, E., Schou, P.K., & Grünwald, E. 2021. Controlled by the algorithm, coached by the crowd – How HRM activities take shape on digital work platforms in the gig economy. *International Journal of Human Resource Management*,32(12): pp. 2643–2682.

Whittaker, R.H. 1970. *Communities and Ecosystems*. Macmillan.

PART IV
DIGITAL TRACES OF WORK

14

After Vanity Metrics

Critical Analytics for Social Media Analysis

Richard Rogers

Introduction

'Vanity metrics,' as they are critically termed (Ries 2009), measure the performative work one carries out on social media. Posting on social media and subsequently displaying and maintaining like, view and follow counts have been critiqued as both distracting modes of engagement as well as performance in a 'success theater'. Each of these critiques is considered in turn in this chapter. The notion of vanity metrics implies another project, however: how one may consider reworking the metrics. In an undertaking called critical analytics, I propose an alternative metrics project akin to altmetrics in science but rather one designed for measuring actor activity around social issues and causes in social media. These measures for social research seek to highlight other modes of engagement (than distraction or vanity) in social media. The critical analytics put forward are a means to analyse dominant voice, concern, commitment, positioning, and alignment of actors using social media to work on social issues and causes. In all, critical analytics seek to contribute a conceptual and applied research agenda to orient the study of social media use and activity metrics.

The Object of Measurement in Social Media

Vanity metrics, be they view, like, or follower counts, are arguably measuring what could be called 'distracted modes of engagement'. Despite the apparent contradiction, this distracted engagement is captured in new terms that describe the use and users of social media as well as the web more generally. 'Flickering man', 'ambient awareness', and 'continuous partial attention' respectively emphasize the intellectual, social, and interpersonal effects of the reprogramming of our attention. Each describes a specific configuration of new media (be it the web and Google, social media and especially Twitter, and the smartphone) with operating systems and apps that push notifications and alerts, and number badges requiring one to click them to reset to what we might call 'calm modes of engagement'.

Richard Rogers, *After Vanity Metrics*. In: *Research Methods for Digital Work and Organization*.
Edited by Gillian Symon, Katrina Pritchard, and Christine Hine, Oxford University Press. © Oxford University Press (2021).
DOI: 10.1093/oso/9780198860679.003.0014

'Flickering man', as elaborated by Nicholas Carr in *The Shallows: How the Internet is Changing the Way We Think, Read and Remember* (2010) is a critique of how new media affect the intellect. His point of departure recalls *Otherwise Engaged*, a well-regarded play published by the English playwright Simon Gray (1975). The drama revolves around the trials and tribulations of an intellectual, a theme frequently taken up in Gray's oeuvre. The play opens with him cueing up Wagner's *Parsifal*; his intention is to listen to the opera music. As it happens, Simon is interrupted by a mix of professional and personal relationships, a cast of characters one likely would have as friends, followers, or connections in social media, and from whom one would receive postings and notifications in newsfeeds of their activities and updates. One by one the alerts and notifications drop in. First, his tenant comes by to request help, followed by his brother who asks for advice about a job offer, then a journalist-friend and his girlfriend who desires a publishing contract. Through a jarring phone call, he learns an old schoolmate is down on his luck, and finally his wife enters and notifies him she has other plans for their relationship. As Simon's attention is pulled one way and then another, he gradually falls apart, and is transformed from a so-called 'contemplative man' to a 'flickering man', as Nicholas Carr described certain effects of new media on thinking. Ultimately, at the play's end, we find Simon can no longer engage, for he has lost his ability to focus. Social media distracts, but if one considers the listener being separated from opera listening, rather than engaging the mind, it also debases culture according to Andrew Keen (2007) and others.

Writing in a blog post that precedes the book, Carr describes our coming incapacity for 'deep reading' (and presumably 'deep listening' to *Parsifal*) as a product of the web:

> Contemplative Man, the fellow who came to understand the world sentence by sentence, paragraph by paragraph, is a goner. He's being succeeded by Flickering Man, the fellow who darts from link to link, conjuring the world out of continually refreshed arrays of isolate pixels, shadows of shadows. The linearity of reason is blurring into the nonlinearity of impression; after five centuries of wakefulness, we're lapsing into a dream state
>
> **(Carr 2007)**

For Carr 'flickering man' exhibits a browsing or 'skimming' behaviour rather than a capacity for focused reading or flow (Csikszentmihalyi 1997; Carr 2008). Such a change in reading behaviour is attributed to new media, and more specifically to the linked documents of hypertext built into the web. Flashing as well as densely linked web pages invite one to move on unswervingly to the next piece of content. '[The web] injects ... content with hyperlinks, blinking ads, and other digital gewgaws, and it surrounds the content with the content of all the other media it has absorbed' (Carr 2008). Flickering man is primarily a subject born of the web. Even more to the point, Carr argues, there is less memory recall; we no longer know by being well read or having developed encyclopedic or other forms of deep knowledge. Instead we 'Google', which refers to the reflexive activity of searching for an answer or fact checking instead of taking a moment to consider other strategies for thinking of a response. 'Google is making us stupid' (in the title of one of Carr's (2008) articles), because learnedness has been replaced by a knowing that is instantaneous, automated, and tethered to machines. The other illustration given is that some new trivia (or mind) games, which once relied on memory, are instead Google-assisted.

Flickering man is a late web construct, and may be distinguished from ambient awareness, the second term of interest here, which is rather a product of social media and especially Twitter. 'Ambient awareness' refers to knowledge gained through 'short-form status updates' (Thompson 2008). Clive Thompson, author of *Smarter Than You Think: How Technology Is Changing Our Minds for the Better* (2013), adopts the term from human–computer interaction and ubiquitous computing, where it refers to environments designed to respond to the presence of people. Thompson rehabilitates the seeming banality of Twitter users' 'what-I-had-for-lunch' postings by arguing that all together the accretion of posts is a 'sophisticated portrait of your friends' ... lives, like thousands of dots making a pointillist painting' (Thompson 2008, 48). Indeed, Twitter, as conceived by Jack Dorsey and others, was originally a means by which people would continually provide status updates to their friends and intimates, ever remaining remotely in touch (Sarno 2009). Whilst such smartphone use has been critiqued for privatizing public space, the capacity to follow another at a distance results in a form of remote intimacy termed 'co-presence' (Schivelbusch 1986; Ito 2005; Urry 2007). It is an SMS or messaging relationship with a significant other where the text may not be well formed or the image not well composed. Rather, the meaning-making is more connectionist than substantive, where the key content of the message is ambience, or being dropped into the other's space and frame of mind.

Arguably, with the rise of social networking platforms, the person(s) with whom one is co-present have been expanded greatly. They include Facebook friends and other social media connections that widen the number of intimates and friends to a kind of Dunbar flock (of 100–200 individuals) who fill one's 'following space' (Gonçalves and Perra 2011). The Dunbar number refers to the quantity of people one can meaningfully keep in one's active circle of acquaintance. Not only are they sufficiently engaged and engaging so as to be seen and read, these people in one's online circle also increasingly co-determine one's media (and news) exposure, if, as is found and reported, one relies on social media for not just social but societal information (Gottfried and Shearer 2016).

Finally, the third notion is 'continuous partial attention', a term coined by Linda Stone (2009), who defined it as an artificial sense of constant crisis, enabled by the smartphone. So as to not miss anything (at work), one is continuously 'half' on one's phone and half paying attention to the task at hand, although there is a hierarchy in concentration: 'we keep the top level item in focus and scan the periphery in case something more important emerges' (Schwartz 2011). The smartphone, even when placed face down on the table or in one's pocket or bag out of deference to the individuals in the social setting, nevertheless has a presence that commands one's partial attention, whether through interface, sound, or haptic alerts. The attention granted to the phone is also continuous in the sense that it has extended beyond work to the social scene. Wherever one is attuned to the phone, Stone calls it a form of attention that is neither synchronous nor asynchronous, describing it as 'semi-synch' mode. Media thereby become not extensions but so-called partial 'amputations' to cognition (Lin 2009).

Having explored how vanity metrics measure what could be termed 'distracted modes of engagement', I would like to turn to a discussion of what they purport to measure. Indeed, behind the metrics are particular assumptions about social media use and the online performance they encourage (Gerlitz and Lury 2014; van Doorn 2014; Beer 2016).

Why Measure Social Media Activity?

What is social media for and why measure social media activity? First, to attract attention and connections, one performs in social media in a fashion characterized by Jenna Wortham in the *New York Times* as 'success theater', that is, showing others that you are successful. Marieke van Dijk (2014), the Dutch design researcher, similarly calls social media 'opschepmedia', Dutch for 'media for boasting'. Here social media becomes a front-stage space for the presentation of 'the self we would like to be' (Goffman 1956, 12).

Second, social media may be used to build a 'productive network', and it is instructive to refer to the early debate concerning whether it should be called social network or social networking software, where the latter would represent a more utilitarian description as to its purpose and the former reflect friends 'in real life' (boyd and Ellison 2007). If it is social networking software, one is expected to actively network, thereby making the software more productive for the self. Productive networking, now migrated online, refers to connective value, where worthwhile ties are forged. Indeed, productive networking has been built into the business connection platform, LinkedIn; it is also present in Twitter as well as Facebook, even though they are arguably oriented less towards overtly gainful opportunities.

How may that network be put to productive use? There are two main forms of productive networking with connective value frequently associated with social media. One set, often related in popular intellectual essays on social media, reintroduces the work on weak ties, referring to the classic Granovetter (1973) study, which discusses not only opportunities in networking with those to whom one is linked but not close, but also how networking with strong ties (and frequent recourse to them) can be detrimental to building a broader following.

In a popular debate sparked by Malcolm Gladwell on the value of social media and its potential for social change, the key point concerns whether a commitment to 'join the demonstration at the square' can result from social media use (Gladwell 2010). Does the online following hit the streets? The debate reintroduces and ultimately upholds the slacktivist thesis, or the critique of online engagement that liking and sharing are low-cost, feel-good forms of solidarity only (Morozov 2009). But one contribution to the debate stands out for its pinpointing of where the purpose of social media actually lies: '[The] unemployed should spend their time chatting with distant acquaintances on Facebook' (Lehrer 2010). However crude, it is a direct translation of the productive value of weak ties, and summarizes the idea that platforms are social networking sites and have productive networking value for business employment (rather than for social movements).

A third purpose of social media (for those keen on developing metrics) is to capture and propagate consumer futurism, which refers to one of the early discoveries of the use of social networks for marketing—the existence of 'cliques' and brokers, or the 'highly-between' individuals (as they are termed in network science), influencing cohorts with his or her new purchases or interests. Here particularly connected users seed desire in others, or what people will want to consume in the near future. A particularly successful connection on social media can elicit 'niche envy', where one covets the other's entrance privileges and access levels (Turow 2006).

The combination of these particular social media purposes—success theatre and self-projection, productive networking and consumer futurism—furnishes social media use with value and an urgency to be measured. More poignantly, considering one's online scores, a social media user can become impressed with his or her attractiveness to others, which is how vanity is often defined. The visibility of scores brings to mind Baudrillard's (1990) notion of statistics as particular forms of wish fulfilment. 'Vanity metrics' become fulfilling measurements of attractiveness to others. One implication for such metrics is that they invite one to continue to perform for the score. Such outcomes raise the question of whether the metric measures or in fact prompts behaviour.

The Desire for Social Media Performance Metrics

Vanity metrics not only gauge but also encourage all the desires of vanity: celebrity, influence, and coolness. In the success theatre of social media, heightened socialness, together with increasing connectedness, breed what is termed 'micro-celebrity', or the treatment of the audience as 'fan base' (Marwick and boyd 2011; Senft 2013). Daniel Boorstin, the former American Librarian of Congress, once famously defined celebrity as the quality of being well-known for being well-known (Boorstin 1961). The accompanying critique in that work concerned how celebrity is fashioned by fame rather than granted by greatness. Social media metrics propagate this loop of well-known-ness and construct celebrity as notoriety rather than greatness

276 Critical Analytics for Social Media Analysis

by keeping score and displaying it in number badges, follower counts, and similar. The micro in the term micro-celebrity is apt here in the sense that it is a product of minor fame indicators.

Networks are productive not just by manufacturing displays of metrified micro-celebrity but also in that they output influence. Indeed, the second aspect of vanity metrics derives from ideas of 'influencers' in networks or the 'clout' a particular person wields that is construed as palpable influence. In *Linked: The New Science of Networks* and elsewhere, Barabasi (2002) discusses how networks of influence can be thought of in popular terms as a handshake distance measure. How many handshakes away is one from the CEO of a major corporation and thus from the largesse he or she may be able to dispense? One's placement in the network may be measured according to the path length from other nodes and being 'highly between' means being particularly well placed such that one's distance to others of interest is shortest (Freeman 1977). Betweenness centrality becomes an influence score in social media when viewed as productive social networking platforms. One's influence is measured as such and the influencers thereby become identified, valued, and marked up.

Finally, the last discussed desire behind vanity metrics relates to consumer futurism, trending, and ultimately coolness. Networks can measure rising relative novelty (or the trending in Twitter's 'trending topics') as well as those who spread it (to future consumers), but it is the adjudication of trend and acting upon it one way or another as a style statement that could be considered 'coolness' (Liu 2004). How has it become associated with the online as a source for spotting it? As Alan Liu has pointed out, the 'cool' has resided online since the advent of the web; it has been a category of website since the earliest directories were made to organize the web through 'cool site of the month' awards and other similar taxonomies such as the 'weird' in the early (and contemporary) Webby Awards. More recently, with the rise of the so-called filter bubble where content is recommended based on one's own preferences, trends, too, have become personalized (Pariser 2011). Twitter's trending topics are based on one's own geography and other 'signals', which in a sense displaces and distributes trends from a broader societal scale and scope into the smaller networks of the micro-celebrities and well-niched, who then would be expected to spread them.

The argument thus far is that the web, social media, and smartphones, whilst distracting, constitute modes of engagement that are measured and outputted in the form of vanity metrics. The measurements are vanity metrics for they take seriously front-staging or success theatre activity in social networking sites as productive and valuable. The attractiveness of vanity metrics lies in the desires they seed and reflect in the self but also in the promise of the identification of trend and trendsetters, in a realm associated with the cool.

From Vanity Metrics to Critical Analytics

I would like to put forward an alternative to vanity metrics, however, that could be construed as an agenda or a proposed pathway for an altmetrics project for social media (rather than one for novel academic citation analysis, whence the term is borrowed (Priem et al. 2010). 'Critical analytics', as it is termed, is a proposal for an alternative to vanity metrics, which begins with a shift away from social media as a productive social networking site for self-presentation only. Rather, it also could be viewed as a space for studying 'social issue networking'. On the streets, in meeting houses, and in pamphlets but also online in forums, websites, blogs, comment spaces, and now, increasingly, on social media platforms such as Facebook, Twitter, Instagram, and elsewhere, causes are put forward, taken up (or ignored), pledged to, rearticulated, and rallied around. Metrics could be devised for social media that do not build on it as vanity space but as one for this kind of social issue work. Whilst the proposed metrics below are by no means fully formed, social issue networking would at least consider (1) the particular actors that give voice to the issue with the greatest strength; (2) the issue areas or fields taking up the concern and those ignoring it; (3) the longevity or durability of actors' concern; (4) its specific articulation as well as counter-articulation; and (5) the set of actors who specify the concern in the same manner but who may not be allies. In this rendering of the issue space to be charted are thus dominant voice, concern, commitment, positioning, and alignment. In the following I briefly explain these 'critical analytics' by way of a series of illustrations.[1] All together, these and other altmetrics for issue work in social media provide alternatives to measuring vanity in spaces of self-presentation, although boastful uses of social media should not be dismissed entirely or even fully separated from critical uses.

Dominant Voice

Among the measurements for social media and other online media put forth here are, first, dominant voice, capturing the sources considered most impactful (although not necessarily credible) within that issue space. Which sources are given in an (authoritative) issue space, and of those, which dominate and which 'speaking subjects' are cut down or marginalized (Foucault 1972)? One particularly stark illustration of the study of dominant voice is an analysis of the sections of the newspaper where the HIV vaccine is most discussed. In 2009 the very prospect of creating a vaccine that would protect those without HIV-AIDS or treat those with it was being debated. In leading US newspapers, as a group of researchers and I found, an HIV vaccine was discussed at a much greater proportion in the business rather than in the health sections (see Figure 14.1). Here the authoritative space is the news, and the dominant voice is business news, although it is worthwhile to state that whilst the health section may be marginal, an HIV vaccine is not just a news item. It is also an issue that is part of a larger global health, intergovernmental, and transnational nongovernmental agenda, as is evidenced in Figure 14.2.

The Gates Foundation (like the news) is also an authoritative space; it is among the largest private foundations in the world funding projects in issues related to global health and development. In a comparison in 2014 between the issues on the Gates

business

Fig. 14.1 Rendition of mentions of HIV AIDS vaccine in leading US
newspapers, 2009, business and health sections compared
Analysis by students at the University of Amsterdam, May 2009.

funding agenda and the issues of concern to the actors in the global health and development field more broadly (as found on their websites), it is notable that certain
issues are nominally funded and others are inevitably not (see Figure 14.2). Among
the un-funded issues (so to speak), high on the agenda of the field actors, are poverty,
food security, and climate change. As caveats, it is important to mention that the
un-funded issues may be covered by the Foundation in other terms, as the analysis
concerns the issue language employed by the actors, rather than broader categories
or groupings. Such an ethnographic starting point or heuristic takes seriously how
the actors in the field deploy terms, which I will revisit when discussing positioning
below. The un-funded issues also could be described as broad issues outside of the
admittedly wide scope of 'global health'.

In both illustrations—business dominating the discussion of an HIV vaccine, and
the global health and development field highlighting issues un-funded by the Gates
Foundation—the dominant voice analysis opens up a discussion of potentially significant attention deficits. It is also a means to insert the language and agendas of
the non-dominant voice, in the tradition of 'counter-mapping' where materials, often land maps, are created to challenge dominant representations and power relations
(Peluso 1995).

Concern

Concernrefers to whether a person or organization (or sets thereof) are present or
absent within the issue space. Who is doing or occupying the issue, and who has de-
ferred? That is, for which actors is it or is it not a matter of concern? The becoming of
a matter of concern has been summarized as the 'redirection of attention' by publics
(Latour 2008, 48). As groups of children's rights, social justice, ICT4D, or other

Gates and Gates grantee issues compared and ranked.

HIV/AIDS
Malaria
Poverty
Vaccines
Tuberculosis
Maternal Health
Infectious Diseases
Cancer
Food Security
Global Health
Immunology
Child Health
Epidemiology
Climate Change
Public Health
Cell Biology
Immunisation
Microbiology
Brain Sciences
Molecular Biology
Reproductive Health
Water and Sanitation
Hunger
Parasitology
Vaccine Development
Agricultural Development
Malnutrition
Newborn Health
Population Health
Adolescent Health
Diarrhea
HIV Prevention
Infection

Influenza
Neglected Tropical Diseases
Neuroscience
Vaccination
Abortion
Basic Life Sciences
Chagas
Clinical Trials
Experimental Medicine
Leishmaniasis
Maize
Nutrition
Pneumonia
Reproduction and Development
Animal Health
Cardiometabolic Science
Genetics
Genomics
HIV Treatment
Human African Trypanosomiasis
Malaria Transmission
Malaria Vaccines
Sleeping Sickness
Structural Biology
Vector Borne Diseases
Youth Issues
HPV
Agriculture
Bioinformatics
Biological Threats
Chlamydia
Clinical Sciences
Congenital Disorders
Crop Research
Education
Endocrinology
Equitable Trade
Governance
Health Surveillance
HIV Strategic Information
HIV Technologies
Human Health
Independent Media
International Public Health
Malaria Diagnostics
Malaria Treatment
Plant Science
Quality Education
Rural Development
Solid Waste Management
Strong Communities
Vector Biology
Womens Health

Fig. 14.2 Funded and 'un-funded' issues by the Gates Foundation, according to an analysis of the issue agendas (found on their websites) of the Foundation as well as its grantees. Resized according to frequency of mentions and shaded according to funded (in grey) and un-funded (in black)
Analysis by Digital Methods Initiative, 2014–2015.

issue-oriented NGOs go about their work of creating campaigns, toolkits, graphic animation videos, serious games, and other action formats to seize the attention of their fellow issue professionals 'in the bubble' (as it is often colloquially said) and the general public outside of it, events transpire where a decision must be made whether to make an issue into a matter of concern. Should attention be redirected towards it? In other words, should there be concerted efforts to make it into a matter of concern? The significant nuclear accident in 2011 in Fukushima, Japan, caused by a tsunami, led to the release of radiation, including a spread of radiated water off the coast. As the events were happening, a group of action researchers and I asked the question, to whom is this particular issue a matter of concern? By measuring the mentions of 'Fukushima' on the websites of Greenpeace and WWF, we created an indicator of the extent to which it is a matter of concern to leading environmental NGOs as well as NGOs concerned with species (see Figure 14.3).

Issue professionals and others may pose the question, what kind of an issue is Fukushima? Is it primarily a nuclear issue, or perhaps a political one in the sense that a particular Japanese political party is invested in nuclear power whilst others are firm opponents? What could Fukushima do to an issue? In the event Fukushima

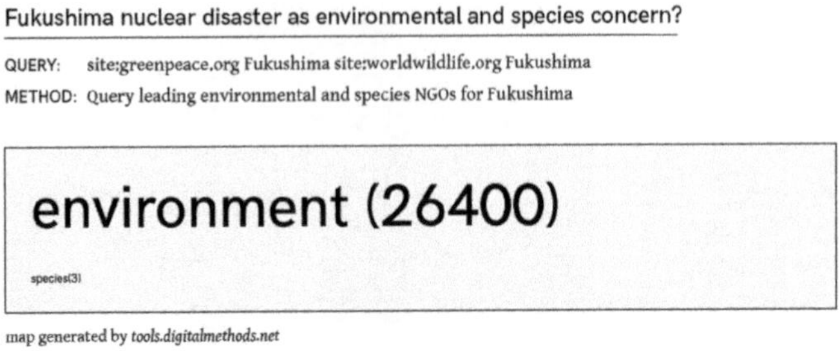

Fukushima nuclear disaster as environmental and species concern?

QUERY: site:greenpeace.org Fukushima site:worldwildlife.org Fukushima
METHOD: Query leading environmental and species NGOs for Fukushima

environment (26400)

species(3)

map generated by *tools.digitalmethods.net*

Fig. 14.3 Source cloud of Greenpeace and WWF, resized by the quantity of mentions of Fukushima, March 2011
Source: Lippmannian Device, Digital Methods Initiative, Amsterdam.

resonated greatly with Greenpeace and hardly at all with WWF. This finding indicates a skewed distribution of concern towards the environment and away from animals or marine life, at least in the immediate aftermath, according to the technique. From the points of view of the NGOs as well as how Fukushima was made into a particular type of issue, it should be remarked that in the aftermath both Greenpeace and WWF have been active in the anti-nuclear issue space in Japan, with campaigns based on the lessons from Fukushima. The critical analytics here are snapshots relating not only to whether but specifically to whom an issue is a matter of concern at a given time. Moreover, one can ask, who is absent and who may be subject to cajoling into joining at another given time, when another snapshot may be taken? Longitudinal concern, or stringing together snapshots of concern, is the subject of 'commitment'. It refers to concern over time despite lessening (rather than increasing) attention, as related below.

Commitment

Commitment is the longevity or persistence of concern: do actors move into and out of the issue space as trend followers without qualms, or do they abide by their concern? That is, for how long is it a matter of concern to the actors? Indeed, in addition to who deems an issue a matter of concern (or whether the issue is present or absent in the actor's communications), the related question for the issue concerns longevity or perseverance, despite lessening attention by others. Longevity may be inconvenient, especially if other issues arise that may be receiving more attention and may thereby seem more attractive. Funders may have left the previous issue; should you, too? In describing commitment, one may differentiate between the citizen who must care for a community beyond oneself and a consumer who needs to care only for the self (Suleiman 2003).

As an illustration of studying commitment as a form of critical analytics, I share an analysis into Greenpeace's longevity of concerns, undertaken on the basis of its campaigning behaviour, as expressed on its website. The analysis is undertaken using the Internet Archive, the large online repository of websites from the past.[2] It employs a capturing and rendering technique developed to create a screencast documentary of the frontpage of a website over time in the style of time lapse photography (Rogers 2013). Having captured the website frontpages over a seven-year period, which issues could be said to persist (Greenpeace as citizen), and which are more fleeting (Greenpeace as consumer)? In this manner of a commitment mapping, it was found that Greenpeace is remarkably consistent in its main issue campaigning; from 2006 to 2012 (the timeframe of the mapping) Greenpeace did not waver from its campaigning for 'Nuclear', 'Oceans', 'Toxics', 'Forests', 'Climate', and 'Peace and Disarmament', as the menu items on the website read (see Figure 14.4). In each year those main issues are present, whilst a smattering of others appear and disappear (genetic engineering and sustainable trade) or appear and remain, only to leave the frontpage years after the analysis (agriculture). Year-on-year campaigning for the same issue demonstrates a resistance to issue fatigue.

The daily appearance of the menu item and the content that must be generated to sustain it, lest it becomes 'empty', could also be described as a commitment device. The device is an issue-sustaining formula such as a United Nations calendar, with its annual HIV-AIDS day on 10 December (and numerous others).

The question remains, however, whether content activities bear out such a finding of commitment. Remaining within the realm of website analysis, one can also

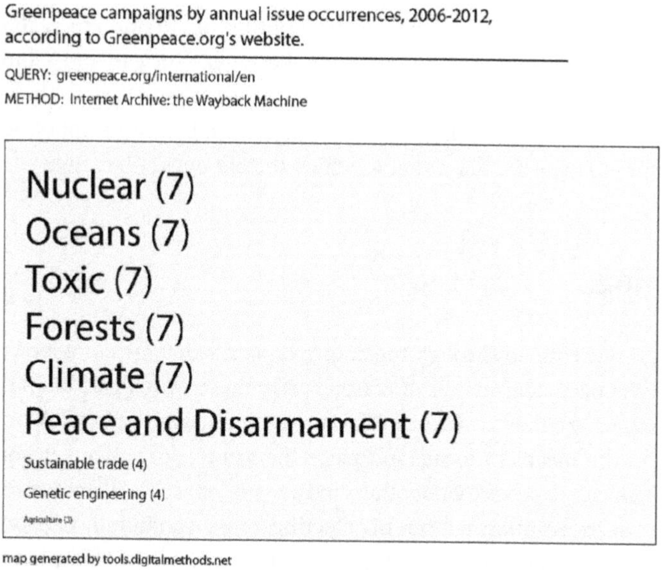

Greenpeace campaigns by annual issue occurrences, 2006-2012, according to Greenpeace.org's website.

QUERY: greenpeace.org/international/en
METHOD: Internet Archive: the Wayback Machine

Nuclear (7)
Oceans (7)
Toxic (7)
Forests (7)
Climate (7)
Peace and Disarmament (7)

Sustainable trade (4)

Genetic engineering (4)

Agriculture (3)

map generated by tools.digitalmethods.net

Fig. 14.4 Issue cloud of Greenpeace's issue commitment, evidenced by consistency of campaigning for the same issues over a seven-year time frame, 2006–2012.
Source: Achive.org. Analysis by Anne Laurine Stadermann.

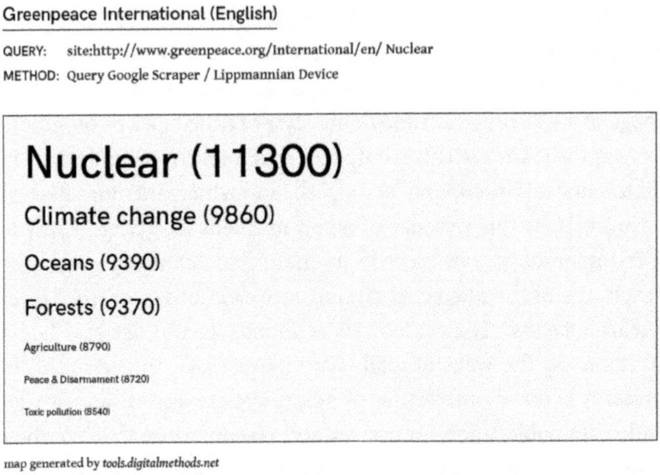

Greenpeace International (English)

QUERY: site:http://www.greenpeace.org/International/en/ Nuclear
METHOD: Query Google Scraper / Lippmannian Device

Nuclear (11300)

Climate change (9860)

Oceans (9390)

Forests (9370)

Agriculture (8790)

Peace & Disarmament (8720)

Toxic pollution (8540)

map generated by tools.digitalmethods.net

Fig. 14.5 Issue cloud of Greenpeace's distributed attention to its issues on the basis of Google results' page counts per issue, on its website, greenpeace.org, 2012
Source: Lippmannian Device, Digital Methods Initiative, Amsterdam. Analysis by Anne Laurine Stadermann.

query the Greenpeace website for all of the main campaign keywords, so as to create a snapshot of the number of pages dedicated to each (see Figure 14.5). In the event, in 2012, Greenpeace shows a fairly even distribution of attention to each of the issues (where attention is page count per issue), however 'Nuclear' and 'Climate' have more copy (by some 2000–3000 pages with mentions) than 'Toxics'. Thus commitment, as longevity of concern, is also continually tested by the advent of new causes and techniques to measure the extent to which the old ones still matter.

Positioning

Positioning is determined through the choice of words that are employed to denote and discuss the particular matter of concern. Are these words part of an agenda or stance-taking, or are they conscious efforts to step outside the fray? A positioning analysis seeks the means to locate and place the actors' purposive keyword choice (or issue language) vis-à-vis that of others in the same space (Williams 1976). Rather than an exercise in reception, it is one of detecting (and meaningfully interpreting and plotting) issue space insertions by actors. In social media when #blacklivesmatter is met with #alllivesmatter, the actors are injecting a counter positioning or, as described by Akrich and Latour (1992), an anti-programme into the space of a programme. One could call it a sponsored insertion if undertaken by political lobbyists or operatives, or even a debate if there are views exchanged, but great sifting work is required to unearth the artful agents working in the sub-political realm or in organizing the heap of short texts into what could be called orderly transcripts of a debate.

Rather than detective work or debate mapping, it is described here as positioning analysis; who is joining a particular programme and who is joining an anti-programme, with which nuance and from which location? Positioning as locating is thus not only substantive but also topological in a geographical sense. Geo-coordinates often accompany digital media, and one may place content in a (seemingly) straightforward geographical sense, however much pinpointing location (and visualizing it) are fraught with issues of density (concentration of points or dots), tiling (the sizes of the map's area components), and other complicating factors.

One example may serve as an illustration of such positioning analysis. When the US Supreme Court ruled in favour of same-sex marriage in 2015, on Instagram (as well as Twitter and across social media), the hashtag #lovewins and #celebratepride and the counter-hashtags #jesuswins or #loveloses could be said to position those deploying them in the societal issue space (see Figure 14.6). One lauds the decision with a programme and another derides it with an anti-programme. Here the critical analytics concerns how actors are positioning themselves (with the programme, with the anti-programme or efforts at neutrality) as well as geo-locating such positionings. It also should be noted that such oppositions should be nuanced for there may be multiple programmes, anti-programmes, and also other acts in that space such as users spamming, trolling, and hijacking.

Those joining programmes and anti-programmes are often considered issue-specific 'hashtag publics', and described as 'bursty joiners' and leavers, or otherwise fleeting participants (Bruns and Burgess 2015; Rambukkana 2015). One contribution of these publics that demonstrates their relatedness is the memetic; it refers to content sharing similar characteristics in form and substance, made with knowledge of the other content and circulating in the space (Shifman 2014). With #jesuswins comes a cascade of crosses and red shades of colour and this may be contrasted to the abundant use of rainbow imagery over at #celebratepride. The meme and counter-meme are furnished by the competing uses of filters, the original Instagram feature, and source of its popularity.

Working with the hashtags, one may chart the use of #celebratepride and #jesuswins (as well as related hashtags #lovewins and #loveloses) on Instagram, where related hashtag analysis would confirm that clustered hashtag publics, whilst in camps, also nuance their positioning into one particularly religious cluster (#jesuswins with images of the cross) and one against the ruling and same-sex marriage where #loveloses expresses sentiment against the validity of same-sex marriage. When locating (geographically) the posts, densities in particular parts of the USA (including the Bible Belt) are noted, albeit with far fewer postings than #lovewins, which also resonates outside of the USA. Here the analysis substantively (through a combination of hashtag and visual (meme) analysis) and geographically positions the reactions to the court ruling.

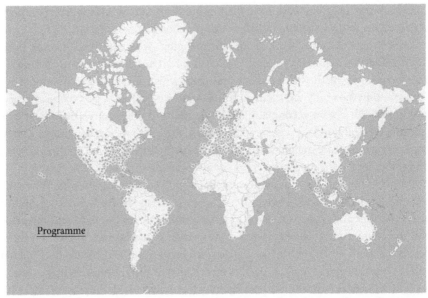

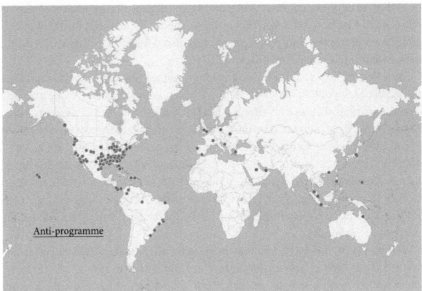

Fig. 14.6 Geo-location plotting of Instagram users of competing hashtags after the US Supreme Court Ruling on same-sex marriage, July 2015

Analysis by Bastiaan Baccarne, Angeles Briones, Stefan Baack, Emily Maemura, Janna Joceli, Peiqing Zhou, and Humberto Ferreira, Digital Methods Summer School 2015.

Alignment

Lastly, alignment is a term for group formation through positioning. That is, who else is using the same issue language and therefore shares a similar position? They may be strange bedfellows, in the sense of not belonging to a particular area, field, coalition, partnership, and so forth, but their choice of language aligns them with others who elect to employ the same terms. The use of the term 'alignment' (and perhaps the usefulness of the analytics) are drawn from Walter Lippmann's description of how publics decide which side to take in political affairs. Rather than making meticulous study of a social issue and the options facing those in the business of policymaking, they look instead for 'coarse signs of where [their] sympathies ought to turn' (Lippmann 1927, 64). In this reading the 'coarse signs' are particular keywords or terms actors use when discussing an issue. When multiple actors use the same language, or when publics do so, they align. Is the barrier between Israel and the Palestinian Territories to be called a 'security fence' or an 'apartheid wall'? When security fence is used, it is the Israeli position, whereas apartheid wall is the Palestinian. Other terms could be construed as measured side-taking (separation wall), efforts of reconciliation (separation fence), or neutrality (barrier) (see Figure 14.7).

Alignment refers to the company a keyword keeps. Who else is deploying that particular issue language, and thereby is associated so as to be in line with another? One aligns oneself on the basis of shared language. Whether in utterances captured by the media or replayed from the parliamentary floor, shared language becomes Lippmann's 'coarse sign'. How should we consider the more general study of the company kept by keywords? One could ask, which NGOs (however disparate in their issue orientation) are aligned when it comes to discussing Internet access as a human right,

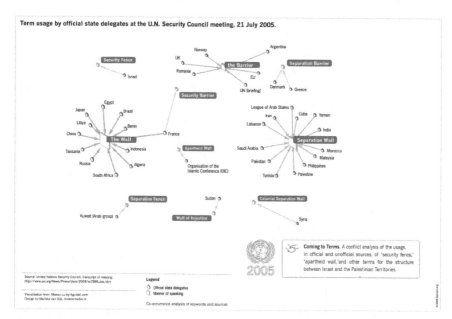

Fig. 14.7 Alignment of countries in the UN Security Council on the basis of the use of keywords for the barrier between Israel and the Palestinian Territories, 2005
Source: Rogers and Ben-David, 2010.

or which national states are in favour of austerity measures in Europe (even though they may disagree on bail outs)? These are analyses of single issues with multiple actors, but one also could analyse multiple issues (keywords) and their actors, seeking clustered alignments of actors.

It should be pointed out that the limitation of these critical analytics lies in their coarseness, to redeploy Lippmann's term. They indicate, according to web and social media data, the significance of actors in given issue spaces according to mention counts (dominant voice). They give a sense of an actor's matters of interest (concern), and the durability of those interests (commitment) on the basis of the issues they choose to mention and continue to mention. They provide a view of an actor's standpoint (positioning) given the specificity of the issue language they utilize, together with their alliances because those actors utter the same (alignment).

Conclusion: Alternative Metrics for Social Media

In summary, building upon 'altmetrics' for science, an alternative metrics project, I propose another altmetrics for social issue spaces, which I call 'critical analytics'. In order to do so, I call for a change in the networks under study by social researchers, that is, a shift from the social network (with its vanity metrics) to the issue network. Critical analytics seeks to measure alternative modes of engagement (other than those for vanity metrics and distracted modes of engagement) such as dominant voice, concern, commitment, positioning, and alignment.

One of the original insights of the altmetrics project in science concerns the significance of social media for the organization of attention to new work. The new science metrics would anticipate scholarly interest in articles published or pre-published, and even projects under development or being blogged about in progress. It grants to the web, and more specifically social media platforms, the status of a near real-time data stream that would not only anticipate interest in new work but also provide indications of impact sooner than the time it takes for print citations to accumulate and be counted (Thelwall et al. 2013). Critical analytics is similarly considered an alternative to existing metrics projects in social media, but the relationship between altmetrics and citation analysis (Web of Science) is different from that of critical analytics and vanity metrics.

Critical analytics borrows the insight that there is professional work being organized and disseminated through social media that does not principally concern the presentation of self and vanity (although there are of course those aspects to science as well as to social issue work) (Bennett and Segerberg 2012). As in the manner that altmetrics sees science networks in social media, critical analytics proposes to see issue networks. Thus, the social network is 'productive' not just for the self and what one would like to be, as well as for business connections, but also for issue engagement analysis.

Critical analytics takes from other online engagement measurement practices, such as media monitoring, the idea that engagement in social media is meaningful and worthy of measure beyond the purview of vanity. Actor impact in issue spaces, the dominant voice measure, is an exercise in actor identification and source demarcation that one could undertake in science or media monitoring, where the actors are authors or opinion leaders and the sources are vetted journals or leading newspapers (respectively). Concern as redirection of attention by publics similarly may be studied in terms of novel pockets of innovation in science (Callon et al. 1983). Commitment could be conceived as longer than expected attention to a news item or unfashionable scientific paradigm, still writing about it after the end of the attention cycle (Downs 1972). Positioning may be thought of as the specific terms used, over and again, in news articles, which signal a slant or an editorial policy in the framing of accounts of an event (Herman and Chomksy 1988; Entman 1991). Alignment could be conceived of as common frames across newspapers, showing how the newspapers were in line with another. In other words, each of the critical analytics could be described as forms of repurposed metrics in science and media monitoring, applied to social media.

That the study of engagement in media evolves with the advent of social media also holds here, too. For each of the critical analytics there are combinations of actors and language, with relationships between them that are plotted substantively, topologically, and stylistically, where the particularities are medium-specific. There are substantive hashtags, geo-located posts, and photos as well as memes expressed through filters. Moreover, the outputs of the analytics also share a visual language with the medium from whence they are derived. There are word clouds, place marker maps, image grids, and other visualizations of the medium. Thus, the analytics and their outputs, whilst sharing provenances and features with metrics from science citation analysis and media monitoring, also contain digital indicators whose means of measure are commonly referred to as analytics. Not just the posing of an alternative to vanity metrics but also the study of engagement in issue work furnishes the critical attribute.

Finally, critical analytics not only serve as a reminder that not all online metrics need to be of the vanity variety, but also furnish a research agenda to catalogue works that could be conceived of as such and to develop additional ones. For example, #Polar scores sorts politicians' tweets, estimating ideology (and its severity) on the basis of hashtag usage (Hemphill et al. 2016). Persecuting.us, by the critical media artist Paola Circio (2012), scores online utterances on Twitter, revealing how polarizing people can be in political discourse and exposing it (Manghani 2017). These projects (and no doubt many others) are demonstrations of how social media usage may be evaluated, but also how metrics can themselves be critical.

Acknowledgements

An earlier version of this chapter was published as 'Otherwise Engaged: Social Media from Vanity Metrics to Critical Analytics', *International Journal of Communication*, 12(2018), 450–72.

Notes

1. Some of the metrics have been developed with the aid of tools developed by the Digital Methods Initiative, University of Amsterdam, https://tools.digitalmethods.net.
2. The Internet Archive is at https://www.archive.org.

References

Akrich, M., and Latour, B. 1992. A summary of a convenient vocabulary for the semiotics of human and nonhuman assemblies In Bijker, W. and Law, J. (eds), *Shaping Technology/Building Society: Studies in Sociotechnical Change* (pp. 259–64). Cambridge, MA: MIT Press.

Barabasi, A.-L. 2002. *Linked: How Everything is Connected to Everything Else and What It Means for Business, Science, and Everyday Life*. New York: Plume.

Baudrillard, J. 1990. *Cool Memories*. Trans. Chris Turner. London: Verso.

Beer, D. 2016. *Metric Power*. Basingstoke: Palgrave Macmillan.

Bennett, W. L., and Segerberg, A. 2012. The Logic of Connective Action. *Information, Communication & Society*, 15(5): pp. 739–68.

Boorstin, D. 1961. *The Image: A Guide to Pseudo-events in America*. New York: Harper Colofon Books

boyd, d. and Ellison, N. B. 2007. Social Network Sites: Definition, History, and Scholarship. *Journal of Computer-mediated Communication*, 13(1): pp. 210–30.

Bruns, A., and Burgess, J. 2015. Twitter hashtags from ad hoc to calculated publics. In Rambukkana, N. (eds), *Hashtag Publics: The Power and Politics of Discursive Networks*. (pp. 13–28), New York: Peter Lang.

Callon, M., Courtial, J. P., Turner, W., and Bauin, S. 1983. From translations to problematic networks: An introduction to co-word analysis. *Social Science Information*, 22(2): pp. 191–235.

Carr, N. 2007. From contemplative man to flickering man. Encyclopædia Britannica Blog, 13 June, http://blogs.britannica.com/2007/06/from-contemplative-man-to-flickering-man/.

Carr, N. 2008. Is Google Making Us Stupid? *The Atlantic*. July/August.

Carr, N. 2010. *The Shallows: How the Internet is Changing the Way We Think, Read and Remember*. New York: W.W. Norton.

Circio, P. 2012. Persecuting.us, website, https://persecutiting.us.

Csikszentmihalyi, M. 1997. *Finding Flow*. New York: Basic Books.

Downs, A. 1972. Up and Down with Ecology. *Public Interest*, 28: pp. 38–50.

Entman, R. 1991. Framing U.S. Coverage of International News. *Journal of Communication*, 41(4): pp. 6–27.

Foucault, M. 1972. *The Archaeology of Knowledge and the Discourse on Language*. Trans. Alan M. Sheridan Smith. New York: Pantheon.

Freeman, L. C. 1977. A set of measures of centrality based on betweenness. *Sociometry*, 40: pp. 35–40.

Gerlitz, C., and Lury, C. 2014. Social media and self-evaluating assemblages: On numbers, orderings and values. *Distinktion: Journal of Social Theory*, 15(2): pp. 174–88.

Gladwell, M. 2010. Small change: Why the revolution will not be Tweeted. *New Yorker*, 4 October.

Goffman, E. 1956. *The Presentation of Self in Everyday Life*. Monograph no. 2. Edinburgh: University of Edinburgh Social Sciences Research Center.

Gonçalves, B., and Perra, N. 2011. Modeling users' activity on Twitter networks: Validation of Dunbar's number. *PloS one*, 3 August, dx.doi.org/10.1371/journal.pone.0022656.

Gottfried, J., and Shearer, E. 2016. *News Use across Social Media Platforms 2016*. Washington, DC: Pew Research Center.

Granovetter, M. 1973. The strength of weak ties. *American Journal of Sociology*, 78(6): pp. 1360–80.

Gray, S. 1975. *Otherwise Engaged*. London: Whitstable.

Hemphill, L., Culotta, A., and Heston, M. 2016. #Polar scores: Measuring partisanship using social media content. *Journal of Information Technology & Politics*, 13(4): pp. 365–77.

Herman, E.S., and Chomsky, N. 1988. *Manufacturing Consent*. New York: Pantheon.

Ito, M. 2005. Intimate visual co-presence. Position paper for the Seventh International Conference on Ubiquitous Computing, Tokyo, 11–14 September.

Keen, A. 2007. *The Cult of the Amateur*. New York: Crown Publishing Group.

Latour, B. 2008. *What is the Style of Matters of Concern? Two Lectures in Empirical Philosophy*. Assen: Van Gorcum

Lehrer, J. 2010. Weak ties, Twitter and revolution. *Wired*, 29 September.

Lin, L. 2009. Breadth-biased versus focused cognitive control in media multitasking behaviors. *PNAS*, 106(37): pp. 15521–2.

Lippmann, W. 1927. *The Phantom Public: A Sequel to 'Public Opinion'*. New York: Macmillan.

Liu, A. 2004. *The Laws of Cool*. Chicago: University of Chicago Press.

Manghani, S. 2017. The art of Paolo Cirio: Exposing new myths of big data structures. *Theory, Culture & Society*, 34(7–8): pp. 197–214.

Marwick, A. and boyd, d 2011. 'To see and be seen: Celebrity practice on Twitter. *Convergence: The International Journal of Research into New Media Technologies*, 17(2): pp. 139–58.

Morozov, E. 2009. 'From slacktivism to activism. *Foreign Policy*. 5 September.

Pariser, E. 2011. *The Filter Bubble*. New York: Penguin.

Peluso, N. L. 1995. 'Whose woods are these? Counter-mapping forest territories in Kalimantan, Indonesia. *Antipode*, 27(4): pp. 383–406.

Priem, J., Taraborelli, D., Groth, P., and Neylon, C. 2010. Altmetrics: A manifesto. Altmetrics.org, 26 October, http://altmetrics.org/manifesto.

Rambukkana, N. 2015. Introduction: Hashtags as technosocial events. In Rambukkana, N. (eds), *Hashtag Publics: The Power and Politics of Discursive Networks*. (pp. 1–12). New York: Peter Lang.

Ries, E. 2009. Vanity metrics vs. actionable metrics. Four Hour Work Week blog. 19 May. http://fourhourworkweek.com/2009/05/19/vanity-metrics-vs-actionable-metrics/.

Rogers, R. 2013. *Digital Methods*. Cambridge, MA: MIT Press.

Rogers, R., and Ben-David A. 2010. Coming to terms: A conflict analysis of the usage, in official and unofficial sources, of 'security fence', 'apartheid wall', and other terms for the structure between Israel and the Palestinian Territories. *Media, Conflict & War*, 2(3): pp. 202–29.

Sarno, D. 2009. Twitter creator Jack Dorsey illuminates the site's founding document. Part I. *Los Angeles Times*. 18 February.

Schivelbusch, W. 1986. *The Railway Journey: The Industrialization and Perception of Time and Space*. Berkeley: University of California Press.

Schwartz, T. 2011. Take back your attention. *Harvard Business Review*. 9 February. https://hbr.org/2011/02/take-back-your-attention.html.

Senft, T. 2013. Microcelebrity and the branded self. In Hartley, J., Burgess, J., and Bruns, A. (eds), *A Companion to New Media Dynamics*. (pp. 346–54). Oxford: Wiley-Blackwell.

Shifman, L. 2014. *Memes in Digital Culture*. Cambridge, MA: MIT Press.

Stewart, J. B. 2016. Facebook has 50 minutes of your time each day. It wants more. *New York Times*, 5 May.

Stone, L. 2009. Beyond simple multi-tasking: Continuous partial attention. Linda Stone blog. 30 November. https://lindastone.net/2009/11/30/beyond-simple-multi-tasking-continuous-partial-attention/.

Suleiman, E. 2003. *Dismantling Democratic States*. Princeton, NJ: Princeton University Press.

Thelwall, M., Haustein, S., Larivière,V., and Sugimot. C. R. 2013. Do altmetrics work? Twitter and Ten Other Social Web Services. *PloS one*, 28 May, dx. doi.org/10.1371/journal.pone. 0064841

Thompson, C. 2008. Brave new world of digital intimacy. *New York Times*, 5 September.

Thompson, C. 2013. *Smarter than You Think: How Technology is Changing our Minds for the Better*. New York: Penguin.

Turow, J. 2006. *Niche Envy*. Cambridge, MA: MIT Press.

Urry, J. 2007. *Mobilities*. Cambridge: Polity.

Van Dijk, M. 2014. Personal communication..

Van Doorn, N. 2014. The neoliberal subject of value measuring human capital in information economies. *Cultural Politics*, 10(3): 354–75.

Venturini, T. 2016. Controversy Mapping: A Travel Companion. HDR dissertation. Lyon: Ecole Normale Supérieure de Lyon.

Williams, R. 1976. *Keywords*. London: Fontana.

Wortham, J. 2012. Digital diary: Facebook poke and the tedium of success theater. *Bits Blog, New York Times*, 28 December.

15

Investigating Online Unmanaged Organization

Antenarrative as a Methodological Approach

Adriana Wilner, Tania Pereira Christopoulos, and Mario Aquino Alves

Introduction

There is a terrain in organizations that is unsupervised, in which employees can express their feelings and fantasies. Gabriel (1995) defines this dimension as the unmanaged organization and stresses that it is a symbolic space for myths, jokes, gossip, caricatures, nicknames, and other forms of narratives that are subjective in their nature. In order to apprehend the nuances of unmanaged organization, researchers need to move away from the technical rational universe they are used to working within and away from dichotomic frames such as control/resistance. Coffee corners are a typical location where those symbolic narratives may manifest within the physical spaces of organizations. In our research, we asked what happens when coffee corners move to the internet. We have investigated blogs, social media and employee review platforms and found that there is a rich resource for researchers to explore in order to understand employees' perceptions about the organizations they work for, whether or not these formal organizations are digital.

Analysing narratives about organizations provided by employees on the internet allows researchers to understand hidden facets of organizational culture and human resource policies and practices. Moreover, it is possible to follow the sensemaking process of organizational change and to anticipate tensions. There is an opportunity to unveil the struggle between different narratives about organizations and to contrast them with official dominant narratives. This kind of research is challenging not only due to the volume of posts but also because of the fragmented and polyphonic nature of testimonials, especially on social media and review platforms. This chapter discusses how to research the online unmanaged organization by collecting testimonials posted by employees and former employees on the internet and analysing them using an approach called antenarrative analysis (Boje 2001). Antenarrative methodology deals with fragmented stories without a beginning, middle, and end and allows the researcher to assemble the pieces of a broader narrative puzzle.

Adriana Wilner, Tania Pereira Christopoulos, and Mario Aquino Alves, *Investigating Online Unmanaged Organization*. In: *Research Methods for Digital Work and Organization*. Edited by Gillian Symon, Katrina Pritchard, and Christine Hine, Oxford University Press. © Oxford University Press (2021). DOI: 10.1093/oso/9780198860679.003.0015

We illustrate the methodological challenges and paths encountered when researching non-hierarchical organizations and the internet with a specific case (Wilner et al. 2016, 2017a). We use the term non-hierarchical organizations to describe organizations employing radical horizontal models without charts, formal positions, and chiefs that were established this way or that later made such a change. We studied four organizations, three of which were digital companies encompassing face-to-face work. This is a rich territory to research the unmanaged organization because, as non-hierarchical organizations are viewed as ideal places to work, employees who criticize the model openly would be seen as ungrateful for complaining about an environment where they do not have someone managing them. When there are no formal channels for open discussion, informal unmanaged terrains become an escape valve.

First, we explain the antenarrative approach. Then, we explain how this methodology can be used in studies about work tracking digital traces left by employees and former employees. Finally, we illustrate the antenarrative approach by presenting how we operationalized it in our research.

The Antenarrative Approach

Narratives about organizations on the internet are usually fragmented and incoherent. How are they articulated and gain order and meaning? David Boje (2001, 9), although not mentioning the internet explicitly, stated that 'the postmodern and chaotic soup of storytelling is somewhat difficult to analyze. Stories in organizations are self-deconstructing, flowing, emerging, and networking, not all static'. This statement fits completely the online set of fragmented, dynamic, and connected narratives we find on the internet. These stories cannot be told within the paradigm of the hegemonic field of organizations focused on the creation of official stories and master narratives, usually with a definite commercial purpose, both for the external public and for the internal public. In this field, those who have power always try to 'dictate' their hegemonic meanings to others through advertising, authorized biographies, slogans, logos, statements about mission and values, images, websites, official communication. Parallel to the construction of hegemonic narratives, small stories left by many different stakeholders also have the potential to eventually gain cohesion in different processes of sensemaking, forming counternarratives that contest master narratives. Usually, counternarratives are viewed as the narratives of the marginalized and defeated, unheard voices trying to contest official master narratives. Most counternarratives are created by the individuals that normally do not have voice in organizational dominant narratives, but generate 'small stories' or 'little people stories'. Small stories are living stories told in the moment. Only when interconnected with other anecdotes do a plot and a beginning, middle, and end arise. Then, there will be a narrative with a coherent pattern that may even eliminate noise from the living chaotic stories and eventually become established and taken for granted.

When analysing the art critic Giovanni Morelli's methodology, Ginzburg (1991) pointed out parallels between the critic's method for analysing a painting, the method of forensic investigation of the fictional detective Sherlock Holmes, and Sigmund Freud's therapeutic method. The similarities of these methods rested on the apprehension of marginal and irrelevant details as revealing keys to the authorship of a painting, or a crime, or the deeper causes of traumatic experiences (Ginzburg 1991). This methodology of an investigation *à la Sherlock Holmes* that looks at details of small stories and the interconnection between them is what Boje (2001) calls *antenarratives*. These antenarratives make bridges between living stories and narratives. When we analyse online posts, we can make sense of those fragmented testimonials by joining the pieces, looking at how they form a dialogue.

Antenarratives, according to Boje (2001), can be seen through a double lens: 'as being before and as a bet' (Boje 2001, 10). One methodological path is to work on the retrospective sensemaking of narratives. This is done by deconstructing narratives, asking what narratives are made of, what are the embedded meanings, and how a narrative could be replaced with polysemous multivocal little stories. The other methodological path, the bet, also an interpretative lens, drives in the opposite direction, from stories to narratives, trying to understand and anticipate narratives. It looks at the network of stories, at the intertextual connection between them, at possible emplotments, at themes that appear and vanish in those nets of stories. Antenarrative is also a dialectical process of anticipating, constructing, and reconstructing counternarratives that exist around the master narratives. It is by principle speculative, a process of sensemaking that takes into account the struggle of different and far from consensual stories, trying to answer the question: 'what is going on here?' (Boje 2001, 13).

The emblematic research on Disney, that (Boje 1995) carried out before systematizing his methodology helps to explain this approach. Boje wanted to understand alternative ways of understanding Disney history apart from the heroic and romantic grand narrative of a successful and harmonic company created and developed by just one man.In order to find the multiple voices that were suppressed in this history, he accessed the Disney archives from 1989 to 1990, from where it was possible to collect documents, audio and video tapes with CEO speeches, interviews,public relations films, working meetings, stockholders meetings, and so on. He found that the romantic corporate,as a storytelling enterprise, documented everything. The corpus he was interested in totalled 2967 lines of text in 116 pages from 21 different sources.With this material, plus books and other texts by different author, he started to look at themes and different voices within those themes throughout history,paying attention to the differences between the CEO's story and other employees' stories and how they dialogued with each other and had different readings of the same themes. This methodology enabled him to capture and construct the diversity of antenarratives behind the monolith that was the official narrative.

Antenarrative Analysis and Internet Stories

Contemporary narratology finds fragmented stories no longer in storytellers of great writings, but in small texts and fragments of internet media messages: reports, advertisements, political and economic comments, biographies, social media posts, and comments, review posts by consumers and employees (Murray 2017). On the internet, researchers can investigate fragments that shape narratives, as what we call 'small stories' are documented in the virtual space. Especially when dealing with sensitive issues, such as the unmanaged organization, internet research opens new ways of collecting and analysing data.

Antenarrative analysis of internet material can be carried out following four antenarrative patterns: linear-antenarratives, cyclical-antenarratives, spiral-narratives, and rhizomatic-antenarratives (Boje 2011, 2014). Table 15.1 summarizes the peculiarities of each pattern.

According to Boje (2001), there are also eight methodological options to analyse antenarratives: deconstruction, grand narrative, microstoria, story network, intertextuality, causality, plot, and theme. These can also be used in combination. Any of these methodological options may be applied to the different antenarrative patterns presented in Table 15.1. In Table 15.2, we briefly explain them and give examples in the context of work and internet.

Table 15.1 Antenarrative patterns and internet material

Antenarrative patterns	Description	Examples
Linear antenarratives	Connects past and future by a way of retrospection-prospection sensemaking in one single movement	Twitter threads, where each tweet is an account on its own, but assembled create a story
Cyclical antenarratives	Connects past and future by a way of retrospection-prospection sensemaking in regular cycles	Daily blog entries
Spiral antenarratives	Narratives that start small and amplify in orbits of a spiral form, with a central force driving them	The emergence of fake news
Rhizomatic antenarrratives	Narrative segments that do not have shape, symmetry, sequence, or repetition, where the assemblage of materiality and human actors is essential	The use of devices like hashtags (#) to tag some issues to some virtual persona (@)

Source: Adapted from Boje (2011).

Table 15.2 Methodological ways to analyse internet antenarratives

Methodological options	Description	Example
Deconstruction	The researcher compares master narratives with small stories to introduce new voices, review hierarchies, give light to contradictions by looking at apparent exceptions and trace subtle meanings, among other methodological strategies. The objective is to, in the end, resituate the narrative considering the richness of multiple points of view. In order to proceed with deconstruction antenarrative methodology, the researcher has to reach multiple small stories and compare them with official narratives published by organizations	Researchers can deconstruct media narratives of an organization by looking on the internet at fragmented stories by employees
Grand narrative	The researcher also uses deconstruction analysis, because he/she compares master narratives with small stories, looking at interplays and possibilities of rebuilding what was once a linear mono-voiced narrative. Grand narrative analysis is interested in the historical and political dynamics of narrative building	Studying, for instance, the emergence of models of organizing brought about by startups such as Uber, the researcher can investigate stories from different stakeholders on the internet to look for the complex dynamics of work relations, in order to make sense of the ambiguities that take place and to restore the master narrative of empowerment and its counter-narrative of work destruction by those new models
Microstoria	The researcher looks at archival records of 'little people stories' as possibilities to resist a dominant narrative and proceeds with an analysis that combines deductive and inductive methods. On the internet, it is possible to look for 'little people stories' in multiple sites and social media	Boje et al. (2016) investigated stakeholders' stories about Burger King looking at the Glassdoor site, which is the leading global source of employee reviews, in order to understand and reframe narratives of organizational change

Continued

Table 15.2 *Continued*

Methodological options	Description	Example
Story network analysis	The researcher makes a map of stories looking at a system in a rhizomatic way	In previous research (Wilner et al. 2017b), we mapped stories on the internet about employees that were dismissed after publishing posts that displeased employers—in order to look for antenarratives about the unmanaged organization
Intertextuality analysis	The researcher analyses the dialogue occurring between different actors and their living stories in connection with master narratives. An intertextual antenarrative analysis of small online stories, combined with other methodological options, can explain how some human resource practices arise, grow, and die and how tensions in work relations develop	It is possible to look at how users interact with a specific post, for instance, of employee whistleblowing, building a counter-narrative
Causality narrative	The researcher investigates dynamics of small stories to build or reframe a narrative with causal attributions	In making sense of what caused a merger failure from the point of view of organizational culture, the researcher can look at internet sites and social media, including Glassdoor, in order to make sense of different possible narratives
Plot analysis	The researcher looks at stories forming or transforming a plot with a beginning, middle, and end with its critical events. A plot has a succession of incidents and events, which are configured and reconfigured into a whole story	The narrative of an introduction of a diversity employee policy may have different characters, events, crises, climax, and resolution from the master narrative released by the organization, and the internet search can help the researcher find small stories about the process
Theme analysis	Researchers look at taxonomies that come from stories and, at the same time, from the theory, to locate possible thematic narratives	The researcher can make sense of stories on the internet about a strike with themes such as the romantic narrative, a chaotic narrative, etc., and identify overlaps and ambiguities between them

Source: Adapted from Boje (2001).

With blogs, social media, and other sites on the internet, it is possible to do this kind of research even when there are barriers to accessing archival documents and interviews inside the organization one wishes to study. We detail this process in the next section, illustrating this with a case from our research on non-hierarchical organizations.

Applying an antenarrative approach in an online context

In this part of the chapter, we will discuss how to apply antenarrative approaches. We used both perspectives of antenarrative analysis, the deconstruction and the construction, the 'being before' and the 'bet', as Boje did with Disney (Boje 1995).

The context

We were intrigued by the dominant narrative about non-hierarchical organizations. Mainstream narratives tend to romanticize the elimination of chiefs and formal positions, condemning models based on hierarchical control (Getz 2009; Hamel 2011; Raelin 2011). According to official narratives spread by pop management and media, non-hierarchical organizations are a solution to the tyrannical and inefficient model of centralized management. In a self-managed organization, as there are no bosses, each employee would define how to contribute to goals and they would spontaneously feel motivated to assume responsibilities. Each employee would be made accountable for results, thanks to a democratic and transparent information system and peer control. Changes in interests and roles would happen by agreement between all. The model of self-managing organizations would also be more efficient, as it would let information flow faster—which would be a quality extremely useful in today's turbulent and unstable environments—as there would be no need to continuously restructure organizational charts.

Academic literature on non-hierarchical organizations developed from the 1960s to 1980s, when radical self-management organizational models were in fashion. During those decades, non-hierarchical organizations transcended the boundaries of unions and social movements and were embraced by privately owned companies, such as W. L. Gore and Morning Star, before spreading internationally (e.g. Brazilian Semco). The experimental models of flat hierarchies that have flourished since then abolishing charts, formal positions, and chiefs were mainly marginalized and in some cases abandoned—one known example is Oticon and its spaghetti organization—but have seen a resurgence recently with technology entrepreneurships desirous of keeping their agile and informal startup roots.

There has been critical research about non-hierarchical organizations (Freeman 1972; Pfeffer 2013; Foss and Dobrajska 2015), but we detected a lack of research based on testimonials from employees, as those authors discussed relevant questions of structure, power, incentives, and results but did not base their research on interviews with different members of flat organizations. We were trying to understand how employees make sense of a model of organization built on idealized assumptions of the self-managed organization. To accomplish our objectives, we set out to deconstruct established narratives of organizations and look at what they are made of (before) and try to foresee what employees were building in stories they left on the internet (bet).

Collecting data

Getting critical testimonials from employees is not easy. Even if employers agree on employees answering researchers' interviews and/or questionnaires, these individuals might feel too insecure to share their thoughts about the organization and have doubts about the confidentiality of their opinions (Das Swain et al. 2020). In the scope of such a study, blogs, social media, and other internet sources provide opportunities for overcoming this barrier and collecting valuable data. To capture these 'little people stories', we decided that a suitable source would be a review platform. Online review platforms have multiplied recently—mainly for consumers—and, among them, there are those sites where employees and ex-employees give their testimonials about companies where they work or worked. Glassdoor is the main global online review platform on work issues. It claims to have 50 million monthly visitors (Glassdoor 2020). Reviewers provide a rating from 1 to 5 for the employer and have the option to award stars according to five facets: culture and values, work/life balance, senior management, compensation and benefits, and career opportunities. After the rating, reviewers give comments about the employer, in three sections: pros, cons, and advice to management. Finally, he/she decides to recommend or not recommend the organization to job seekers and may choose if he/she approves or disapproves of the CEO. The typical pattern of antenarratives of Glassdoor is spiral. Antenarratives start small and gain amplitude with certain issues driving them, as employees' and former employees' testimonials have to fit these predetermined topics.

When searching reviews, researchers need to be cautious. The first care is to check the politics, norms, and the operational logic and system of the platform. In the case of Glassdoor, the company publicizes that there is a verification system to assure that users work or worked for a certain firm. There are standards to prohibit companies from incentivizing or coercing employees to write positive reviews, and users can only post once a year. Glassdoor also claims that the system detects content that violates standards and users can easily flag questionable content. After content is flagged, it is checked by moderators, and, according to the platform, this process results in a 10 per cent rejection of flagged reviews. However, it is important to stress that Glassdoor states on its site that the number of users and posts exceeds the capacity to proceed with a complete check.

As Glassdoor was founded in 2007, research based on data from the platform is relatively recent. Landers et al. (2019) were pioneers in examining the validity of Glassdoor ratings. They compared overall and facet ratings from Glassdoor with US federal surveys and found validity for the overall satisfaction rating, but not for the five different facets. They suggest that Glassdoor information can be used, but cautiously and combined with other sources. There are several quantitative studies comparing job satisfaction indicators from Glassdoor with financial results (Huang et al. 2015; Luo et al. 2016; Ji et al. 2017; Moniz 2017; Das Swain et al. 2020), reaching the conclusion that there is a correlation between those indicators and the performance of firms. Several rankings were created in recent years in partnership with Glassdoor, such as the MIT SMR/Glassdoor Culture, published by MIT Sloan Management Review, that gives insights about organizational culture using reviews published on Glassdoor.

Research on consumer reviews shows that, usually, individuals who write online reviews have extreme opinions, whether these be on the positive or negative side (Hu et al. 2009), as they only write when they are emotionally involved. Glassdoor claims that it minimizes this underreporting bias by requiring users to submit a review after they view three pieces of content on the site. This mechanism guarantees that practically every user writes a review. In research by Schoenmüller et al. (2019) evaluating 25 review platforms, 21 were more polarized than Glassdoor.

Considering the research about and on Glassdoor, we found that the platform could be used for our purposes, since the platform had mechanisms to avoid bias and we could take additional steps to guarantee that our data and analysis would be consistent. How could it be done? Glassdoor indicates if the review is from a former employee or current employee and whether from a part-time or full-time employee. According to Moniz (2017), former employees are more willing to write negative comments about their ex-employers and part-time employees feel more detached from their companies compared to their full-time counterparts, which influences the evaluation of organizations. To deal with this bias, we decided to consider only full-time employees and we also separated reviews into two groups: employees and former employees. We decided to include ex-employees because we wanted to take into consideration workers who had a full experience but might be more critical about the model, but doing this separately allowed us to detect differences and analyse whether they compromised the analysis.

There is a wider concern about using social media data for academic purposes, both in quantitative and qualitative studies. In research with users, Williams et al. (2017) found that they did not feel comfortable about the use of their posts for academic studies without their authorization or without anonymization of information. The last guideline published by the Association of Internet Researchers (AoIR) (Franzke et al. 2020) draws attention to aspects such as obtaining informed consent and pseudonymizing and anonymizing data. However, in the case of Glassdoor, open content is already anonymized. It is not possible to track authors of the quotes, a caution taken by the platform itself. We decided not to cite organizations reviewed, even though information on Glassdoor is public and available for organizations, employees, former employees, job searchers, and any other stakeholder.

We investigated four organizations from different countries and sectors. Three of these organizations are digital, in the retail, games, and human resources services—all of them founded at the end of 1990s. The fourth is an industrial organization that produces technological inputs for different industries, founded in the 1950s. We decided to have multiple cases in order to investigate if there were similarities between flat organizations independent of size, sector, or country.

We extracted all reviews from the four organizations chosen from January 2015 to May 2016. We searched these organizations and used the filter of full-time employees to get our data. Then we transferred all reviews in the time period chosen using basic commands of copy and paste.

We began reading 'little people stories' of employees, looking for themes, different perspectives that represented those themes and language used, according to critical discourse analysis (Fairclough 2003). We proceeded with an abductive approach when looking for themes, which means we moved from theory to empirical material and from empirical material back to theory and so on. In two of the four organizations, themes and perspectives were repeating before we reached the end of comments, which assured us that we had reached a point of saturation. Repetition of themes and narrative perspectives gave strength to our research. If more and more reviewers were mentioning the same issues, it seemed reasonable to infer that those questions were important.

We collected testimonials from 88 employees and 59 former employees for organization 1, and 69 from employees and 47 from former employees for organization 3. In the case of organizations 3 and 4, as they are small businesses, we had to extend the period analysed for all posts until May 2016. Even with this extension, it was only possible to collect 9 reviews for organization 3 (7 from employees and 2 from former employees) and 19 for organization 4 (8 from employees and 11 from former employees). There was a repetition of themes and perspectives in organizations 3 and 4 if we considered each organization and compared them with the two bigger ones. For that reason, we decided to keep them, but we stress that if we had extended the scope to more evaluations new aspects might have emerged.

It is important to mention that, considering the size of our sample, we were able to proceed with a manual qualitative analysis, but when we deal with internet posts, that is not always possible. According to Latzko-Toth et al. (2017), the rise of Big Data gave too much emphasis to quantitative approaches, leaving concerns about how deep they can go. On the other hand, how do we deal with large amounts of data in qualitative studies? Our approach was to limit the scope of data collection in order to retain the depth of manual qualitative analysis.

Another point we want to stress is that, even though individuals must give their personal information to Glassdoor, their reviews are anonymous. This characteristic comes with an opportunity for researchers— as it is possible to explore impressions about very sensitive issues—and also with a challenge—as reviewers take lower risks of being punished or criticized in comparison to non-anonymous testimonials. For this reason, we were very cautious in our analysis, looking for perspectives that were representative of themes and not for outliers—for instance, a specific problem with one chief, department, or location that was not pointing to more general issues.

Simultaneously, we collected documents that presented the 'grand narratives', as we wanted to contrast the official narratives with antenarratives that arose from Glassdoor. Our search started on organizational websites and on the internet for mission statements, reports, handbooks, messages for employees (disclosed to the public), and case studies submitted for prizes. We also interviewed a representative from each organization as part of the research. We read official documents and transcripts of interviews looking for themes in the same way we did with employees' comments, going back and forth to theory and also back and forth between employee data and employer data. The analytical difference was that, in the case of employees, we were departing from stories to sew together possible antenarratives (microstoria methodology), and in the case of employers, we were departing from narratives and deconstructing them in order to understand their composition and contrast them with the perspectives from employees (deconstruction methodology). In the following section we are going to explain this process of analysis.

Antenarrative analysis

As mentioned, we proceeded with an abductive approach, going forth and back to the literature with a thematic perspective (theme analysis). The research literature mentioned questions of power disputes, leadership, employee's performance evaluation, accountability, and efficiency, issues that were also themes within reviews and company documents and interviews. Proceeding with a preliminary analysis, we went back to the data and found additional themes that appeared in both official narratives and 'little people stories'.

One such theme was related to *motivation and shared values*. When we searched within this theme, we reviewed fragments of narratives relating to it and found there was a common perspective, built upon the idea of self-motivation, autonomy, and a 'common project' that would arise naturally from the model. One review mentioned an 'innate drive of each person to reach his or her full potential' and a culture that 'welcomes different viewpoints', while another said 'there is little need to invest in motivating employees that are empowered'.

Reviews extracted from Glassdoor offered different perspectives on this issue of *motivation and shared values* and, as soon as we found the theme important, we went back to our dataset to identify relevant reviews. We then looked for repetitions balancing richness of narratives and consistency of data. We found three different perspectives for this theme. We outline them below, in order to illustrate how we proceeded with a thematic analysis:

- A first perspective was aligned to the official narrative, even repeating official language. For instance, when reviewers write 'a management model that allows value sharing between people' and 'we are a community that engages', they almost repeat the official statement that employees 'practice shared values and are engaged in meaningful common project'.
- The second perspective considered that it was hard to have an 'innate drive' of self-motivation, so problems would arise, but organizations could not be fully blamed. As one reviewer said, 'it can be difficult to motivate people who are unwilling to motivate themselves', while another stated that the model 'assumes that these people (so unique and full of singularities) will be able to serve common interests that they barely know and understand'.
- The third perspective was opposed to the official narrative in a more radical way. For instance, a reviewer said that it was easy to get along 'as long as your ideas don't challenge the status quo', while other wrote that they 'use their unique culture as a weapon', and a third mentioned 'dogmatic thinking'.

The three perspectives that we identified in relation to the theme *motivation and shared values* were repeated in other themes, but new perspectives also appeared. To illustrate this, when we analysed questions of power, within the theme denominated as *internal struggles*:

- The first perspective repeated the official narrative that there was no space for struggles as everyone was in the same plane,
- The second perspective pointed out problems that were out of the control of organizations such as that people 'have an ego' and 'make mistakes'.
- The third perspective accused the model of 'harassment and bullying'.

In addition to these three perspectives, a fourth perspective challenged the official point of view arguing that there was nothing substantially different in the organization compared to hierarchical organizations—'only other companies lack the hypocrisy I've seen here', as one employee said.

Having found this new perspective, we went back to other themes to see if the same fourth perspective was present. In the case of the theme *leadership*, we found this repetition, for instance, employees mentioning that in the end the owner decided. A reviewer said: 'I do not believe the owner will leave the core in the hands of 160 employees, it is obvious. But taking decisions behind closed doors and saying they were made in consensus is a large baloney'. By going forth and back to the themes, we continued adding perspectives.

We also analysed aspects of language. The grand narrative was full of metaphors, such as 'sharing the steering wheel' and we found that reviews, especially those that matched the third perspective, also used metaphors, such as that culture was a 'weapon', 'a cult', a 'party line', or 'high school'. While supporters sometimes used the first person ('I'm proud to be a part of this FAMILY'), neutral or opposed comments sometimes used the third person ('they promote "honest and open communication" yet people get fired after you hear them voicing concerns ...'). This analysis helped us to find links between 'little people stories' and to compare them with official grand narratives. We started to understand that some employees felt they fitted or were longing to fit the grand narrative, while others did not feel part of it, and when using the third person ('they'), different antenarratives were being connected by sentiments of anguish, frustration, cynicism, and/or revolt.

Intertextuality was also present, with reviewers dialoging with organizational narratives (intertextuality methodology). Supporters repeated official narratives most of the time and even used the same tone. For instance, a technology organization states in its manual for new employees how to prepare for trips that the company regularly organizes for its employees 'Step 1. Find someone to watch your cats; Step 2. Board our chartered flight; Step 3. Relax by the pool. Step 4. Relax by the pool some more.' A reviewer that recommends the organization uses the space for cons to mention 'Company doesn't yet have an office in Hawaii' and the space of 'advice to the management' to write 'N/a. Maybe I should use this space to advise myself ... Uh, use breath mints more often. Remember to smile' (the manual also mentions bowls of fresh fruits, massage rooms, and other 'things around the office'). Critical reviews also dialogued with grand narratives. For instance, a reviewer said 'You are un-WOWing your internal customers', as a reference for the culture of 'WOW' to external customers.

We were eventually able to identify five antenarratives (theme analysis) about non-hierarchical organizations that we contrasted with the official narrative. We reconstructed the official narrative joining themes from the four organizations and we presented it as the 'good flat organization', based on an idealized vision of a non-hierarchical model. According to the narrative, a non-hierarchical organization would be naturally collaborative and harmonic; employees would be 'empowered', 'engaged', 'responsible', they would share the same values, and they would not fight because they would 'transcend power'. The narrative assumes that when the organization turns at least formally non-hierarchical, questions that were in the shadow will come to light automatically solving dilemmas of power, leadership, and efficiency, for instance.

As the master narrative gives no space for nuance, employees have to deal with the ideal image and they do it in different ways. With microstoria analysis, we were able to interpret those, arriving at the five antenarratives we present next to illustrate the results of our thematic analysis. We called the first antenarrative 'We are in the boat', using our language analysis, as reviews from supporters who feel or try to convince themselves and others that they are part ('we') of the narrative. The second narrative, 'the fault is human nature', dialogues with the grand narrative, but considers that letting human beings manage themselves will not naturally solve organizational problems, but on the contrary result in some problems. It is a Hobbesian antenarrative, which does not blame organizations but instead human nature. The third antenarrative, 'there are problems with this model' also dialogues with the

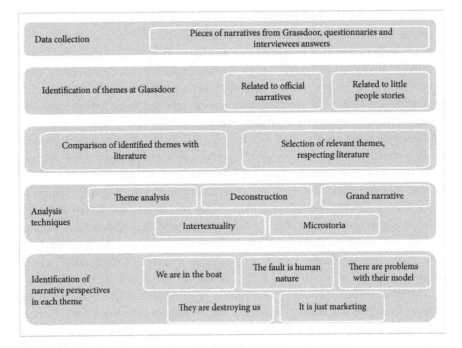

Fig. 15.1 Methodological approach of the research
Source: The authors (2020).

grand narrative, but in a different way. It is not a question of human nature, but of the design of the model. The fourth antenarrative, 'They are destroying us', detaches ('they') from organizational models with anger and frustration in order to deal with a model designed to be perfect and not questioned. And the fifth antenarrative, 'it is just marketing' develops the idea that non-hierarchical models in essence do not differ from hierarchical organizations. Figure 15.1 illustrates our methodological approach. The general methodological approach was planned, but not all analytic techniques were predicted. We found intertextuality important while looking at our dataset and realizing how quotes interacted with one another and with official documents.

Additional challenges

Some characteristics of researching sensitive narratives online are worthy of further comment. Unlike coffee corners, blogs, social media, and internet platforms are not private spaces and what is posted online can be accessed anytime by anyone. In our initial research (Wilner et al. 2017b), we found that physical spaces like coffee corners are somehow safe for employees but cannot be managed by organizations, allowing employees to have a terrain to vent in order to cope with the 'emotional labor'

(Hochschild 2012) of their functions. In other words, organizations provide a space for employees to freely express their emotions in order to guarantee self-control in the frontstage at work. In contrast, online unmanaged organizations have no clear boundaries and cannot be managed either by employees or by organizations.

The reach of posts can go beyond that which employees imagined, but the increase in the amplitude of those symbolic narratives can give a larger space for employees to manifest and interact about their feelings. At same time, even though organizations have no control over what their members post, they can supervise and punish them not only for work-related content but also for general behaviour (for instance, posts that manifest any kind of prejudice in any context). The surveillance does not have the same effect when manifestations are anonymous. Even though organizations may try to identify who is behind a message posted on Glassdoor, in most cases they are not able to do so. As we explained above regarding the methodology we used, analysing anonymous posts needs caution. It is important to separate perspectives that repeat themselves from unique perspectives, analysing if the latter make sense in the context of the whole analysis.

Another characteristic of online narratives is that users on the internet compete for other users' attention. It is important to evaluate the specific media used in the research in order to understand the impact, following the McLuhan aphorism that 'the media is the message' (Fiore and McLuhan 1967). We carried out background research about the Glassdoor platform, the validity of reviews and the function in order to proceed with the research. In the case of our research, we did not find evidence that users would write dramatic content just to draw the attention of readers, but this aspect needs to be considered when researching online narratives.

One other aspect is intertextuality. We mentioned that we looked for intertextual connection between the grand narrative and the 'little people stories', but there was also intertextuality between different reviewers ('I agree with other reviewer …'). Unlike coffee corners, the online unmanaged organization has no physical boundaries. Anyone can come in and leave, and in the case of Glassdoor this means that any individual who works or worked for the organization can write a review after reading reviews of other people with whom he/she would never drink a coffee. And unlike coffee corners, what is said in a moment becomes persistent—as if all that is said unsupervised would accumulate in a file. This intertextuality changes the message. Reviewers might make sense of what was written before to write their review, building the antenarrative together in a different way than they would do if they only had the physical world in which to vent. As antenarratives get support and cohesion, they might turn into counternarratives or even grand narratives.

Characteristics of internet narratives were analysed by different methodological options. Deconstruction, microstoria, intertextuality, and theme analysis were applied as ways to identify different narrative perspectives, giving emphasis to different points of view. We looked for a diversity of stories, looking for individual perspectives, but as this is an interpretative approach, we could not say that it is possible to eliminate our own perspectives. It is possible to say that the methodology implicates us not only in identifying antenarratives but, in the bricolage of 'little people stories', in building antenarratives.

We consider that our methodology is not generalizable, which would be a grand narrative itself. Analysis performed according to the principles we proposed should consider different contexts and their particularities. As we assumed, the research is socially constructed, thereby implying that the social context of analysis is always the primary target. Bateman (2019) recommends that one way to address this issue is to start the analysis from communities of practice involved in producing such an idea or object of analysis. This will contribute to identifying contextual, relevant choices to be considered. Besides, contextual viewing conditions should also be an object of analysis, as the researcher is part of the narrative building process.

References

Bateman, J. A. 2019. Towards critical multimodal discourse analysis: a response to Ledin and Machin. *Critical Discourse Studies*, 16(5): pp. 531–39.

Boje, D. M. 1995. Stories of the storytelling organization a postmodern analysis of Disney as Tamara-land'. *Academy of Management Journal*, 38(4):pp. 997–1035. Available at: https://pdfs.semanticscholar.org/5190/4d70a2063cf47af6a7d35d7c3c4fe7138b57.pdf.

Boje, D. M. 2001. *Narrative Methods for Organizational & Communication Research*. Sage.

Boje, D. M. 2011. *Storytelling and the Future of Organizations: An Antenarrative Handbook*. New York, USA: Routledge.

Boje, D. M. 2014. *Storytelling Organizational Practices: Managing in the Quantum Age*. Routledge.

Boje, D. M., Haley, U. C. V., and Saylors, R. 2016. Antenarratives of organizational change: The microstoria of Burger King's storytelling in space, time and strategic context. *Human Relations*, 69(2): pp. 391–418.

Das Swain, V., Saha, K., Reddy, M. D., Rajvanshy, H., Abowd, G. D., and Choudhury, M. 2020. Modeling organizational culture with workplace experiences shared on glassdoor. In *Proceedings of the 2020 CHI Conference on Human Factors in Computing Systems*, Association for Comp uting Machinery, New York, NY, United States, (pp. 1–15).

Fairclough, N. 2003. *Analysing Discourse: Textual Analysis for Social Research*. Psychology Press.

Fiore, Q. and McLuhan, M. 1967. *The Medium is the Message*. New York: Random House.

Foss, N. J. and Dobrajska, M. 2015. Valve's way: Wayward, visionary, or voguish? *Journal of Organization Design*, 4(2): pp. 12–15.

Franzke, A. S., Benchmann, A., Zimmer, M., Ess, C. and the Association of Internet Researchers. 2020. *Internet Research: Ethical Guidelines 3.0*. Available at: https://aoir.org/reports/ethics3.pdf.

Freeman, J. 1972. The tyranny of structurelessness. *Berkeley Journal of Sociology*, 17: pp. 151–64.

Gabriel, Y. 1995. The unmanaged organization: Stories, fantasies and subjectivity. *Organization Studies*, 16(3): pp. 477–501.

Getz, I. 2009. Liberating leadership: how the initiative-freeing radical organizational form has been successfully adopted. *California Management Review*, 51(4): pp. 32–58.

Ginzburg, C. 1991. Chaves do Mistério: Morelli, Freud e Sherlock Holmes. in Eco, H. and Sebeok, T. (eds), *O Signo de Três* (pp. 89–129). São Paulo, Brazil: Perspectiva.

Glassdoor. 2020. About us. Available at: https://www.glassdoor.com/about-us/ (accessed 25 November 2020).

Hamel, G. 2011. First, let's fire all the managers. *Harvard Business Review*, 89(12): pp. 48–60.

Hochschild, A. R. 2012. *The Managed Heart: Commercialization of Human Feeling*. 3rd edn. University of California Press.

Hu, N., Zhang, J., and Pavlou, P. A. 2009. Overcoming the J-shaped distribution of product reviews. *Communications of the ACM*, 52(10): pp. 144–7.

Huang, M., Li, P., Meschke, F., and Guthrie, J.P. 2015. Family firms, employee satisfaction, and corporate performance. *Journal of Corporate Finance*, 34: pp. 108–27.

Ji, Y., Rozenbaum, O., and Welch, K. 2017. Corporate culture and financial reporting risk: Looking through the glassdoor. *SSRN*. Available at: http://dx.doi.org/10.2139/ssrn.2945745.

Landers, R. N., Brusso, R. C., and Auer, E. M. 2019. Crowdsourcing job satisfaction data: Examining the construct validity of Glassdoor.com ratings. *Personnel Assessment and Decisions*, 5(3): p. 6.

Latzko-Toth, G., Bonneau, C., and Millette, M. 2017. Small data, thick data: Thickening strategies for trace-based social media research. in *The SAGE Handbook of Social Media Research Methods* (pp. 199–214). Los Angeles, CA: Sage.

Luo, N., Zhou, Y., and Shon, J. 2016. Employee satisfaction and corporate performance: Mining employee reviews on glassdoor.com. in *Proceeding of International Conference on Information Systems* (ICIS).

Moniz, A. 2017. Inferring employees' social media perceptions of corporate culture and the link to firm value. *SSRN*. Available at: http://dx.doi.org/10.2139/ssrn.2768091.

Murray, J. H. 2017. *Hamlet on the Holodeck: The Future of Narrative in Cyberspace*. MIT Press.

Pfeffer, J. 2013. You're still the same: Why theories of power hold over time and across contexts. *Academy of Management Perspectives*, 27(4): pp. 269–80.

Raelin, J. A. 2011. The end of managerial control?. *Group & Organization Management*, 36(2): pp. 135–60.

Schoenmüller, V., Netzer, O., and Stahl, F. 2019. The extreme distribution of online reviews: Prevalence, drivers and implications. *Columbia Business School Research Paper*, (18–10). Available at: http://dx.doi.org/10.2139/ssrn.3100217.

Williams, M. L., Burnap, P., Sloan, L., Jessop, C., and Lepps, H. 2017. Users' views of ethics in social media research: Informed consent, anonymity, and harm. in *The Ethics of Online Research* (pp. 27–52). Emerald Publishing Limited.

Wilner, A., Christopoulos, T. P., and Alves, M. A. 2016. Leadership in organizations without chiefs: idealization and frustrations. *32nd European Group for Organization Studies*. Naples, 22 June.

Wilner, A., Christopoulos, T. P., and Alves, M. A. 2017a. Organizations without Chiefs: narratives and counter-narratives of totemic leadership. *33rd European Group for Organization Studies*. Copenhagen, 6 July.

Wilner, A., Christopoulos, T. P., and Alves, M. A. 2017b. The online unmanaged organization: control and resistance in a space with blurred boundaries. *Journal of Business Ethics*, 141(4): pp. 677–91.

16

Tinkering with Method as We Go

An Account of Capturing Digital Traces of Work on Social Media

Viviane Sergi and Claudine Bonneau

Preamble

Consider Table 16.1, summarizing the repertoire of working out loud (WOL) practices, based on a fuller version presented in our own research.

In this table, we see neatly delineated categories (bold and numbered) described in an explicit way and pertaining to the phenomenon labelled 'WOL'. To generate such a table, one can suppose that a phenomenon was vaguely known and recognized as understudied, that data were collected and analysed following the appropriate guidelines, and that results were reduced and condensed into these categories, illustrating and elucidating, albeit partially, what the phenomenon is. Reading this table, we come to understand that the categories it presents document and describe the variety of forms that this phenomenon of 'WOL' can take. The table is clear and ordered. If the categories had been messy, fuzzy, and equivocal, it would be normal to think that something had gone wrong with the method, the development of the table, or the writing or editing of the text in which it appears (or any combination of the four).

Yet this table only reveals part of the story: an important part, of course, but certainly not the whole story. It does not show the work of generating the material that will be considered as 'data', nor does it display the sensemaking work needed to see and make categories from data. It retains no trace of all the attempts that preceded it. It is a fixed image, a destination reached. The process of producing the data is made absent as such tables, which are fixed representations, are developed. Many things get lost due to such absences: the doubts, the lingering questions, the failed attempts, the epiphanies, or the dissatisfactions (you should hide all of these). This might be said of any table, figure, or visualization, and most certainly of our table. This is part of the invisible expectations that come with methods and data presentation, that most of us have internalized. But what is further invisibilized by these generally undiscussed

Viviane Sergi and Claudine Bonneau, *Tinkering with Method as We Go*. In: *Research Methods for Digital Work and Organization*. Edited by Gillian Symon, Katrina Pritchard, and Christine Hine, Oxford University Press.
© Oxford University Press (2021). DOI: 10.1093/oso/9780198860679.003.0016

Table 16.1 Reworked based on Sergi and Bonneau (2016, 388)

Form of WOL	Action of tweets
1. Exposing	
1.1 Work in development	**Producing traces of work processes**
1.2 Difficulty	
1.3 Interaction	
2. Contextualizing	
2.1 Environment and resources	**Creating and maintaining an ambient awareness**
2.2 Day-to-day tasks	
2.3 Expertise	
3. Documenting	
3.1 Progression	**Planning the course of action**
3.2 Method	
3.3 Goal	
4. Teaching	
4.1 Ways of doing things	**Transforming the experience into reusable knowledge**
4.2 Lessons learned	
4.3 Best practices	
5. Expressing	
5.1 Feelings	**Creating a cathartic space**
5.2 Mockery	
5.3 Complaints	
6. Thinking in a reflective manner	
6.1 Consideration	**Making judgements about what has happened**
6.2 Dilemmas	
6.3 Assessment	

expectations are the questions about methods: of *actually* performing the method, doing the study, and documenting its findings.

This is the primary aim of our chapter: to present, as it emerged, the method that we developed to document what we have called 'working out loud' (WOL) on social media. But a second objective is to reflect on our method, because it had to be (at least partially) invented as the research itself progressed. As John Law (2004, 144) puts it, 'method is always much more than its formal accounts suggest'. But what is left outside such formal accounts of method? Inspired by STS (science and technology studies), one could say that method is always a question of practice, hence always implying a dose of adjustment, bricolage, and innovation, and we agree with this view. Nonetheless, we faced a number of challenges with this study, and the method we present here required more tinkering than we expected. This tinkering shared similarities with the object of our inquiry: it was nothing radical or magistral, but rather mundane. It nonetheless affected how we proceeded, as we had to adjust and adapt our approach, and had to reflect on just how our method could be stretched. This led us to reflect on the fact that maybe the problem resides in the assumption that tinkering with method is an issue. Beyond the specificities of researching work practices in a qualitative fashion on social media, our chapter can be read as an invitation to think about the 'mess' that accompanies methods in action, and the requisite imagination that might be needed to face it. Inspired by Law (2004), our chapter will hence explore both sides of the method we developed for our study: its structure and its lack of structure.

But First, the Object of Inquiry and its Emergence

Before reaching the heart of the matter, let us begin by situating the inquiry we pursued and its main object. For a few years now we have been exploring how people use, in a fully voluntary way, social media (mainly Twitter and Instagram) in the course of their mundane work activities. We have named this practice 'working out loud' on social media, which we define as a 'communicative and sociomaterial practice where individuals voluntarily turn to public social media platforms to share what is part of their daily work' (Bonneau et al., 2021, 51). Our inquiry focused on ordinary uses of social media, in relation to work activities and situations.

From the onset of our study, we wanted to distinguish our object (e.g. informal uses of social media) from mandatory uses (e.g. corporate uses prescribed by an organization), professional practices (e.g. marketing content production or community management), and other promotional uses (e.g. branding or self-branding), which abound on social media. We were also less interested in the purely technological aspect of social media uses. When we began our study, the idea of 'bring your own device' (BYOD, see Cisco 2012) was becoming more widely discussed, as organizations were recognizing that their employees came to work with their own mobile phones and were using them, either for their work or in spite of policies limiting or prohibiting access to public social media such as Facebook. Social media such as Twitter, and later Instagram, were already integrated into the life of a large number of working individuals, so we came to suspect that these might be the site of mundane narrations of work. Consequently, this is what we place at the heart of our exploration: what people share, about their work and in the course of their work, on social media. The work in question does not necessarily imply an obligation to use social media. We were rather interested in the ordinary use of these digital media by workers of all kinds to communicate something about their mundane experience of being at work. Inspired by various strands of literature that have already documented the richness of mundane work activities (such as workplace studies and studies on computer-supported collaborative work, see for example Sachs 1995; Star and Strauss 1999; Heath et al. 2000), we aimed to understand not simply what people did *with* social media, but *on* social media. This sensitivity for the mundane experience of work came with a strong belief that what features in ordinary life is not banal and thin, but rather undervalued (Brekhus 2000) and at the very root of practices, which makes it worthy of exploration.

This exploration relies on the collection of user-generated digital traces available on social media platforms. Like Bowker (2007), we consider the content generated by social media users as traces of their online activities (rather than limiting our definition of 'traces' only to the metadata these activities generate). The content production (writing a tweet on Twitter, posting a picture on Instagram) is the activity, and the content itself is a trace of this activity, along with related metadata (e.g. author, timestamp, geo-location, etc.). In our case, we focus on the content generated by WOL on social media, and consider it not only as traces of online activities, but also as traces of the work activities they describe. On social media, these traces are typically multimodal. First, they can include textual elements such as captions, comments, and hashtags. Second, they also include graphical elements that are produced through different visual communication modes mobilized by social media users who publish not only photos, but drawings, collages, GIF animations, emojis, memes, artistic creations, inspiring quotes, and poems presented as images. Finally, these traces can include audio and video material.

We would have liked to include actual examples of posts that we collected from Instagram that belong to WOL to illustrate some of its dimensions, but this was not possible for copyright reasons. But to give the flavour of these posts, we here briefly describe three of them. A first example is an Instagram post of a lab researcher performing tissue culture in a laboratory, sharing her reflections on an aspect of her work in the lab (illustrating the dimension *Thinking in a reflective manner—Dilemma*). In the caption that accompanied the photo, this person wondered if there might be a better way to ensure a sterile environment while generating less waste. A second example is that of a musician showing a picture of his workspace. He explains in the caption why his workplace changes frequently during the course of his work activities (illustrating the dimension *Contextualizing—Environment and resources*). Finally, as a third example of WOL, we collected the post of an artist showing her progress on a new piece by sharing a picture of an unfinished painting and describing it as a work in progress in the caption (illustrating the dimension *Exposing—Work in development*).

We did not begin our research with the definition of WOL presented above, nor with a precise idea of what would be shared on social media. Successive rounds of data collection and analysis led us to progressively document the richness we suspected from the start of our study. While we had a hunch that people at work might be using public social media to narrate their work experience, this idea first had to be sustained and then further specified. Our exploration of WOL was fuelled by the relative absence of research attention (at the time, 2012 and 2013) given to informal uses of social media in the context of work, and by our own use of social media. Furthermore, our familiarity with workplace studies, CSCW studies, and practice studies in general (Nicolini 2013) shaped our thinking. Of the two of us, Claudine first forayed into empirical material to bring this impression to light, which led her to identify something that she labelled 'working out loud' on social media (Bonneau 2013). After recognizing that what she observed was shaping up to be a distinct phenomenon,

Viviane joined her to continue defining its contours. But even if we had a label and a general sense of what WOL entailed, we felt that this mundane use of social media could still be documented more thoroughly.

Our joint exploration of WOL pursued a number of objectives. First, we wanted to interrogate what we know about formal uses of social media in work situations, given that the vast majority of studies of uses of social media had been conducted around enterprise social media (ESM) and/or specific issues, such as knowledge sharing or collaboration (Majchrzak et al. 2013; Leonardi and Meyer 2015; Leonardi and Vaast 2017). We aimed to go beyond issues and formal processes by asking ourselves one question: in addition to what has already been demonstrated, do people *also* use public social media, such as Twitter and Instagram, to talk about their work, whether or not these uses have any connections to their organization's recognized tools or mandatory practices (such as using Slack or Microsoft Teams)? This question already foreshadows the challenge of data collection we outline later in this chapter. It might be relatively easy to say that people are using social media to share thoughts and experiences about their work, but who is doing this? More precisely, what are they sharing? As we collected more data (see the section 'Data collection in the wild' for more details), we were able to identify a number of dimensions of WOL, showing that while people engage in it they perform a variety of *actions* (such as exposing, teaching, and reflecting) that showcase different *facets* of work (themselves as workers, work context, or work processes) and share details about their own *experience* of being at work (which include embodied and temporal aspects of work, and elements pertaining to the atmosphere in which they are working). These dimensions were not posited a priori, in a theoretical fashion, and they gradually accumulated as we cycled between data collection and analysis.

At the same time, pursuing this inquiry came with its own specific methodological challenges. Because we did not know all the facets of WOL when we began our study, we were not aware that we would have to invent the methodological approach needed to provide an answer to our initial question. If we began with the platforms themselves and not with individual workers, how could we find data that could help us in our documentation process? Here is the crux of the matter: we decided from the start that our inquiry would be qualitative and focused on the practice of WOL, and we would not begin by selecting individuals already known to be using social media in the mundane fashion that intrigued us. As is still the case today, many, if not most, studies of or on mainstream social media platforms such as Twitter rest on big data approaches, collecting and analysing very large datasets (Brownlie and Shaw 2019). Opting for a qualitative exploration of social media was a conscious choice, and a necessity. Assembling large datasets on Twitter, for example, is based on the a priori identification of either specific keywords or hashtags frequently used by those who publish content related to the research theme, then extracting the corresponding publications by adding other segmentation parameters if necessary, such as sociodemographic and temporal criteria. When we began data collection, we had none of these defined a priori keywords or hashtags, and this was not a problem:

not knowing the scope of the phenomenon, we did not want to limit ourselves right from the start with a few hashtags or keywords. This was also part of the excitement of data collection, that we would have to 'hand pick' our data and discover the variety of hashtags used by people (the excitement would wane a bit when we were faced with the questions such data collection entailed; see the next section). Furthermore, as researchers interested in the uses, practices, and experience of work, we were also slightly dissatisfied with these quantitative studies, which left out many aspects of work and working that we considered important to keep present and make visible. Indeed, the heterogeneity and variability of online practices, including non-standard, extreme, or fringe cases, are often ignored, diluted, or misinterpreted by automated quantitative analyses (Highfield and Leaver 2015). This was a second, and strong, objective that characterized our study of WOL: try to capture the variety and richness we suspected lay underneath this emergent label of 'working out loud'. Over time, this aim was reinforced by the publication of studies stressing that social media are effective channels for exposing affective, embodied, or aesthetic dimensions of various experiences, including work (e.g. Laestadius 2017).

Hence, while our initial impulse for conducting this research was to explore how workers use social media to narrate their work as it is happening, we did not begin our investigation with an idea about what, exactly, people may be sharing on social media. It is our empirical exploration and analysis, inspired by digital anthropology (Miller 2018) and digital ethnography (Hine 2015), that led us to uncover that what people were sharing really allows us to grasp the daily texture of work: here a worker reflecting on the task at hand, there an employee sharing his emotional state following an event at work, another one showing what goes on 'behind the scenes' of her work setting, for example. But how did we find this material, constitute our data, and analyse it? We will now present the approach that we had to devise to collect the digital traces necessary for studying WOL. This will then lead to a discussion about the bricolage and serendipity involved in this data collection.

Invisibilized Aspects of Research Work

The next two paragraphs, taken from another of our texts, summarizes the methodological approach we used to collect and analyse a corpus of Twitter messages. We decided to quote this description extensively, as it presents all the main steps we followed.

> *Our methods rest on a qualitative approach, inspired by digital ethnography (Hine, 2015) and is based on the manual collection of three small corpus of posts between 2014 and 2017: 200 Twitter posts from workers and professionals in several domains; 20 social media profiles of artists, mainly mobilizing entries on Instagram, but also posts on Twitter; and 150 Instagram posts from workers and professionals in several domains. Such*

a 'small/thick data' approach allowed us to capture the specificities of the phenomenon under study, since we explored the 'traces in their 'native' format, as they are envisioned by social media users (Latzko-Toth et al. 2017, 204).

On an operational level, we connected to Instagram and Twitter platforms with our own accounts and manually extracted data from the user interface. We began the data collection with the general aim of documenting the kind of work practices taking place on social media. We began this general data collection process by using the site search engine to find posts using work-related hashtags (e.g., #work, #working, #showyourwork, #shareyourwork) [this description of our approach simplifies how we proceeded; see details later in this chapter]. Using a snowball sampling approach on the posts we already collected, we were able to find new users through their comments and to find other hashtags describing work contexts (e.g., #workingforaliving, #behindthework). In order to collect posts in various professional areas, we also performed queries on Instagram's and Twitter's internal search engine after asking ourselves, 'Who would share his or her work and what would he or she say about it?' For example, we searched for domain-related hashtags such as 'nurse', 'firefighter', 'accountant', etc. All posts collected were captured using a screen capture tool and were documented in a log, along with their date of publication, URL, and details about how we found them and field notes. Qualitative textual analysis was used to proceed to a manual thematic coding of each post in an open and inductive manner (Miles, Huberman, & Saldana, 2013). We considered posts as 'holistic units, in which images/videos, text, emoji, and hashtags should be interpreted together' (Laestadius, 2017, 588). Therefore, our analysis considered the visual and textual elements of posts together, using the descriptions, hashtags and comments to contextualize the pictures. For example, the hashtag #deadline adds a temporal context that would not be considered if only images content were analyzed.

(Bonneau et al., 2021, 51-52)

While these quotes present all the formal steps, many details of what we experienced are missing. We omitted some details because, in most articles or book chapters, they are not necessarily needed, having to do with minor technicalities of conducting a study. Other aspects have also been left out of this description, including those pertaining to the actual experience of following what appears above as a clear protocol—questions that arose, emotions that we felt, or trials and tribulations. Both dimensions—the small tricks we devised and our personal experimentation—are usually kept hidden when it comes to presenting the methods chosen and followed for a study. This has to do with the *style* of methods: it is expected that methods be clear (so they can be easily understood and evaluated), structured (so their logic and rigour can be appreciated), and precise (so they can be reproduced). Would a murky, fuzzy, and imprecise method still be considered an appropriate method for scientific research? The natural (naturalized) answer is no. These characteristics also apply to the written presentation of methods, where the writing is instrumental in producing these qualities for the reader who has not been part of the study. Yet, the written quality of a methods section is rarely considered because it is supposed to be 'simply' retelling what was done, and how. Seen from a different epistemological point of view, however, the neutral and detached tone that we most frequently find in methods sections can be viewed as performative: it contributes to giving an impression of neatness and rigour. But saying that this way of presenting methods sections is performative does not make it any less real, as Law and Urry (2004) remind us. Rather, this idea highlights that the way methods are presented and represented plays an active part in shaping what we think of, and expect from, methods. It also can invisibilize part of the work of doing research, which echoes the concept of invisible work.

Generally speaking, invisible work is by definition work that is not perceived and not recognized. As Nardi and Engeström explain, invisible work covers:

> (1) work done in invisible places, such as the highly skilled behind-the-scenes work of reference librarians, (2) work defined as routine or manual that actually requires considerable problem solving and knowledge, such as the work of telephone operators, (3) work done by invisible people such as domestics, and (4) informal work processes that are not part of anybody's job description but which are crucial for the collective functioning of the workplace, such as regular but open-ended meetings without a specific agenda, informal conversations, gossip, humor, storytelling.
>
> **(Nardi and Engeström 1999, 1).**

Yet, as they also discuss, the invisibility of these forms of work (a list that could be expanded) does not mean that this work is inconsequential, marginal, or unimportant. In fact, the 'drama' of invisible work lies in its mundane, tacit, and sometimes highly personalized character, sometimes even in its dirty nature,[1] making it difficult to formally recognize. This tension between visible and invisible aspects of work points towards a larger issue, that of the gap and tensions between the formal and the informal realms in organizations—in other words, between prescriptions and practices. Understanding both realms and, more importantly, their interrelations in various settings appears to be a key research programme that is still brimming with possibilities, especially in today's context where work and organizations are both undergoing a series of significant changes, many of them technological in nature. We also consider that cultivating an attention to invisible work should not be limited to the objects of our studies but should also be encouraged in our own work and practice. This goes for tasks that tend to disappear from presentations of completed research projects, but also applies to aspects that have been relegated to the sidelines of doing 'correct' research, such as affect. As Gherardi et al. remind us, 'Affect is relevant for organization studies mainly for its potential to reveal the intensities and forces of everyday organizational experiences that may pass unnoticed or pass in silence because they have been discarded from the orthodoxy of doing research "as usual" ' (Gherardi et al. 2019, 309).

If this implies making these aspects of organizational and work experiences visible in research, we consider that it also applies to our own work as researchers. We thus attempt, in these pages, to shed light on aspects of research work that may be discussed more informally (after a presentation, for example), but are most often kept out of our texts.

Data Collection in the Wild

Given that we started with the idea that WOL is done in a non-prescribed, informal, and personal way—a wide variety of persons can use their social media platform of choice to share observations, snapshots, or micro-experiences of themselves at work—we quickly realized that the phenomenon we saw appearing in the material we were collecting knew no boundaries. 'Narrating' one's experience of work might sound like a specific activity, but we were confronted with the challenge of actually finding these snippets of experience. Unless specific users have already been identified and selected, as the first step of the research (which was not our case), finding the material on Twitter or Instagram implies performing searches or queries through their respective search engines—and it was there that the challenge made itself the most visible: what keywords should we be entering to 'get' our data?

Indeed, 'working out loud' is the name we gave to all the tweets we found and kept as 'data' after we started to analyse the material collected. Our compass during rounds of data collection was our definition. It was not possible for us to know in advance the keywords that users would be using when narrating their work on social media, for three main reasons, as discussed below.

WOL is not a label that workers are familiar with, although they might be performing it, hence they do not spontaneously use an explicit hashtag like #workingoutloud or #WOL. Nonetheless, this did not prevent us from exploring if workers were using such hashtags, which led us to discover that some do, and that there is even a practice labelled 'WOL', however this was developed by a consultant and presented as a way to structure collective discussion of work between workers (Stepper 2015). But while tweets or posts on Instagram may include the #workingoutloud (or #WOL) hashtag, this was not specific enough to our study (as it was mainly used in organizations who were familiar with the consultant's method) and not diffused in a wide enough fashion to cover most instances of what we had defined as WOL.

The fact that most of the relevant material that we found did not include the #workingoutloud hashtag confirmed our intuition that the phenomenon we were trying to describe could not be narrowed down to one or two widely used or even stabilized hashtags. We also kept in mind the conclusions of a number of qualitative studies conducted on Twitter: most tweets do not come with hashtags, 'Hashtags are far from the only way people communicate on social media' (McCosker and Gerrard 2020, 5) and selecting only material that includes specific hashtags may be limiting (boyd et al. 2010; Tufekci 2014). Hashtags have also been seen as 'insider's lingo' (Baym 2015), which might explain their limited spread. Finally, studies on hashtags have revealed that they should not be seen as traditional keywords (used for example to categorize) as there is a creative aspect to their elaboration (no one has to use a 'designated' hashtag and can create his or her own) and a complexity in their form (hashtags can be a word, a string of words, a sentence, an acronym, etc.). These elements make hashtags a weak criterion for initially including or excluding content collected on social media in the kind of qualitative research our study belongs to. This does not mean that we discarded hashtags and did not pay attention to them, but rather that hashtags were not our primary mechanism of collecting data.

Our progressive exploration revealed that the words that may be used to talk about one's daily activities or experiences vary in a significant way between workers and work contexts. For example, a scientist doing experiments in a lab will not talk about a repetitive and boring task with the same words as an accountant or a visual artist—although the adjective 'boring' may be present in all instances. At the same time, all of them are communicating something about their experience at work, namely that they are performing a tedious activity.

Because our interest was in informal, non-mandatory use of social media, we could not specify in advance the names of companies or organizations where we knew that WOL would be happening.

Taken together, these observations led us to conclude that WOL could be done by any working person, in any work context. Farmers, jewellery makers, nurses, sanitation workers, sailors, tattoo artists, coders, academics, entrepreneurs, carpenters, punk musicians, cake decorators, antique collectors, welders, dancers: these people could be working out loud on social media—and they were, as we progressively discovered. In other words, we discovered that we were dealing with a social practice that was defined by its fully open-ended nature: virtually anyone can be working out loud on social media, as the only two requirements to do so are to use a public social network and be willing to share a microscopic glance into daily activities, experiences, or challenges. Studies—even mobile, digital, or multi-sited ethnographies—usually start with an idea of where the field is, even if this field moves and expands. On the contrary, our field had—and still has—no clear(er) boundaries. This of course could be said of any field, as the performative understanding of research defining a 'field' is an act performed partially by the researcher. However, we consider that our focal phenomenon was even less 'boundable' in an a priori fashion. Guided by our theoretical influences (workplace studies, practice studies, CSCW studies), our initial definition of WOL was the main element that guided us through our 'construction of the field' (Amit 1999). It was voluntarily inclusive to allow us to take account of a wide spectrum of work-related tweets and posts, but, at the same time, it excluded material that consisted of content curation (e.g. selecting and sharing content that already existed, even if it was work-related) and promotion of finalized realizations (for instance, journalists or scholars referring to their latest publications, or musicians promoting their newest single available for download or purchase). We should also highlight that our study was driven by our curiosity for this phenomenon and, contrary to a number of other studies on and of social media, we were not interested by the practices of specific individuals over time. Our inquiry was thus phenomenon led, rather than user led, which contributed to widening its scope.

An exploration fed by our imagination

Realizing that WOL may be a practice highly difficult to bound in an a priori way reveals something about the phenomenon we studied and underscores a key feature of our methodological approach: we had to use our imagination and our growing understanding of what workers could be sharing on social media in an active fashion as we collected the data. This created a sense of wonder for us, as we were surprised each time we went on Twitter and Instagram to perform searches, but it also raised doubts about the material we encountered and our ways of encountering it. Our affective experience echoes what Abidin and de Seta recently highlighted about digital ethnography:

> The bundle of methodological choices called 'digital ethnography' is an unstable construct, a nested toolbox of practices filled to the brim with potentialities and failures. Nearly any researcher who chooses to adopt an ethnographic approach to digital media ends up dedicating some thought to the anxieties, challenges, concerns, dilemmas, doubts, problems, tensions and troubles that result from practicing it.
>
> **(Abidin and de Seta 2020, 11)**

Interestingly, Abidin and de Seta evoke the bricolage of digital ethnography, and the affective experience of building on an approach that may not be as stable as we might want it to be. This was clearly at the forefront of our inquiry, as we were keenly aware of the unstable nature of our method when we went on Twitter and Instagram to collect data and faced questions, which came with affective responses, sometimes enjoyable and sometimes uncomfortable. This is where the tinkering took place: when we launched a search with a keyword and it did not produce anything, when we had to imagine what could characterize 'work' in various settings, when we looked at tweets or posts about very mundane elements and had to ask ourselves, 'Is this too mundane?' We tried to stay open to these feelings, as they can feed back into the general process of doing research (Locke et al. 2008; Sergi and Hallin 2011). Doing so, we also had to develop a way of collecting, naming, ordering, and treating the material that we found through searches and queries on each platform, and by clicking on hashtags[2]—which also involved a dose of bricolage as we discovered what we needed to preserve from these digital traces.

While we have not kept records of the very first queries we performed, our initial explorations of WOL allowed us to gradually discover a number of hashtags (and keywords, as we also looked for these words without the hashtag sign) that would prove relevant to come back to. However, rather than systematically collecting all publications found through these hashtags, we used them as one of the means at our disposal. Looking back on our approach, we can see that these hashtags mainly belonged to two broad categories. The first refers to the act of working and showing the work or some part of the work (location, time, intensity), while the second revolves around specific professional activities, as exemplified in Table 16.2.

Table 16.2, although rather detailed, should not be read as exhaustive, as a complete list of possible hashtags and keywords would be virtually impossible to develop. Indeed, given the flexibility and possible personalization of hashtags, we are still finding new relevant hashtags with each round of data collection. We opted for a long list of examples to show the wide variety found in hashtags used by people when they talk about their work and their work experience on social media. With the exception of #showyourwork and #working, which we used early on, all of these hashtags have accumulated as we progressed. While there is room for a great deal of variation in these hashtags, over time we noticed a structure, especially for the examples shown in the right-hand column. Discovering this structure came about as we tried searches on Twitter and Instagram, with more or less success, and replicated them from activity to activity. Once we discovered that people were using the structure #[domain]life, as in #accountlife, #surgeonlife, or #farmerlife, we played with it and generated novel activities to explore.

Two elements must be noted here. First, given the fully exploratory approach that characterized our work, our aim was to maximize the variety, and not to document the intensity, of a specific form WOL can take. We also did not aim to identify domains of activities where it might be more prevalent than in others. Once we tried a keyword or hashtag, we perused the results at the time the search was performed, and we captured the instances that fit, broadly speaking, with our general definition of WOL. We never collected all the posts associated with a keyword or a hashtag, as all of the queries we performed led to an amount of data that could not be handled in a qualitative manner.[3]

Indeed, the collection of all posts would have confined us to the coding and counting of posts, whereas our research objectives required analytic breadth and depth (Pritchard 2020). We limited ourselves to looking at a few dozen results or so, as this was enough to document a new dimension or add to an already identified dimension of WOL. Second, launching a search and getting results rarely directly produced content that we could simply collect. Tweets and posts had to be considered one by one, and a preliminary analysis had to be conducted, because keywords

Table 16.2 Categories and examples of hashtags used to find material

Hashtags centring on the act of sharing something related to work	Hashtags revolving around professional activity
#showyourwork	#[domain], as in #musician,
#shareyourwork	#farmer, #workingmom,
#shareyourworkspace	#AircraftMechanic,#sciencegirl,
#working	#maledancer, #digitalnomad
#amworking	
#workhard	#[domain]life, as in #accountinglife,
#somuchwork	#developerlife, #entrepreneurlife,
#WorkingOnSunday	#architectlife, #aussielogger, #barberlife,
#stillatwork	#lifeatsea, #startuplife
#freelance	
#workfromanywhere	#[specific activities] #coding,
#workingfromhome	#shiprepair, #shooting, #estateliquida-
#nightwork	tion, #instashipping, #screenwriting,
#workworkwork	#teaching, #digitaldrawing
#behindthescenes	
#behindthedesk	
#goodtimesatwork	
#attheoffice	
#funattheoffice	
#officelife	
#workselfie	
#overtime	
#myofficedesk	
#getitdone	
#hustling	
#dailygrind	
#ilovemyjob/#ihatemyjob	
#coworkinglife	
#worklifebalance	
#lovewhatyoudo	

and hashtags were sometimes used in a way that did not correspond to an instance of narrating one's work. For example, an accountant on vacation may tag one of her posts #accountantlife but uses it to refer to her time at the beach. This also contributed to making data collection time consuming, an aspect that should not be underestimated when conducting qualitative analysis of posts on social media.

In sum, we had to use our imagination, in an abductive fashion, to think of spheres of activities and look for instances of WOL. Using our imagination made our method 'move'—and this movement was fundamentally required by our object of inquiry: it changed form depending on the affordances of each platform, the highly personal ways Twitter and Instagram were used by each person, the context in which their short narration was happening, etc. We expected WOL to vary when we started this research, but did not anticipate the scope of the variation. Accordingly, our method had to display some fluidity, as our focal object was fuzzy and fluid (akin to Law 2004). Describing acts of imagination is not easy and, in our case, this imagination took the form of questions. Most of these revolved around asking ourselves who could be narrating their work experience of work (e.g. a captain) and what kind of words or hashtags this person might use. These questions were first shaped by theoretical elements related to the concepts of practice and of invisible work. As we progressively refined our definition of WOL, we also incorporated its dimensions into our data collection work. We also made use of our own experiences of being at work. Combined, these empirical, conceptual, and experiential aspects nourished our exploration.

This process might give the impression of cherry-picking; however, we argue that it was rather abductive in the way it unfolded. Abduction, as developed by Peirce (1905), involves oscillating between empirical phenomena and theories and knowledge and 'is the type of reasoning in which scientific creativity is manifest' (Anderson 1986, 145). Abduction is not pure intuition, but insight emerging in a context influenced by the researcher's thinking and current ideas, hence this oscillation. Theoretical or conceptual dimensions may have guided our work, but they remained to be specified, in their expression and variability, on social media. For example, recognizing that affect is constitutive of practice (e.g. Gherardi 2017; Gherardi et al. 2019) implied that we should look, for example, for expressions of affect and descriptions of environments as related to the experience of working and being at work. It also invited us to be attentive to the ways we were affected as we looked at possible material, investigating our own reactions to posts. These reactions included surprise related to the discovery of 'patches' of data (i.e. a keyword or hashtag that opened up many tweets or posts that could be considered as instances of WOL), which in turn stimulated our search for more data and our thinking about this practice. While we knew we wanted to pay attention—empirically and theoretically—to affect, the ways this concept manifested itself in tweets and posts were not further specified and needed to be documented in all their possible forms, spurring an open interrogation of what could belong to affect (conceptually) and of how it could appear in WOL (empirically).

Constituting data

Finding material that could help us document WOL was one thing, but we had to be able to collect this material in a stable way. If every tweet has its own hyperlink, just like every Instagram post, we knew from the start that we would have to find a way to capture the content we wanted to analyse, and not simply rely on bookmarking this hyperlink. Not only do social media platforms change over time, but content can disappear easily. For data collection on Twitter we relied on Tweetdeck, a free Twitter client (other tools exist; we suggest that researchers consider these various options based on the specifics of their data collection, before committing to one tool).

Tweetdeck presents Twitter content in columns, which can include saved searches (such as a hashtag that we wanted to follow) and also 'collections', a column in which tweets can be 'saved'. We used this function to create a deposit of possible tweets to include. After closer inspection, tweets that were set aside were then transformed into screenshots, to be analysed. For Instagram, we could not rely on a tool similar to Tweetdeck. We thus conducted several rounds of data collection, making screenshots as we found material relevant for our analysis. Data collection on both platforms hence led us to create libraries of tweets and posts that were each carefully numbered. We used either Word documents or Excel spreadsheets to compile information about each instance, including a column for first ideas that emerged as we came into contact with the tweet or post. Figure 16.1 is an example of a spreadsheet we developed to document how we found material. This table shows how we kept track of our data collection, facilitating both repetition and variation in our approach.

We can say that it was only after these first steps—finding, setting aside, selecting, and screenshotting that this material was transformed into 'data' to be analysed. In this sense, we can say that our data were produced, but such production is not a fabrication: it only reveals how scientific work proceeds, as Latour (1987) eloquently demonstrated. A second screening of the data happened when we analysed the material, as some of the collected posts sometimes turned out to be only remotely connected to WOL. This proved a constant challenge with our exploration of this

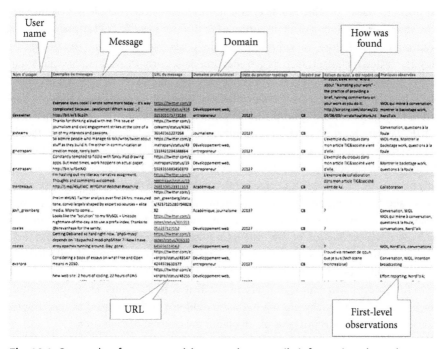

Fig. 16.1 Screenshot from a spreadsheet used to compile information about the material collected, identifying the different categories of information recorded.

practice, as the borders between working out loud (narrating one's experience of work or sharing a mundane aspect of work) and branding/promotion could be fuzzy in some instances. As mentioned previously, we strived to keep what we call an 'open proximity' between the material and our definition of WOL. However, since we refined the dimensions of this definition as we proceeded, we consider that this process was one of co-construction: making an aspect of WOL emerge, conceptually, in our analysis led us to look for more instances of it in new tweets or posts.

A Few Ethical Challenges

Our research involved collecting data in a passive way, as we did not have direct interactions with the authors of the posts. Such unobtrusive collecting of posts voluntarily shared on social media not only brings methodological challenges but raises a number of ethical questions that must be addressed in the early stages of the research design. We cannot cover all of these challenges in an exhaustive manner in this chapter, but we briefly examine some ways to mitigate risk for (unknowing) research participants. As stated in the *Ethical Guidelines* developed by the Association of Internet Researchers (AoIR), we need to 'ensure that no more data, especially sensitive and personal information, is collected than is strictly necessary' (Ranzke et al. 2020, 12). Since the objective of our research was to study the content of WOL posts in order to reflect on this practice, and not to analyse the sociodemographic profile, status, or intentions of their authors, we did not need to collect their personal information. Therefore, we collected only the posts themselves, and did not record any associated metadata, such as geo-location data. Also, we decided to collect only public posts found on public accounts, where users likely have no expectation of privacy. In such cases, the use of research data without gaining informed consent from users may be justifiable (The British Psychological Society 2017, 8). Furthermore, particular care must be taken in minimizing the potential harm users could face by having their public posts circulated in another context. When reproducing the collected posts in academic publications and presentations, we remove all references to any personally identifiable information that could reveal their identities, by blurring faces, and taking out any markers (usernames, locations, etc.). In order to prevent readers from identifying the posts by placing text in a search engine, we also include only partial reproduction of the Instagram posts, by cropping the images and texts. Such treatment addresses the concern of the traceability of anonymized collected data via search engines (Whiting and Pritchard 2018). However, while these precautions help to protect participants, they are not sufficient to guarantee copyright compliance, which explains why our WOL posts could not be reproduced in this chapter, considering that it was not possible to obtain the consent of each user.

Concluding Remarks

As Law (2004) reminds us, there will always exist a gap between method as performed and accounts of method, as guided by the traditional principles of academic
writing. But as Nardi and Engeström reveal through the concept of invisible work,
'[w]ork is, in a sense, always invisible to everyone but its own practitioners' (Nardi
and Engeström 1999, 2). This clearly expresses that no one understands work in a
fuller and finer way than the person who practises it. Combined, we suggest that
these two ideas should inspire us, as researchers, to expand our thinking about our
methods, both performed in situ and over time, and described in our texts. Most of
the time, no one 'sees' our research as it emerges. A method may be chosen and devised in advance, prior to its enactment, but it rarely means that it will not require
adjustments, tinkering, or even gradual invention. This invisibility is tacitly accepted.
In this chapter, as in our research on 'working out loud', we wished to question this
accepted invisibility. What is made invisible escapes inquiry and may impoverish our
understanding of social and human phenomena. Of course, this does not mean that
everything should be exposed or made transparent. However, we argue that when
it comes to reflections about method, it might be fruitful, in some cases, to discuss
more explicitly how the *doing* of research proceeds.

   In the case of research, many reasons explain this invisibility, and, as we have argued in this chapter, the way we tend to construct and develop our methods sections,
in our texts and in our presentation, contributes to such obfuscation. One could say
that this is normal, as all the details about how a specific study was conducted, from a
daily and processual view, can never be fully captured, partially resist being put into
words, and may not even be consequential enough to be included in how we communicate our results. We can certainly agree with this critique, but we also believe
that there are times and places to reveal what goes on 'behind the scenes' of methods,
as this says something both about the method itself, and the knowledge it helps to
produce. The aims and spatial limitations of the traditional journal article may not
allow for such a discussion, but texts reflecting on methods, and classes devoted to
methodology, should open up this 'behind-the-scenes' view of research, as it is constitutive of inquiries and of their results. As Van Maanen et al. (2007) remind us,
what fundamentally gets hidden in most presentations of results is this very process
of discovery. Furthermore:

> [p]racticing organizational researchers know ... that any narrative suggest-
> ing an orderly, standard model of the research process is rather mislead-
> ing. What seems apparent to those who have carried out organizational
> research projects is that method can generate and shape theory, just as the-
> ory can generate and shape method. There is a back-and-forth character in
> which concepts, conjectures, and data are in continuous interplay.
>
> **(Van Maanen et al. 2007, 1147)**

Keeping this back and forth visible may be difficult when writing a text that aims to communicate research findings retrospectively. As we have aimed to show in the presentation of the method we devised, keeping theoretical, methodological, and empirical concerns side by side and considering how they can inform each other is fruitful. This is especially the case when it comes to phenomena that are simultaneously banal, ephemeral, fuzzy, fluid, and distributed.

In sum, we conclude by arguing that it might be especially relevant to simultaneously think about the appropriate methods to inquire into digital phenomena and to cultivate an open and imaginative approach to method altogether. Along with the need for reflexivity (Abidin and de Seta 2020), such imagination in terms of methods may enrich our understanding of digital phenomena and help us with our development of methods well suited to the ever-changing digital realm.

Notes

1. One example of what could be at the same time characterized as dirty, mundane, invisible, and digital work is the work performed by workers who are paid to do content moderation, patrolling various platforms to remove offensive material (of a violent or pornographic nature, for example). See for example 'The trauma floor' on The Verge' (https://www.theverge.com/2019/2/25/18229714/cognizant-facebook-content-moderator-interviews-trauma-working-conditions-arizona) and 'The laborers who keep dick pics and beheadings out of your Facebook feed', on Wired (https://www.wired.com/2014/10/content-moderation/) for a description of what this difficult work entails.
2. On Twitter as on Instagram, hashtags are active as hyperlinks, and clicking on one generated a page with all the posts that include the hashtag.
3. For example, a search with the hashtag #farmerlife generates 295,302 posts, as of 24 May 2020.

References

Abidin, C., and de Seta, G. 2020. Private messages from the field: Confessions on digital ethnography and its discomforts. *Journal of Digital Social Research*, 2(1): pp. 1–19.

Amit, V. 1999. *Constructing the Field*. London: Routledge.

Anderson, D. R. 1986. The Evolution of Peirce's Concept of Abduction. *Transactions of the Charles S. Peirce Society*, 22(2): pp. 145–64.

Baym, N. K. 2015. *Personal Connections in the Digital Age*. John Wiley & Sons.

Bonneau, C. 2013. Travailler à haute voix sur Twitter: quand la collaboration informelle emprunte un réseau public. *TIC & Société* 6, (2): pp. 1–19.

Bonneau, C., Endrissat, N., and Sergi, V. 2021. Social media as a new workspace: How working out loud (re)materializes work. In Mitev, N., Aroles, J., Stephenson, K., and Malaurent, J. (eds), *New Ways of Working: Organizations and Organizing in the Digital Age*. Palgrave. (pp 47–75).

Bowker, G. C. 2007. The past and the internet. In Karaganis, J. (ed.), *Structures of Participation in Digital Culture.* (pp. 20–36). New York: Social Science Research Council.

boyd, d., S. Golder, and G. Lotan. 2010. Tweet, tweet, retweet: Conversational aspects of retweeting on Twitter. In Sprague Jr., R. H. (ed.), *HICSS 2010 Proceedings of the 2010 43rd Hawaii International Conference on System Sciences.* (pp. 1–10). Washington, DC: IEEE Computer Society.

Brekhus, W. 2000. A Mundane Manifesto. *Journal of Mundane Behavior,* 1(1): pp. 89–105.

The British Psychological Society. 2017. Ethics Guidelines for Internet-Mediated Research. Retrieved from www.bps.org.uk/publications/policy-and-guidelines/research-guidelines-policy-documents/research-guidelines-poli.

Brownlie, J., and Shaw, F. 2019. Empathy rituals: Small conversations about emotional distress on Twitter. *Sociology,* 53(1): pp. 104-122.

Cisco. 2012. BYOD and Virtualization: Insights from the Cisco IBSG Horizons Study. Retrieved from http://www.slideshare.net/CiscoIBSG/byod-and-virtualization-insights-from-the-cisco-ibsg-horizons-study.

Gherardi, S. 2017. One turn … and now another one: Do the turn to practice and the turn to affect have something in common? *Management Learning,* 48(3): pp. 345–58.

Gherardi, S., Murgia, A., Bellè, E., Miele, F., and Carreri, A. 2019. Tracking the sociomaterial traces of affect at the crossroads of affect and practice theories. *Qualitative Research in Organizations and Management: An International Journal,* 14(3): pp. 295–316.

Heath, C., Knoblauch, H., and Luff, P. 2000. Technology and social interaction: The emergence of 'workplace studies'. *The British Journal of Sociology* 51(2): pp. 299–320.

Highfield, T., and Leaver, T. 2015. A methodology for mapping Instagram hashtags. *First Monday,* 20 (1). Retrieved from https://firstmonday.org/ojs/index.php/fm/article/view/5563

Hine, C. 2015. *Ethnography for the Internet: Embedded, Embodied and Everyday.* Bloomsbury Publishing.

Laestadius, L. 2017. Instagram. In Quan-Haase, A., and Sloan, L., (eds), *The SAGE Handbook of Social Media Research Methods* (pp. 573–92). Sage Publishing.

Latour, B. 1987. *Science in Action: How to Follow Scientists and Engineers Through Society.* Harvard University Press.

Latzko-Toth, G., C. Bonneau, and M. Millette. 2017. Small data, thick data: Thickening strategies for trace-based social media research. In Quan-Haase, A., and Sloan. L. (eds), *The SAGE Handbook of Social Media Research Methods* (pp. 199–214). Sage Publishing.

Law, J. 2004. *After Method: Mess in Social Science Research.* Routledge.

Law, J., and J. Urry. 2004. Enacting the Social. *Economy and Society,* 33(3): pp. 390–410.

Leonardi, P. M., and Meyer, S. R. 2015. Social media as social lubricant: How ambient awareness eases knowledge transfer. *American Behavioral Scientist,* 59(1): pp. 10–34.

Leonardi, P. M. and Vaast, E. 2017. Social media and their affordances for organizing: A review and agenda for research. *The Academy of Management Annals,* 11(1): pp. 150–88.

Locke, K., Golden-Biddle, K., and Feldman, M. S. 2008. Making doubt generative: Rethinking the role of doubt in the research process. *Organization Science*, 19(6): pp. 907–18.

Majchrzak, A., Faraj, S., Kane, G., and Azad, B. 2013. The contradictory influence of social media affordances on online knowledge sharing. *Journal of Computer Mediated Communication*, 19(1): pp. 38–55.

McCosker, A., and Gerrard, Y. 2020. Hashtagging depression on Instagram: Towards a more inclusive mental health research methodology. *New Media & Society*, OnlineFirst, retrieved from https://doi.org/10.1177/1461444820921349

Miller, D. 2018. Digital anthropology. *Cambridge Encyclopedia of Anthropology* (pp. 1–16). Retrieved from http://doi.org/10.29164/18digital

Nardi, B. A., and Engeström, Y. 1999. A web on the wind: The structure of invisible work. *Computer Supported Cooperative Work (CSCW)*, 8(1): pp. 1–8.

Nicolini, D. 2013. *Practice Theory, Work, and Organization: An Introduction*. Oxford University Press.

Peirce, C. S. 1905. [Letter] To Signor Calderoni, on Pragmaticism. *CP* 8: pp. 205–13.

Pritchard, K. 2020. Examining web images: A Combined Visual Analysis (CVA) approach. *European Management Review*, 17(1): pp. 297–310.

Ranzke, A. S., Bechmann, A., Zimmer, M., Ess, C., and Association of Internet Researchers. 2020. Internet Research: Ethical Guidelines 3.0. Retrieved from https://aoir.org/reports/ethics3.pdf.

Sachs, P. 1995. Transforming work: Collaboration, learning, and design. *Communications of the ACM*, 38(9): pp. 36–44.

Sergi, V., and Bonneau, C. 2016. Making mundane work visible on social media: A CCO investigation of working out loud on Twitter. *Communication Research and Practice*, 2(3): pp. 378–406.

Sergi, V., and Hallin, A. 2011. Thick performances, not just thick descriptions: The processual nature of doing qualitative research. *Qualitative Research in Organizations and Management: An International Journal*, 6(2): pp. 191–208.

Star, S. L., and Strauss, A. 1999. Layers of silence, arenas of voice: The ecology of visible and invisible work. *Computer Supported Cooperative Work*, 8(1): pp. 9–30.

Stepper, J. 2015. *Working Out Loud: For a Better Career and Life*. Ikigai Press.

Tufekci, Z. 2014. Big questions for social media Big Data: Representativeness, validity and other methodological pitfalls. In Weng, L., Menczer, F., and Ahn,Y. Y. (eds), *Proceedings from ICWSM '14: 8th International AAAI Conference on Weblogs and Social Media* . Palo Alto, CA: AAAI Press.

Van Maanen, J., Sorensen, J. B., and Mitchell, T. R. 2007. Introduction to special topic forum: The interplay between theory and method. *Academy of Management Review*, 32(4): pp. 1145–54.

Whiting, R., and Pritchard, K. 2018. Digital Ethics. In C. Cassell, A. Cunliffe, and G. Grandy (Eds.), *The SAGE Handbook of Qualitative Business and Management Research Methods: History and Traditions* (pp. 562–577). Sage Publishing.

17

Organizational Culture in Tracked Changes

Format and Affordance in Consequential Workplace Documents

Andrew Whelan

Introduction

Anyone accustomed to working through the circulation and joint production of documents will have experience with tracked changes: the word processing feature which records edits to documents and affords the production of comments in their margins. Rather than being an anterior or preparatory form of and site for work, the proposition put forward here is that tracked changes are a primary digital residue of work: a location in which to analyse the articulation of workplace culture and politics. In organizationally significant documents, tracked changes marginalia make visible the interpretive schemes by which staff and management express their understandings of the work that they do, and their respective objectives in the organization of that work.

In methodological terms, tracked changes in such documents are naturally occurring empirical data evidencing workplace relations. These data require both a contextual frame, by which they can be situated relative to the organization and its processes, and an analytical frame, by which the data can be scrutinized and interpreted. In this chapter, institutional ethnography is utilized to provide the former, while ethnomethodology furnishes the latter. The methodological contribution lies in conducting a close, ethnomethodologically informed reading of tracked changes comments and discussions, where this reading is conducted within the institutional ethnographic frame, which emphasizes the organizational significance of such documents.

The chapter is set out as follows. I begin in the next section by situating the research methodology relative to relevant literature. I then discuss tracked changes in a consequential workplace document. I describe the document and its local organizational significance: a draft workload model specifying the weighted hours allocated to various academic labour tasks (lectures, tutorials, and so on). I present pertinent

Andrew Whelan, *Organizational Culture in Tracked Changes*. In: *Research Methods for Digital Work and Organization.*
Edited by Gillian Symon, Katrina Pritchard, and Christine Hine, Oxford University Press.
© Oxford University Press (2021). DOI: 10.1093/oso/9780198860679.003.0017

examples of tracked commentary on this document, describing the strategies they evince. I move from the discussion of specific instances to the broader implications of the readerly logics they instantiate.

The methodology applied involves looking at the communicative traces of a specific kind of work (the work of workload negotiation), and looking at those traces in a specific kind of way. There is a precedent for this kind of analysis in the study of literature. In 'genetic criticism', researchers study unpublished drafts of texts (Kinderman and Jones 2009), with attention usually on the development of the text across versions. The interest here, however, is in backchannel communication via commentary on *iterations* of the draft, rather than the development of the draft.

The argument, borne out by the data and the analysis, is that scrutinizing backstage communication processes such as tracked changes in significant workplace documents produces insight into how work is locally understood, organized, described, and negotiated. This leads to a more general discussion of document format and affordance, in an organizational sense. The analytical section thus ends with commentary on how tracked changes are tacitly used in workplace processes as a communicative tool, without reflexive acknowledgement of this use or its implications. I conclude the chapter detailing some of the drawbacks and merits of the methodological approach.

Applying Institutional Ethnography and Ethnomethodology to University 'Admin'

I refer briefly to three bodies of relevant literature here: institutional ethnography, ethnomethodology, and critical university studies. Institutional ethnography and ethnomethodology are properly understood as methodological approaches. Critical university studies embraces a range of methods; it functions here as a contextual backdrop, furnishing an intellectual and political orientation to local and structural problems of workplace (dis)organization.

Originally developed by Dorothy Smith (2005), institutional ethnography is now widely used in healthcare, education, and other institutional contexts (Burstow 2016; Doll and Walby 2019; Russell and Reid 2019). One of the key aspects of institutional ethnography is its explicit engagement with how organizations are structured and mediated through the circulation of texts (Smith and Turner 2014). 'Texts' are described in institutional ethnography in a broad sense, including email, video, images, and other classes of documents more familiar to studies of work (letters, spreadsheets, forms, and so on). Smith and other institutional ethnographers point out that the replicability of texts is a key feature of the coordination of complex social action across space and time. Hospitals, for example, are recognizable as such across geographical spaces in significant part because their activities are coordinated by reference to networked software, forms, databases, and standardized coding systems instantiated in paper and digital documents. Institutional ethnography directs attention to how administrative technologies such as mundane workplace documents organize social relationships. An excellent example of this is the idea of the institutional circuit or accountability circuit (Johnson and Bagatell 2019, 2). An institutional circuit

> locates sequences of text-coordinated action making people's actualities representable and hence actionable within the institutional frames that authorise institutional action. In institutional circuits, institutional work comprises mining actualities selectively to identify aspects, features, measures, and so on that fit the governing frame (sometimes called a 'boss text').
>
> **(Smith and Turner 2014, 10)**

An institutional circuit is governed by a 'boss text'. A boss text is a document which functions as an overarching framework guiding action, for instance, a policy document or a piece of legislation. Boss texts proliferate subsidiary texts in a kind of textual hierarchy. These subsidiary texts are designed to capture specific organizational activities, in order to produce reporting or audit information, demonstrating that organizational activity accords with the boss text.

Institutional ethnography is both a methodological orientation, guiding researchers to documents and documentary processes in organizations, and a political and ontological project. One of the central objectives of institutional ethnography is to empower people by cultivating greater appreciation of the structures by which their governance is coordinated, including specifically bureaucratic structures. Alongside this political orientation, associated particularly with feminist praxis, institutional ethnography has ontological implications insofar as it emphasizes documents as key structuring elements in organizations. Documents coordinate doings. This ontological aspect of institutional ethnography is partially derived from ethnomethodology.

This brings us to the second relevant body of literature: the ethnomethodological 'studies of work' tradition, especially with reference to documents. This orientation, derived from the pioneering ethnomethodological research of Harold Garfinkel (1967), exhibits a phenomenologically informed approach to social practices in various contexts, including work, broadly understood (Garfinkel 2005; Liberman 2013; Rouncefield and Tolmie 2016). As the name implies, ethnomethodology seeks to explicate vernacular 'members' methods' of making sense of the world and of presenting and negotiating accounts of what they are doing and why.

Ethnomethodologists developed methodologically and analytically robust research in conversation analysis, on the organizational structure and design of conversation in both informal talk and especially talk in institutional contexts (Hutchby and Woofitt 2008; Heritage and Clayman 2011; Arminen 2017). A body of work was also developed in membership categorization analysis, on how social categories (for example, 'research active') are developed and morally constituted in talk (Jayyusi 2014; Fitzgerald and Housley 2015). Conversation analysis and membership categorization analysis are fine-grained empirical approaches to social action, concerning both the seen-but-unnoticed structure of local social exchange, and the normative and political aspects of identity categories mobilized and instantiated in talk.

Another strain of this literature directs attention to activities oriented to documents and how documents are used in specific social contexts. This has involved both ethnomethodology of reading practices (Rooksby 2016; Watson 2016), and ethnomethodological attention directed to how documents are used in and shape proceedings at the local level (Garfinkel and Bittner 1967; Llewellyn and Hindmarsh 2010; Mondada and Svinhufvud 2016). The approaches and analyses presented across this literature facilitate the analysis below. Ethnomethodology provides foundations from which to address, among other things: how parties orient to each other and to the communicative context of the document itself; how they interpret the document's implications and its relations to other such documents; how they exhibit and locate their expertise so as to justify preferred courses of action; and how they conduct alignment with and invoke others (real and imagined).

There is a third relevant body of literature: critical university studies, or CUS (Petrina and Ross 2014; Gill 2016; Newfield 2016; Alvesson et al. 2017). CUS spans education policy (Marginson 2013), critical pedagogy (Giroux 2020), the hierarchies of race and gender in the university (Gutiérrez y Muhs et al. 2012), the political stakes of the contemporary university (Chatterjee and Maira 2014), and positions on the value of progressive education (Docherty 2011; Connell 2019). There is work on acceleration in the academy (Vostal 2016), on the academic labour process (Sutton 2017), and on how technological work processes and quasi-market disciplinary mechanisms reconfigure academic labour and value (Lorenz 2012; Williamson 2020). As academic work is unbundled and casualized, bibliometric and audit technologies, including student surveys, function to constrain and discipline academic labour (Burrows 2012; Sharpe and Turner 2018; Thiel 2019). CUS has produced valuable insight on both the political economy of the university (Bousquet 2008), and the Foucauldian aspects of contemporary academic administration (Ball 2003).

While compelling critical insights have been furnished by this literature, CUS has been thin on the practical granularity of how academic labour is negotiated, accounted for, and organized, despite interest in labour intensification of the sort workload deliberations might mitigate or exacerbate. CUS is valuable here in that it explicitly addresses the cultural, political, and economic problems at the work site. The dominant form of explanation in this literature, however, is 'up', by reference to overarching constructs such as neoliberalism. The analysis presented here is intended to avoid the reduction upwards, by showing how local processes, communicative strategies, and discursive positions produce the conditions which other critics name as 'neoliberal' without detailing close engagement in local contexts, and without specific methodological interest in providing such engagement.

My references to this literature are motivated in the sense of 'workers' inquiry' and 'dig where you stand' (Lindqvist 1979; Ovetz 2020): I hope to cultivate empirical insight into how the local context is structured. While the relationship between institutional ethnography and ethnomethodology is evident (Smith 2005, 67), and while institutional ethnography has paid close attention to the negotiation of documents, my synthesis of these approaches accords with the material available to me. In other contexts, similar documents might be available in similar states of preparation. The context, however, is likely to determine what kinds of literatures would best situate the workplace practices under consideration.

The Workload Document in Organizational Context

This section describes the organizational context for the research. The documents I analyse are derived from a committee: the Faculty Workload Reference Group (FWRG). The FWRG is mandated to devise a workload model for Faculty ratification. The work of the committee occurs in a specific context. A university restructure amalgamated what were previously several small faculties into much larger units. What were previously distinct faculties of Law, Arts, and Creative Arts became one large faculty. This faculty housed, under the one administrative roof, a range of disparate teaching and research practices, which were managed in stable and separate administrative and accounting mechanisms prior to the restructure. Part of the challenge for the FWRG lies in formulating commensurability across practices historically organized and costed in distinct ways (e.g. the distinction between a tutorial in the humanities, and studio practice in the creative arts).

In institutional ethnographic terms, the institutional circuit around the workload model is as follows. At the apex point of the hierarchy is the 2009 *Fair Work Act*. The *Fair Work Act* is Commonwealth of Australia industrial relations legislation, setting out the conditions under which employers and employees negotiate Enterprise Bargaining Agreements, usually referred to as EBAs or EAs. Accordingly, the local 2015 university Enterprise Agreement requires faculties to have standing workload models, have these models ratified by the Faculty, and have FWRGs formulate them. The relevant section of the EA, current at the time the data were produced, is set forth below:

25.4. Faculty Workload Models

25.4.1. The Executive Dean or equivalent of each faculty shall be responsible for maintaining a workloads model for the faculty. The development of an appropriate workload model consistent with this Agreement will be the responsibility of each faculty workload reference group and subject to ratification by academic staff in a faculty meeting or by other faculty survey.

25.4.2. The faculty workload model will;

25.4.2.1. Encompass the elements of research, learning and teaching, and governance and service and be based on 48 (minus public holidays and concessional days) out of 52 weeks per year;

25.4.2.2. Indicate the normal balance between the elements of academic activity that are relevant to that faculty.

25.4.3. Faculty workload allocations shall be published and be available to all staff within each faculty including on the faculty's intranet site.

25.5. Faculty Workload Reference Group

25.5.1. The Faculty Workload Reference Group will consist of the Executive Dean or nominee, a Head of Department or Associate Dean or equivalent person, and two staff members of the faculty; one appointed by the NTEU Branch and one elected by the academic staff of the faculty.

25.5.2. In addition to the role of the Faculty Workload Reference Group in developing the faculty workload model, the Reference Group will also monitor the equitable distribution of workloads across the faculty and in the first instance attempt to resolve any disputes in respect of workload allocation.

25.5.3. The Faculty Workload Reference Group will meet at least twice a year following the distribution of workload allocation and prior to the publication of the timetable for the next teaching session. Academic staff within the faculty will be notified four weeks in advance of the meeting and will be given the opportunity to submit issues for consideration.

25.5.4. Each Faculty Workload Reference Group may make such administrative arrangements as may be necessary to administer the workload standards in this Clause.

(University of Wollongong 2015, 21)

Triggered by federal legislation, the EA is the boss text, mandating the FWRG to produce the workload model. The model then generates 'subsidiary' documents: forms designed to capture individual academics' workloads per semester, spreadsheets describing allocations and temporal 'credits' and 'debts' across semesters and years, email negotiations about teaching allocations and so on. The workload model has indirect but real effects on other documents usually considered to be at some remove, including research- and teaching-related documents. For instance, in specifying assignment word counts, course outlines conform to the model in that word count is an expression of estimated hourly weightings for teaching, which include marking. While not visible to teaching staff, the workload model is the mechanism aligning work allocation to budget.

The model is consequential to staff. How much teaching and marking is involved in a given semester or year for any member of permanent or fixed-term teaching staff is determined with reference to the model. While the workload model has nominal stipulations about research time, research productivity, and administrative load, attention is usually on teaching and how teaching activities are defined and counted (research activity is in any case captured by other mechanisms).

The clauses from the EA above set out the composition of the FWRG. They also stipulate that the workload model must be established by the FWRG and *ratified* by academic staff. The requirement to ratify is one of the reasons why establishing a working model is difficult. Teaching staff want a model accurately describing (and not increasing) their work; management want a model that will not increase costs (that is, decrease workload). As the balance between these goals is difficult to accomplish, it is difficult for the FWRG to produce a model staff will ratify. In the school in which the research was conducted, the last time a workload model was ratified was approximately 10 years ago. At the time of writing (2021), following another restructure, this school continues to refer to a document known as the 2012 interim model. The work of the FWRG analysed here did not culminate in a workload model.

There are several important features to note about the work of the FWRG, pertaining to the primacy of the document. When the FWRG is understood to be active, the draft workload document is treated by all parties as an accurate and direct representation of the FWRG's progress. The document *is* the work of the FWRG. The FWRG works textually, both 'live' and via email or otherwise remotely. The document directs interaction, both proximal (in FWRG meetings) and distal (in the 'shape' or value it gives to work practices beyond it). It is a kind of proto-contract, eliciting 'retrospective-prospective' orientations.

Production of the document is owned by the FWRG, but the document is public in that anyone can ask about it (or see it 'under the counter'). The document is an accountability totem (see Sabri 2013). The document also has a relatively autonomous affective life for staff: its contents intimate possible local futures, and favourable progress is understood as an indicator of the goodwill and health of the relationship between staff and management.

While responsibility and author function are ascribed to the committee, key individual figures (not committee members) held exclusive editorial prerogatives over the text itself at *almost* all times. While versions of the document consistently built up marginalia and edits, the committee did not directly amend the text of the document without tracking, either together, or individually. This was not derived from a concern about version control. It was understood that committee members would make decisions about changes to the document, which those key administrators would then apply to the text. Put bluntly, control of the text does not lie with the committee.

There are some descriptive concepts helpful for contextualizing the draft workload document and its salience. The first, derived from John Law's (2004, 33) *After Method*, is 'hinterland'. In the social study of science and related areas, hinterland is used to refer to those aspects of a technology, process, etc. which are now sedimented or reified, and therefore opaque, invisible, or 'black boxed'. Part of the research agenda is to explore the hinterland: to excavate the organization of the organization, through paying attention to the documentary processes and deliberations which culminate in a workload model. The second concept is that of 'negotiation erasure' (Kameo and Whalen 2015, 256). This is a term used to describe how the hinterlands of documents are elided. For example, administrative forms do not describe or reference the processes through which they came to be. In bureaucratic contexts, this back end is invariably obscured from view. Administrative documents thus solidify, coming to appear durable and stable across space and time. Once negotiations have been concluded, the hinterland of the document is obscured through negotiation erasure. The document enters what Smith refers to as 'textual time': the deliberations giving rise to it (and, importantly, the lived practices it works to define and cost) are detached from it, its history becomes invisible, the model comes to self-evidently stand as neutral and legitimate with respect to the activities that it represents, and which it will come to organize (Smith 1990, 74–5). Such documents are not disrupted without a formal process by users or by those who own the document and its processes.

Workplace Communicative Strategies in Tracked Changes Commentary

I was a member of the FWRG from 2014 to 2017. During that time, I received around 970 emails regarding the committee's work. I attended eight formal FWRG meetings, and two faculty forums, presenting and discussing the draft workload model for the benefit of the faculty. I attended multiple informal meetings with committee members and with other interested parties. I saw nine distinct iterations of the document (excluding 'doubles': copies of the same version from different members with tracked changes). At the end of my service on that committee, I came to reflect on what had and had not been accomplished in that time, given the committee had not put forward a new model for ratification. Workload modelling is a concrete manifestation of the themes in the critical university studies literature, and so I returned to the media of the committee and began to scrutinize it, wondering whether it might helpfully contribute to that literature somehow.

There is, unfortunately, no neat formula or 'recipe' for conducting analysis of this kind, although what follows is deeply informed by the ethnomethodological writing referenced above. I read tracked commentary as forms of action or invitations or exhortations to action: looking to see what a given comment was *doing*. I searched for identifiable strategies and repeated gestures in the comments and began to classify and name them. I sought to understand and explicate the literacies and rationalities underlying these strategies and gestures. I paid close attention to how those writing the comments navigate and utilize the terrain of the text and the broader textual environment. I looked at comments to see how, in their design, they articulate and seek to legitimate distinct and not always compatible local positions and perspectives. I scrutinized comments in their contexts, with adjacent 'turns' and replies, as elements in conversational exchanges. I considered how comments, produced for the audience of the committee, exhibited diplomacy, and antagonism. In short, through close reading of the data, I sought to explicate the ethnomethods or 'members' methods' the data instantiate. My personal recollection of the committee informed my institutional ethnographic description. I used a software program to anonymize commenters, partly because the ethnomethodological interest is in *how* things are said rather than *who* says them. Individual commenters cannot therefore always be identified (other than as 'Reviewer 1'), but it is nonetheless possible, as we will see shortly, to identify and allocate the approaches consistently taken by the parties to the document.

In order to exhibit the discursive and interactional strategies and organizational priorities voiced in tracked commentary, I turn now to some specific forms of intervention, sequenced according to their scope relative to the text. The sequence builds up from 'atomic' aspects of the text to forms of intervention demonstrating contrasting styles of reading the document on the part of FWRG members.

The most basic level of tracked changes is associated with text layout and form, and produced by the word processing program as it records incremental formatting and editing. This produces comments like the following:

Deleted: where necessary
Formatted: Left, Right: 0 cm, No bullets or numbering, Allow hanging punctuation
Formatted: Indent: Left: 1 cm, No bullets or numbering

At a level above this, we find editorial observations regarding misnumbered items, queries about unwieldy text and so on:

Also see comment 4 above. There is no box for 'new subject' in this table.

This comment points to a mismatch between information in the draft presented in textual and in tabular form: an omission in a table of a time allocation specified in the text. The comment exhibits tacit, prospective awareness of documentary sedimentation or 'stickiness'. We can thus read commentary both as direct input into the draft, and for how FWRG members orient to the document, including notably how they orient to it as a durational process. For example:

Subject amendments that sit outside of the definition of Less Significant amendment to Courses and Subjects (Course and Subject Approval Procedures—New Courses and Significant Amendment to Existing Courses

This comment represents *stepwise anterior referential definition*. It specifies a definition by indexing a local policy document: Course and Subject Approval Procedures. In institutional ethnographic terms, this comment is about and on the 'border' between this document and the broader documentary terrain. The workload draft is internally and in commentary shaped by mobilization of other documents, at varying levels of proximity or distance, which may in stepwise fashion predefine or entail how definitions in the draft are formulated. Indexing other documents in this way enhances the stickiness of definitional text: where this indexing is effective, such definitions are accepted as non-negotiable. Sticky text speeds up deliberations by rendering discussion of some topics redundant. Simultaneously, sticky text extends the life of the document itself, as it 'steps' to inform following documents. The stickier the document becomes, the faster it enters 'textual time', organizing practices around it.

The strategy of stepwise anterior referential definition is used by all parties, such that definitions can be queried or contested if different definitions can (or cannot) be found in other local university documents hierarchically 'above' or 'diagonal' to the workload model in the institutional circuit. Consider the following invocations of the boss text:

> It is hard to understand this range. Is a semester 13 weeks, or 16, or something else? Whatever it is, it should be consistent, and only one number.
> Does it allow for lower loads in 'ordinary' semesters for people who teach also in summer session?
> In the 2015 EB at 25.4.2.1, the clause regarding workloads, 48 weeks is specified, so it is not clear why there are numerous different ranges in the document.

The comment immediately below this reads:

> This is straight from the enterprise agreement-see clause 2.6

Here a comment and its response both reference the Enterprise Agreement for definitions of the length of the semester (the response directs the reader to a clause in the workload model, which in turn cites the EA). The length of the semester has implications for the 'density' or 'compression' of hours. Attending to the ethnomethods of how committee members address this issue highlights two linked strategies used by teaching staff to express and legitimate their criticism of the model. I refer to these strategies as practice-based warrant, and prospective proxying.

> This is counting actual teaching weeks only. But things happen before and after the semester (subject outlines, tutors, set readings, marking, chasing up recalcitrant grades, withhelds, etc.). A great deal of activity takes place outside the 13 weeks. So it will be argued that either (a) we should model based on a 16 week semester, which would take the weighted figure to 20 hours per week ($32 \times 20 = 630$), or (b) we should have larger weightings.
> That is, the weightings are insufficient for the real hours.

The comment above concerns the weightings allocated to contact hours, the core mechanism of the draft model. The draft model allocates hypothetical hours to different teaching modes. These hypothetical hours can be before the contact hours (preparing lectures, etc.), or after (such as marking). The argument, that the weightings inappropriately 'squeeze' teaching activities, is one we could anticipate from teaching staff. It is justified by description of the practicalities of teaching preparation, administration, and assessment outside the bounds of the semester. This is *practice-based warrant*, whereby those most familiar with the work point out that the 'on paper' weightings do not capture the realities of practice.

The linked strategy, specifically in the phrase 'it will be argued that', is *prospective proxying*. Prospective proxying involves commenters implying that the model in its current form will not pass ratification. Again the document is oriented to as a durational process. This strategy is future-oriented: it conjures future opposition (from others) in the present. The reader is to understand that resolving the issue in the present will produce a more harmonious future. In another instance:

> These are very high and people will likely reject the document on those grounds.
> Is this given by the research active policy or the APF?
> The alternative numbers are more likely to get through ratification.

This example permits some more insight into prospective proxying ('people will likely reject'), considering how membership categorization analysis and conversation analysis describe how categories are produced and do moral work, and how alignment is expressed. With both 'it will be argued that' and 'people will likely reject', the following strategically significant features are evident: the vaguely threatening prospect is of future opposition from others (from an invoked category of experienced, and possibly combative academics). Those predicting that opposition thus use indirection: they 'channel' the prospect of opposition, rather than directly mounting it. They thereby dis-align from membership in the category of experienced academics (which they represent, and with whose joint experience their objections are legitimated), providing prognoses on their likely perspectives, whilst aligning to the joint project of ratification. This evinces a rhetorical or discursive strategy, but it is also a fundamentally social accomplishment and event.

The prospective proxying in the above instance is combined with a possibly rhetorical query in pursuit of an anterior referential definition. The clause being commented on enumerates the number of publications required per annum. The query seeks a source for the numbers: the Research Active Policy, or perhaps the Academic Performance Framework (APF), two other university policy documents. If the numbers can be shown to have been drawn from such a document, they might stick. If not, they will be problematized further.

Another strategy evident in the comments is the *expedience warrant*. It is expedient to have a concise, flexible, and navigable document. For this reason, the kind of granularity entailed by the comment to which the warrant is issued is counselled against. This strategy is directed to streamlining the document and the process of its production.

> This is too detailed for this document and will lock it to a point in time depending on workload processes in the schools. In good faith and as confidential documents the spreadsheets used by the schools can be reviewed by the FWRG.

The expedience warrant works to omit unnecessary elaboration or excessively detailed description from the draft. That which the expedience warrant truncates is often of great interest to staff: matters such as procedure, discretionary authority on the managerial side, and so on. Although the FWRG's work is institutionally mandated, the expedience warrant acknowledges that discussion in tracked commentary risks becoming a quagmire. In the example above, the expedience warrant blocks an unwieldy proposal, but does so with an assertion of the 'good faith' future for the FWRG, which is also a validation of the FWRG. The FWRG is where such matters would be discussed—not the workload model, for all to discuss.

Another strategy, commonly but not exclusively used by committee members representing management, is *deferral*:

> **Flagged for FWRG discussion**
> To be discussed by Chair and FWRG

Deferral is the execution of the expedience warrant. Deferral both acknowledges the validity of the prior comment, and forecloses further textual intervention by invoking the hierarchy of committee members ('the Chair') and presence required to address the comment.

Some gestures and strategies (for example, boss text invocation, or manoeuvres around stepwise anterior referential definition) are used by all parties. These are put to different ends, however, corresponding to how they are deployed within distinctive reading logics. These are reading for accountability and 'justice' (the 'paranoid' reading), indulged in most frequently by teaching staff, and reading for concision and flexibility, as practised by members representing management. This is a simple and predictable classification. Its relevance lies in how it can expose limits to reading strategies, especially the paranoid reading, given the organizational context in which that strategy operates.

Here we see a complementarity between ethnomethodological analysis of tracked marginalia ('inside' the document) and institutional ethnography of the workload document and its institutional circuit ('around' the document). The production of the draft encourages teaching staff to view the document critically. The staff's preoccupation with explicating the detail in the model, enculturated by their institutional position, limits their grasp of the longer-term effects of their strategy for dealing with the document. 'Paranoid' reading may lead to unwitting complicity with the managerial imperative to cost efficiency. Two examples can demonstrate this.

> There is still no account for whyseminars [sic] are weighted this way, or why a tutorial couldn't just be called a seminar. People will probably ask about this.

Here prospective proxying, in the service of the paranoid reading, is used to query the distinction in weighting between seminars and tutorials. There is a question of 'justice'. The time of disciplines conducting seminars has more value. From the perspective of staff in disciplines conducting tutorials, this discrepancy is unfair and arbitrary. Perhaps their tutorials could be relabelled as seminars, to enhance their temporal value. Perhaps this is a reasonable line of questioning. It is a line of questioning, however, which accords with the budgetary objectives management are obliged to meet. The example above illustrates a form of negative solidarity: if I cannot have it, nor should you. Will all tutorials come to be weighted as seminars, or will all seminars come to be weighted as tutorials? Teaching staff should be able to predict the answer to this question.

> This should say what the maximum number of PhD candidates an individual
> academic can have is, and it should also probably stipulate a preferred minimum.
> **Flagged for FWRG discussion**

Here we see another example where the paranoid reading accords with the interests of faculty management. This results in a *specificity trap*. The expectation that the model should clarify and allocate an equitable temporal value (or cost) to academic activities enhances the view and control of management, and expands the range of practices under the domain of commensurable cost efficiency. The paranoid reading is a disciplinary accomplice to managerial control, inviting not only costing, but also further specification of the range of work, for example of how many PhD candidates an individual *should* supervise so as to 'perform' appropriately. The paranoid reading serves the control function.

Ethnomethodological analysis of the design of tracked changes communication makes visible the interactional strategies and readerly logics committee members deploy. Prospective proxying, practice-based warrant, the expedience warrant, and deferral are all 'interior' to exchange within the document, they are textual actions and expressions, directed to negotiation of how the document formulates workload. Situating these strategies and logics in an institutional ethnographic frame permits an assessment of their merits and implications in the broader institutional field.

The Organizational Affordances of Tracked Changes

The section above consisted of an empirically driven analysis and critique of interactional and discursive strategies in tracked changes. Such analysis and critique demonstrate that looking at tracked changes, and looking in this way, is productive to an understanding of the organization and conduct of work. Further benefits to the approach become evident when we take a step back to consider the organizational use of tracked changes. The technology and the routine social practices of tracked changes have organizational affordances, in the same way that other communicative technologies have social, political, and cultural affordances (Tiidenberg and Whelan 2019). The preceding discussion shows that commentary in tracked changes is double-edged. It works, and does not work, as a communicative site. The ways that it works and does not work are related.

It works in that it provides a backchannel for organizational communication, and especially for informal upward communication. Sensitive issues which are difficult to raise publicly, and about which reticence is exhibited in other media (for example, email between staff and management) can be explored in FWRG tracked changes. This is partly because the tracked changes are on the salient document itself, but it is also because of how the circulation of the draft and the technology of tracked changes itself invite this use. Tracked changes thus play an important diplomatic or political role in negotiations about the workload model. The guarantee of this effectiveness lies, paradoxically, in how tracked changes commentary doesn't work.

It does not work in that it is not embedded in any substantive mechanism for ensuring commentary is acted on, or even remembered. The commentary in tracked changes therefore implies a kind of textual immediacy. This commentary, we might say, exhibits the viscosity of organizational documentation. The final workload model will not have any marginalia: its negotiation will be erased. A ratified workload model would exhibit no memory of how the document itself coalesced. At that point, the document will have entered textual time. But at this prior point, where tracked changes are available for view, the document remains liquid. Nothing is completely fixed. There is porosity between the formal content of the document and its marginalia. The time of the document is closer to the immediate. Tracked changes occur in a documentary time which is not the lifetime of the meeting, but also not the static textual time of the final model. Tracked changes occur in an interstitial time.

The informality of tracked changes permits organizationally delicate dialogue. At the same time, this informality consigns that dialogue and its social and political value to oblivion. There is no mechanism whereby the observations expressed in tracked changes flow through to new versions of the process. Old workload model drafts and the labour and commentary invested in them and in their tracked changes disappear. This can be understood as a standard feature of administration: the right to forget. The right to forget gives parties room for manoeuvre when it comes to the next round, or when the committee is reconvened with new membership. At the same time, the onus of recovery of the historical and institutional memory is thereby placed on individual committee members and administrators. Negotiation erasure consistently involves a kind of institutional forgetting about why things are the way they are and how they came to be this way, a fundamental feature of the operation of social power. While the institution and all working parties in it maintain an acute interest in efficiency and economy with respect to workflow and work process, it is incongruous that the very document through which workload is formalized and administered is produced in this ad hoc and technically inefficient way. The perverse satisfaction in this particular case is, therefore, that there is 'organized inefficiency' in the very production of the document ostensibly designed for the purposes of formalizing labour intensification.

Evaluating Tracked Commentary as a Research Site

While the application of institutional ethnography and ethnomethodology to documents is well established, there are various issues to consider in using these kinds of documents. One issue is ethics. It could be ethically problematic to analyse such documents without prior informed consent from those producing the tracked commentary. Were it possible to secure such consent, however, the commentary, and thus the research, would be different. I did not seek prior consent, because I did not consider the material as data until after I left the FWRG. I did not seek consent after the fact either, because the risks to individuals seem negligible to me. Commentary is produced *ex officio*, in terms of incumbency of institutionally mandated roles. The data are anonymized, and there is no analytical attention on the individuals involved. Another issue is access. This concerns organizational and business process confidentiality, and the researcher's orientation to and relationship with the organization, rather than human research ethics. Some level of access is required to know these documents exist and access them. If I had not been on the committee, I might never have given tracked commentary much thought, or reflected on what it indicates about organizational communication.

The documents involved here are quite specific, but many workplaces produce documents in similar ways, which are similarly consequential to local or broader contexts. Researchers conducting fieldwork may be able to access such documents. Depending on operational sensitivity and the stringency of confidentiality processes, some documents of this kind will increasingly be stored in electronic archives. Legislative documents, documents in criminal cases, higher level policy and budget documents, corporate finance documents, documents that circulate through institutions such as political parties, corporate boards, and intelligence agencies, are all likely to be a good deal more sensitive than a draft faculty workload model, and yet to also have similar backchannel marginalia associated with them. The epitextual or paratextual material around these documents is sometimes made available to journalists. Scrutiny by academics is irregular, and indeed, rarer than it should be. Were such scrutiny more common, we might have better insight into how we are governed.

A further issue is that, as with any analysis directed towards mediated communication, the approach described here is bound by software design features which differ across both operating systems and versions of software. Original tracked commentary was assembled using a version of Word which automatically time- and date-stamped all comments. The version of Word on which this document was prepared does not make this information immediately visible. It is not possible to predict how future versions of Word or other word processing software might handle tracked changes.

These issues must be assessed relative to possibly useful features of the approach. There is one immediate and evident useful feature, which is that without this kind of attention, we would not be able to make the concrete observations which have been made here about the paradoxical oddities of irreflexive or 'unmanaged' circulation of documents. There are further benefits relative to the literatures described at the beginning of this chapter. The approach developed here works to sharpen the criti- cal teeth of ethnomethodological orientations to media forms in workplace contexts. The ethnomethods shown in tracked marginalia demonstrate how forms of reading and writing in the workplace can (rightly) be inherently political. This accords with the tacit politics of Garfinkel's position, especially in his early work (Garfinkel 1956; Doubt 1989).

Further benefit derived from the work presented here highlights the role of material media in participation in workplace decision-making, pertinent to critical university studies (CUS) and to the study of work and organization more broadly. CUS often refers to generic, inadequately specified phenomena: 'discourse', 'neolib- eralism', and so on. Tracked changes are an affordance of the design of Microsoft Word documents. This affordance is already ideological or political, insofar as it dis- tinguishes between the body of the text and marginalia, on the text but not of it. This feature of the Word document, skeuomorphic with and derived from the circu- lation of drafts in paper form, has organizational affordances which are more than convenient in their implications. The temporality of document stabilization oriented to tracked changes, the tactical use of tracked changes as a diplomatic backchan- nel, the forms of reading and writing evidenced in tracked changes, are afforded by the technology. This technical aspect of the format of the document is thus conse- quential: media and organizational form are entangled. The analytical approach set out here thus empirically grounds organizational communication and discourse in media forms.

Finally, I hope that the approach described in this chapter will help to develop methodical, analytical, and practical specificity for critical accounts of workplace organization and communication, and for critical studies of the university such as those described at the beginning of this chapter. This would accord with Smith's orig- inal aspirations for institutional ethnography: a sociology for people, intended and designed to enable individuals to see and understand the administrative processes by which they are governed. The hope would be that enhancing such understanding would in turn serve as a means by which workplace decision-making could be made more meaningfully participatory.

References

Alvesson, M., Gabriel, Y., and Paulsen, R.. 2017. *Return to Meaning: A Social Science with Something to Say*. Oxford: Oxford University Press.

Arminen, I. 2017. *Institutional Interaction: Studies of Talk at Work*. London: Routledge.

Ball, S. 2003. The Teacher's Soul and the Terrors of Performativity. *Journal of Education Policy*, 18(2): pp. 215–28.

Bousquet, M. 2008. *How the University Works: Higher Education and the Low-Wage Nation*. New York: New York University Press.

Burrows, R. 2012. Living with the H-Index? Metric assemblages in the contemporary academy. *The Sociological Review*, 60(2): pp. 355–72.

Burstow, B. (ed.). 2016. *Psychiatry Interrogated: An Institutional Ethnography Anthology*. Cham: Palgrave Macmillan.

Chatterjee, P., and Maira, S. (eds). 2014. *The Imperial University: Academic Repression and Scholarly Dissent*. Minnesota: University of Minnesota Press.

Connell, R. 2019. *The Good University: What Universities Actually Do and Why it's Time for Radical Change*. London: Zed Books.

Docherty, T. 2011. *For the University: Democracy and the Future of the Institution*. London: Bloomsbury Academic.

Doll, A., and Walby, K. 2019. Institutional ethnography as a method of inquiry for criminal justice and socio-legal studies. *International Journal for Crime, Justice and Social Democracy*, 8(1): pp. 147.

Doubt, K. 1989. Garfinkel Before Ethnomethodology. *The American Sociologist*, 20(3): pp. 252–62.

Fitzgerald, R., and Housley, W. (eds). 2015. *Advances in Membership Categorisation Analysis*. London: Sage.

Garfinkel, H. 1956. Conditions of Successful Degradation Ceremonies. *American Journal of Sociology*, 61(5): pp. 420–24.

Garfinkel, H. 1967. *Studies in Ethnomethodology*. Englewood Cliffs: Prentice-Hall.

Garfinkel, H. (ed.). 2005. *Ethnomethodological Studies of Work*. London: Routledge.

Garfinkel, H., and Bittner, E. 1967. 'Good' Organizational reasons for 'Bad' Clinic Records. In Garfinkel, H. (ed.), *Studies in Ethnomethodology* (pp. 186–207). Englewood Cliffs: Prentice-Hall.

Gill, R. 2016. Breaking the silence: The hidden injuries of neo-liberal academia. *Feministische Studien*, 34 (1): pp. 39–55.

Giroux, H. 2020. *On Critical Pedagogy*. London: Bloomsbury Publishing.

Gutiérrez Y Muhs, G., Niemann, Y., González, C., and Harris, A. (eds). 2012. *Presumed Incompetent: The Intersections of Race and Class for Women in Academia*. Logan: Utah State University Press.

Heritage, J., and Clayman, S. 2011. *Talk in Action: Interactions, Identities, and Institutions*. Chichester: Wiley-Blackwell.

Hutchby, I., and Wooffitt, R. 2008. *Conversation Analysis*. London: Polity.

Jayyusi, L. 2014. *Categorization and the Moral Order*. London: Routledge.

Johnson, K., and Bagatell, N. 2019. Negotiating tensions on the front line: Circuits of accountability and self-governance in institutional care of adults with intellectual disability. *Work, Employment and Society*, 34(4): pp. 644–60.

Kameo, N., and Whalen, J. 2015. Organizing documents: Standard forms, person production and organizational action. *Qualitative Sociology*, 38(2): pp. 205–29.

Kinderman, W., and Jones, J. (eds). 2009. *Genetic Criticism and the Creative Process: Essays from Music, Literature, and Theater*. Rochester: University of Rochester Press.

Law, J. 2004. *After Method: Mess in Social Science Research*. London: Routledge.

Liberman, K. 2013. *More Studies in Ethnomethodology*. Albany: SUNY Press.

Lindqvist, S. 1979. 'Dig where you stand'. *Oral History*, 7(2): pp. 24–30.

Llewellyn, N., and Hindmarsh, J. (eds). 2010. *Organisation, Interaction and Practice: Studies of Ethnomethodology and Conversation Analysis*. Cambridge: Cambridge University Press.

Lorenz, C. 2012. If you're so smart, why are you under surveillance? Universities, neoliberalism, and new public management'. *Critical Inquiry*, 38(3): pp. 599–629.

Marginson, S. 2013. The impossibility of capitalist markets in higher education. *Journal of Education Policy*, 28(3): pp. 353–70.

Mondada, L., and Svinhufvud, K. 2016. Writing-in-interaction: Studying writing as a multimodal phenomenon in social interaction. *Language and Dialogue*, 6(1): pp. 1–53.

Newfield, C. 2016. *The Great Mistake: How We Wrecked Public Universities and How We Can Fix Them*. Baltimore: Johns Hopkins University Press.

Ovetz, R. 2020. *Workers' Inquiry and Global Class Struggle: Strategies, Tactics, Objectives*. London: Pluto Press.

Petrina, S., and Ross, E. 2014. Critical university studies: *Workplace*, milestones, crossroads, respect, truth. *Workplace: A Journal for Academic Labor*, 23. doi: https://doi.org/10.14288/workplace.v0i23.184777.

Rooksby, J. 2016. Text at work: Mundane practices of reading in workplaces. In Rouncefield, M. and Tolmie, P. (eds), *Ethnomethodology at Work*, (pp. 199–216). London: Routledge.

Rouncefield, M., and Tolmie, P. (eds). 2016. *Ethnomethodology at Work*. London: Routledge.

Russell, L., and Reid, J. 2019. Institutional ethnography in education. In Paul Atkinson, Sara Delamont, Alexandru Cernat, Joseph W. Sakshaug and Richard A. Williams (eds), *Sage Research Methods Foundations*. Thousand Oaks: Sage Publications.

Sabri, D. 2013. Student evaluations of teaching as 'fact-totems': The case of the UK National Student Survey. *Sociological Research Online*, 18(4): pp. 148–57.

Sharpe, M., and Turner, K. 2018. Bibliopolitics: The history of notation and the birth of the citational academic subject. *Foucault Studies*, 25: pp. 146–73.

Smith, D. 1990. *The Conceptual Practices of Power: A Feminist Sociology of Knowledge*. Toronto: University of Toronto Press.

Smith, D. 2005. *Institutional Ethnography: A Sociology for People*. Walnut Creek: Rowman Altamira.

Smith, D., and Turner, S. (eds). 2014. *Incorporating Texts into Institutional Ethnographies*. Toronto: University of Toronto Press.

Sutton, P. 2017. Lost souls? The demoralization of academic labour in the measured university. *Higher Education Research and Development*, 36(3): pp. 625–36.

Thiel, J. 2019. The UK National Student Survey: An amalgam of discipline and neo-liberal governmentality. *British Educational Research Journal*, 45(3): pp. 538–53.

Tiidenberg, K., and A. Whelan. 2019. 'Not like that, not for that, not by them': Social media affordances of critique. *Communication and Critical/Cultural Studies*, 16(2): pp. 83–102.

University of Wollongong. 2015. University of Wollongong (Academic Staff) Enterprise Agreement, viewed 27 November 2020, <https://staff.uow.edu.au/content/groups/public/@web/@personnel/document/doc/uow197995.pdf>.

Vostal, F. 2016. *Accelerating Academia: The Changing Structure of Academic Time*. New York: Springer.

Watson, R. 2016. *Analysing Practical and Professional Texts: A Naturalistic Approach*. London: Routledge.

Williamson, B. 2020. Making markets through digital platforms: Pearson, edu-business, and the (e)valuation of higher education. *Critical Studies in Education*, doi: 10.1080/17508487.2020.1737556

18

Conclusion

Reflections on Ethics, Skills, and Future Challenges in Research Methods for Digital Work and Organizations

Christine Hine, Katrina Pritchard, and Gillian Symon

Introduction

When we first started to work on this volume, we knew that the distributed, multi-modal, and mobile forms of work that we collected together under the banner of digital work and organizations were growing phenomena. The steady increase in digitization showed no signs of abating, as datafication and digital communication colonized work and leisure spaces alike. It was then, and remains, clear that researchers interested in understanding work experiences, management practices, and organizational structures would need to develop skills in investigating digital phenomena and that this need would become more pressing as time went on. We also knew that this enterprise could present ethical challenges, as digital data have the potential to breach expectations of privacy and researchers may repurpose data in unexpected ways. In addition, as we write our concluding comments at the beginning of 2021, reflecting across the chapters collected here and considering their significance, we also have to consider the ways in which the world of digital work, and indeed the world as a whole, has changed in response to the Covid-19 pandemic. In this concluding chapter we first reflect on the ethical stance that our authors have taken in relation to their research, examining the ways in which they have navigated the complexities of public online spaces and proprietary data and looking at developments on the horizon. We also consider the nature of the skills that our authors have brought to bear on their research challenges and reflect on the training, resources, and interdisciplinary connections that will enable future researchers to grapple with the constantly expanding yet diverse and unpredictable terrain of digital work. Finally, we draw together reflections on the impact of the pandemic and highlight the significance of the methods collected here as we move into the post-pandemic phase of research into digital work.

Christine Hine, Katrina Pritchard, and Gillian Symon, *Conclusion*. In: *Research Methods for Digital Work and Organization.*
Edited by Gillian Symon, Katrina Pritchard, and Christine Hine, Oxford University Press.
© Oxford University Press (2021). DOI: 10.1093/oso/9780198860679.003.0018

Ethics and Digital Work Research

As described above, there is an ethical position embedded in our choice of research focus and our decisions on where and how to intervene. There is also a strong ethical dimension to *how* we carry out our research. In this section we draw together thoughts on the ethical decisions that have challenged the authors in this volume as they carry out their research and look to future challenges on the horizon. In doing so, we build on the lively and thoughtful history of discussions across disciplines around the ethics of research into digital phenomena and particularly in relation to business and management research (Whiting and Pritchard 2017). We explore the ethical principles our authors adhered to and highlight their solutions to issues of publicness, vulnerability, and legitimate interest in relation to research into digital work.

Ethical guidelines for digital research focus on the need for researchers to conduct a situated evaluation of their ethical responsibilities on each occasion, rather than being able to apply a pre-existing set of rules determined by the characteristics of the digital platforms being studied. The British Sociological Association (2016), for example, counsels researchers to operate according to situated ethics and an ethics of care, while the Association of Internet Researchers (2019) offers a framework for researchers to evaluate the degrees of publicness of data alongside sensitivity and risk to participants, taking a cross-cultural and pluralist approach to ethics. It is noted that user expectations for privacy often deviate from the objective qualities of platforms. Users cannot, practically speaking, exercise a continual caution about the traces they are leaving, and cannot therefore be said to have consented in any meaningful way simply by using a digital platform in a way that leaves a trace. Gray (2017) calls for researchers to operate with respect, build trust, and expect mutuality, and notes that it is problematic for researchers to behave as if data are simply there for the taking.

From an ethical perspective, using unobtrusive methods online means that individual workers are participating in the research unknowingly, apparently violating one of the fundamental underpinnings of research ethics, informed consent. However, digital data are often assumed to be in the public domain and not requiring consent, in turn, raising the complex issue of the repurposing of data for goals not originally envisioned. Researchers thus need to consider whether scraping and publishing data from platforms is ethically suspect even if practically possible and take specific, nuanced steps to protect the authors of data from harm, whether by protecting anonymity or negotiating consent. Issues of ethics and copyright may also intersect here and researchers' employing institutions, publishers, and funding bodies may wish to have a say. We may also need to operate different sensitivities, depending on whether we are dealing with textual or visual data. In the current volume, and guided by our publishers, we have taken a very cautious approach to the reproduction of social media material, and particularly images without consent, in order to avoid both copyright breach and inadvertent harms. Researchers focused on digital work must take into account power relations and institutional players in the context of working relations and workplace hierarchies but also in relation to the social media platforms. We may need to incorporate into our ethical considerations the changing conditions of mutual visibility in digital contexts that Leonardi and Treem (2020) highlight and note that we should not be guilty of subjecting the participants in our research to inappropriate digital surveillance. We may need to refrain from following people between the spaces reflected in our data if people choose to keep them separate just as boyd (2014) opted not to follow the teenaged participants in her study of social media across online and offline spaces.

For the ethnographers in this volume who visited face-to-face settings (Bailey at al, Coletta, and Grommé) the most challenging ethical issues were posed by shadowing participants at work, raising concerns as to whether they were truly able to consent freely, or were constrained by existing work hierarchies and whether consent can be maintained as participants switch between relatively public and relatively private activities across different devices and platforms. Grommé found that sometimes it was important to respect privacy, rather than pushing to what is hidden behind a participant's screen. As Bailey and colleagues note, it is also difficult to anonymize fieldnotes when you describe activities with such detail and specificity. Their solutions involved care over the sharing of their raw data and focusing their observations on participants who did not seem unduly concerned by the attention. Unlike some contexts of digital interaction we might observe, at least in this instance the participants were fully aware they were being observed and the researchers could adjust to visible signs of concern in response to the intrusion.

Arguably, autoethnographers tread a particularly complex ethical territory. For Badger, the key ethical issue was the covert nature of the research as he took on a full participant role as a delivery rider. He was open about his researcher status with fellow riders that he wished to interview, but did not disclose his study to the owners of the platform and also could not gain consent for all of the fleeting interactions that made up the experience of being a delivery rider. The focus of his observation is the platform and his own experiences with the platform. He notes that it is unlikely the platform would have given permission for an overt study, also that taking this position required extensive and ongoing ethical review from his university. Direct involvement in the setting where digital traces are produced can inform ethical sensitivity: Whelan analysed the comments on a document that he had himself been involved in constructing and hence was able to evaluate the context and assess the availability of the in-text comments for scrutiny. Hine discusses some of the different positions that autoethnographers can take in relation to consent, key among them being a sensitivity to the others implicated in an autoethnographic account. This concern does not change in any fundamental sense when the autoethnography deals with digital activities, but the digital context potentially increases the scope of those drawn into the autoethnographic account and the autoethnographer needs to take responsibility for determining what it is appropriate to say about them.

A number of our authors set out to conduct fully consented research in which participants cooperated in data collection with full knowledge of the researchers' intentions although it is notable that even here there were concerns about the extent to which consent could be comprehensive. In the study reported by Rozas and Huckle the ethnographer attempted to make participation overt, through declarations of their researcher role both when co-present in person and on digital platforms associated with the community. The limitations of the awareness that can be built in this way in large events and forums are acknowledged. Jarrahi and colleagues stress the importance of informed consent, not just at the outset of participation but throughout the diary-keeping and beyond. The authors point out that diary methods may encourage over-sharing by respondents and that the opportunity to withdraw data may therefore be necessary. It is also important to consider whether diary data may capture the voices and images of third parties beyond the consented participants. For Willment, the travel blogs that are the focus of this netnography were viewed as public sites and hence available for study without consent—however, in this case the study was conducted overtly with informed consent for interviews and to study the activities of travel bloggers across blog posts and other social media. Pseudonyms were used, but it is noted that quotations from blogs could be traced back to their origin and hence full anonymity could not be promised to participants whose material was quoted and this was drawn to the attention of participants. Beyond the core set of participants, comments left on blogs were treated as available for analysis by virtue of being posted in the public domain, but usernames were obscured.

Beyond consent, Savage and colleagues framed their participants as partners in the research. This action research required a close attention to the activities of workers on the platform in question. The researchers aimed to ensure that workers were paid appropriately for the efforts they put into the study via the platform itself. They also protected anonymity and focused on the behaviours of the collective rather than interrogating the behaviours of any individual. This does not, however, solve wider ethical concerns with the ownership and application of the data generated in this way. The researchers propose a way forwards that would involve an open repository of such data accompanied by provision for equitable access to tools aimed at helping crowd workers.

Whilst those dealing directly with participants focused on consent, and alongside that, respect, trust, and appropriate recognition or anonymization for the context, somewhat different solutions were operationalized by many of those dealing with publicly available social media data, especially at scale. Castello et al. provide a useful overview of the complex territory that surrounds ethical decision-making on the use of social media data. They highlight in particular the importance of careful risk assessment focused on the potential for privacy infringement and harms to users of social media. In the specific case they described, the researchers took a cautious approach in which the social media data were not viewed in isolation but were part of a complex of research methods. Consent from the main actors was acquired in the context of one-to-one interviews, whilst the research was made overt to a broader array of social media users through announcements within the social media platform. Finally, the researchers sought to protect the data through anonymization, taking into account that a direct quotation can be searchable back to the original context in which it was made. Sergi and Bonneau included only publicly available posts in their study and advocate taking steps to reduce the identifiability of any examples published, by blurring images and removing identifying text. Jemielniak and Stasik similarly highlighted that we cannot assume that public tweeting means that a user should be singled out for attention by researchers. Their solution was only to use direct quotations from tweets that are already highly visible, for example from figures with a public profile. This decision highlights the need for nuance in addressing the 'publicness' of social media data since even public tweets may need sensitive treatment when we transfer them to a research context. There is also a temporal dimension to ethical choices, since publicly available data may subsequently be amended or deleted from its original context.

Beyond concerns for privacy, some data that researchers might access online may have potentially serious consequences for the security of digital workers. This is so for the discussions collected by Bucher and colleagues from Reddit. Although participants already use nicknames, and hence their real identity is anonymous throughout, the researchers advise taking a cautious approach towards anonymity, removing any details that could potentially lead to identification and using pseudonyms for nicknames. This is particularly important here since the discussions often relate to critical perspectives on employers. A similar approach was taken by Wilner and colleagues analysing data drawn from Glassdoor. The comments on Glassdoor are made anonymously, thus precluding any attempt by the researchers to gain informed consent for their use. The researchers did not use the names of the organizations in presenting their analysis and took care not to present unusual or identifiable examples.

The authors in this collection have thus taken various stances on the publicness and availability of digital data and have sought to develop situated, nuanced, and above all ethically careful approaches to their data and their relations with participants in the research. In addition, a developing ethics in relation to the platforms that enable and constrain so much digital work is also apparent. The ethical stance in Rogers' work relies upon giving us the tools to undertake a critical analysis of issues of voice and attention within social media platforms, rather than simply accepting as givens the conditions that the platforms create. This is an ethic of examining the otherwise taken-for-granted of public discourse as enacted online, and as such often focuses on institutions rather than private individuals and takes these as available for critique in virtue of their publicness. Such a stance connects with an important live issue on research ethics as they come into contact with issues of data protection, proprietary ownership, and governance. Researchers in digital work have increasingly argued in recent times that it is necessary for them to be able to scrutinize the operation of digital platforms without an a priori constraint on the research agenda from the terms and conditions of those platforms. This issue will continue to be argued as the wider debate on the appropriate forms of governance and scrutiny for digital platforms continues to develop and it is one with which our ethical review bodies will need to grapple.

Skills and the Digital Work Researcher

As digital work becomes an even more important focus of research scrutiny, it is timely to consider what critical and technical skills researchers will need to draw upon due to the specifically digital nature of the phenomena they study and what training will be needed as a result. We take for granted that these researchers will need thorough grounding in the principles and practice of social science research according to the nature of their discipline. Methodological principles endure across settings and a strong competence in research design, rigorous analysis, and critical thinking is needed whatever the context. Indeed, some researchers will need to be competent in more than one method: methodological mixing has been common-place within Internet research (Hine 2015) and the research agenda of digital work post-pandemic, as Budhwar and Cummings (2020) note, is likely to contain large and complex problems that require multi-disciplinary attention. From reviewing the chapters in this volume we can see that there are some competences and foci of training that would be particularly useful to develop, although these competencies need not all reside within a single researcher and collaborations will also be key.

For researchers who observe work (whether paid or voluntary), there is a recurrent question around the extent to which they need to be or become competent in that domain of work themselves, whether in order to gain access to the setting or to be able fully to explore their research agenda. Bailey and colleagues reflect on their efforts to acquire sufficient technical understanding and vocabulary to be able to follow the flow of work that participants carried out and understand the significance of their actions. Notably this was a team-based ethnography, allowing for activities to be shared out and complementary roles taken, such as observing the same activity for different aspects. Grommé was also present in the physical location as an observer but often unable fully to be a participant in the work because of the need for specific technical skills and the confidential nature of the work. However, there was a focus on developing an understanding of the work through observing and interacting as far as possible and attending to the role of various technological platforms and devices in the work. For an ethnographer who works to step into the role of participants, greater demands are placed on technical competence. As autoethnographers, Badger and Hine both had to be able to carry out the digital work that they sought to understand. Badger needed to develop the skills to hold down the job that he was studying and take on the physical risks that this entailed, but in addition had to develop skills of fieldnote taking whilst performing the job, all on a single device. To achieve this he added in additional tools such as the use of Strava to track journeys and a Go-Pro camera to record video, alongside the apps necessary to do the job. He used text and voice notes, photos and screenshots, building a complex array of different components to his fieldnotes, which in turn required him to develop additional skills of building synthesis across multiple sources.

Ethnographers need an additional skill set beyond technical understanding to follow the activities of participants, in that they need the skill to maintain their own research agenda too. Hine reflects on the demands on the ethnographer to develop the skills needed to operate effectively in the setting and to appreciate the experiences of other participants whilst also maintaining a reflexive distance to be able to comment on the experience and connect with broader social and cultural themes. This inevitably limits access: some domains are accessible to an autoethnographer, but only if we are plausibly able to gain membership and acquire the skills. This means that some domains may be out of reach of autoethnography unless we can recruit existing members to analyse their own experiences. In the study described by Rozas and Huckle, the ethnographer had previously been a full participant in the community as a software developer. This provided access into the scene and also a level of technical understanding of activities that would have been difficult for someone without a technical background to acquire quickly. As they reflect, the insider role does bring drawbacks, however, in the potential for over-familiarity leading to a neglect of issues that could be investigated and also the biases that come from having over-familiarity with one specific role. Key to Coletta's methodological point is that the ethnographer needs to develop the skills of alternating between immersion in the various temporalities of the field and the temporal structures of their own fieldwork schedule. Coletta was part of a team conducting the ethnography: this required the team to develop the means to coordinate the work of data collection and synthesis across the researchers, including shared spreadsheets and team sessions working together on the data.

Some researchers draw on what might be termed everyday competencies of the digital world. Whelan's method, for example, involved applying an ethnomethodological lens to the traces captured in the 'track changes' feature of word processing software. Technically speaking, therefore, the method draws on the everyday competences of the user of word processing software. Willment's netnography required a familiarity with the blogging platforms and social media sites that travel bloggers made use of, and the ability to save and take screenshots of material as it was encountered in order to maintain a record of the fieldwork. After identifying the sample of Glassdoor reviews of interest, Wilner and colleagues downloaded these using a simple copy/paste operation: a technique that was suitable here because the sample was relatively small and the text of the reviews was the key interest rather than the data having any complex network structure that needed to be preserved. A manual qualitative analysis was carried out. The only technical skills required were an ability to use the search and filter facilities of the site. Jemielniak and Stasik set out to showcase the use of tools for scraping and analysing Twitter that do not require the researcher to develop programming skills. Nonetheless, there is a considerable degree of skill to acquire in choosing the right tools and the right data to provide meaningful results and developing the understanding required to interpret the results. Tools for social media scraping and analysis are quite volatile, as are the social media platforms themselves, and the availability of free-to-use tools depends on developers having the resources and commitment to maintain them. Whilst using such tools may not require a highly technical background, it does come with a need for a degree of investment in developing and maintaining awareness.

It is useful to read Jemielniak and Stasik's advice on using ready-made tools for scraping and analysing social media alongside the discussion by Castello et al. about the scope and affordances of big data analysis using social media data and the need for a careful development of research strategies. It is also important to remember that methodological approaches often do not come to us ready-made, especially when we are re-purposing existing tools. Sergi and Bonneau discuss the process of 'tinkering with' method as we go along, developing methodological solutions in tandem with the process of research. The researchers used an emergent search strategy on social media platforms, gradually refining their understanding of the data of interest and developing search strategies that enabled them to locate them—for Twitter this was facilitated by Tweetdeck, a tool that allows for saved searches. Data capture was done manually, using screen capture and logging details of the post and user in Word or Excel, followed by a manual thematic analysis of the resulting dataset. Technically-speaking, nothing beyond basic user skills is required but methodologically speaking a careful process of sifting and refinement is going on. As emphasized in the Introduction, researchers need to understand the ways in which 'data' are shaped by platforms such that the phenomena of interest take different forms in different contexts. This is as true for images as text, as demonstrated in Pearce et al.'s (2020) work on visual representations across platforms.

Some researchers who are interested in digital work build on tools that are becoming widely used across the social sciences for gathering data from participants. As Jarrahi and colleagues recount, various different technological approaches to collecting diary data are available—from simple spreadsheets and text-messaging to more complex multi-modal approaches and tailored solutions. In this study the diary was implemented using survey platform Qualtrics and participants were emailed a link to remind them to complete the diary survey. They could complete multiple choice and open questions and add photos. The diary needed to be tested on multiple devices and platforms. Qualtrics provides a relatively easy to learn platform for hosting a diary that means researchers do not have to code their own app. This diary approach works best if participants have constant access to a suitable device—in this case, since the study focused on nomadic workers, their access to a suitable device could pretty much be guaranteed, but this would not always be the case for other participant groups. We note that such approaches have considerable utility for capturing reflections on the experiences of digital work when researchers' ability to spend time with participants in physical spaces is relatively limited, for example as dictated by the social distancing measures attendant on the pandemic.

For other researchers in this collection, a distinctive set of digital research skills that require further competence in programming come to the fore. This is particularly the case where the research is conducted at a greater scale than ready-to-use tools can support or where the researcher needs greater control over the parameters or assumptions embedded in their analytic tools. Rogers advances a 'critical analytics' of social media, examining the nature and role of the performance metrics provided by social media platforms and proposing an alternative approach focused on exploring the networking of social issues across such platforms. Rogers outlines a set of analytic concepts that comprise a critical analytic stance—operationalizing these concepts draws on a set of tools for scraping and visualization of data from social media platforms. These tools require a close understanding of and skill in engagement with the social media platforms and often also programming skills to develop suitable tools for scraping and visualization. This is particularly the case in the methods developed by Savage and colleagues for action research with platform workers. Their approach depended on a substantial array of technical skills, including the use of JavaScript to develop the browser plug-in to collect data on worker behaviours, database development skills to connect with the plug-in and collect the data, and also data science skills to analyse the patterns emergent in the data.

This requirement to draw on an extensive array of technical skills to conduct research is particularly the case when studies employ multiple methods. Castello and colleagues assembled methods that drew on a number of different technical and analytic skills, including both qualitative and quantitative, spanning large-scale and automated and in-depth, hands-on approaches. The study also spanned multiple social media platforms, scraping data via the API. Their automated analysis involved the use of NLP (natural language processing) to identify sentiment within social media posts, with the algorithm refined through qualitative analysis. Bucher and colleagues also took a multimodal approach to the analysis of social media data, focusing on the presentation and sharing of images in addition to their analysis of the emotion-work done in text. The researchers conducted a large-scale analysis of online community using data mining techniques. They wrote their own script to scrape the data using Python to access the Reddit API and then filtered the resulting dataset using a custom dictionary to identify posts relevant to their research questions. Programming language R was then used to clean and standardize the data before conducting a clustering analysis to identify a network structure of clusters of dictionary terms often discussed together. A qualitative analysis of these clusters was then carried out to explore the meanings within each cluster. By combining the large-scale approach of cluster analysis drawing on programming techniques for scraping, cleaning, and analysing the data with an inductive qualitative analysis, the authors aimed to explore both the structure and meaning within the data. However, they acknowledged that a large multidisciplinary team of researchers may be needed in order to provide the necessary array of skills.

The Covid-19 Pandemic and Future of Digital Work

The research methods, skills, and ethical sensitivities displayed by the contributors to this volume are set to become more relevant than ever for business and management research. The societal crisis of the Covid-19 pandemic and the measures taken to control the spread of the virus have in a short time produced a 'radical transformation of the space-time of everyday life' (Fuchs 2020, 378). Notable within this transformation have been changes in the organization of working life for many people. In the space of a few months, the proportion of the population working digitally from home underwent a massive upshift as, in response to the restrictions on movement and interaction designed to reduce the spread of Covid-19, many people started to work at home in response to government advice. Whilst it is fortuitous that suitable digital technologies were available to make it possible for many people to achieve their working tasks without going to a physical office, it must be acknowledged that this shift to home working has not been easily achieved. The mere availability of suitable technologies does not mean that organizations or individuals are ready to use them. Such a rapid transformation placed immense pressures on organizations to implement change at pace and entailed huge strains on workers often adapting to non-ideal conditions and lack of resources and often at fear for their livelihoods. Home-working, for many, entailed juggling the demands of caring and home-schooling. Having previously been a choice or luxury for many who practised it, working from home became in many cases an enforced practice (Waizenegger 2020). Whilst the immediate shift to digital working from home was a response to the specific requirement for social distancing, these changes may be difficult to reverse in full when restrictions are lifted. Whilst some workers will return to the office, there are widely held views that working from home will endure beyond pandemic-related restrictions (Nagel 2020). Attendant on the increase in the number of people working digitally from home, there was also an increase in the extent of datafication as an increasing array of daily activities and work tasks were being conducted via digital platforms (Risi et al. 2020). This aspect of the digital shift may also be difficult to reverse. These challenging times have brought us a radical and possibly enduring shift in the numbers of people engaged in distributed forms of digital work and in the extent of daily working activities conducted via digital platforms.

Such a shift brings challenges for researchers hoping to understand and influence for good in the realms of contemporary working practices. Budhwar and Cummings (2020) counsel that urgency to do research should not lead to compromised rigour. They suggest that we need to take care to develop new research instruments and methods that attend to current circumstances but also that we need to be conscious of the different cultural contexts within which our research must operate and be careful to examine the provenance of data that might become available. This point about critical attention to the underlying phenomena that scrapable data represent has been apparent throughout the chapters in this volume and should, we hope, help future researchers to rise to the challenge that has been identified. Budhwar and Cummings (2020) also highlight that many of the problems that management researchers are facing are large and complex:

> in the rapidly emerging 'new-normal', the present and future of relevant work processes and dynamics of working away from traditional work set-up and effective interactions with different stakeholders can't be comprehensively studied adopting a single discipline lens.
>
> **(Budhwar and Cummings 2020, 441)**

The current volume anticipates this need for multiple methodological lenses. We span perspectives that scrape existing data traces of digital work and those where new data are generated to illuminate the working experience. In the process, we offer ways to examine digital work from both the perspective of emergent organizational structures and working relations and from the ground-up as a meaningful aspect of everyday lives. This array of approaches has much to offer future researchers who grapple with the multi-faceted legacy of the pandemic for working lives.

Among the many challenges attendant on the pandemic has been the realization that we are not all impacted in the same way. In practice, whether or not home working was deemed possible (and this decision often relied on the needs of employers) depended on the kind of work that one did. Knowledge workers have often been able to take their work away from the office while frontline workers have disproportionately experienced the health risks of continuing to work together with co-present colleagues and in public-facing roles. The pandemic cast a new focus on social inequality and this comes with responsibilities for researchers. Bapuji et al. (2020, 1206) argue that in the context of the pandemic 'management research—including the research on inequality—needs to take a societal turn and shine light on the ways in which organizational practices contribute to inequalities in society.' This focus on inequality, they argue, includes differential consequences of the pandemic across groups of workers, according to which work can be digitized and which must be performed in person, but also due to differential effects on outsourced work and gig work. Across the chapters in this volume, the authors consider a variety of different contexts in which digital work arises, from low-paid platformed labour and gig work through to highly skilled and high reward forms of professional knowledge work. Each circumstance offers up a different set of methodological challenges and a unique form of digital trace of the work being done. An array of candidate methods for the study of digitally related work are presented here, offering a resource upon which to build future tailored solutions for new contexts and also to develop comparative approaches that delve into emerging forms of inequality.

In addition to the prospect of inequalities across different organizational forms, there are also challenges that proceed from inappropriate assumptions that are placed upon workers about their access to suitable conditions for working at home and the availability of resources to do so. There is a gendered and intersectional dimension to inequalities in access to and experience of digital work in the pandemic (Özkazanç-Pan and Pullen 2020). Inequalities also operate on both a sectoral and global scale. Outcomes are not deterministic and are highly dependent on 'local situations, resources and circumstances' (Bandi et al. 2020, 5). Mexi (2020) argues that we need to be actively planning for a future of decent digital work and that if we are to do this, we need to understand what is going on in depth and detail. This will require research methods that are able both to understand patterns and emergent structures of digital working and to interrogate the experience of that work and the circumstances under which it is carried out. While much of this research may use methods that draw on born-digital data of the kind captured by many authors in this volume, it will still be important for at least some researchers to use ethnographic methods to immerse themselves in the complex multi-modal reality of working situations, as the ethnographers in this volume demonstrate.

In addition to the gross inequalities that may be exacerbated in a shift towards digital work, it is also important to attend to more subtle or insidious diversity across the experience of work and the organization of working relations. In this regard, Wang et al. (2020) highlight that it is still unclear whether the future of digital knowledge work will move towards digital forms of Taylorism or towards empowered autonomous workers, suggesting the need for a research agenda that diagnoses and intervenes in the direction of travel. In the current volume, the action research described by Savage and colleagues is very much in this spirit. From an organizational perspective, George et al. (2020) look at the radical shock offered by the pandemic and describe a pressing new urgency for a research agenda looking at how organizations are able to work effectively in distributed forms. Among the changes to explore are subtle, but nonetheless significant, changes in the form of working relations: as we discuss in the introduction, Leonardi and Treem (2020) describe an explosion in behavioural visibility attendant on the shift to digital working. This behavioural visibility describes the extent to which we can be seen and judged through multiple interacting forms of communication and data thanks to increasing digitalization and datafication. Leonardi and Treem (2020) suggest that we need a multi-pronged approach to empirical investigation of the phenomenon: sophisticated data scraping and analysis on what forms visibility takes and how it varies; interrogating algorithms and regimes of quantification that create the data and present it to us; qualitative research into the motivations that produce the data and the inferences people draw from them; and critical analysis of the power structures that are manifested and reinforced. Across the chapters in this volume, authors demonstrate methods in action that rise to this array of challenges, spanning approaches from the cross-contextual comparative approach that activity theory takes to distributed organizations in Rozas and Huckle's chapter to the detailed attention to the working practices of a single document by Whelan.

The emerging research agenda for the study of work and organizations post-pandemic has digital work and organizations at its heart, but is also attentive to the inequalities that both lie within that phenomenon and suffuse the question of who does and does not have access to digital work. Many of those who have described the emerging research agenda have highlighted an ethics of enquiry that seeks not simply to describe emerging phenomena but also to intervene in shaping directions of travel to alleviate inequalities and avert harm. Much has been done in emergency mode in recent times and sometimes considerations of the desired direction of travel and the unexpected consequences of expedient change has been sidelined, but it is possible for the future to be more measured. Careful, rigorous, and ethically sensitive research into digital work by suitably skilled researchers will be a part of that process. We anticipate that the methods described in this volume will assist with that agenda.

References

Association of Internet Researchers. 2019. Internet Research: Ethical Guidelines 3.0. https://aoir.org/reports/ethics3.pdf

Bandi, R. K., Klein, S., Madon, S., Monteiro, E., and Ranjini, C. R. 2020. The future of digital work: The challenge of inequality. In Bandi, R. K., Ranjini, C. R., Klein, S., Madon, S., and Monteiro, E. (eds), *IFIP Joint Working Conference on the Future of Digital Work: The Challenge of Inequality* (pp. 3–10). Cham: Springer.

Bapuji, H., Patel, C., Ertug, G., and Allen, D. G. 2020. Corona Crisis and inequality: Why management research needs a societal turn. *Journal of Management*, 46(7): pp. 1205–22.

boyd, d. 2014. *It's Complicated: The Social Lives of Networked Teens*. New Haven, CT: Yale University Press.

British Sociological Association. 2016. Statement of Research Ethics—Digital Research Ethics. https://www.britsoc.co.uk/media/24309/bsa_statement_of_ethical_practice_annexe.pdf

Budhwar, P., and Cumming, D. 2020. New directions in management research and communication: Lessons from the COVID-19 pandemic. *British Journal of Management*, 31(3): p. 441.

Fuchs, C., 2020. Everyday life and everyday communication in coronavirus capitalism. *tripleC: Communication, Capitalism & Critique. Open Access Journal for a Global Sustainable Information Society*, 18(1): 375–399.

George, G., Lakhani, K. R., and Puranam, P. 2020. What has changed? The impact of Covid pandemic on the technology and innovation management research agenda. *Journal of Management Studies*, 57(8): 1754–8.

Gray, M. L. 2017. Big Data, Ethical Futures. Anthropology News https://anthrosource .onlinelibrary.wiley.com/doi/epdf/10.1111/AN.287

Hine, C. 2015. Mixed methods and multimodal research and internet technologies. In Hesse-Biber, S. N. and Burke Johnson, R. (eds), *The Oxford Handbook of Multimethod and Mixed Methods Research Inquiry* (pp. 503–21). New York: Oxford University Press.

Leonardi, P. M. and Treem, J. W. 2020. Behavioral visibility: A new paradigm for organization studies in the age of digitization, digitalization, and datafication. *Organization Studies*, 41(12): 1601–25.

Mexi, M. 2020. The Future of Work in the Post-Covid-19 Digital Era. Social Europe Blog. https://www.socialeurope.eu/the-future-of-work-in-the-post-covid-19-digital-era

Nagel, L. 2020. The influence of the COVID-19 pandemic on the digital transformation of work. *International Journal of Sociology and Social Policy*, 40 (9/10): pp. 861–75.

Özkazanç-Pan, B. and Pullen, A. 2020. Gendered labour and work, even in pandemic times. *Gender Work and Organization*, 27(5): 675–76.

Pearce, W., Özkula, S. M., Greene, A. K., Teeling, L., Bansard, J. S., Omena, J. J., and Rabello, E. T. 2020. Visual cross-platform analysis: Digital methods to research social media images. *Information, Communication & Society*, 23(2): 161–80.

Risi, E., Pronzato, R., and Di Fraia, G. 2020. Living and working confined at home: Boundaries and platforms during the lockdown. Journal *of Cultural Analysis and Social Change*, 5 (2), article 12.

Waizenegger, L., McKenna, B., Cai, W., and Bendz, T. 2020. An affordance perspective of team collaboration and enforced working from home during COVID-19. *European Journal of Information Systems*, 29(4): 429–42.

Wang, B., Schlagwein, D., Cecez-Kecmanovic, D., and Cahalane, M. C. 2020. Beyond the factory paradigm: Digital nomadism and the digital future (s) of knowledge work post-COVID-19. *Journal of the Association for Information Systems*, 21(6): 1379–401.

Whiting, R., and Pritchard, K. 2017. Digital Ethics. In Cassell, C., Cunliffe, A. L. and Grandy, G. (eds), *SAGE Handbook of Qualitative Business and Management Research Methods* (pp. 562–79). London: Sage.

Index